FRANZ BOAS

*Critical Studies in the
History of Anthropology*

SERIES EDITORS

Regna Darnell
Stephen O. Murray

FRANZ BOAS

The Emergence of
the Anthropologist

ROSEMARY LÉVY ZUMWALT

UNIVERSITY OF NEBRASKA PRESS

Lincoln

Library of Congress Cataloging-in-Publication Data
Names: Zumwalt, Rosemary Lévy, 1944–, author.
Title: Franz Boas: the emergence of the anthropologist / Rosemary Lévy Zumwalt.
Description: Lincoln: University of Nebraska Press, [2019] | Series: Critical Studies in the History of Anthropology | Includes bibliographical references and index.
Identifiers: LCCN 2019004038
ISBN 9781496215543 (cloth: alk. paper)
ISBN 9781496217455 (epub)
ISBN 9781496217462 (mobi)
ISBN 9781496217479 (pdf)
Subjects: LCSH: Boas, Franz, 1858–1942. | Anthropologists—Germany—Biography. | Anthropologists—United States—Biography. | Racism in anthropology.
Classification: LCC GN21.B6 Z86 2019 | DDC 301—dc23
LC record available at https://lccn.loc.gov/2019004038

Set in Arno Pro by Mikala R. Kolander.

Dedicated to Ludger Müller-Wille
Scholar of the Arctic and of Franz Boas
Friend and colleague

Contents

Illustrations

Series Editors' Introduction

Regna Darnell and Stephen O. Murray

Although there have been many biographies of Franz Boas over the years since his death in 1942, the breadth of his six-plus decade career has eluded the capacity of any single biographer to capture its complexity or to fully assess his contributions across academic disciplines, the professionalization of American science in universities, and his public activism. Previous efforts have ranged from uncritically laudatory to unmitigatedly disparaging or have focused on limited parts of his oeuvre such as race and diversity, political activism, disciplinary contributions to anthropology, linguistics, folklore, education, and Native American Studies.

Rosemary Lévy Zumwalt combines a conversational and readable style with a systematic and comprehensive revisionist account of Boas and Boas scholarship. Familiarity with Boas's diverse disciplines and the employment of a professional translator for the German that was his first language allows her to unpack his evolving theories and methods for contemporary audiences in a range as diverse as Boas's own.

The first work, *The Emergence of the Anthropologist*, begins with Boas's family background and the Germany of the times in which he was born. Like Tristram Shandy, his birth is not the beginning of the story. Zumwalt, like Douglas Cole before her, chose a "natural" cutoff date of 1906, when Boas left the American Museum of Natural History to concentrate on developing anthropology as an academic discipline and training a cadre of students who shared his vision for Americanist anthropology. In terms of his professional achievements to this point, documentation is relatively straightforward, in that Boas's career remained largely within the bounds of anthropology as understood in the late nineteenth and early twentieth centuries. But to Boas himself, it was far from straightforward.

The story crisscrosses continents, national traditions, and disciplinary actors and includes multiple disappointments and dead ends. Zumwalt has searched out and incorporated Boas materials from archives throughout the United States as well as from his papers at the American Philosophical Society, often relying on her own translations. Much of this material is previously unknown in English-language sources. It fleshes out Boas's early education and the fluid character of the disciplines he explored before opting for anthropology as his primary professional identity. The path from psychophysics, physical geography, cultural geography, and physical anthropology to cultural anthropology and ethnography emerges as a gradual one, each new set of interests retaining insights and methods from his prior endeavors. Boas was not alone in this fluidity; his mentors also pursued research questions and developed methodologies not clearly bounded by disciplinary labels. The social sciences were not as discrete as those of their descendants familiar to us today. Boas adopted important parts of his mature position from each of these directions. Throughout his career, he would continue to incorporate methods and perspectives from other disciplines (e.g., applying Indo-European linguistic techniques to unwritten Indigenous languages of the Americas).

Zumwalt's treatment of Boas's cartography and ethnology among the Eskimo (now called Inuit in Canada) of Baffin Island is particularly detailed and revealing, drawing extensively on the geographic researches of Ludger Müller-Wille. The transition to the Northwest Coast and the interaction of the region's cultures and languages would occupy Boas for the rest of his life. Zumwalt chronicles his anxiety at separation from his family to establish a baseline that fieldwork collaborators and students could pursue under his direction from afar.

Later recollections of Boas by later generations of colleagues, students, and his own children and grandchildren inevitably focus on the mature Boas, on the often more self-confident, aloof, and formal persona of the public intellectual at the forefront of his discipline. This volume captures the uncertainties and vicissitudes of his earlier career, in which later successes were only ambitious dreams. Zumwalt interweaves the professional and the personal, revealing the love story of Boas and Marie as well as the conflicts of loyalty Boas suffered balancing his family in America against often conflicting loyalties to his parents, sisters, and other family, as well as to colleagues and mentors remaining in Germany. Zumwalt uses his own words to highlight the poignancy of his struggles in this early period: his difficulties in learning English, precarious employment, and failure to realize his grand ambitions quickly. Readers are led to consider the period in his life before the end of the story was known. We see the young Boas from his own point of view.

Shaping Anthropology and Working for Social Justice, the forthcoming second work of this biography, turns to the more mature and decisive Boas, professionalizing Americanist anthropology according to his view of its proper scope and expanding his influence through the students he trained at Columbia. Zumwalt emphasizes the continuity between the early idealism of Europe's 1848 failed revolutions that Boas acquired from his mother and took with him into professional practice as well as in his personal life. Tendrils extending beyond his home discipline increasingly led Boas out of the ivory tower: his political commitments, played out across continents, and his passionate belief in anthropology as holding a key to solving the problems of living in challenging times. Though his emphasis moved from antiracism in America to resistance to Nazi oppression, Zumwalt argues that Boas remained rooted throughout in the elusive values of the early years chronicled in the present work that sets the stage.

Acknowledgments

I am grateful to Davidson College and Agnes Scott College for providing me with sabbatical leave for the research and writing of this book. For this project, I was named a John Simon Guggenheim Fellow and a Mellon Resident Research Fellow at the American Philosophical Society. I am grateful also to the staff of the Agnes Scott College McCain Library—especially Director of Library Services Elizabeth Bagley, User Education Librarian Casey Long, Access Services Coordinator Debbie Adams, Access Services and Interlibrary Loan Coordinator Stephany Kurth, and Administrative Coordinator Marianne Bradley. I thank Esther Muench for her German translations and Ira Jacknis for his generous help. I am enduringly grateful to the staff of the American Philosophical Society—Beth Carroll-Horrocks, who was the manuscript librarian when I began my research; Charles B. Greifenstein, associate librarian and curator of manuscripts; and the visionary and energetic Martin Levitt, librarian emeritus. I am grateful to Jocelyn K. Wilk of Columbia University Archives and to James Stimpert, senior reference archivist, Johns Hopkins University, Sheridan Libraries, Special Collections. I thank Fordyce Williams, coordinator of the Clark University Archives, for assistance on my research on Franz Boas at Clark University; and Kenn Harper for help with my research on Esther Bein and her family and on Minik and the other Inuit from Greenland. I am also indebted to Thomas Ross Miller, who has researched the history of sound recordings in the North Pacific, and Marilyn Graf, archivist for the Indiana University Archives of Traditional Music, for assisting me in obtaining a digitized copy of the wax cylinder recording made by Boas on June 6, 1897. I am very grateful to

Kendra Meyer, digital lab manager at the American Museum of Natural History, for identifying illustrations for me. I thank my mother Dorothy V. Zumwalt, who, into her 103rd year of life, listened to me read aloud the next draft. I thank my husband, Isaac Jack Lévy, who is a constant source of encouragement to me and whom I trust always to be my first and best editor. I also recognize four Boas scholars whose works serve as a foundation for those of us who follow them: George W. Stocking Jr. (1928–2013), Douglas Cole (1938–1997), Herbert S. Lewis (1934–), and Regna Darnell (1943–).

I am grateful to those who have assisted me at the University of Nebraska Press: Matt Bokovoy, senior acquisitions editor; Heather Stauffer, associate acquisitions editor; and Ann Baker, editorial, design, and production manager. In particular, I want to thank Emily Shelton for her careful copyediting.

I dedicate my book to Ludger Müller-Wille, consummate scholar of the Arctic and of Franz Boas. A kinder, more gracious, more knowledge-able person I could not have found to assist me, as he did, at every stage in the process of writing this book.

Introduction

Franz Boas was born in Minden, Westphalia, on July 9, 1858. He was directed on the path from his birthplace in Minden to his adult life in New York through the intellectual grounding provided by his family and by the German educational system. He was to become one of the central founders of anthropology in the United States. Franz came into his family as the only son, beloved by his parents, his sisters, and all his relatives. The intellectual components so crucial for his later successes emerged from his mother's careful instruction in the Fröbel kindergarten that she had helped to found in Minden, and from the many months she devoted to homeschooling her son because of his ill health. In his youth Boas looked forward with anticipation to accomplishing great things—to studying, exploring, writing, living the life of the scientist who was always creating, always learning, and always breaking new ground. Just a few months before his seventeenth birthday on April 9, 1875, he wrote to his sister Antonie (affectionately called Toni), who had cautioned him against being "too ambitious," that "I tell you, if I shall not become hugely famous later on, I would not know what I should do. It seems terrible to me to have to spend my life unknown and unnoticed by people. But I am afraid that none of these expectations will ever be fulfilled. I am scared myself of such thirst for glory, but I cannot help it." This "thirst for glory"— elsewhere described by Franz in another letter to his sister as a need to "do something exceptional"—led the young boy to dream of traveling to Africa; and, later, as a teenager, of voyaging to the North Pole or the South Pole. His quest would find fulfillment when he departed with great fanfare from Germany for Baffin Land on board the *Germania* in 1883.[1]

Franz Boas's tenacious character would be crucial for the path he charted for himself toward excellence in physics, geography, ethnography, and then, more broadly, anthropology. Once taken with an idea, he would not give up in spite of all difficulties thrown in his path. Boas himself remarked on this singular personality trait, his "persistent will," in a letter to his family, written while on board the Boskowitz during his 1888 fieldwork in the Pacific Northwest Coast,

> Instinctively I think back to my own years between 20 and 30 and can say that I am rather satisfied with them, even if the ideas of those days did not always remain the same. But I can say that I am on the way to carrying out some of them and that some of them were replaced by new ones. Although there were many disappointments, I have seen many of my highest hopes fulfilled, and I have seen that a persistent will leads to its goal either one way of another. Ten years ago I was a young, dumb student, easily influenced by others, weak of character, yet with the best intentions and given to the influence of the moment. I hope that I have improved since.[2]

Franz Boas had a singular goal as he moved into his adult years: to establish himself with professional flourish in a challenging world. In 1884–85, when he was not successful in finding a position in the United States, he returned to his family home with a bruised and chastened ego but also with a determination that would not be diminished. After time at home and then in Berlin, Boas earned his *Habilitation* in June 1886, a degree that would entitle him to teach at a German university. Departing in July 1886 for a visit to Marie in New York, Boas was never to return to his homeland again, save as a visitor. He found his way to the Northwest Coast to begin fieldwork among the American Indians—to collect languages, folktales, and myths and to make a collection of items to defray his travel expenses. He returned to New York, found employment as an assistant editor at *Science* magazine in 1887, and married his beloved Marie. From the time of their marriage in March 1887 through the next decade, Franz and Marie would start their young family and move from job to job. In 1889 they moved from their New York City apartment to a house in Worcester, Massachusetts, for Boas's job as a docent in anthropology at the newly founded Clark University. From Worcester, they moved to Chicago in 1892–93, for Boas's position as chief assistant in the department of anthropology at the World's Columbian Exposition (WCE), and in 1894 as temporary chief curator of the Columbian Museum in Chicago. Boas returned in 1894 to Marie and the children, who had preceded him back to New York. They left behind their baby Hedwig, who had died in his arms in their Chicago apartment and lay buried in a cemetery that, for the rest of his life, Boas visited every time he passed through Chicago. When he returned home, Boas suffered a mental collapse from the years of strain and unrelenting work. His doctor, Abraham Jacobi, ordered him to rest. Boas complied by working for only six hours instead of all day long. Soon he was off to the Northwest Coast and to California for a series of jobs, supported by various sources of funding. Eventually, with Frederic Ward Putnam's unceasing support, Boas found his way in 1896 to the American Museum of Natural History (AMNH) as assistant curator of ethnology and somatology. With boundless ambition and a wide ethnographic embrace, Boas crafted a plan for exploration of the Northwest Coast and Siberia. He and Putnam convinced the president of the AMNH, Morris K. Jesup, to finance the lavish undertaking, the Jesup North Pacific Expedition (JNPE).

Working from the AMNH, Franz Boas's vision for anthropology was, as a professional discipline, grounded firmly in a museum with strong links to a university. While he had taught on a temporary basis at Columbia College, the undergraduate division of Columbia University, as a lecturer in physical anthropology in the faculty of pure sciences from 1896–98, Franz Boas desired to have a permanent base in the university and to retain his position at the AMNH. Boas envisioned teaching all the professional anthropologists in his classes at Columbia University and then having these anthropologists employed at the AMNH and elsewhere in the United States. In 1899 he was appointed to a full-time position at Columbia University as the chair in anthropology in the newly created department of psychology and anthropology. With the fortitude and sheer stubbornness born into him and imbued in him by the *Herzensbildung*—the cultivation of the heart—he attained his goal.[3]

My work twines together the strands of the personal and the professional and reveals, through the palpably accessible prose of his letters and journals, his love for his fiancée and then wife, Marie Krackowizer, and for the field of anthropology as he shaped it. This is a love story that draws within its embrace the members of the Boas family, who served as an integral part of his professional development and as a sounding board for challenges in his research and the conflicts in his work life. The lives of colleagues and friends are also woven together with Boas's as he moved through life's struggles until he was able to obtain a position at the AMNH and finally at Columbia.

For Boas the heart of his life story lies in his unpublished letters, diaries, and field notes, made available when they came like a treasure to the American Philosophical Society in a gift from Boas's daughter, Helene Boas Yampolsky, in 1961–62 and from his son-in-law, Dr. Cecil Yampolsky, in 1964. Here lies the richness of detail to fill the void that Alfred Louis Kroeber identified at the time of Boas's death: "There is little on public record or floating in tradition regarding the youth of Boas. Without being secretive, he reminisced little . . . : the present and the future absorbed his interests." By 1947 Robert Lowie had learned from Boas's son-in-law that the early correspondence from Boas's years as a student had been preserved "and that they reveal the nascent investigator's ardor for research." Lowie continued, "Publication of the correspondence would be a great boon, for it is likely to reveal intimate glimpses of the writer's personality, such as are all too rarely vouchsafed by his monographs and books." Precisely such an undertaking is underway with *The Franz Boas Papers: Documentary Edition*, headed by project director and general editor Regna Darnell.[4]

I have written *Franz Boas: The Emergence of the Anthropologist* as a way to trace the stepping-stones that lead to the development of Boas's vision for anthropology. I underline the tenacity of his efforts, the passions of his life, and the toll the struggle took on him. I begin then with the infant Franz and follow him up to his employment at the American Museum of Natural History and Columbia University. I desire to show how the loves of Franz Boas led him from his childhood to adulthood, to a shaping of American anthropology in deeply important channels, with the acuity of his mind and the sharpness of his vision.

Note on Translations

All translations are from German unless otherwise indicated. The children of Franz Boas, Helene Boas Yampolsky and Ernst Boas, translated many of the letters in the Boas Papers and in the Boas Family Papers. When these translations from the American Philosophical Society are cited, the translator is not indicated. Indeed, often the translator is not known. For new translations undertaken for this work, the following abbreviations for translators are used: Esther Muench (EM), Ludger Müller-Wille (LMW), and Rosemary Lévy Zumwalt (RLZ).

FRANZ BOAS

1

Ardently Desired Boy

Young Boas and His Family

Of her son Franz, Sophie Boas recalled, "'The ardently desired boy was born July 9, 1858. He was a weak child. He wouldn't cry and after the doctor spanked him, he greeted this bad world with energetic cries. And these energetic cries were significant for his life.'" Following Ashkenazi custom, the parents named their first son Franz Uri Boas, after his paternal grandfather, Feibes Uri Boas—with the "F" of Feibes and of Franz symbolizing the continuity of the first name and "Uri" bequeathing the Hebrew name, the meaning of which is "my fire," "my light," derived from "God is my light." Franz grew to dislike his middle name and never used it.[1]

The year before Franz's birth, Sophie and Meier Boas had lost their first-born child, Helene (b. June 1852), at age five. A second daughter had been born to them in July 1854; Antonie (or Toni, as she was affectionately called) would be Franz's beloved older sister.[2] In an autobiographical essay that he wrote at age nineteen Boas remarked, "Shortly after I was born my parents took in a little two-year-old girl [named Lina] who stayed in our house for nine years [until 1867] and whom we were accustomed to consider as a sister." Likely his parents' grief over the death of Helene was eased by this little girl and by the arrival of baby Franz. Just a few days after Franz's third birthday, his mother gave birth to a baby boy named Ernst, who died of whooping cough in his first year. Franz wrote, "I have only very dim recollections of him, but through his death a brother was taken from me forever; later, to be sure, I got two more little sisters, [Hedwig (b. 1863) and Anna Margaret (b. 1867)], but I never again have had a brother."[3]

Franz Boas assumed all of the expectations that his parents had for their only son. As Cole writes, "Without quite stating or perhaps yet realizing it, Franz was now and forever the only son of Meier and Sophie. He wore a heavy mantle of parental expectation and filial responsibility." Franz Boas repaid these expectations in his respect for and loyalty to his parents, as expressed in the following birthday wishes to his father, written when he was eleven years old: "I promise to make you happy by always being obedient and that I shall try to become a worthwhile person. I wish you all the best in this world and I am sure you love me as much as I do you."[4]

Franz Boas's paternal ancestors, as Brilling notes, likely came to Westphalia in the last decade of the seventeenth century from the Rhineland and southern Jewish communities. They lived in Werther in the county of Ravensberg, and in Bielefeld, both in the northern part of Rhineland.[5] Following the order in 1808 to take a last name, Bendix Feibes Aron Levi, who then resided in Lübbecke, took the name of Boas, while his relatives in Werther took the name of Weinberg. As Brilling remarks, it is not known why Bendix Feibes selected the biblical name of Boas from the Book of Ruth, nor why his relatives in Werther took the name of Weinberg.[6] Perhaps the adoption of a new last name seemed a novelty to Jews, maybe even slightly superfluous to the first bearers of the patronymic of Boas and Weinberg. Possibly also the relatives didn't know the last name that the others had chosen, nor perhaps did they see any need to agree upon their selection.

Bendix Boas became a successful textile merchant in Lübbecke and was well established in the Jewish community where he served as *Mohel*, one who performed the circumcision as part of the ritual of *Brit Milah* that, on the eighth day after birth, ushered the baby boy into the covenant of Israel. His sons were among those he ritually circumcised. Bendix Boas allowed the third of his four sons, Meyer (b. 1803), to study medicine in Göttingen and thus to enter "the only academic discipline" to which Jewish students had access in Germany at that time. Meyer Boas was to practice medicine in Büren (1836–51) and then in Paderborn, where he died on March 13, 1881. Brilling writes, "He belonged to the first academic Jews under the Westphalian Jews in his family. He was the great uncle of Professor Franz Boas," and he appeared as "Dr. Boas (Paderborn)," on the genealogical chart, dated March 1, 1930, compiled by Franz Boas's maternal first cousin, Richard Kaufmann of Munich.[7]

Bendix Boas was a merchant specializing in drapery cloth and fabric. He passed on his business acumen to his son, Feibes Uri Boas (1798–1836), one of his seven children, who moved from Lübbecke to Minden to marry Karoline Frank (1802–81). Karoline was the only child of Joseph Meyer, who had "named himself 'Frank' in the time of Napoleon after his place of origin, Franken," or Franconia. In his eighties Franz Boas related the following family story to his son, Ernst, who recorded it as follows: "F. B.'s father's mother's father [Joseph Meyer Frank] was born in Sommerach on the Main [in lower Franconia]. At the age of 13 he was given one Thaler and told to make his way in the world. The first night out a teacher stole his Thaler. Some woman took him in. He sailed down the Rhine on a raft and settled in Holland, then in western Westphalia, first in Hausberge, then in Minden." On his own at the age of thirteen, at which a Jewish male was considered an adult, Joseph Meyer Frank learned hard lessons, encountered meanness and kindness, and managed to find his way in the world. On April 14, 1808, he became a citizen in Minden, when he paid "7 Thaler 19 Groschen," and signed an oath of loyalty to "His Majesty of Westphalia." Concomitant with becoming a citizen of Minden and taking the last name of Frank, Joseph Meyer Frank purchased a house in 1808.[8]

Following Prussian law, through his marriage in 1821 to Karoline Frank, the only child of Joseph Meyer Frank, Feibes Boas was permitted to apply for and was granted "*Bürgerrecht* [citizenship rights] from the city manager" of Minden on September 12, 1821. Having studied for one semester at the university in Münster, Franz Boas's paternal grandfather, Feibes Boas, became a textile merchant and opened a store on the Obermarkt. As Lehmann recalled, Karoline's grandparents "had a textile store, [with] clothes and linen fabrics, but they were also forced to sell porcelain [made by] the Royal Porcelain Factory Berlin . . . , because otherwise as Jews in Minden, Westphalia they could not buy a house, or were not allowed to open a business."[9] Lehmann reflected further, "Grandfather Feibes Boas died very young allegedly as a result of a common cold"; or perhaps, as she remembered from the testimony of Dr. Jahn, the military medical physician, from tuberculosis, since her father, Meyer, was exempt from military service because "his father had tuberculosis." Karoline Frank Boas was "extraordinarily well educated, she spoke fluent French," and was said to have served "one time as an interpreter for Jérôme-Napoléon, King of Westphalia."[10]

Fifteen years after her marriage, Karoline Boas was a widow with five children. Being the second oldest, Franz's father, Meier, was just two months shy of his thirteenth birthday. With what must have taken steely courage and composure, Karoline placed an announcement in a newspaper of her husband's death and of her intention to carry on the family mercantile business of Feibes Boas:

> It has pleased the benevolent Creator, in His unfathomable decree, to free last night from this earthly life my beloved husband and tender father of 5 children not yet of age.
>
> I bring to the many friends and acquaintances knowledge of this great loss to me and, with this notice, pledge that I will continue unaltered the business that has operated for several years and ask that the trust they gave to him who is now eternal be kindly transferred to me.[11]

The family of Sophie Meyer, Franz Boas's mother, had also been in trade for several generations. Her forebears came from an old Westphalian-Jewish family from Petershagen, located seven miles north of Minden on the Weser River, a bishop principality under whose protection "since 1550 one of the oldest Jewish communities in Westphalia was created." Thus, the maternal relatives of Franz Boas had resided in the environs of Minden for several hundred years. The Jews of Petershagen were allowed, as stipulated in their letters of protection, to deal in "trade goods of all kinds," and, more specifically, to trade in livestock, to slaughter and sell the meat, and to run pawn shops.[12]

Jonas Meyer (1787–1851), married Jette, née Menke (b. 1792), at some point after 1808 and moved to Minden, where their daughter, Sophie, mother of Franz Boas, was born on July 12, 1828.[13] Settling in Minden, Sophie's father, Jonas Meyer, purchased a four-story Westphalian half-timbered structure in 1820. This impressive building served both as a home to what would be his large family and as a location for his "grocery store, beer brewery and grain store." Lehmann extracted the following description from her mother's letters: "No doubt, Minden was then a small farm town. The parents had a cow, servants, and maids, and they were for the most part financially well off, although there were supposedly setbacks with the grain business. His wife Henriette, née Menke (called Jette) [1792–1851], came from a small Brunswick town, Gifhorn. She seems to have been a fine woman, gentle and always mediating between father and children." Jette Meyer gave birth to eleven children, four of whom died during childhood. All of the children were provided with good educations: the boys attended the Gymnasium and the girls, Sophie (1828–1916), Berthe, and Fanny (1834–56), went to the Minden *Töchterschule*, the secondary school for girls. Lehmann noted, "The parents were devout Jews, kept a kosher house, but didn't cut themselves off and associated themselves with Christians, too." Jonas Meyer was "often irascible." Sophie, who adored her mother, "tried everything in her power to make her hard life bearable." During her free time at home, Sophie helped her mother care for the large family by knitting socks for the boys and stockings for the girls, for "at that time there were no knitting and weaving machines. All of this work had to be done at home." Sophie's mother was busy preparing her daughter's dowry by having yarn spun and linens woven.[14]

Sophie's high school record noted her outstanding achievements. Her teachers wrote that she was a "model student, among the best the school ever had, and [that] her departure left the staff with deep sadness and an earnest wish that her future would be as blessed as it deserved." Given religious instruction by Rabbi Edler, Sophie "was as a young girl devout and religious, especially during the time when she was confirmed, between 14 and 16 years old." Sophie was a member of "the Jewish club, 'Union,' where they danced, put on plays and cultivated all forms of social life."[15]

Prior to her marriage to Meier Boas, Sophie was drawn into the intellectual and political foment that culminated in the revolutions of 1848. She and her younger sister Fanny participated in the Minden revolutionary circle. Abraham Jacobi, a central figure in the movement, would later play a major role in the development of Franz Boas's professional life and become his uncle through marriage to his mother's sister, Fanny. Born to parents with few resources—the district records of 1851 described his father as belonging to the "'uneducated, ordinary village Jews'"— Jacobi had been a sickly baby, not expected to survive. Jacobi's mother was determined that her son should escape their meager circumstances and made sure that he received an education. Jacobi's father was a close friend of Franz Boas's maternal grandfather, Jonas Meyer. Jacobi journeyed to Minden from the neighboring village of Hartum to attend the Gymnasium and was welcomed into the Meyer home, where he was a close friend of Sophie's brother, Abraham Meyer, who had been born the same year as Jacobi. In exchange for the family's hospitality, Jacobi gave lessons to eleven-year-old Jacob and likely also to ten-year-old Fanny.[16]

Jacobi and the Meyer brothers were fortunate to be able to attend the Minden Gymnasium. Recognized for its excellent faculty, it was the first Protestant secondary school established in Westphalia. Douglas Cole notes, "Under Dr. Siegmund Imanuel, a converted Jew from Hamburg and the school's director from 1822 until his death . . . , the Gymnasium's prestige had grown as its curriculum was reformed, its staff strengthened, and a more practical Realgymnasia program added." Among the teachers were several with progressive political opinions. "The liberal and democratic [ideals] of one of these, Gymnasium teacher Theodor Herzberg," Cole writes, "found fertile ground in Jacobi and the young student remained in touch with Herzberg and the younger Meyers after he left Minden to study medicine."[17]

During his 1849 summer vacation in Minden, Jacobi rejoined the revolutionary group. This democratic Jewish association union consisted of Jewish political dissidents, among whom were Sophie, Fanny, and their youngest brother, Emil. In 1850–51 Jacobi began work with the Communist Bund in Cologne and maintained "an intense correspondence with Sophie and her younger sister." In one letter Jacobi enlisted Fanny's help in selling lottery tickets to benefit German revolutionary exiles in Switzerland; he enclosed a list of sympathizers that included Franz Boas's father, Meier, and his uncle Aron. Sophie and Fanny, at the latter's instigation, formed their own Kränzchen, or reading circle, "in October 1850 to read and discuss political literature." In January 1851 Sophie travelled to Stuttgart to meet with a leading Jewish revolutionary, Louis (or Ludwig) Kugelmann, originally from Lemförde, a small town north of Minden, who had been part of the Minden political circle. The following month Jacobi sent Sophie and Fanny a copy of *The Communist Manifesto* to read and discuss.[18]

Sophie's life changed dramatically with the death of her mother, Jette Menke Meyer, on February 5, 1851. As she explained in a letter to Jacobi, dated March 8–12, 1851, she was now called upon to be completely practical. While she acquiesced to her new circumstances, she felt bereft, not only because of her mother's death but also because of the loss of her intellectual and political connections. She wrote, "'What I do now, I do gladly; it makes me happy, as is fitting to any girl, to be busy, but it does often make me terribly sad that I must sacrifice so much of my previous intellectual life.'" She had begun her letter with an "'expression of sympathy for the political exiles,'" and with a positive view on dire political circumstances. "'The consciousness of our impotence, our inability to do even the smallest thing, would completely defeat us if we did [not] hold up the hope for a better future.'" The next day Sophie wrote about the blind spot that the revolutionaries had for the position of women: "'Sometime, perhaps after centuries, when all humanity is recognized as human, even the yoke under which women are burdened will be broken. They too will lift themselves up, elevated by circumstances and the times, and rise to the place that is their due.'" She emphasized, "'Believe me, my friend that then and only then will you all be able to be happy.'" She concluded with a plea for the inclusion of women in the revolutionary movement and with a statement of women's power: "'Do not leave us so alone, we too have strength.'"[19]

Jacobi continued in both his medical studies and in his revolutionary work. In May 1851 he was in Berlin to take the state medical exam and possibly also to help found a branch of the Communist Bund. As he later recalled, "'The moment I put my foot in Berlin where I had to take my state examinations, I was invited to the city jail by a dozen irresistibly courteous constables. Mistaking me for a star of political magnitude, the authorities had included my name with that of K. Marx . . . and [several] others.'" Jacobi was carrying letters from Sophie and Fanny, so the Minden police carried out a search of the Meyer home in June 1851. Herzig includes the transcript of Jacobi's trial, in which Jacobi commented on Sophie Meyer's letter from May 24–25, 1851, "that this . . . four-page-long letter clearly showed that he overtly told his two friends [Sophie and Fanny] all he knew about his Cologne friends." Compelled to testify in court about their involvement in revolutionary activities, "Sophie and

Fanny being just women, their political activities—reading, discussing and distributing 'revolutionary material,' Fanny even selling tickets for a lottery to support wounded and refugee revolutionaries—were not being prosecuted any further and in the police records their activities were being played down." Harmless they might have been, but their Kränzchen "was forbidden and dissolved."[20]

Jacobi remained in captivity for eighteen months, moved as he was between prisons in Berlin, Cologne, and Bielefeld. While he was incarcerated in Bielefeld's Sparrenberg Castle, Sophie and Fanny managed to visit him. Finally, he was charged with lèse-majesté, the crime of insult against a sovereign, and sentenced to six additional months in the state prison at Minden. On the eve of his release, a kindly jailer tipped him off: the authorities planned to arrest him again on another charge. So, with the assistance of the jailer, who released him from prison very early in the morning, Jacobi fled Minden. Along with many other "major exiled democratic leaders in most of Europe," he went to England, first visiting Karl Marx in London and then staying with Friedrich Engels in Manchester.[21]

Unable to practice medicine in England, Jacobi sailed for America in October 1853. He settled in New York City and lived among German compatriots in the large population of political refugees, many of whom were affectionately called "48ers." Fanny Meyer, who was engaged to Jacobi, traveled to New York in the company of her brother, Jacob, to marry Jacobi. Tragically, Fanny died in 1856 at the age of twenty-two while delivering their first child, a boy, who survived only one day.[22]

Franz Boas's forebears had established themselves in the Prussian city of Minden, Westphalia, on the Weser River. His parents, Meier and Sophie, both from well-to-do merchant families, married in August 1851 and made their first home on Ritterstraße in the upper city. Meier Boas worked in the mercantile business that had been in his family for at least three generations. Mid-ninteeenth-century Minden had a small Jewish population with approximately 200 Jews among the 12,252 inhabitants (85 percent Protestant, 13 percent Catholic, and 2 percent Jewish). The Jewish merchants, specifically those of Minden, had been channeled into the mercantile trade by Prussian legal statutes for well over one hundred years and made a smashing success of it. Among the leaders in the "textile and clothing industry," as listed in the 1857 business directory for Minden, were ten Jewish firms. Most of the Jews were middle- or upper-class merchants with "a few bankers [and] a sprinkling of artisans and professionals." Integrated into the "civil society of the city," Minden Jews still maintained a strong social identification among themselves. While the city had no ghetto, or *Judengasse* (Jewish lane), and thus the Jews were not forced to live in tight proximity with each other, still they were connected by social, economic, religious, and kinship ties.[23]

Sophie was married six months after the death of her mother, in August 1851, and her father died two months later. She had stepped aside from her political work but, along with her husband, she maintained the ideals of the 1848 revolutions in her home, passing them onto their children. Toward the end of his life, Franz Boas remarked, "The background of my early thinking is a German home in which the ideals of the revolution of 1848 were a living force. My father, liberal but not active in public affairs; my mother, idealistic, with a lively interest in public matters, the founder . . . of the kindergarten of my home town." For Boas these ideals were threaded throughout his life as "equality of opportunity, education, political and intellectual liberty, the rejection of dogma and the search for scientific truth, and identification with humanity and devotion to its progress."[24]

Sophie's work to establish the Fröbel kindergarten in Minden was closely linked to these egalitarian ideals. The method of instruction was based on the educational model developed by Friedrich Fröbel, with a focus on the education of the whole child, the belief in the "innate human goodness and perfectibility" of children, and an active engagement with nature, where the child would learn through playing, as well to plant seeds and care for gardens. The metaphor of the garden was core to the approach of Fröbel, who had created the term "kindergarten" to signify a garden of children or a garden for children, and each Fröbel kindergarten had a long strip of land for the children to cultivate and plant. Sophie remarked on this at the Minden kindergarten, established in 1860 in a space provided by the apothecary Faber: "The good size space, a large room with a large garden, is nicer than in the place where I had a kindergarten before."[25]

With one teacher, one assistant, and Sophie's active participation, the school had enrolled thirty-eight kindergarteners by 1861–62. Among these were Franz, his sister, Toni, and probably some of the Meyer cousins. Franz remembered fondly, "There we were entertained with little games and talks, which at the same time were directed toward awakening our minds, especially our interest in nature by games which imitated animal life, and by keeping our own flower beds which we had to sow, water, and care for." He added, "I do not know whether my love for nature which I possessed very early and still do possess stems from this or whether it was awakened at home where my mother kept us children busy not only as in kindergarten but also made us observe nature." Franz's mother recognized and nurtured her son's love of and talent for the natural sciences. Boas recalled years later his mother reading to him from "the children's books by Hermann Wagener which dealt with our immediate environment, the phenomena which met the child in the room, the yard, the woods, and with the animals and plants in the woods." He continued, "I always very eagerly drank in the content and was as happy as a king with these hours of reading aloud, for I could not read as I was not yet five years old." Emotionally very close to his father as well, the ten-year old Franz would ask "to take a walk with him, and would say, 'Let's talk smart.'"[26]

Both of Boas's parents had been raised in observant Jewish households. His maternal and paternal grandparents, Jonas and Jette Meyer and Feibes and Karoline Boas, followed Jewish dietary laws, observed the Sabbath, and adhered closely to religious ritual observances. For Boas's parents, the hold of Jewish law lessened. Lehmann recalled her mother saying that "her father had tormented his children so much with his piety, that it reversed itself, and all his children [had become] freethinkers." Meier Boas's "drift from tradition . . . began during his apprenticeship in Bonn where his faith was shaken when he saw his master, behind closed shop doors, selling on a Saturday. It suffered further erosion when, in a Bonn restaurant, he did not eat kosher and found that 'heaven did not fall to earth nor did his mother suddenly appear threateningly before him.'" While Boas's father had put aside strict adherence to dietary laws, nonetheless, years later, when Franz was away from home attending university in Bonn, he wrote his father to thank him for the package of food he had received: "Don't worry, old man, about my buying anything of the pig since you take such good care of me." In contradistinction, Boas's mother had sent him "Pumpernickel und Schinken"—pumpernickel and ham, for the Westphalian dinner he would serve to his friends in Heidelberg.[27]

While Hedwig Lehmann had stressed that "our parents were free thinkers," she also emphasized that "the children got religious instruction." At the age of eighteen, Franz wrote Toni about the freedom of viewpoints in his family and the regret he felt for not having had religious education: "Everyone can go his own way, and one does not hamper a family member's views." However, he missed an intensity and honesty of intellectual exchange in their family. "We don't seek to share our views with each other. One . . . knows little of the other's opinion and even less how he reached it." He continued, "Thus, no one of us really knows what views Papa has—religious as well as political. He votes for the National Liberal Party, but that's all. I'm terribly angry that I've never had proper religious education. Everyone should be familiar with that nowadays. I don't think that it would have changed my views if I had studied it properly. I'd love to take religious classes after my exam, though—preferably Judaic and Christian. But this won't happen." Franz concluded, "In this regard, you've had it much better since you enjoyed religious education before you got confirmed."[28]

In what might seem an incongruous addition to family celebrations, Meier and Sophie Boas introduced the secular celebration of Christmas and other Christian holidays into their home. The children embraced Christmas with utter exuberance. Franz wrote his uncle with details of their celebration: "We spent a beautiful Christmas. We had a tree and fine presents. I got a tool box from Papa and Mama; Masius's Nature Studies, 1st and 2nd volumes from Uncle Salomon; Far and Near, or Sketches from all parts of the world from Uncle Julius; some transfer pictures from Toni; and patterns for fret work for Toni and me, and something I wanted very much—a geologist's hammer." Franz was particularly fond of the books by Hermann Masius because "one can learn Latin, Greek, Italian and other languages from the footnotes."[29]

While, in his younger years, Boas felt he had missed out on religious instruction, in his later years he had a different perspective. Of his parents' religious ties, Boas wrote in 1938, "My parents had broken through the shackles of dogma. My father had retained an emotional affection for the ceremonial of his parental home, without allowing it to influence his intellectual freedom." He concluded, "Thus I was spared the struggle against religious dogma that besets the lives of so many young people."

Still, while Franz and his sister, Hedwig, stressed how slight the hold of Judaism was on their father, Meier Boas continued to attend the celebration of Jewish holidays in his parents' home and "kept the Jewish holidays in old tradition and for filial affection to his old pious mother." He also served as head of the Minden Jewish community and thus maintained contact with both his coreligionists and his heritage.[30]

As with other German Jews, the Boas family valued religious customs. There was, nonetheless, a countervailing pull toward modernization and toward a merging with the mainstream of German society. This process of "integration into German society," or *Verbürgerlichung*, had been underway since the late eighteenth century. "German and Minden Jews," Cole writes, "were already deeply assimilated into economic life, if less so into German culture and society. To the emerging generation, full emancipation and assimilation did not necessarily mean an end to their Jewishness, but it certainly meant a decline in its significance." Shulamit Volkov writes of the gradual transition of German Jews from the benighted and legislatively restricted group of the eighteenth century to "full and equal citizens, full *Bürger* in Germany" in the latter part of the nineteenth century. "The story of Jewish entry into bourgeois society," Volkov opines, meant becoming part of the *Bürgertum*. This entailed the adoption of "a culture, widely conceived as a system of norms and values." For entry into the Bürgertum, Volkov identifies four criteria, all of which came to apply to the Jews of Minden, and explicitly to the Boas family from the late eighteenth century into the nineteenth: to change the community's occupational structure—that is, to abandon "the traditional role as small trader," and to move into commerce and industry; to learn and to use the German language; to attain the ideal of learning (*Bildung*); and to manifest the "bourgeois ethos and pattern of moral behaviour (*Sittlichkeit*)." Thus, the exchange of Christmas presents marked more than the Boas family's secular adoption of a mainstream German religious celebration: wrapped in those Christmas presents were the markers of becoming *like* their German-Christian neighbors—*like* but not *just like* them, for the Boas family did not put aside the celebration of Shabbat on Friday evenings around the family table of Franz's paternal grandmother, nor the children's religious training with Rabbi Edler. Likely Boas and his family observed the fast of Yom Kippur, the atonement for sins, for Boas wrote to his parents the day following the ending of the fast that "atonement is happily passed."[31]

Sophie's childhood home would become her married residence in 1862. She moved back with her husband, Meier, eight-year-old Toni, and four-year-old Franz. Lehmann recalled her birthplace with fondness: "We lived in the old house of our grandparents, which originally was a genuine Westphalian farmhouse, with a barn [on the first] floor and many lofts and a few small rooms, a yard and an adjacent building for livestock and grain." The family shared the spacious residence with Sophie's brother, Abraham Meyer, his wife, Bertha, and their four children. Lehmann remarked, "Because Minden had been a fort until 1871, one could not live outside the gates and the walls. So my mother's brother Abraham Meyer remodeled the house," and succeeded in designing two very elegant residences. For the young Franz, his sisters, and his cousins, this home provided places for ready-made fantasy and adventure. The lower part of the house fronted on Market Street, opposite the military Hauptwache; stairs ran up the four stories to the Opferstraße in the upper city. Thus Franz, his three sisters, and the Meyer cousins—Julius (b. 1855), Theodor (b. 1857), Willy (b. July 24, 1858), and Adele (b. ca. 1863)—could run from the lower town to the upper town and pass the ground floor where the family businesses were housed, up through the family residences to the Opferstraße. On the ground floor Abraham Meyer had his mercantile warehouse and his grain store, complete with a small courtyard and the *Hinterhaus*, the original barn that he used for the storage of grain. Boas's father, Meier, also had his office and a shop on the lower level. Meier worked in partnership with his brother, Aron, in supplying merchandise for Minden's rural population until 1865. That year Meier began work with Sophie's younger brother, Jacob Meyer (1834–1906), who lived in New York and operated "a lace and fine goods import business in Lower Manhattan." As a representative in Germany for his brother-in-law's fashionable imports, Meier provided merchandise for "the fashionable world of Minden." Lehmann recalled, "No one could be happier than my father to get out of running the small-town store where he felt out of place."[32] With this change in his business, Meier Boas made frequent long trips to Belgium, France, and, in 1869 to New York, and he entered more actively into the successful family network of trade in fashionable goods that connected relatives throughout Europe and across the Atlantic.

On their floor of the building, the Boas family had the four front bedrooms: "Two were facing the market, one was pitch dark, it was Toni's room, and our dining room and children's room faced our neighbor's large sloping roof." The children found it to be "an ideal room"; they could climb out the window onto the flat roof of their uncle's office to "see the market and our yard" below, and Franz and Willy planted a garden there. As Franz wrote to his aunt in April 1870, "Just think, I have planted a garden on the roof next to the children's room. I have sown all kinds of flowers and almost all of them have their first little leaves." The next year he wrote to his sister Toni, "My garden on the roof is in quite good order and your rubber tree grows well." In her description of the layout of the house, Lehmann recalled that "from the front a long corridor led into the back room past the kitchen. It was a large bedroom where our parents slept with Aenne in her crib and a small room for Franz and me with a built-in bathtub, naturally without running water, and then another very small room, Franz's private room where he did all of his experiments and schoolwork." Lehmann remembered that Franz's room could hardly hold all of the students who came to study with him when math assignments were due. "But," she added, "he helped everyone," and continued, "The same residence was for the Meyers with six children, . . . so ten children all grew up together in the house."[33]

The cousins were great friends, particularly the boys, Franz and Willy, who were the same age. Willy Meyer had been born just two weeks after Franz and the two were raised as siblings. "Both children," Lehmann recalled, "got nurses who were peasant girls." Close in age, the two cousins, Hedwig and Adele, were also fast friends. The built-in bathtub, located in Franz and Hedwig's room, served as the children's playful means of communication between the two residences. As Lehmann said, "We discovered that the drain of our bathtub was a wonderful speaking tube over to the Meyers, thus we often sat in the bathtub," speaking into the drain to the Meyers children on the floor below. With multiple uses, the bathtub was topped with a board and "covered with a cloth and used as a table" during the day. Then there was the quotidian use for the tub: "Early in the morning Matilda, our young maid at that time, came with a big kettle of hot water from the kitchen. Then the battle began: who takes a bath first? There was a partition screen around Franz. He, as the older one who had to leave for school earlier, demanded his right." The others did not wait quietly; rather, "the pillows were missiles and flew over the screen."[34]

Boas's childhood health problems began when he was four years old and coincided with the family move to Sophie's childhood home. This large, old structure was complete with a store for the sale of grains and numerous rooms for their storage. Possibly young Franz developed allergies to mold and dust and other environmental antigens, although this diagnosis was not, of course, available to the nineteenth-century medical profession. Julia Liss suggests another explanation, that his ill health derived from familial tensions. "It does not seem unlikely," she writes, "that his difficulties reflected the conflicts he experienced in thinking about his own future, which played themselves out in the dynamics of his family relationships." While one can never be certain of their origins, his health challenges did begin when he was four and lasted throughout his teenage years, ending when Boas went to university and his family moved to their newly built residence in Minden.[35]

As Boas wrote, "In this year [1862] I became very sick so that the doctor sent us to the country. We went to Clus. As we lived there many weeks I had the opportunity to become acquainted with the woods and, to be sure, I noticed much there owing to a book of Wagner." His sister Hedwig spoke of this time: "Franz was only four years old when he went with his mother in the forests of Bückeburger-Klus. They gathered flowers; he made his first Herbarium. His parents gave him a book with colored pictures from domestic wild flowers and he found out how to draw a parallel between them. He could not yet write; his mother wrote the names which he told her under the dried flowers. Father and mother were very proud of their little boy." Klus provided a pastoral woodland setting, just four kilometers east of Minden; Sophie Boas took her son there to recuperate from his severe and unrelenting headaches, for which the doctors of the time had no treatment save for rest and fresh air. They stayed in "a very simple inn," which had been part of the "an old hunting seat of the Fürsten of Bückeburger." The next summer, as Boas recalled, "We again lived in Clus and my cousin Willy Meyer lived there for a while. Again as in the previous year I occupied myself entirely with the pursuit of nature and, to be sure, in moderation so that my cousin was also taken in by a love of it. From then on for a still longer time we gathered plants together and chiefly sought to gain a knowledge of natural history."[36]

At age six, after they had completed kindergarten, Franz and his cousin Willy Meyer were given private lessons by Herr Permeier. As Boas wrote in his CV, their teacher "prepared us so well that we could be admitted into the fourth class of the Bürgerschule" in Minden, and they remained at this school for the next two years (1865–67). As with most Prussian schools, classes were coeducational.[37]

Boas remembered being enchanted by *Robinson Crusoe*. As he recalled, "Owing to this book I got a great longing to see and get acquainted with foreign countries, a longing which has not left me. At that time my desire was always directed towards Africa, chiefly to the tropics, and I still remember very well that I ate as much as possible of certain foods which I did not like in order to accustom myself to deprivations in Africa." As a young boy of thirteen, Franz had written to Toni of his plans following graduation to travel to the North Pole or the South Pole, as well as to Australia or Africa, "but—but—but, I have to make sure wisely to use the time I'm given for study for without being equipped appropriately what fruits would such a trip bear?" Boas also recalled his fascination with fairy tales: "The stories of Red Riding Hood, Snow White, and similar ones I could read and read a hundred times without getting tired. My favorite was always Sleeping Beauty and the fairy tale of the Seven Ravens."[38]

At the end of the school year in 1867, Franz and Willy visited the Minden Gymnasium, as was requisite. Lehmann remarked, "All boys must visit it before they come into the *Gymnasium* at nine years old." Franz wrote to his Uncle Jacobi, "At Easter I was accepted in the Gymnasium. It is much nicer here than in the lower school because Latin is giving me much pleasure.... Now I will tell you about my German class. At the last dictation I stood first. You can imagine how happy I was." With a strong focus on languages, the Minden Gymnasium required students in the academic program to take Latin every year, with French added the second year and Greek the third. Students also took courses in German literature, history, geography, science, and mathematics. In Minden, as in other German cities, the neohumanist Gymnasium served as a "comprehensive school in its lower grades and as a well-nigh exclusive university preparatory school in its higher grades."[39]

Franz wrote to his father in Latin and in French about his grades, as well as to his uncle, whom he addressed "Avunculus amatus!" He detailed his progress in his first year in Gymnasium in a letter to Uncle Jacobi: "I have been promoted, third in the class, to the Quinta and my report reads: Latin, German, Natural History, Geography—very good; writing—satisfactory; singing—quite good; behavior—very good. Mama and Papa say it is a good report and you can decide for yourself if you also think it good." In a more playful mode, Franz wrote, "This morning between 8:30 and 10:30 I ran around in the snow and rain for America." The following year Franz told his uncle again about his report card. All was good or satisfactory, save for deportment, where, it was noted, that he was "sometimes sleepy in school, otherwise good." With enthusiasm, eleven-year-old Franz was putting his interests to work: "I have for some time been working out a little lecture in natural history whose theme is: What is the origin of the tides; life in the sea; the origin of the earth; fossils and the difference between land and water animals. The hardest is still to be done, namely fossils and the difference between land and water animals."[40]

With his move to the Gymnasium, Franz's focus shifted to physical geography and zoology. As he recalled, "In the winter when we received zoology instruction, I turned entirely from botany and zealously put my entire efforts in zoology." Fascinated by the skeletal structure of the animals, and much less interested in their external attributes, he acquired the bodies or heads of "geese, ducks and hares." He added, "The mice and frogs had to wait." His sister Hedwig remembered vividly how he loved "to gather rats, mice, [and] frogs." Franz's mother, ever supportive of his interests, "gave him a pot, where he could boil animals. Then he cut the bones out and composed them again. Sometimes he dissected them too."[41]

Lehmann also remembered the beautiful mountains that surrounded Minden: "Every day free of school the boys were going to the Porta Westfalica or climbed up the Wittekindsberg," a mountain that rises just to the west of the port and overlooks the Weser gorge. She continued, "Franz never went without his botanizing box, a net to collect butterflies, [and] a hammer to discover fossils. Very early he was beginning to collect stones and the stone cabinet plays an important part in our youth." Franz, his cousin Willy, and his schoolmate and close friend Carl Dröge dug and planted a garden close to Minden, as Boas recalled, "on an unoccupied cliff." He remarked, "We carried out this plan with great zeal; for a long time, this place formed our point of association, until one time finally we found to our great sorrow that it was destroyed." He had a herbarium in which he grew mosses, lichen, and other plants. In a thank-you letter for what must have been a Christmas gift, Franz wrote to his uncle and aunt, "The herbaria that you sent us gives me great pleasure. How strange that you, dear uncle, should know that I have so much pleasure and interest in nature study. I had already started a moss and flower herbarium several years ago."[42]

While Franz's boyhood was replete with hobbies and adventures— all linked to his academic interests and to the *Bildungsideal* (educational ideal) that his mother espoused—he continued to suffer from health challenges. At age ten he had been in Gymnasium for just a short time when he had headaches so bad that he was kept out of school for six months. His sister Hedwig remarked, "He was a nervous child, [and] often had a headache. The doctor advised the parents to go with the boy to Helgoland. So the mother and son went!" Located on the North Sea, Helgoland was then, as it is now, a seaside island resort known for its healthful climate. Under British rule from 1807 to 1890, Helgoland was a tourist resort for upper-class Germans; Sophie and her son stayed there for two months. Franz wrote to his uncle Salomon of the journey: "Papa and Hete accompanied us to the station, and it was touching to see how Hete, weeping, embraced us for the last time, and Papa took a gentle farewell from us." They traveled by train to Harburg and then by boat to Hamburg; from there they departed on a fourteen-hour trip by boat to Helgoland. Franz remarked on the "dust clouds on the heath" in Lübbeke and "the beautiful harbor" in Hamburg with the ship "masts . . . unspeakably long and dense." He and his mother stayed overnight in the Alster Hotel, "illuminated with thousands of gas flames," and they could see the small steamers as they "sailed back and forth" in the harbor. Franz continued, "The next morning when we sailed for Helgoland, it was quite stormy, but I became seasick only at the last moment. . . . The second day when we went to the dunes we found some algae, but on the subsequent days we found much more. We often took sails on the ocean but the company was so boring that I would have preferred to stay home. On the last day we caught a sea anemone, which kept until we reached Hamburg." Franz said that they "had a happy reunion" at Bückeburg, where they were met by his father and his sisters Hete and Aenne. He concluded, "For today this letter which your loving Franz has written is ended."[43]

As Franz recalled, "I loved equally [the sea] in calm and in storm [and] also the wealth of the animals and the plants in the sea." His sister Hedwig related that her mother and brother "gathered sea-stars, sea hedgehogs, sea-devils, sea grass, [and also] went fishing with the fishermen." One summer Sophie took both Franz and Toni to Helgoland for health reasons. Lehmann recounted, "At that time Helgoland was British territory, and I remember that the two had great difficulties at customs, because the authorities did not want to believe that a large, very heavy suitcase contained stones. As always Franz had collected fossils; he later gave the beautiful stone collection to the Minden Gymnasium."[44]

While Sophie and Franz were relishing the sea and its bounty on their trips to Helgoland, Meier Boas was at home in Minden, full of worry. He wrote his wife, "I hope that our Franz has completely recovered. Yesterday I spoke with the doctor and told him about our child. He recommended to me once again that we should not at the present time fatigue him. . . . He should go outside to play. . . . Now you will do all of this. We want the children truly to be cared for." He recalled that while he was in Hamburg with Franz they went together "to the zoological garden and the aquarium, [but] that was well before the main concern" with his health. Even when Franz was in good health this was enough for him for one day. He continued with his advice: "Do not point out to him that which excites him. At any rate, each evening, take a walk to St. Pauli but don't go to the theater."[45]

With constant bouts of illness and concerns about keeping up with his schoolwork, Franz continued in Gymnasium. In 1871, when he was in the Obertertia—equivalent to the ninth grade—Franz became so ill that "all learning for a long time had to be entirely stopped," and he was "immediately sent to the country." This set him back in his school years, particularly in "Greek grammar and in the use of Latin which one gains in the Tertia."[46] At the same time, his sister Toni became very ill. She had moved to Jena in 1870 to spend the year with the Weichardt family in a pension for young girls. For seventeen-year-old Toni, this time away from home was intended to be what "every girl of a well-to-do family [did] for one year." A serious and accomplished musician, she was studying piano and, in addition, learning English from Lisbeth Weichardt. Cole writes that Toni also received "private instruction in Latin and drawing" and that "Toni was happy at the Weichardts', but by the end of October she began to suffer from what was diagnosed as rheumatism in her left hand and wrist. She wrote that Mama was not to worry, that the camellia baths and wristlet had already improved her condition and that she was back to the piano. But the ailment worsened, with the inflammation affecting her hip." Franz remembered this time: "My eldest sister had become sick there while she was in a pension, and since the doctors would not permit her to be taken to Minden, my mother spent her time partly with us and partly with my sick sister." On these absences from home, Sophie would leave the household in the care of Bertha Lütge, who would add short notes about the children—Franz, age twelve; Hete, seven; and Aenne, three—in the letters written by family members in order to reassure the mother about the health of her children who had remained in Minden.[47]

With Meier's work necessitating travel, the strain on the entire family was palpable. Sentimental and emotional about his family, Franz's grades began to slip. His ranking went from third in his class to sixth, a change that for his parents and for himself was of great concern. Nonetheless, he was promoted to Obertertia following the Easter break. Cole recounts, "Scarcely had the new class begun after the Whitsun holidays when he was struck by a recurrence of severe headaches." Franz wrote Toni, "'My headaches came back yesterday during Greek Extemporary so I have to leave school.'" Cole continues, "He was sent to the Porta countryside, but the next month, with both Toni and Franz in need of their mother's care, Sophie took all the children to Jena."[48]

Lehmann reflected, "Our mother went with us children to Jena, to Prof. Siebert's Sanitarium, where Toni now lived." Franz recalled, "Because of my illness we all had to go to Jena, . . . neither of us children could do without our mother's care." The family stayed in Jena for one year. Franz empathized deeply with his sister. He wrote his aunt, "Poor Toni, I am so sorry for her. She has been in bed over a quarter of a year and there is still no change." Franz benefited from the "continuous stay in the fresh air." He wrote, "I became healthier and by October [1871] I was again able to take regular school lessons." Franz's mother and father had grown concerned that he was falling behind in his education, so they enrolled him in the Zenkersches Institut, a private school for boys run by Professor Gustav Zenker. In Jena there was no choice other than the Zenkersches Institut, since there was no public gymnasium. Boas recalled that he learned nothing in this school, because he was enrolled for only two months and the class was not as advanced as the one he had been attending in Minden. During this period Franz's real education occurred in the botanical garden at the University of Jena, where he made the acquaintance of the botanist Dr. Johann Dietrich, private scholar and curator of the university herbarium in the botanical garden, who took a great liking to "this clever boy."[49]

Dr. Dietrich taught Franz about "the rudiments of physiology and anatomy of plants" and instructed him on the use of the microscope to study the structure of plants. With Dietrich's authorization, thirteen-year-old Franz was admitted to the museum and to the Jena botanical garden, where he was able to explore the greenhouses and to study the geographical distribution of plants. Franz remembered this time: "In the beautiful botanical garden in Jena I got to know many exotic types and at my frequent visits in the garden one of the guides took a fancy to me and showed me all the rarities of the garden. . . . At the same time by taking many excursions with my younger sisters. . . . I got to know the surrounding country well." Six years later Franz recalled this period of his life: "Because of these lessons I acquired such a preference for botany that it almost stifled all my other hobbies." He continued, "This instruction had very great value for me because it became clear to me that true science does not consist in describing single plants but in the knowledge of their structure and lives and in the comparison of all classes of plants with one another."[50]

Franz's parents removed him from the Zenker Institute and made arrangements for his return to Minden. From a child's perspective, Franz thought this was due to his parents' concern about his lack of progress in school. As Cole relates, the parents were indeed concerned, but not solely because Franz wasn't progressing: "Though her letter that raised the need to remove Franz from Zenker's institute has not survived, Meier's resigned reply suggests that it touched upon the question of Franz's Jewishness." Meier had written Sophie from Minden, "By the way, the Zenker affair does not exhibit the bad character that you think. Such coarseness sadly happens everywhere and from this regrettably our children cannot be protected. They must scrape through as their parents have." As Meier further reflected on the arrangement for his son, he came to agree with Sophie that their son should be taken out of the Zenker Institute: "The more I think about this, I believe that Franz should be in school here in the fall, he should go to Finsterbusch. . . . I don't want the child to be with unfriendly people." Since Meier wouldn't "be going on any long trips," he would be in the position to "watch out against his physical stress and to care for his intellect." Additionally, as he pointed out, they had relatives in Minden to help with settling Franz in at the Finsterbusch residence. Meier remarked on the difference in quality between the private institutes and the public Gymnasia: "It appears that there prevails an entirely different character in the Gymnasium than in these private institutions."[51]

Not at all happy about the possibility of taking a room with Finsterbusch, Franz returned to Minden. He had no desire to lodge at the Minden Töchterschule, the girls' high school, where Ludwig Finsterbusch, who had served as director from 1866–73, had rooms to let. As he wrote his mother, "I don't want to be with Finsterbusch. I would get homesick there more than ever for Jena and for you. For . . . one sits in a boarding house like a prisoner, and if you were to insist, you—as certain as two times two is four—would receive a letter in the first eight days in which I wrote that I couldn't bear it there any longer. I wouldn't be able to socialize with any boy. No one would come there, and I wouldn't be able to go to anyone." He pleaded to be allowed to stay at the Meyer house, and his cousin Willy also wrote a letter to his aunt Sophie, asking her to allow Franz to stay with him. At first it appeared that Franz would get his wish: there would be no room available for him until two soldiers had vacated their rooms in mid-March. However, a young woman lodger gave up one of her rooms. Meier wrote Sophie, "So Finsterb[usch] is possible, our wish has come to pass." Since Franz had been staying with his father alone, Meier confessed, "I must admit, it is a bit scary to me also to have the child with me alone." Franz's father was sending "over his bed this morning. It is not necessary that all of his things be taken there. He can fetch what he uses from our house." And he observed again that "naturally all the family members look after him."[52]

Meier wrote Sophie, "The young one will accustom himself hopefully very well at Finst[erbusch]." He told his wife about the plans for Franz to be with the family: "This [Shabbat] evening Franz will go with me to Grandmother [Karoline] to eat and in the morning and all Sunday he will be with the Meyers." He detailed his arrangements to take Franz to piano lessons, to English lessons, and to Rabbi Edler for the "one-hour weekly lessons." Regarding their major worry, Meier remarked, "How extensive is his lagging behind, I do not yet know, his extemporaries will show this."[53] Meier's worries about his son were eased by a dream that he related to Sophie: "When one sits so alone, and an unveiled dream comes, one slips happily over the gloomy past and the way is lit to the future towards one's glorious wishes. I saw our student son visiting the university. Yes, yes, in Bonn or else Heidelberg or else another lovely spot." Meier wrote Sophie about his return to Minden from a business trip, "I am happy to be arriving in Minden [to be with] Franz. . . . Franz is with the Meyers until I come to the house to pick him up. His and the children's pleasure in seeing each other again was extraordinary."[54]

As a result of all the school that he had missed, Franz was behind the other students, particularly in Greek and to some extent in mathematics. He reflected on this lonely and uncomfortable time: "I never felt really at home at Mr. Finsterbusch's house. I was worried about my sister who was then very sick and I longed to be at home. All my work availed me of nothing, since our teacher had forgotten that I had missed the whole class and he required the same of me as of the other students, and if I did not know as much, he explained it as laziness." He wrote a very sweet and sad letter to his sister Hete, who was in Jena with their mother, and his other sisters, Aenne and Toni: "First of all you must excuse my writing in pencil, but I have no ink. It is not right that you cry so often. Right now I am in a mood in which I should like to cry all the time. I am always alone here, no one visits me and when I do go home it is always for only a few minutes." This difficult period ended with a wonderful memory. In April 1872, Franz recalled, "After a quarter of a year my parents came back to Minden with my sister and very happily I went home." While this time was "almost the hardest period of my life," memories of it had nearly vanished when Franz wrote his recollections at the age of nineteen.[55]

Able to return to the Gymnasium in 1873, Franz was in the Obersekunda, equivalent to the eleventh grade. Because of the "great gaps" in his education, he was held back. He wrote, "As I was once again not well this winter my parents decided in spite of my strong opposition to leave me another year in the Secunda since they feared that I was not measured to the demands which the Prima would put on my working strength." In a more nuanced reflection on the decision, Franz's father wrote to his sister Toni that he was "a very undeveloped boy," and that both Meier and the teacher had doubts about moving Franz up.[56] When it was finally determined that Franz would stay "one more year in Secunda"—meaning that he would have spent a total of three years at that level—he wrote Toni that he despaired of having "to plough through all that boring stuff one more time." In all, Franz had missed close to two years in Gymnasium due to illness, "half year each in Quinta and Secunda and over three-quarters of a year in the Obertertia."[57]

In April 1875 Franz was promoted to Prima for the last two years of study in Gymnasium. In October 1876, when he entered his final year, the Oberprima, at the Minden Gymnasium, he wrote, "'Now the good time ends and the work begins.'" He abandoned all his "side studies" and focused entirely on "assimilating everything that was offered to us in school." Franz was preparing for the dreaded *Abitur* examination that stood "'like the Alps'" before him and would mark the end of secondary education. Franz and his four other classmates, called *Abiturklasse*, had to take the Abitur to qualify for admission to university.[58] He wrote his sister Toni, "As the exam pushes me, I just hope I will be able to survive it and will come through." Under intense pressure, Franz sought some relief and understanding through writing long, detailed letters to Toni about his studies and his thoughts. He agonized over his father's desire that he study medicine. "You have chosen the ideal life profession," he wrote, "which you quietly follow, while I have the solid inner conviction that medicine certainly is not the right field for me and that I will never excel at it." He continued, "My main interests do not find nourishment in it, so I will always remain as a physician hungering, hungering for knowl-

Ardently Desired Boy

edge, hungering for understanding. And I'm sure if I followed my studies, I . . . could still do something good in my profession." Franz continued, "I trust in my strength. . . . I can now really cry out with . . . Hutten: 'Ich hab's gewagt!' 'I have dared it!' And a bold game I tried." In response, Toni cautioned Franz against assuming too much self-assurance. Franz replied,

> You think namely because of the content of my previous letter, I would have too much self-confidence. I can't deny that I have faith in myself, but I haven't had that always. Only recently have I. And you know why? Because for me, self-confidence and hope are the same. . . . Because if my strength doesn't get me another profession, I have to go through my life as a doctor, and for that I'm simply not made, albeit you don't want to hear that. And that's why I trust in my strength, and I want to work until I have attained that purpose. . . . I just want to work until I have achieved something.[59]

The weeklong examination schedule was grueling: "The five candidates began the process on Saturday, January 20, 1877, with a Latin dictation. More Latin followed on Monday. Tuesday was taken up with religion so Franz had the day off. Then, day by day, came French, mathematics, German and history, and Greek." All five passed but none with enough distinction to avoid the oral examination that was scheduled for the morning of February 12. Franz was required to "explain Archimedes's principles and other axioms. Greek came after lunch . . . and finally history. Franz had to recite Lycurgus' legal contributions and compare it with the laws of the Roman decemvirs [ten men] and Moses, then present a narrative of the Vandal invasions and the Crusades, and recapitulate the phases of the French Revolution." At 5:30 in the evening, all five students were told that they had passed. As Cole recounts, "Franz ran straight home. 'How I ran down the stairs or up them, I don't know, but faster than ever before.' His father, arms outstretched, awaited him. The noise brought the Meyers up from below, but Franz was dispatched to tell Grandmother Boas and Aunt Emilie (Aron's widow), while Meier hurried to telegraph the good news to Toni." As Franz wrote, "'I will never forget Darwin's birthday, the day of our examination.'" The students in the lower class, the Unterprima, hosted a raucous celebratory party for the successful five. As Franz wrote Theodor Meyer, the students drank and celebrated from "8 in the evening to 3 in the morning . . . and we all had a great time." The next day they were hung-over and had to take a walk to work it off.[60]

Franz was delirious to have passed his examinations. Müller-Wille observes, "His grades were quite mixed, the average fairly low." With the scale going from 1, which was the highest, to 6, with 5 and 6 being a failure, Boas received the following: "German, satisfactory or 3; Latin, 3; Greek, 3; French, 3; History, good or 2; Geography, 2; Mathematics, excellent or 1; Physics, 2; Physical Education, quite good, about 2." Müller-Wille concludes, "The grades clearly show why he was specifically interested in Mathematics, he knew his strength which bore out later in his career." Also remarking on his grades, Cole notes that Boas's handwriting was judged to be "'ugly and untrained.'"[61]

Sophie wrote Abraham Jacobi about the intense relief and joy that came with the successful end to Franz's Abitur: "At last the great worry is off our shoulders. The boy has passed his examination very well." She continued, "I never feared that he would not pass, but four weeks ago he had a severe throat infection that ran him down so terribly that I feared his body would not stand the strain. Thank heaven he held out but he looks like a walking corpse." The townspeople shared in their joy: "We are being congratulated from all sides. You know how in a small town everyone knows everyone's business."[62]

Mingled with the struggle to prepare for the Abitur, there had been another challenge for Franz: the battle between what the father wanted for the son, and what the son wanted for himself. Lehmann summarized this conflict succinctly: "My father wanted nothing so much as for his son to be a doctor, but Franz's heart at that time was set on becoming a mathematician." In the thick of the conflict, Franz wrote to Toni, "I don't think that I'm very much up to medicine. . . . Toni, please, don't talk with anyone of what I am writing." He added, "You may talk with Uncle Jacobi . . . only." The struggle was prolonged and intense, and Franz attempted a respectful resignation to his father's wishes. In the concluding passage to his twenty-page statement for his curriculum vitae, he framed the dilemma, "Recently the question has become more and more pressing what I want to become. From youth on my favorite desire was to be able to study natural science and when I learned mathematics and physics, both these sciences were what appealed to me most." With words that scarcely veiled the tension between father and son, Franz wrote, "But I cannot carry out these desires, since my father believes that it would be no sort of study for earning my daily bread." With resignation, Franz conceded that "for that reason I have decided, if without preference, on applying myself to the subject lying next to my interests, medicine." In the next sentence, he pulled back to "the chief reason why I have no desire for medicine is that my favorite sciences are the comparative, and medicine has little to do with them." With tenacity of spirit, Franz determined "to hold open the possibility of later perhaps being able to transfer to another subject I will as far as it is possible study mathematics along with [medicine]. If I can still apply myself to another study, it must happen in the next two years, for until then I chiefly listen to general natural science lectures." As Müller-Wille explained in a personal communication, "It was compulsory to end the cv strictly with an explanation of what one wished to study, what profession one hoped to attain, i.e. the *Berufsziel* [professional goal]." Thus, Boas concluded, "so I hope with my whole heart that this desire which determines my whole life will still be fulfilled for me."[63]

There was intense pressure on Meier Boas to change his mind—from his wife, his son, from Jacobi, and, finally, from representatives of the Minden Gymnasium. The director of the Gymnasium, the science teacher, and the members of the school board visited Meier and Sophie to pressure Meier into allowing his son to pursue the study of science and mathematics at university. The representatives from the Gymnasium conveyed to Franz's father their view that "it would be wrong not to let the boy study what he wanted." Franz's science teacher, Professor Dr. Julius Florens Banning, a well-known and published botanist, was among this group. As the instructor of "all the science classes," Banning would have been particularly loath to lose a student to medicine in whom he saw such promise. He had recognized Franz's gifts, had assigned him "extra work," and had gone "botanizing with him." Director of the Minden Gymnasium from 1861–85, Dr. Otto Gandtner—who subsequently became the curator of Bonn University and a member of the Leopoldina Academy—had read Franz's curriculum vitae "with exceptional interest and satisfaction." He clearly had heard Franz's plea in the concluding paragraph to be allowed to pursue his interest in science. Müller-Wille notes in a personal communication the "extraordinary range and renown of his teachers (several with doctorates), some of whom enticed him to push forward."[64]

Sophie conveyed the conversation to Jacobi. Franz had been given "a great mathematical problem for his first task for the examination." Sophie exuded pride: "His work was so successful that the director and the teacher maintain that he has a genius for mathematics, that his knowledge by far exceeds that of the usual graduate, and that he should become a docent," that would involve taking a professional teaching position at a university. While Meier "saw no future for his son in the profession," he compromised and agreed to allow Franz to begin the study of mathematics and sciences at university and would "not stand in his way when he learns later that the study of medicine does not satisfy him."[65]

Both mother and son exalted at the successful resolution of this crisis. Sophie Boas wrote her daughter Toni, "Best of all, Papa won't bar his way any longer if he doesn't want to stay with medicine. It even seems to me as if he's struggling with himself as to give [Franz] instant approval to follow his heart in his studies." Repeating his refrain, "Ich hab's gewagt!," Franz wrote Toni that, like Ulrich von Hutten, "I have dared it!" For Franz it was the daring of standing up to his father and saying "that I want to study mathematics and science." Franz continued,

> I have already talked to Papa a few days ago when he came back, ... but he told me we must wait for the letter from Jacobi, and today it came. He wrote that they must leave the decision to me, and Papa said, I should decide, he didn't want to stand in my way. I didn't think too much of the whole responsibility resting on my shoulders, and I said, I want to study mathematics and science. So now the whole future is in my hands and let us hope that I'll succeed. I dared! Now I will study first mathematics, chemistry and physics and I will go to Heidelberg, we will see each other hopefully in four weeks from now.[66]

With perspicacity Franz Boas had articulated at age nineteen in his curriculum vitae challenges and perspectives that he would carry forward to his scholarly work as a young man and later to his professional work as an anthropologist. He recalled his time in Klus, when, as a young child of four, his mother read to him from the nature books of Hermann Wagner. While he loved these books and relished the world of flora and fauna their words and illustrations opened to him, he reflected on a challenge for his young mind: "Still all these books had the disadvantage of teaching me to pay attention to details only, while they awoke no understanding at all for nature in general. This may also have been due to the fact that I was too young then to be able to have an eye for more than details, an ability which in any case I lacked for a long time." Franz had created the "herbarium of various kinds of moss." Held in the moist soil and within the glass frames of the herbarium was the beginning of a comparative approach: "Perhaps, however, it shows also that I possessed the inclination to compare isolated things with each other." When he was twelve years old, Franz had occasion to learn the complexities of botany from Dr. Dietrich of the University of Jena. Of this experience Franz wrote, "This instruction had very great value for me because it became clear to me that true science does not consist in describing single plants but in the knowledge of their structure and lives and in the comparison of all classes of plants with one another." Thus, the comparative approach to science that would become so important for the Boasian stamp on anthropology began for him in the lush botanical gardens of Jena when he was twelve.[67]

As a young boy and a teenager, Franz Boas's education combined the classical schooling of the Gymnasium with the wonderful serendipity of his pursuit of his own interests, whether in Helgoland, Klus, or Jena, or on days free from school in Minden. The greater part of his serendipitous and creative education occurred during his bouts of headaches as a child and the requisite medical absences from school. Of course, in his adventures he was often led by the hand by his mother, who had laid the foundation for his love of nature in the Fröbel Kindergarten that she had helped to establish in Minden and who had willingly even given him a pot to boil animal carcasses for dissection. Along with the pursuit of adventures and hobbies, Franz also endured emotionally trying times. With resilience and fortitude, he pulled through what he referred to as "almost the hardest period of my life" with only faint memories of the challenges. His ability as a young man to let trauma recede to a faint memory and to remember fully the happiness he experienced would serve him well in the difficult years to come. At nineteen Franz Boas had clarity of vision for his future. "In three years," as he wrote Toni, "I will become a doctor; a year after, the state exam; and I will habilitate as a Privatdozent, so I now think." He pondered, "Will it be so, what do you think?"[68]

Years before, Franz had written Toni about his desires for his future work, "I want to become an African traveler and explore all its unknown countries. I feel completely drawn to it. I want to get to know the people and their customs and habits, even those already-known peoples, the Galla, Banda, Kaffir, Hottentots; its flora and fauna and the countries' geologic conditions." He worried about the choice of profession, as it would be connected with his course of study: "If I study botany I'm forced to become a teacher—something I wouldn't enjoy. It's actually not right to say that since I don't know anything about being a teacher. But if I, indeed, were a teacher then I'd have to kill all my lovely time with the dumb schoolboys and would not rise above others." Then Franz added, "It'd be different if one could become a professor or something like that right away." In his letters as a young schoolboy, Franz returned repeatedly to what he did not want to become: "I don't feel like becoming a doctor, and a businessman—that wouldn't gratify me at all." He concluded, "I think, I'd always feel unhappy if I weren't to do something exceptional."[69]

2

Student Life into Its Deepest Depths

Boas at University

Boas arrived at the Ruprecht Karl University of Heidelberg in April 1877. He wrote his mother about attending the lecture by Robert Wilhelm Bunsen, the great chemist whose name came to be affixed to his invention, the Bunsen burner, "When I went to him for the first time, I had a very strange feeling. He was the first great scientist I had ever seen, and to sit at the feet of such a master and listen to his words is an even more beautiful feeling." Boas continued, "There is always a tremendous stamping of feet when he enters and when he leaves." In a letter to Toni, Boas wondered if he would ever be greeted in such a way. "But," he reflected, "that is a long way off." After two months in Bunsen's class, Boas wrote his parents that "the longer I've been listening to Bunsen the better I like him." Boas added, "He's especially good when he does a dangerous experiment. He then gives a friendly smile and says, 'You see, gentlemen, this experiment is very dangerous, but now I'm doing this and that so it's completely safe,' and usually this is followed by a big smashing explosion." In a recent lecture, Boas had taken five pages of notes: "At the end I could hardly keep up."[1]

Boas had elected to go for one semester to Heidelberg, "the dream city of so many students" in the nineteenth century. He wanted to "spend occasional Sundays and holidays with Toni," who was studying piano at the Lebert and Stark Conservatory of Music in Stuttgart. "I've now arrived safely in Heidelberg," Boas wrote Toni. He spent his first days acquainting himself with the city, buying supplies and finding lodging in a house in the old city that had about a dozen student lodgers.[2] Boas found Heidelberg "a pretty city" and remarked on the ancient walls, "where once walked princes; the trees rooted in the cracked walls make the ragged shape of the torn walls appear wild and give the dead ruins a new life." On his climb up to the castle, Boas became melancholy and homesick: "I thought of all my loved ones that I've left back home, of the many years I've lived in my parents' home, and how we always shared good and bad times. I also thought that everyone must go his own way, that we ought to find jobs, one here, the other there, and as I had this thought, I firmly concluded that the friendship that we've always had with each other should never die and that you should continue to be confidant of my joys and pains as always." The following day Boas hiked the Philosopher Trail up to the mountain called Heiligenberg and marveled at the view: "You can't imagine how beautiful it is up there. Today it was so still and quiet, only the birds sang; below lay the old-town Heidelberg, across from the castle." On his second of many visits to the castle, he watched as a plaque was set in the ground. It read, "At this place Goethe sat, musing in the autumn days in 1814 and 1815." To his friend Reinhard Krüer, he wrote, "I tell you this is a glorious region, in the Neckar valley, surrounded by mountains, and at the beginning of the Rhine plain. And then the lovely ruined castle, which in itself is wonderful. . . . I am already sorry that I shall not stay here for longer than half a year, but that can't be helped so I will make full use of this one semester."[3]

Boas described his living space in a letter to his mother and included a sketch of its layout: "It is a long, narrow room with a small sleeping room." He had rented a brand-new piano, which arrived on his return from his visit to the castle. He immediately sat down to play some variations of Felix Mendelssohn, as well as everything else he could remember by heart. He anxiously awaited "the arrival of his books from home" so that he could have the rest of his music. Of the location of his lodging, Boas wrote, "I live almost exactly opposite the University," with only a ten-minute walk to the science laboratories.[4]

Boas went to the university on Friday of his first week in Heidelberg to register for his classes. He signed up for Moritz Cantor's analytic geometry and Immanuel Fuchs's differential calculus, both of which met twice a week; Bunsen's chemistry, which met five times a week; and, after being urged by Fuchs, he enrolled in a mathematics seminar that met six times a week. Boas's academic schedule went from Monday to Saturday, with seventeen classes per week. Fuchs had taken a special interest in Boas, with his obvious mathematical gifts. "I was with Fuchs," Boas wrote his mother, "who teaches differential and integral calculus. The man was very friendly, offered me a chair and talked to me about my previous experience, advised me to attend the seminar, which I will do." He also suggested that Boas join the mathematics club, where Boas happily met other students who shared his interest in mathematics. Boas also signed up for kettledrum lessons on "Tuesdays, Wednesdays and Fridays at 11 o'clock"; but by June, due to the heat, he found no pleasure in playing the kettledrum. He also began taking Russian. "I can pretty much read it," he told Toni, "and I hope that I'll have learned this language in a year. You will surely think, 'Gosh, what nonsense. He should rather learn something else.' But it's no nonsense but a long-cherished plan that I now execute."[5] In a letter to Reinhard Krüer, who was completing his last year at the Minden Gymnasium, Boas wrote, "Yesterday afternoon I matriculated. Just think I had to wait my turn for four hours, there was such a crowd there. Then I listened to a beautiful speech and had to inscribe my name in a huge book, after which I received my registration card." He also told about going to see Bunsen to register for his course: "I had imagined him quite different. He is blind in one eye and quite deaf, but runs upstairs like a youth."[6]

Boas had found his way around Heidelberg, settled into his rooms, and lined up his courses, but he was missing his friends. "I only wish I had some acquaintances," Boas wrote Reinhard, "for I am so very much alone." At the castle, some students had approached Boas about joining their fraternity but despite his loneliness he would not choose to affiliate with them because they were "very common persons." Members of the fraternity Burschenschaft Alemannia zu Heidelberg again approached Boas, as he told his mother, "to win me over." Passing a few hours with them, Boas decided that they were a "quite coarse society" and that he would have nothing to do with them. "I asked them straight out if they were men of principle," he told his mother, "which they negated, smiling coldly. That's when I thought, 'You won't get me then.'" He had two reasons for not joining a fraternity: he intended to stay in Heidelberg for only one semester, and he had promised Uncle Jacobi that he would not join during the first semester. He added in his letter to his mother that he was "pretty desperate" to make some friends.[7]

Boas was finding no one he liked, and those he had met did "not seem particularly nice." He told his mother about meeting "Steinfeld from Rinteln and a certain Levi—you see, noisy Jews," and a boy from Berlin, who was a chemist. He met a student with whom he would play four-hand piano, since he had not yet found anyone who played violin or cello. Boas remarked, "I did not get his name, but I am sure he is a Jew." He had also made friends with Neisser, a neighbor who was in his math class and "with whom I am learning to cram." Boas had begun a friendship with another neighbor, Alfred Polis, about whom he wrote, "Now I associate mostly with Polis, a chemistry student, with whom I spend most evenings. In the evening he knocks on the ceiling of his room, which is my floor, that I should come down, and in the morning I must wake him up by stomping my boots on the floor. . . . To show that he is awake, he then knocks on the ceiling."[8] Boas was trying to distance himself from Levi, who, though "quite a decent man," had taken up with, as Boas noted, "a very unbearable Jewish society." He continued to play piano with the young man, Heimann, whose last name he had finally learned. One month later, Boas was still lamenting that he could not find "a nice circle of friends." He liked Polis very much, but the latter studied so much that Boas saw little of him. He reflected ruefully to his parents, "Truly, if I had not promised you not to affiliate [with a fraternity] in the first semester, I would now certainly join."[9]

Boas's attempts to distance himself from other Jews—from the "*lauten Juden*," the loud-mouthed Jews as Douglas Cole translates it, or "the noisy Jews"; and from the "intolerable Jewish Society"—was nested within what John Cuddihy calls *The Ordeal of Civility*. "The secularizing Jewish intellectual," Cuddihy observes, had as "the focus of his concern . . . the public behavior of his fellow Jews." Cuddihy continues, "The anguish of acculturated Jews" lay in the "loud" and unrefined manners of other Jews. Leonard Glick observes, "Most German Jews were profoundly ambivalent and at times overtly antagonistic toward the new Jewish immigrants from Eastern Europe. Gerson Cohen remarks, "Whatever else German Jews sought to be as Jews, they passionately sought to be urbane Jews and urbane Germans, loyal and dignified *citizens* with a distinct identity as Jews." The Eastern European Jews ran smack up against "this passionate quest" of the German Jews and found it unintelligible and irritating. "German Jews, for their part,"

Cohen continues, "had their own bill of grievances against East European Jews, whom they often found to be uncouth, uncultured and offensive.[10]

Thus, for Franz Boas at nineteen, fresh from his sheltered home in Minden, his encounter with Jews steeped in Jewish culture, in *Yiddishkeit*, was a shock. In sum, he was repulsed. At the same time, he undoubtedly felt threatened that non-Jews would elide him, Franz Boas, who they would know to be a Jew, with the bunch of "noisy," "intolerable" Jews. Lionel Trilling expressed the split between German Jews and East European Jews as follows: "The German Jews . . . were likely to be envied and resented by East European Jews for what would have been called their refinement." It wasn't that Boas denied his Jewishness. After all, the first sentence of his curriculum vitae prepared for his exit from the Gymnasium read, "My name is Franz Boas and I am the son of the merchant M. Boas and his wife Sophie Boas, née Meyer, of Hebrew religion." Of Hebrew religion, yes, but of secular Judaism, Franz Boas was from a refined, acculturated, and intellectual family.[11]

Boas was attending lectures regularly, though his parents were concerned that he was "slacking off." He assured them that he was working hard, going over his work for each class, and fulfilling his obligations each day. He wrote his mother about his classes, "You ask me if I liked the mathematics lectures; I must confess, until now, I haven't liked differential calculus, it is to die for boring by this teacher. The material in and of itself is interesting but Fuchs is horrible so far. Cantor, however, pleases me well, he makes it a bit fresher and more interesting than Fuchs, but he cannot compete with Bunsen, because Bunsen has the best presentation of all the teachers that I have heard so far, so calmly and clearly he speaks." Boas concluded his overview of his professors: "Fuchs also speaks quietly, but so quietly that you fall asleep." After *Pfingstferien*, or Pentecost vacation, he purchased a differential calculus book and "suddenly understands what it is all about." He also had begun to attend Kuno Fischer's lectures on aesthetics. He wrote his parents of Fischer as "a very famous lecturer, so clear and concise!" Boas admitted that it was hard for him to take notes because he had difficulty "with such abstract things" in separating "the essential from the nonessential."[12]

Boas's parents frequently asked their son if he was happy with his choice of study or if he regretted having given up the chance of studying medicine. Boas responded, "You always ask if I like my studies, whether I would not rather become a doctor. I will never go back on this; my studies are the most beautiful thing I can imagine." What was better, he asked, than "to explore . . . the laws of all phenomena, the cause of all things?" Then he added, "If I can only learn enough." Daily he became more and more aware that the field of study he had selected was enormous. Boas travelled to Stuttgart to visit with Toni and to hear her play, and she came frequently to visit her brother in Heidelberg. He wrote his parents, "What she has learned of the piano is simply colossal; she plays like a true artist." At the end of May Boas had received a night letter, signed by Uncle Mons, asking Boas to meet him at the station at 10:30 p.m., "I went to the station, to pick up uncle and . . . there stood Papa! I think I could utter only a word in amazement." He added, "Since I've left home, I haven't been as happy as I was that evening when he arrived." Together, father and son travelled to Stuttgart to visit Toni.[13]

Through these visits with his sister and father and the frequent exchange of letters with his parents, Boas let his family know about the aspects of his life at the university about which they would approve, but he sought to shield them from other areas. While he had assured his parents of his punctilious study habits, to his friend Reinhard he candidly related, "You have no idea what a loafer I have become and how much time I spend in cafés. . . . When the weather is bad I stretch out on the sofa for an hour or two and read." In another letter to Reinhard, Boas playfully remarked, "Don't imagine I spend my whole time grinding at my studies. I believe that Bacchus and Venus can be well satisfied with me." Then, in perhaps a more honest appraisal of his feats, Boas observed, "We sacrifice to Bacchus more than enough here. Venus has turned away from me completely."[14] While his parents might not have approved, they certainly could understand their son's behavior with respect to frequenting cafés, stretching out on the sofa to read novels, and drinking—even to excess—with his friends. However, Boas's participation in another aspect of German student university culture would come to horrify them: *Mensur*, student dueling, also known as academic fencing. As an independent, Boas was accommodated in his dueling by fraternal organizations that allowed two unaffiliated duelists to borrow the weapons and armor swathing and to fight following the completion of all other scheduled duels of the fraternal organizations.

Samuel Clemens visited Heidelberg during the summer of 1878. Writing under the pen name of Mark Twain, he described a duel that was similar to those in which Boas had participated. Two "strange-looking figures were led in from another room," he wrote. "They were students panoplied for the duel. They were bareheaded; their eyes were protected by iron goggles which projected an inch or more, the leather straps of which bound their ears flat against their heads; their necks were wound around and around with thick wrappings which a sword could not cut through; from chin to ankle they were padded thoroughly against injury; their arms were bandaged and rebandaged, layer upon layer, until they looked like solid black logs." The goal of the duel was to inflict greater and more serious wounds on the face of one's opponent than one received. The two participants were "placed face to face," with their seconds swathed and ready for dueling near their sides. With a student as umpire, another student with a "watch and a memorandum-book to keep record of the time and the number and nature of the wounds; a gray-haired surgeon was present with his lint, his bandages, and his instruments," the duel would begin. In their fencing, the duelists, heavily swathed and unable to move, stood in place, face-to-face.

> The instant the word was given, the two apparitions sprang forward and began to rain blows down upon each other with such lightning rapidity that I could not quite tell whether I saw the swords or only flashes they made in the air; the rattling din of these blows as they struck steel or paddings was something wonderfully stirring, and they were struck with such terrific force that I could not understand why the opposing sword was not beaten down under the assault. Presently, in the midst of the sword-flashes, I saw a handful of hair skip into the air as if it had lain loose on the victim's head and a breath of wind had puffed it suddenly away.

And so the duel would proceed until one duelist inflicted serious damage on the other, or until a draw was called and the duel rescheduled so that the insult precipitating the duel could be rectified and honor restored. The surgeon stood by with supplies to patch, bandage, or sew the wounds as necessary. Clemens observed the results of one such duel: "A good part of his face was covered with patches and bandages, and all the rest of his head was covered and concealed by them." Students, Clemens said, liked to be seen in the street with fresh scars and bandages covering their faces and heads. Indeed, Clemens remarked, "newly bandaged students are a very common spectacle in the public gardens of Heidelberg." Students particularly prized wounds on their faces "because the scars they leave will show so well there."[15]

Boas wrote Reinhard about the encounter that lead to a challenge to a duel: "Yesterday I received a double challenge and have accepted, and it will happen in three weeks, and the horrible part is my opponent is an old skilled fencer. This is how it happened." Boas described how he shared the rental of his piano with another student who practiced "études at least two hours a day." The residents of the house complained to the landlord and "suggested that he practice at another time when it would not disturb them so much." Boas said that he "would have been glad to be rid of him, but he would not go, for he had paid his share for this month and would not take it back." Boas continued, "Yesterday when he began to play there began a terrible racket in the court before my window. . . . I became furious and yelled at them out of the window that they should come to my room and play their children's symphony. . . . They immediately sent me a challenger who demanded that I take it back. I declared my willingness provided they would tell me that the caterwauling was not meant as an affront to me. They answered I could take that as I would, i.e. it was meant for me, whereupon I accepted their cards." He concluded, "I shall certainly be wounded." To insure secrecy, Boas did not send this letter until Reinhard had left Minden, since Boas was afraid that his friend "might accidentally" give him away to his family. Following the duel, Boas told Reinhard, "I shall write a few words, because I may not do more. You probably read the postcard with difficulty in which I told you I had had a wound in my scalp." Boas continued, "A piece four cm. long and one and one-half cm. wide was cut out of my scalp but I gave my opponent three cuts from ear to nose that required eight stitches." Boas said that he would be coming home on August 4th and would probably be bandaged "because the cut heals slowly." Reinhard wrote Boas in elation about the outcome of the duel. Boas replied, "What the devil

Student Life into Deepest Depths

is the matter. I write that I have dueled and been cut, and you rejoice that I have cut someone else. It is true my opponent is still in bed, while I was able to go out the day after the duel, but nevertheless I was cut."[16]

While recovering from his wound, Boas was visited by his mother's best friend from childhood, Betty Lehmann, and her son, Rudolf, who was three years older than Boas and who would years later become his brother-in-law, when Rudolf married Hedwig in 1885. In her account of her brother's younger years, Hedwig Lehmann told the story she had heard of Franz's visit to the hotel where Betty and Rudolf Lehmann were staying: "Franz did not take his hat off when he visited them, and Rudolf told Franz how rude he was. He then confessed that he had a scar on his head and he was afraid that his parents would learn about it!" From this initial encounter, Franz and Rudolf began "a great friendship that lasted a lifetime." The two shared interest in philosophy and spent holidays together on walking tours in the Weser Mountains or at the Boas home in Minden.[17]

Having begun the semester at Heidelberg in such a lonely fashion, Boas ended with good friends. He wanted to treat them to "a Westphalian-Pumpernickel dinner," consisting of pumpernickel rye bread, Westphalian ham, other condiments, and *Korn* liquor. As he prepared to leave Heidelberg for home, Boas gave his friend Reinhard Krüer advice about his time ahead at university:

My dear boy,

Enjoy yourself when and how you can, what then will you do at the university? Enjoy things when you can, and be sad when you must, but not too long. How long can you enjoy your youth before the duties bear down on you? Therefore, be happy when you can, enjoy the beauties that Hamburg offers and particularly our mountains and forests.

Boas reflected in an expansive and slightly boastful fashion, "I tasted Heidelberg to the very bottom and am now very happy to return to Minden although I am almost sorry to leave Heidelberg. . . . Truly in my first semester I have learned student life into its deepest depths—duel, the jug, etc." He concluded, "I would never have believed that of myself when I left Minden." As if to prove his point, Boas said that he would have to spend three days in the student jail because "one morning at three o'clock, when not quite sober, I put out a lantern."[18]

To his parents he wrote about this frolicsome and drunken evening. At the meeting of the mathematics society, of which Boas was a member, they "had a huge and lively debate about everything." He explained, "There is always a 12 o'clock curfew, so we moved to the cellar and there . . . drank until about two o'clock. Of course, we all were, as we climbed up from the cellar, no longer quite sober, and tottered dreadfully but very happily through the streets. When we got to the park, we suddenly got the idea to put out the lanterns." Boas continued, "This went very well, but eventually I was unlucky and got caught." Likely, he said, he would have to spend time in "the detention room." He concluded by asking them not to be angry with him, even though they hadn't expected "such tricks from your Franz." Boas reassured his parents, "You need not be afraid that I will come home with a beer belly. . . . I've not become a souse."[19] At the end of the semester, Boas appeared before the university police and was sentenced to three days in the *Karzer*, the student jail. University students were regarded as among the elite and therefore were "endowed with a special judicial code of honor" that set them above the public authorities. Very accommodating, the constable worked with the student to arrange a convenient time. Boas left Heidelberg without having met his obligation for detention, and with "his scalp wound unhealed, on August 3, 1877."[20]

With fear and dread, Boas finally told his parents about the Mensur and his resulting wound. Addressed "Dear Parents and to you only," the letter began, "For a long time I've had a secret like a stone on the heart, that I had to hide from you until now. Namely I have fought a Mensur." Hoping to minimize their alarm, he minimized his injury: "I've not been cut in the face." He begged them "not to lose your confidence in me for I am still just as good and you may therefore trust me just as well as before." In a tumble of words, Boas told of his first duel in which he suffered a cut to the head that "will probably not yet be healed by the time I come home." He assured his parents that he had done "everything to avoid Mensur," but "I was really too proud," and the students who were taunting him from the street refused to apologize. Ending his missive,

Boas wrote, "Thank God that the heavy burden on my soul is lifted, . . . do not be grieved about it, I could not act otherwise. . . . Please, please write me right away that you are not angry with me, and if you can, that my actions were justified, but write me." Boas's father responded immediately: "First we are worried that you have a wound on your head, which will not yet be healed when you come home. That must be bad indeed. I am asking you *immediately to give* us a complete and truthful account." His father said that he would talk personally with his son about the whole episode. He continued that, while one cannot acquiesce to "an injury to one's honor," clearly Franz did not grasp the concept of honor. Meier queried, "And have you now saved your honor by having been struck by your offender?! [I'll have more to say to you] in person." Assuring Franz that their love for him had not diminished, he leveled, "But we follow your life and your deeds now with much greater concern than we thought was necessary." He concluded, "Write us *immediately*, how it is with the injury."[21]

The homecoming from Heidelberg was unhappy for Boas. He had to face the serious displeasure of his parents, but an even greater sadness awaited him. His dearest friend Reinhard Krüer drowned while swimming in the Weser River three weeks after Franz's return to Minden. Franz joined in the search for the body. Along with others, he plied the waters of the Weser for four days when at last they found the body of Reinhard, which had floated far downstream. At the memorial service, Krüer was eulogized as "'the best student of his class, full of freshness and life, a respected youth, enthusiastic about all that was good and beautiful.' The funeral was on August 29, and the entire Gymnasium and many from the city walked behind the bier to the cemetery." In the hope of diffusing their son's deep sadness over the loss of his friend, Meier and Sophie Boas quickly made plans for him to be bundled off to Berlin by train the very evening of the funeral. Uncle Mons met him and "took him on a holiday to Denmark and kept him busy in a whirl of visits to friends, relations, and the sights of the city."[22]

Boas returned to Minden from his trip to Denmark on September 20 and left one month later for the Rheinische Friedrich-Wilhelms Universität in Bonn, where he would stay for four semesters. At the end of the semester in Heidelberg, Boas had written his mother that he was going to shift his emphasis from chemistry to physics: "I intend to go to Bonn all right," but mostly for the professors. He said he didn't want to attend lectures in physics at Heidelberg because "I can hardly do better anywhere than in Bonn with Clausius." He would also take organic chemistry that was boring as it was taught at Heidelberg. He wrote his parents, "If only physics and organic chemistry would be better here [in Heidelberg], then I would stay and work with Bunsen in the winter." Boas reflected, "The only thing I missed this semester with lectures, is that I have not taken the history of mathematics, but it over-lapped with Fischer's [philosophy of aesthetics], so I did not do it." He continued, "I have learned enough now to see what subject I want specifically to choose." While interested in physiology, he settled on physics.[23]

Boas's coursework over the two years at Bonn was recorded in the Leaving Certificate of October 25, 1879, signed by Rector Johannes von Hanstein, University Judge Brinkhoff, and Dean Gerhard vom Rath. For the winter term of 1877–78, Boas took experimental physics, a seminar in physics, and theory of electricity with Rudolph Clausius; organic chemistry laboratory with August Kekulé; integral calculus with Hermann Kortum; and geography of America and Asia with Theobald Fischer. In the summer term of 1878 he studied elements of algebra and took a seminar in mathematics with Rudolph Lipschitz and continued in the theory of electricity and a seminar in physics with Clausius. In his second year at the Rheinische Friedrich-Wilhelms Universität in Bonn for the winter term of 1878–79, Boas took a new course with Clausius on the mechanical theory of heat; a course with Lipschitz on the theory of energy; a course with Kortum on differential and integral calculus; a seminar in physics and a seminar in botany from vom Rath; history of modern philosophy from Jürgen Bona Meyer; and microscopic botany from von Hanstein. In the summer term of 1879 Boas took a course in comparative anatomy with Franz von Leydig. Appended to the list of courses was the following note, "Of the student no incriminating matter is known with respect to civil and academic matters."[24]

During his first term, Boas served his three-day sentence in the student jail in Bonn for having extinguished the streetlights in Heidelberg. His father had written him with the news that "'the nemesis for your Heidelberg student pranks had come knocking' in the form of a police enquiry." On Friday, November 30, 1877, Boas reported to the student jail to serve his time. When he was released, he wrote his parents:

> It is truly fortunate that I did not need to sit there any longer, because then I would surely have gotten ill because there is such a horrible stench in the air . . . and it is terrible, to be so alone for three days, to sit spellbound. . . . Willy is really a good guy, he . . . visited me three times, though actually no one is allowed [to visit] in the Karzer, but the keeper is not inhuman. In addition, I could not sleep at night in the bed because of the stench, so I was happy as I came out again.

He spent Monday "walking around all day outside." With the time spent in detention, Boas's record was cleared.[25]

Determined not to find himself alone again and without friends, Boas joined the Burschenschaft Alemannia zu Bonn. Founded in 1844, this was the same fraternal organization to which his cousin Willy Meyer belonged and to which others from Westphalia were recruited. Explaining his decision to join the fraternity, Boas wrote Toni, "'I cannot be alone. If I were, I would think too much about the past, about what cannot be altered.'" Years later, his sister, Hedwig Lehmann, reflected on this time in her brother's life: "These were wild and happy years for Franz. Every vacation he came home with new 'Schmisse' [dueling scars] and our mother was especially unhappy that his handsome face was being marred. He also made debts, but my father allowed him to have his way." Lehmann continued, "I do not believe Franz studied much during his first year in Bonn. The fraternity took all of his time."[26]

Boas's letters home were replete with accounts of his activities with "the Burschenschaft, his initiation . . . , the annual founding celebration with Old Boys . . . , the weekly Kneipe nights and fencing practice . . . and business meetings." In February 1878 Boas told his parents about the *Commers*, the Burschenschaft ritual, involving ninety participants, all singing and pledging oaths of solidarity, with drinking prohibited until after midnight. Once midnight had passed and the students were no longer bound by the prohibition against drinking at the Commers, everyone copiously imbibed. "I stayed until two o'clock and went home relatively sound," Boas wrote. At nine o'clock in the morning, he got up, shaved, went for a little walk with two of his friends, and then returned to the tavern again for the official morning pint.[27]

Boas described his "wild" behavior during *Fastnacht*, a celebration preceding Ash Wednesday, similar to Carnival, that was marked by excess of drink and bawdy behavior. "You really mustn't be cross with me," Boas wrote his mother, "but I have been horribly raucous these days, in a way I never thought I could. But I'm happy that it's now over; I could not have lasted one more day." He described the rollicking Fastnacht-fun he had had with his fraternity brothers that involved heavy drinking and flirtatious encounters with young women. In the evening they gathered in a large pub, moved all the tables together, and spent the night drinking, talking, and singing. Boas described Fastnacht as "really the one and only fraternity celebration among all students." Gathered with students they didn't know at all, they drank *Brüderschaft* (brotherhood) whereby the participants toasted each other, linked arms, and drained their glasses, all the while looking into each other's eyes. They then shifted from the formal address of either *Sie*, or the last name preceded by *Herr*, to the informal *Du*, or by using the first name. "That evening I got home at three o'clock; you can imagine that I wasn't all that sober anymore." On the following day, Boas and his friends went to Cologne, where the festivities dwarfed the razzle-dazzle in Bonn. On Tuesday, the day preceding Ash Wednesday, Boas "rollicked the most." He began the day with heavy drinking, went home to sleep because he had drunk too much, "but, instead of my room, I ended up in the living room of my landlords with whom I had planned to go to the costume ball." Eventually he made it to the costume ball, and "danced until two," then went to the pub, and drank until Wednesday morning. Forthrightly, Boas admitted "that was a horrible night, one over which I have a terrible moral hangover. . . . Now, I've come to my senses, I was rather crazy these days and celebrated Fastnacht wilder than anyone; it's good that that happens only once." He added, "But I had great fun."[28]

At Bonn, instead of hiding the results of his duels from his parents, he wrote home about them. During the Christmas vacation of 1877 Boas's mother had begged him to give up dueling. However, by January 1878 he told of "an 'elenden Blutigen'—a miserable cut—which required him to stay home for a day." In February he wrote his mother of his inability to forego the Mensur because of his attachment to the *Couleur*, a term that referred specifically to the headgear and ribbons worn by the members of his fraternal organization, but more generally to the sense of camaraderie:

Dear Mama,

We have already talked a lot about the dueling over Christmas, and you know what I think of it, but I cannot give up the whole wonderful life here in the Couleur just because of this one thing that I maybe don't like.

In a postscript, he added, "I'm very well again. . . . After some time, one won't even be able to see anything of my scar."[29]

Boas told his parents about his visit to the Bonn synagogue that had been erected to replace the old, eighteenth-century structure. On the previous Friday evening and on Saturday, the Reform synagogue was dedicated with all due ceremony through services, a banquet, and a ball. "I was invited," Boas wrote, "but politely declined for various reasons, because first I saw no reason for me to celebrate and then I thought that I would not know anyone there." Boas related, "On Saturday morning I was met by *einer von uns* [one of us], Springerum who wanted to go to the synagogue, but didn't want to go alone, and we went together"—thus, Boas had explicitly identified himself as being Jewish (admittedly, solely in a letter to his parents). Boas described the synagogue: "The building is truly stunning—beautiful and tasteful up to the smallest details." The entrance was from the Judengasse, the Jewish Lane, through a front structure supported by "magnificent red sandstone pillars." The expansive interior space was divided into three sections by "beautiful columns of red sandstone"; an aisle down the center separated the women's section and the men's. Located at the back was a gallery with space for the choir and the future organ. Always an aficionado of good music, Boas remarked that the choir sang fairly well. "The cantor," Boas wrote, "also has a beautiful voice." Particularly appreciative of Rabbi Dr. Emanuel Schreiber, Boas observed that he "is a very liberal man and his sermon I liked fairly well. I might go back again." He was annoyed with himself, he admitted, "not to have accepted the invitation, because I saw what I had partially considered—that one of the girls from our dance circle of last winter, [Fräulein] Hirth, was a Jewess, and surely enough had come that evening. If I had known that, I would certainly have gone."[30]

By July Boas wrote his parents about the real reason he had attended the dedication of the Bonn synagogue: "I confess, back then I did not go to the Synagogue to attend the ceremony, but in order to see her." He missed his opportunity to be able to see Fräulein Hirth socially at the ball because of "foolish pride and fear." He recounted how he went out one day with Springerum, crossed the street, and they encountered her, "Of course, I blushed up to my ears. . . . Furthermore, I was so frightened that I almost fell, and I then realized . . . how much I was looking forward to the moment when I saw her." He admitted to his parents that he was tormented by emotion: "I have days when I'm half-crazy and will not tolerate being at home, and I search for as loud a society as possible, while [on other days] I prefer to be quiet." And then, in exasperation, he exclaimed, "Oh, what good are all the words, when I cannot describe my heart to you." All for naught was his raging emotion: Miss Hirth was to go to England, and Boas to Kiel.[31]

In his fourth semester at Bonn, Boas asked his parents about Toni: "Has she come home, or must she stay longer in the abominable Kiel?" By August 1879 he had learned of her renewed health crisis. Toni had been under the care of Dr. Johannes Friedrich August von Esmarch, director of the surgery unit at Kiel. He wrote his parents, "Poor Toni has truly too much misfortune, first this, then that. I certainly knew about the misfortune of winter, but surely hoped that the evil would not return. All the more was I frightened and stunned by the news of her new disease." He was consumed with worry "that she has to sit so alone in the far distance without having someone with her." But he was "pleased that she has nice, amiable people there who take care of her."[32] One month later, after finishing his semester at Bonn, Boas told his mother, "I will probably not go back to Bonn" for the next semester, but rather go to Kiel where, as he said, he could "learn enough." The caveat—that he "could learn enough" at Kiel—was telling. Instead of going to the Friedrich-Wilhelms-Universität of Berlin, as he had earlier planned, to study with the eminent Professor of Physics Hermann Ludwig Ferdinand von Helmholtz and to do "research in the best laboratory in the country," he went to Kiel, "a small, undistinguished university with inadequate and rudimentary laboratories and whose single physicist had no great reputation." Boas wrote his parents from Kiel as soon as he had joined Toni, "I happily arrived here last night at 12 o'clock and first went to the university this morning at 8 o'clock to check everything out, then off to Toni with whom I stayed until 11 o'clock." He continued, "She had a very bad day after the change of dressing yesterday—the changing takes hours," and she was running a high fever. With all her discomfort, still he found her "to have improved greatly since the last time, dear Mama, you were here." The fainting spells and nausea had passed, and she wasn't suffering from severe headaches.[33]

Boas would study physics with Professor Gustav Karsten, physicist and mineralogist, in his "dark and ancient" physics institute. Cole notes, "Kiel was remote from the centers of German physics, and it suffered neglect by a Prussian ministry whose main attention was devoted to Berlin." The discipline of physics failed to flourish during Karsten's forty-three-year tenure at Kiel, and the courses he offered attracted very few students. While less than happy in his work with Karsten, Boas had been pulled back to his passion for study by Theobald Fischer and Benno Erdmann. Fischer had moved from Bonn in 1879, when he received a call to the Christian-Albrecht Universität in Kiel to serve as professor of geography. Erdmann, a specialist in Kant, had also been called to Kiel, though he from Berlin, to occupy the chair of philosophy. Boas remarked to his parents that Fischer was "'*very* friendly,' offering support in every way." In addition, Boas worked with Professor of Mathematics and Astronomy Georg Daniel Eduard Weyer, Professor of Mineralogy Arnold von Lausalx, and zoologist Karl Augustus Möbius on the "Geographic Distribution of Sea Mammals."[34] Karsten was interested in the practical applications of physics for work he was doing with another of Boas's professors at Kiel, Möbius. Together they served on the Kiel Commission that "established a chain of permanent observation stations along the German Baltic and North Sea coasts . . . to examine Baltic fisheries" and to make observation on "weather, currents, and properties of the water and plankton." With his interest in the properties of water, Karsten assigned Boas his dissertation research on just this topic, the optical properties of water. Boas had hoped to study a mathematical and theoretical problem, "the 'Fehlergesetz,' C. F. Gauss's law of the normal distribution of errors," but he resigned himself to follow the guidance of his professor.[35]

Boas's frustration at having to work on a topic not of his own choosing was intensified by the numerous problems he encountered with the equipment for his experiments and the questionable results of his research. He suffered ill health from exposure to the "abominable frost and snowy weather" when gathering his data. As Cole recounts, Boas had "to spend time in a boat on Kiel's harbor, sinking zinc tubes with attached mirrors or porcelain plates into the sea." He also spent a great deal of time "in Karsten's laboratory, passing both sunlight and artificial light through tubes of distilled water." Apologizing for not having written earlier, Boas told his parents of his frustrations: "My work hasn't made any progress in recent days since I had to bury myself with experiments on the creation of a suitable blue light. Yesterday, I fortunately found the right arrangement." He struggled to keep his water samples pure and uncontaminated, since impurity would change "'the transparency of water.'" Always at the point of exhaustion, he was working hard on his "observations and calculations." He wrote, "You can't imagine how happy I'd be if I were to reach a conclusion . . . since my work would be then fairly valuable if nothing else, at least I could be rather pleased." Boas discarded two photometers that did not work before finally solving the problem by fixing one himself that would be sensitive enough to measure the intensity of light.[36]

Hedwig Lehmann observed that Boas "had more peace to work away from fraternity life," when he had moved to Kiel. "I remember," Lehmann wrote, "that he made many unsuccessful experiments and that our father grew very impatient." Boas, himself, was impatient: "I wish the horrible dissertation were finally finished. I have no desire to work on it any more!" To his parents, Boas described the problems he was having with the equipment to measure light: "I see myself forced to give up my dissertation entirely and to start anew. Why you ask? Well, because no true Photometer exists. After I have plagued myself all these months as to how I shall get to the heart of my light measures (Photomate, light measurements) finally I see the light, namely that the principle is entirely wrong." He continued, "However, I can take solace that Helmholtz and other people have made the same mistake, but the method still remains incorrect. I then thought of a new one which had been used earlier in similar form, but on the same day a work was published proving the inaccuracy of this method." He resolved not to worry but to start "a new work with fresh courage." Up to this point, his research had demonstrated "the inaccuracy of this method." He exclaimed with a German proverbial expression, "Mein Latein ist ganz zu Ende!" (My Latin is all at an end—I am at my wits end) and concluded that, after a whole day, he could not solve his problems in spite of "a thorough review of photometric methods." He hoped it would go better: "My results so far, I will write now and publish in Poppendorfs annals." Boas did indeed publish "Ein Beweis des Talbot'schen Satzes und Bemerkungen zu einigen aus demselben gezogenen Folgerungen" (A proof of Talbot Principles and remarks on some conclusions drawn from it) in Poggendorff's *Annalen der Physik und Chemie* (1882).[37]

Ten days later Boas wrote his parents, "There is no more unpleasant situation than to find oneself in such a dilemma as I was in, and besides to have so much work during the whole thing. I had no real desire to do anything. I have practically completely arranged my new instruments." Not wanting his student to waste time in starting his research anew, Karsten advised Boas to append his research concerning the photometer to the research regarding the color of water. With this approach to his dissertation difficulties, Boas said, he would finish his research that semester. In a letter to Toni in which he was telling her of a celebration for one of his instructors, Boas wrote, "Just now I hit upon an equation for my calculations. I shall quickly make a note of it before I forget." Seemingly, he had written down the equation before beginning the next sentence: "Thank heaven, now because of this equation I am in a position to solve my problem. I still must see if the final equation permits a solution. If that is the case, I shall jump over the table three times. Then I can finish my observations any time I wish and shall have a fine dissertation. May I succeed!" In a postscript he noted, "Now I must compulsively calculate until I know whether the equation is solvable." By March he was encouraged by the progress of his calculations; he had "approached the question from another angle in order to give the equations a better form." Clearly pleased, Boas noted, "Undoubtedly, I shall get a result on the reflection of light against colored bodies which will be of some interest after all, even though I won't manage to find a solution to the entire question. I have to admit that I'm downright sick of all the counting and will thoroughly regenerate when I'm with you." In anticipation of his visit home after an absence of over six months, he added, "I have so little time to see you, alas. You can't imagine how much I long to see you."[38]

During the work on his dissertation, Boas had developed an interest in psychophysics, but he had not had time to pursue it. He had encountered "certain photometric difficulties" that led him to "psychological questions" about perception. Erdmann encouraged Boas "to execute the work at once and to bring it to him." Thus, Boas wrote a short paper on the interpretation of sensations that was published as "Über eine neue Form des Gesetzes der Unterschiedsschwelle" (A new form of the law of the difference threshold) in *Pflüger's Archiv* (1881).[39]

While Boas's parents shared their son's concerns about his academic work, their worry focused intensely on the Mensur. Meier Boas counseled his son on the dangers of dueling in response to insults from anti-Semites. In November 1880 he wrote, "'I know that you are very sensitive on this point, and it is easy for an attack to be made on you that you think you cannot avoid. I warn you, my dear son, to avoid such things. Ignore provocation; do not believe that you can improve the position of the Jews through your personal intervention. Always remember that we have only one son and do not let yourself into anything whose outcome you cannot foresee.'" Boas's father was aware that "the Jewish question was so much discussed in the capital and elsewhere and . . . he had read about student provocations leading to duels." Meier Boas was referring to the anti-Semitic movement headed by Adolf Stoecker, known as the "Berlin movement." Stoecker, a Lutheran pastor who became Imperial Court Chaplain in 1874, declared himself "'the founder of the anti-Semitic movement,'" and reached the apogee of his political suasion in the 1880s.[40]

Boas assured his father in a way that was likely only to cause him further concern: "'I remain unmolested since every student here knows that I would not be shy to defend my affairs with the sword.'" He wrote,

Dear Papa!

To allay your fears, I hurry to respond promptly to your letter I've just received. Since I only socialize a little and only meet close acquaintances you do not need to worry that I'd ever find myself in situations of such kind to which you refer. Giesbrecht and another one of my acquaintances and I are of the same opinion on such things, and I can talk with them candidly. With friends, on principle, I avoid any conversation that could lead to heated discussions, be it politics, religion or whatever.

Boas concluded his letter, "I promise you once again always to stay far away from all occasions in which I as a Jew would be exposed to insults."[41]

Boas could not restrain himself. In January 1881 he wrote to his parents that "a splendid anti-Semitic action happened to me." Boas and his friend Wilhelm Giesbrecht had gone to a tavern where "several close and not-so-close friends had seated themselves with us." The topic of anti-Semitism had come up, and they were making fun of some anti-Semitic men they knew. Boas continued, "The door opened and in comes one of the 'Führer' who knew one of us very slightly. He asked permission to sit at our table. One good-hearted freshman stammered something like, 'Fine,' and he sat down. Of course, I immediately took my beer and sat at a nearby table saying that I could not sit at the same table with this man. What happened? All but this dunce got up with comments of cold adieus and let him sit there. I have never enjoyed myself so much." The fact that the tavern had been crowded added to the embarrassment for the individual and the amusement for Boas and his friends. "This good young man," Boas remarked, "will be careful not to become Führer of a political movement anytime soon." He only regretted "that this person was not another 'Führer' with whom I was once quite well acquainted," and who continued to greet Boas in a warm fashion while Boas intentionally ignored him. These young men were connected with the right-wing student organization the Vereine Deutscher Studenten, Union of German Students, that was circulating an anti-Semitic League petition. Boas said that he had eschewed confrontation with them but rather had "his friend, Giesbrecht, circulate 'a stinging declaration' . . . that had garnered forty signatures" against the *Judenhetzer*, the Jew baiters.[42]

Müller-Wille notes in a personal communication, "The Vereine deutscher Studenten (vds) was a consolidation or union of student associations which were on the right, anti-Semitic, and nationalistic. They were founded by associations in Berlin, Halle, Leipzig, Breslau, and Kiel on August 6, 1881, at the time at which Boas finished his doctorate." Norbert Kampe remarks on the "new student anti-Semitism" that was especially manifest in Protestant northern Germany. Against such a backdrop, Boas's promises to his parents to avoid conflict were for naught. "Unfortunately I am bringing this time for the last time again a few cuts," he wrote, "one even on the nose!" Wanting to avoid a fuss, Boas emphasized that the duel was unavoidable: "I hope you will not say too much about it, because with the damned Jew baiters this winter one could not survive without quarrel and fighting." He concluded, "So until the day after tomorrow. I am happy as a fish to come to you. I can hardly stand it here."[43]

Boas returned to Kiel after Pfingstferien and reassured his parents that he was living a "secluded" life with "regular hours." He had one friend from the previous semester, he said: "I am not entirely alone. It would otherwise have been boring this summer." By July his mother was still worrying that her son was dueling. Boas wrote her, "Dear Mama, your fear that I have again dueled is not founded. I am no longer a student and have really had enough of it." Boas spent his time preparing for his doctoral examinations. He exclaimed, "You can't believe how very afraid I am of the exam. I only wish it were over!" He confessed, "You can imagine that even though it may be of no use, I am reviewing until the last instant." Still, his work progressed "lustily." He told of his plan of study, "Today I reviewed 1/3 of the general geography, 1/5 of the history of Philosophy, about 1/4 of the Physics, and 1/3 of the special earth science." He added, "I do not expect to flunk, but whether I shall get a decent rating is another matter."[44]

In mid-July Boas told his parents that he expected to "be invited to the exam" by the middle of the following week. "At last! Thursday evening at eight o'clock latest (as it seems now) you may expect my telegram. . . . Because of all this, I feel so stupid, as though a mill wheel were turning in my head." He said that "the entire faculty will be invited to the exam." On Friday, July 22, 1881, Boas made his "official visits" to the dean and to his examiners. As he explained to his father, on Saturday, July 23, he went "with fear and trembling to the university." His oral examination, presided over by Dean and Professor of Chemistry Albert Ladenburg, was held between six to eight thirty p.m. He continued, "You cannot imagine what fear I had before the beginning of the exam. Gradually a certain balance came back to my feelings. I was finally finished at 8:30 and it was high time since I began to suffer from amnesia, i.e. I could not find the words that I wanted to use." His dissertation advisor Gustav Karsten asked him "some very unpleasant and very specific things" regarding the "transmission of water waves," a comparison between "the old and the new electro-dynamic machines," and the "different phenomena of the polarization of light in the atmosphere." Boas confessed, "At first I was very frightened and could hardly get a word out, but it went better later on." Theobald Fischer examined him on "different kinds of terrain con-figuration" and on "the facts about the ebb and flow of the sea and about the theory surrounding it." Fischer also asked Boas to discuss the "gen-eral geography of islands," "the geography of New Zealand," "the most noted farm states of North America and China," and "the conditions for a cultural development of Siberia." Fischer concluded with questions about "the ethnography of Northern Asia." Professor of Mathematics and Astronomy Weyer examined Boas in mathematics, specifically in "mathematical geography" with a focus on "the art of projection." With relief Boas wrote, "Finally Erdmann finished off with philosophy. He asked first about psycho-physics, then went into logic and let me give a short development of materialism. With that I was released and after ten minutes was told that I had passed the exam." Then everyone gathered for wine and cake.[45]

Boas was hoping for "a decent middle grade." Later the same day Boas wrote his father, "Dear Papa! I just found out that I received the 'best' for my dissertation and second best for my exam." As Ludger Müller-Wille conveyed to me, Boas received summa cum laude for the dissertation and magna cum laude for the oral examinations. With the latter weighted more heavily, he was awarded the overall distinction of magna cum laude. Before he could be promoted to doctor, Boas had to have two hundred copies of his dissertation published for distribution to all universities in German-speaking countries. On August 9, 1881, with all the professors assembled, Dean Ladenburg presented Boas with his diploma, with the notation in Latin that the dissertation was "a spec-imen diligentiae et acuminis valde laudatur" (a specimen of acumen and diligence greatly praised). Boas then gave a talk on "Evolution and Structure of Coral Islands."[46]

As he told his parents, his dissertation was complete, "and though it isn't anything special, it is at least tolerable"; or as he wrote in another letter, his dissertation was "ein mäßiges Opus," a moderate piece of work. He dedicated this 1881 "Inaugural Dissertation," *Beiträge zur Erkenntniss der Farbe des Wassers* (Contributions to the knowledge of the color of water), to his "dear parents." On the frontispiece, he began, "In July 1858, I, Franz Boas, of Mosaic Confession, was born in Minden i./W," and he continued with a brief summation of his educational background, the universities he had attended, and a listing of the professors under whom he had studied. In gratitude to his professors, he concluded: "To all of them, I express herewith my heartfelt thanks." In the introduction to the dissertation, Boas began: "Observation shows us that in layers of small thickness seemingly completely colorless and transparent water often assumes a very intense color at greater depths, which, however, is by no means similar in different waters." He scribed the different nuances, "from the deepest indigo blue to sky blue and green- to yellowish-brown and dark brown. Who has not heard of the beauty of Lake Geneva, the color of which competes with the blue of the sky!" He continued with references to the "bright blue" of the Central Asian salt sea, of the indigo blue of the sea off Sumatra, of the aqua blue of "the lake Yoyoa in Nicaragua, the hot springs of Reykir in Iceland, as well as those in Yellowstone Park and the sparkling [hot springs of] Te Tarata in New Zealand." Concluding his introduction, Boas focused on the two themes for investigation: the absorption of light in water, as discussed in chapter 3, and the polarization of light reflected from the water, discussed in chapter 4.[47]

Boas was candid in his dissertation about the shortcomings of his investigations and the limitations placed on his research by the inadequacy of the equipment. He ended chapter 3, "Investigation of the Absorption of Light in Water," with the following assessment: "A drawback to my method of observation was that, aside from sodium light I could get no homogenous light source intense enough to allow a comparison of shades of intensity." With lithium light, it had worked, but "the flame's greater brightness is all too short-lasting" to be useful. He continued, "It was therefore necessary to resort to an expedient for the other colors." Boas drew "an ordinary gas lamp" close to his eyes and placed "an absorbent medium" in front of it, "which ideally would let homogeneous light through." In similar fashion, he indicated at the end of chapter 4, "The Polarization of the Reflected Light from Water," that "probably the degree of polarization is also dependent on the depth of the blue color of the sky, so it is all the greater, the bluer the sky." He concluded, "About this I did not arrive at a definite decision, since the number of bright days was quite low." Similarly, Boas explained the shortcomings in the tables presented in the appendix. At the bottom of table 1, he noted that a single asterisk marked an observation that did "not fit into the series," because, while recording the data, "a small, white cloud passed before the sun," and two asterisks marked an observation that "gave erroneous results because the water suddenly moved strongly."[48]

Boas had written his parents in May 1881, "'If someone had told me a few semesters ago that I would submit such a dissertation, I would have laughed at him. But one learns to be content.'" On the cusp of the festivities, Boas wrote his mother, "Dear Mama, I have just now happily passed my promotion and am really now doctor, Magna cum Laude. . . . Tonight, we tipple." Totally dependent as he was on his parents for all funds, he admitted to his father, "I want to submit the work as soon as possible. That will cost some awful coins! All at once, I have to put 200 Mark on the table." Meier Boas sent his son a draft for more than 267 marks to cover expenses.[49]

The university years for Boas and for other students were a rite of passage into the manhood of the educated elite, and manhood it definitely was, since women were not admitted to German universities in the nineteenth century. According to Arnold van Gennep, the rite of passage marked a change from one cosmic or social state to another with those undergoing the transition set apart from ordinary life in a liminal period, garbed in special costuming—such as the special-colored caps and sashes of the fraternal organizations—subject to ritualized conduct, members of an age grade, and with elders overseeing the imparting of esoteric knowledge. For the university student, this was a passage from the social status of *Abiturienten* (gymnasium school-leavers) to that of *Akademiker* (university graduates). Indeed, even the Latin meaning of *Abitur* conveys this change of status: "about to depart," "one who is going to depart." In the liminal period the university students reveled in "the social freedom of student life," and the "escape from parental authority"; they enjoyed to the fullest their "*Burschenzeit* [rowdy youth]." In this burst of release from the strictures of Gymnasium study, the university student signed up for classes but was not required to attend, purchased texts but was not required to read them, and completed courses but was not required to take examinations. Away from the demanding eyes of the Gymnasium instructors and the watchful eyes of parents, the students loafed through "the first few semesters," and apart from "drinking and dueling," might occupy their time with "an avid browsing in contemporary literature and . . . a sampling of different lectures by famous professors." Certainly Boas followed this pattern of loafing, as he wrote to his Gymnasium friend Krüer, "You have no idea what a loafer I have become and how much time I spend in cafés. . . . When the weather is bad I stretch out on the sofa for an hour or two and read."[50]

Integral to student culture, the university student duel flowered most fully during the period of the Second Empire of Wilhelm II (1888–1918), but certainly was in full swing earlier in 1877–81, when Boas was a university student. Paired with excessive drinking, the Mensur, a carefully choreographed ritual of violence, provided the training grounds for German manhood. As McAleer notes, "The Germans were Europe's most tenacious and serious duelist—serious, because the most striking aspect of the German duel was its deadliness." In the postuniversity Mensur, the combatants, with their dueling pistols in hand, shot to kill. Firmly grounded on the principle of *Standesehre* (professional or caste honor), the duel guarded "the collective honor of German society's upper strata" and maintained "group solidarity over and against the lower orders." In every *Ehrenhandel* (affair of honor, duel), "the participants were representing not only their own interests but those of their class." The fraternal organizations with their ritualized duels set apart, as Hobsbawm elucidates, "the 'old boy,' 'alumnus' or 'Alte Herren,'" members of the social elites, from the influx of middle-class students that flowed into the German universities from the mid-1870s to the mid-1880s.[51]

In the university student duel, the intent was not to kill the opponent in order to expunge the insult as it was in the postuniversity duel, but to stand one's ground, to wield the sword, and to slice the opponent's face more severely than one's own face was sliced in a ritual of facial scarification. Many scars would last a lifetime as marks of passage into German manhood. McAleer maintains, "The *Mensur* was a discipline in which there was neither winner nor loser." However, from Boas's accounts as a participant, the number and length of the slices on the face were crucial in determining who left the Mensur dueling ground with honor restored. Boas included the measurements of his wounds in his letter to Reinhard Krüer (a cut in his scalp "four cm. long and one and one-half cm. wide") and the facial cuts he inflicted on his opponent ("three cuts from ear to nose that required eight stitches"). To his parents, he included a description of his wound as "an 'elenden Blutigen,' a miserable cut." Additionally, Boas engaged in a rematch because his honor had been insulted: the members of the opposing corps had ruled the initial match unsatisfactory. With echoes of the student code of honor, he emphasized to his parents, "If you knew student relationships better, you would understand how severe this insult is." Thus, there were those who prevailed in the Mensur. Their performance was evaluated by those in attendance, by the members of their group, by those of the other group, by the student umpire, and by the student keeping a record of the number of cuts and the time of the duel in the memorandum book.[52]

The blood flowed, the wounds healed, the scars remained, and those in the brotherhood celebrated with drinking bouts of astounding excess: "Rabelaisian quantities were consumed in single sittings on command and in unison with the group, improvised vomatoriums and pissoirs at close ready, while rollicking challenges to 'beer-duels' flew about the table." The affiliated university students were members of one of three dueling associations: "the *Landsmannschaften*, the oldest; the *Burschenschaften*, the least conservative; and the *Corpsstudenten*, the most elite." Belonging to the least conservative in Bonn, the Burschenschaften, Boas was steeped in the collective nature of the organization. He wrote to his parents in February 1878, "'I would never have thought such close ties between the whole group were at all possible. We are 21, constantly together. You would think there would be cliques formed, and certainly one is closer to some than to others, but we stand all for one and one for all.'" Whether as the rallying cry of *The Three Musketeers*, "All for one, one for all," or as the purest expression of Émile Durkheim's collective effervescence, where the individual becomes subsumed in the frenzied excitement of the group, Boas's identity was merged for a time with his Alemannia. As an example of the immediacy of the brotherhood, Boas explained to his parents how the etiquette of address showed emotional closeness: "Our relationship with the old boys is a really nice one. Here comes a man to us, all foreign to me, and he calls me by my first name right away, and we have a bond, drawing us close and closer."[53]

The time came for the serious university student to ease out of the debauchery of his initial years. After three or four semesters of heavy drinking and frequent dueling, the student could declare his status as "honorary" in the fraternal organization. The timing of such honorary and inactive status coincided with the impending examinations—indeed the *only* examinations the students took—and then these were optional, "administered at the end of the three-year college term." These comprehensive and demanding examinations called for disciplined preparation. In a conveniently timed move, Boas departed Bonn for Kiel, where he was freed from the activities of his fraternity and where he could return concertedly to his studies. While Boas left his raucous fraternity activities behind in Bonn, he did not leave behind the engagement in the Mensur. The rituals of manhood that he had played out in Heidelberg had become for Boas more serious in Bonn and Kiel. From a duel over insults about piano études, the engagements escalated to fights over insults about his Jewish heritage. From Heidelberg, where Boas expressed his own anti-Semitic views about the "lauten Juden," the noisy Jews, and "intolerable Jewish societies," to Kiel, where he was fighting duels in response to "Jew-baiters," the circuit illustrated Boas's own journey into the Jewish self—in large measure, and necessarily so for a minority group, a self as defined by others. In Minden Boas was viewed as an acculturated Jew from an upper-middle-class family; in the anti-Semitic climate of Kiel in 1879, he was viewed simply and stereotypically as a Jew.[54]

The upswing in anti-Semitism and the insults to which Boas was subjected coincided with the rise of economic challenges in Germany. Undergoing a rapid process of industrialization with the growth of the naval and shipbuilding industries, Kiel was "strongly Protestant and nationalistic." While pervasive in Kiel, anti-Semitism was not limited to this northern seaport city but was present elsewhere as well. For university students there was an added lever to anti-Semitism that entailed the rise in the number of Jewish students from 1870 to 1885, with a slight dip in 1890 and a rise again in 1895. The educated middle-class Protestants reacted to the increasing numbers of Jewish students "with overt and covert anti-Semitism," and, among other actions, founded the nationalistic and anti-Semitic Vereine Deutscher Studenten, Union of German Students, in the 1880s.[55]

Frederick the Great and Wilhelm von Humboldt had prepared the ground for the German Enlightenment and Jewish emancipation at the turn of the nineteenth century. They saw "the price to be paid by the Jews for admission into German society [as] the repudiation of their Jewish identity." With a shared goal, the German liberals and German Jews of the nineteenth century aimed for complete assimilation of Jews into German society, but the two sides had different interpretations as to what this assimilation meant. For the Jews it meant retaining their Jewish identity and merging with the German nation; for the liberals it meant absorption of the Jews into German society with no trace of their Jewishness remaining. The majority of the German people shifted from the ideals of the German Enlightenment, from the quest for "shared humanity toward which *Bildung* must strive," to a concept of a shared soul of the German people, a *Volksgeist*, a folk or national spirit, that excluded all that was not purely German. As Glick emphasizes, "The German *Volk* were envisioned as rooted in soil, culture, and tradition, and the connections between racial ancestry, land, and cultural inheritance were perceived not as abstraction or metaphor, but as a literal and absolute bond that could not and must not ever be dissolved." Certainly, Boas and his family were among those German Jews who had assimilated to German culture but who had retained their identity as Jews, though for Franz this remained a vexed and problematic identity. The shared soul of the German people would not include the Boases, or other German-Jewish families like them.[56]

The citadel of German Enlightenment was the university. Upon entering the embrace of the German university, a young man became part of the "central cultural institution of nineteenth-century Germany," an institution that maintained its power by controlling "entry into the professions" through authority over state examinations. Set apart from the noble classes and from the commercial middle classes "by their cultivation," those educated at the university formed "a more cohesive and self-conscious group than other college graduates of Western Europe." Indeed, the Prussian Educational Code of 1794 manifested just such a separation by designating the university class as *Eximierte*, citizens exempt "from the draft, freed from any taxes, endowed with a special judicial code of honor, and permitted marriage with the aristocracy." Of course, the latter privilege, allowance of marriage with aristocracy, would not apply to Boas or to other Jewish students who comprised the 9.58 percent of the academic body. In Germany as a whole, the Jews were "never much more than 1 percent of the total population." As Julia Liss and Kampe point out, they were overrepresented in the university student body. While access to an aristocratic wife was of no consequence to Boas, access to the professions was of dear consequence, and, as a Jew, he was in a precarious position. Konrad Jarausch observes, "Because of greater formal and informal discrimination in other areas, the Jewish minority viewed higher education as an important avenue of emancipation from the ghetto toward the free professions of law and medicine, which were not officially barred, like the Officer Corps."[57]

Boas had elected not to pursue a career in medicine, and he had never considered law, nor had he any desire to be part of the elite Officer Corps. He was, however, keen on pursuing university teaching and research. For a Jew, "the price for admission" into the profession of teaching in secondary and higher education "was cultural assimilation into academic Germany, and the cost of professional success (obtaining a full professorship) often was as high as complete amalgamation by conversion." Boas's mentor Theobald Fischer made reference in a letter of December 21, 1884, to a discussion they had had in Kiel about Boas's converting to Christianity, "and I told you that I would consider such a move quite superfluous."[58]

With all the dueling and drinking, blood and beer, there was nonetheless a crucial intellectual core to the university training that "served as the stage in the formation of an individual *Weltanschauung* [worldview], a basic outlook on society and polity." Grounded in the classical study of the Gymnasium and continued in the university, this intellectual core combined "the cultivation of reason and aesthetic taste" and derived from a fulfillment of the inherent capabilities of the individual flowering to its fullest in spirit and intellect. Franz Boas's sense of self was grounded in

Bildung and was steeped in a wide-ranging intelligence that quested for a fulfillment of that which was innate within him, whether as the young child collecting lichen and mosses or as the young man collecting sea water samples.[59]

Years later, in his letter of acknowledgment on the presentation of the *Festschrift* marking his twenty-fifth anniversary of the receipt of his doctorate, Boas wrote, "The honor that you have bestowed upon me leads me to look back, and to think to what I may owe the success that has seemed to you to warrant the expression of such high appreciation. I believe I am not mistaken if I see one of its sources in the early training to independent thought and action that I owe to the German universities." Boas noted the danger for some students in "the sudden transition from strict school discipline to the freedom of the university"; there were those who succumbed "to the temptations of an uncontrolled life." He continued, "Many others—and I count myself among them—are intoxicated by the new life, and require time and increasing maturity to find their place; but when they find it, they stand on firmer ground, better able to cope with the problems of life and of learning than those who have never left the guiding hand of the master."[60]

After having completed his Gymnasium examinations and on the threshold of university life, Boas had written to his sister Toni, "Now in truth, the school years are finished. The ideas that moved me up to now have been completed and new ones will pull me through life. . . . What does the future hold for me . . . ? At least I do not worry. I have no wishes for all my wishes are met. The exam is happily over. I can become what I want; my heart, what more do you want?" Franz signed the letter "Your Brother, who floats in seventh heaven." In becoming "what I want," Boas was fulfilling the essence of *Bildung*, an efflorescence from within, a fulfillment of the inner being.[61]

3

In Heaven, in Love, and Separation

Preparing for the Arctic Voyage

Boas had one year of service as a volunteer in the army: an option for university graduates who entered reserve officer training in place of the three years of service. In July 1881, before undertaking his military service (or his "slavery," as he called it) and fresh from his doctoral examinations, Boas was able to join his mother, Hete, and Aenne in the Harz Mountains for a holiday. Hedwig Lehmann recalled this time: "In summer our Uncle Jacobi came . . . to visit our parents. Mrs. Krackowizer came with her children Marie and Alice to Germany, to take her daughters to . . . the boarding school in Stuttgart. . . . Uncle Jacobi . . . invited our mother, Aenne, Marie, Alice and me to . . . the Harz Mountains, and our newly minted Doctor Franz went directly to Harzburg." Lehmann collapsed into one sentence a romance that took from July 1881 to April 1883 to blossom forth: "And then it happened, that Marie and Franz concluded a partnership for life."[1]

After they had declared their love for each other Franz wrote Marie, "When I first saw you coming down the street . . . , I did not realize how quickly you would capture my heart. I do not think it took a whole day before you had won me entirely." He continued, "I can say that not one minute of those few beautiful days has been lost and do you know what I like to think about most? The Regenstein, the horse cart and the Teufels-brücke [Devil's Bridge] the last morning as we enjoyed the last beautiful minutes together." Marie recalled this time and queried, "Did you really love me already in the Harz?" She admitted, "How frightened I was before you came! The girls had told me so much about their beloved brother and on top of that he did not at all like to spend time with strange girls.

I wanted at first to stay out of your way. But you were so different from the terrible picture that I had made of you." Recalling her most treasured memory, she asked if he remembered "while the others were already going back to the wagon, how we ran to the other side to see what was there." She continued: "And the morning on the Devil's Bridge while we leaned on the banister and I wanted to throw your hat into the water, which you willingly subscribed to. How you looked at me! But at that time I did not fully understand how to read your eyes even though I liked to look into them. Only as I was separated from you longer, it became clear to me that I loved you, you only." Following the time in the Harz Mountains, Uncle Jacobi, Emilie Krackowizer, and her two daughters spent two days in Minden as guests at the Boas home and then they left for Austria, the country that had been the home of Ernst Krackowizer before he fled to America as a refugee from the revolutions of 1848. After their visit to Austria, the Krackowizers settled in Stuttgart, where the girls attended school. During their correspondence, Franz sent Marie "a fifteen-page notebook recalling the holiday in cut-out caricatures and humorous verse and she thanked him playfully as 'his enthusiastic (?) botany student.'"[2]

Entering the army as lance corporal of the infantry regiment, Boas reported to military duty at the fort in Minden on October 1, 1881. He wrote his mother, who was away at Wiesbaden recuperating from an illness, "I arrived here the day before yesterday and immediately threw myself into soldiering." The next day he would receive his uniform and present himself "along with three other volunteers . . . to the instructing lieutenant." They would serve "daily from 8–11 and from 2–4, from 4:30–5:30 for instruction." As a one-year volunteer, Boas was able to live at home with his family. Boas's father had built a large two-story house in 1878, on land made available after the city's fortified walls were taken down. While the house was under construction, Boas had written to his parents about "looking forward to my peaceful, lovely study, the elegant music room [and] the garden. . . . And the location is so convenient that it's almost in the city!" To his father Boas wrote that once "Villa Boas" was constructed and they were sitting in the garden receiving visitors, he mustn't "scramble" about so much, but rather enjoy the "lovely house of your own." Boas had helped his family move from their old house on the Market to the new Villa Boas and then he left for Kiel. In his mind it did not become home to him until he lived there during his year of military service.[3]

In a letter to Uncle Jacobi, Boas wrote, "Soldiering is really quite disagreeable. It keeps me busy six or seven hours a day, and so I can find no more than four hours for decent work, and you know how little one can accomplish in this time." Boas was appreciative of being able to spend time at home: "Since I went to the university I was never here for any longer period, and the little girls, Hete and Aenne, have grown big in this time. I rejoice every day that I can again learn to know my sisters." During his year of military service, Boas shut himself in his study in the evenings and continued his work. His mother wrote to her brother, Salomon Meyer, that Franz had spent the whole Christmas season in his room studying: "He won't allow anything to disturb him. . . . For him there is only science." She reflected, "If he remains healthy only then do I know certainly that we have great pleasure through him." Marking the months in service right along with her son, she wrote, "The first quarter of his slavery is thankfully almost over." Then, as if counting her blessings, she concluded, "The only good thing of the matter is that we have him once more for ourselves, before he moves on in life and in the distance."[4]

Working in the military during the day and holed up in his study at night, Boas was also carefully charting his "plans for work for the coming years." He wrote to Jacobi, "I hope that my plans will have sufficient interest for you that I can tell you about them. Perhaps you remember the things I told you once on our wonderful Harz journey. These matters I have made the goals of my scientific career. I am certain that I do not lose sight of this for one moment." Boas continued, "You may remember that, in a few words, it is the mechanism of the life of organisms and especially of peoples that is before my eyes." He felt, however, that he needed "to keep this goal as a distant one," because he had first to acquire knowledge of the methods of study and to establish himself in his field. He said he was going to "clean up the studies" he had undertaken in psychophysics: he had published one paper in *Pflügers Archiv*, "and one or two more will follow." Boas continued, "Then I will leave psychophysics in peace since it leads me too far afield" from the study of human geography. "As my chief work," Boas wrote, "I have another plan, to study what influence the configuration of the land has on the acquaintance of peoples with their near and far neighbors. . . . But I believe it essential to become acquainted with two other sciences, physiology and sociology, for I believe that even a geographer cannot feel quite sure of himself until he has studied these." As if steeling himself to ask, Boas expressed the need for help from Jacobi in finding a position: "Of course it is not my purpose just to sit down and do nothing but study for I wish also to employ that which I have learned up to now. . . . I cannot and do not wish to do this at Papa's expense, and must look around for a position." Boas said that "with great difficulty" he could "achieve an appointment as a *Privatdocent* with a stipend." Finally, Boas wrote, "Now it is your fault that Johns Hopkins University sticks in my head as a desirable place to work . . . for . . . one or two years. Do you think it possible for me, and that I am competent enough to get a fellowship there? (At last I have said what I have been trying to say for a quarter of an hour)."[5]

Jacobi did all he could to assist Boas in obtaining a fellowship at Johns Hopkins. In March 1882 he wrote an encouraging letter: "I do not think it would be hard to get a stipend. However, I cannot say much about it without closer inquiry." He asked Franz for "a statement of your expectations," for a list of the "public or private recommendations," for some reprints of articles, and for an indication of the "direction of your work now and for the future." Jacobi concluded, "The stipend is only for $500, which is something for Baltimore." Johns Hopkins University President Daniel Coit Gilman wrote a cordial letter to Boas: "Although we have never met I know you so well through our mutual friends . . . as well as by your professional standing that you need never offer an excuse for asking any information which we can give." With approximately one hundred applications for the fellowship program, Gilman cautioned, "All we can promise to *any* candidate we promise to *all*, fair consideration." He concluded on the positive note: "I wish we might see you here." Having received a copy of the letter, Jacobi wrote Boas asking him to send his materials immediately to Baltimore for receipt by May 12, 1882.[6]

Boas also sought advice from his mentor Theobald Fischer about his plans. In enthusiastic support, Fischer wrote, "If you can get a position at Johns Hopkins University, it would be beneficial to you. . . . A two-year stay in the United States would expand your intellectual horizons." Enclosing his letter of support, Fischer added, "I write it intentionally in

German because any decent person must understand English and German." Fischer advised Boas that "above all before the commencement of actual work you must go forward at a rapid pace with preliminary work, which is the inspection, collection and sifting of the raw data." He concluded, "Through detailed studies of the migrations of the Eskimos, you can, in fact, promote important science."[7]

On April 10, 1882, Boas sent materials to Jacobi for the Johns Hopkins fellowship application. In his statement of objectives, Boas noted the shift of interest during his university years from mathematics and physics to geography: "By studying the natural sciences I became aware of other questions which prompted me to take up geography. This subject fascinated me to such an extent that I finally chose it as my major study." In a crucial revelation of his change of perspective, Boas wrote, "In the course of time I became convinced that a materialistic point of view, for a physicist a very real one, was untenable. This gave me a new point of view and I recognized the importance of studying the interaction between the organic and inorganic, above all the relation between the life of a people and their physical environment." Even at this point in his years as a young scientist, Boas eschewed a single-stranded approach to understanding human behavior. For Boas the materialistic approach proved to be a narrow frame that precluded understanding the complexity of human life. Here lay the seeds for the later growth that resulted in the complex study of the physical environment and people's interrelationship with it. He would come to see this as the mutable physical traits of people and the reflection of their lives in language, folklore, and ritual—and, ultimately, as Boas developed the concept, in their culture. His "life plan," Boas said, arose from this orientation and would involve compiling research to answer such questions as, "In how far may we consider the phenomena of organic life, especially those of the psychic life, from a mechanistic point of view? And furthermore what conclusions may be drawn from such a consideration?" In order to undertake such research problems, Boas said, he would need to have "a general knowledge of physiology, psychology, and sociology." He was anxious to complete the smaller projects on psychophysics and meteorology so that, as he said, "I may give all my energy to working on the question which I have chosen as my life's work."[8]

Unable to send Jacobi reprints of his papers, he recounted that, in addition to several others, he had published "a small paper," on "A Proof of Talbot's Statement," in *Annalen der Physik und Chemie* (Annals of physics and chemistry) in 1882. His present focus was on "the relationship of the migration of present day Eskimo to the configuration and physical conditions of the land." Acknowledging that this was "a very extensive piece of work," he explained his approach: "I am taking it up chiefly from a methodological standpoint, in order to discover how far one can get studying a very special, and not simple case, in determining the relationship between the life of a people and the environment."[9]

Boas waited anxiously for news from Johns Hopkins. In May he wrote his sister Toni, "I wonder what will happen with my application to Baltimore? It must be in their hands for several days already." With excitement, he exuded, "It would be *very lucky* for my scientific career if I could go there." Boas said he could "do practically nothing" all day since he had military duty. He said he was able on occasion to "read something about my Eskimos and afterwards take notes. I still have 140 days." By July, having heard nothing from Johns Hopkins, both Boas and his parents were anxious about his prospects. The family network was buzzing. Franz's mother had received a letter from her sister-in-law Phips, wife of her brother Jacob, who lived in New York and who had heard "that Franz can have no hope for the position in Baltimore for this year." The sister-in-law added, "He may hope for it for next year." Sophie wrote to Jacobi, "I beg you to tell us at once whether this prospect for next year is a figure of speech or whether he can really count on it. My husband has now agreed to furnish funds for further study for one year." Franz, she said, wanted to make plans for his year of study and much would be determined by whether or not he would be going to Baltimore. Appending a note at the end of the letter, Boas recounted that he had journeyed to Kiel during his military leave to talk about "my problems with my professors." Boas continued, "I was in great doubt whether I should try to obtain a practical position in October or whether I should accept Papa's kind offer. I asked them whether in view of my ultimate plans if it would be worthwhile for me to devote some time to study." With the support of his professors, he said, "I shall decide to do so." He reiterated his mother's plea for his uncle to tell him "whether I really have any chances in Baltimore."[10]

When he learned that he had not been awarded a fellowship, Boas was devastated. He sat "as a spirit" in his study in Minden, pouring over "the Eskimo language, [with] a Lexicon." In commiseration, Boas's father wrote him from Berlin, where he was on business: "Mama informed me today that . . . Baltimore is nothing. So another disappointment. You will have to experience more of them. I am also very disappointed since I took for granted that you would get the position." He advised his son, "So now put these ideas away and come up with other plans. Please make use of your time in Kiel to discuss and deliberate thoroughly with your friends there, how you should shape your future." With belief in his son and always generous in his support, Franz's father continued, "If it should be necessary for you to spend another year to fully prepare yourself for your future you can count on me." He concluded his counsel: "Do not let this disappointment depress you. Go with determination on your way." In closing, he wrote, "Enjoy yourself to the utmost. I shall be home by the end of the week. Best Wishes, Your father, M. Boas."[11]

Boas's mood worsened with the required military maneuvers in August 1882. He wrote his parents from the Teutoburg Forest in Bielefeld, where five battalions were quartered in overcrowded and uncomfortable conditions. "I cannot tell you much about our march," he wrote, because "one finally becomes too stupefied to even look around." From the dry, rocky region of Salzkotten, Boas bemoaned, "Yesterday and today we had very long marches through endless deep sand which was very tiring. I kept up very well, my feet held out until today." The end of the maneuvers was in sight, with only a week more of "this plague" and then "three days of brigade exercises . . . not nearly as tiring as the four days of marches."[12]

Finally, his year of active military service came to an end. Boas found lodging in Berlin. Living "a truly regulated life," Boas went daily to the library and returned to work at home when the library closed. He was finishing "a short geographical work about the northern borders of the distribution of the Eskimos" that he was hoping would appear soon in the *Zeitschrift der Gesellschaft für Erdkunde zu Berlin* (Journal of the Geographical Society at Berlin). Continuing with his study of the Eskimo language, he was also learning Danish—an easy language, he said, to acquire.[13]

Boas noted in a letter to his mother that in Berlin he was "right in the middle of the geographical circle and could not have found a better place to spend the winter." Boas had gained initial introduction to the circle of scientists through Miss Hennig, whom he had met at a dinner at the Lehmanns. Miss Hennig worked as an assistant to Dr. Wilhelm Reiß, a geologist and explorer and a prominent member of both the Gesellschaft für Erdkunde zu Berlin (Society for Geography in Berlin) and the Berliner Gesellschaft für Anthropologie, Ethnologie, und Urgeschichte (Berlin Society of Anthropology, Ethnology, and Prehistory). In response to Dr. Reiß's invitation, Boas approached his house with "palpitations of the heart at 12 o'clock and with a well-practiced and prepared speech." However, as Boas wrote, "this was an unnecessary effort, since I had hardly sent my card in when Dr. Reiß appeared in the doorway and welcomed me as though I were a good old acquaintance." Put at his ease, Boas did not have to deliver his "great speech" but "could explain to him quite leisurely," as he said, "who I am and what I want." Dr. Reiß assisted Boas in every way, from setting him up with a cartographer who would instruct him in making maps, to inviting him to the Berliner Gesellschaft für Anthropologie, Ethnologie und Urgeschichte for the express purpose of introducing him to Rudolph Virchow and Adolph Bastian. "As I hear from Miss Hennig," Boas wrote, "he has already told Bastian about me and since he happens to be working on Eskimos just now, he asked Reiß to introduce me to him as soon as possible." Boas playfully wrote, "So tomorrow evening you must hold your thumbs for me so that I might succeed in awakening Bastian's interest in me." When he knew Bastian better, he would give him reprints of his work and "explain to him as clearly as possible the purpose of my studies."[14]

Virchow was the leading physical anthropologist in Germany, and Bastian the leading ethnologist. However, scientific disciplines were not firmly delineated in the nineteenth century. Virchow was claimed by the "science of medicine, anatomy, pathology and anthropology . . . as one of their great men." Bastian had studied under Virchow when the latter first began lecturing at the University of Würtzburg in pathology. In 1869 Virchow and Bastian founded the Berliner Anthropologische Gesellschaft, with a name change the next year to Berliner Gesellschaft für Anthropologie, Ethnologie und Urgeschichte. Virchow served as president; and Bastian served as vice president and as the organizing force for *Zeitschrift für Ethnologie*, the journal of the society. Years later, in the obituary for Virchow, Boas remarked that the Berliner Gesellschaft für Anthropologie, Ethnologie und Urgeschichte "soon became a center to which flowed a flood of anthropological material from all parts of the world, and where important scientific questions were discussed by the most competent authorities." Throughout his lifetime Bastian was a traveler of the world, who took "intermediate sojourns in Berlin, his chosen headquarters." From his travels and "his incessant activity as a collector," Bastian accumulated the "vast treasures" that comprised the collection of the Königliches Museum für Völkerkunde, the Royal Museum of Ethnology, of which he was founder and curator; he also served as president of the Berlin Geographical Society (1871–73).[15]

The evening at the anthropological society yielded a rich reservoir of contacts. "I arrived there," Boas wrote his parents, "at seven in the evening" on Saturday, October 21. Initially, he felt "very unhappy," since he knew none of the men. By his own admission, he was ill at ease in social situations: "I try very hard in social gatherings to be courteous but you know that it is very hard for me." He added, "I hope I shall learn some of this also here in Berlin." Boas was relieved when Dr. Reiß arrived for the specific purpose of introducing him: "The first one whom I met was Bastian. Dr. Reiß introduced me before the beginning of the meeting as the Dr. Boas about whom he had already spoken and who was making himself ready for travel in North America." Bastian engaged enthusiastically in conversation with Boas. As Boas wrote, he "immediately pounced on me with the question [as to] when I wished to leave." Responding in detail to Bastian's many questions, Boas observed, "He seemed to be interested in [my responses] although he did not seem to see the entire thought connection immediately." Reiß gave Boas the key to capturing Bastian's attention: "Dr. Reiß told me later that I must always emphasize my intention to travel in speaking to Bastian if I wish to be sure of his interest." Certainly, he must have been captivated enough, since he asked Boas "to visit him in the Museum where I wanted to go so much." After a "long, drawn out . . . and excessively tiring meeting," the group adjourned to the coffee house. Dr. Reiß appeared again at just the right moment to introduce Boas to Virchow, who invited the young man to sit next to him: "When Bastian saw us sitting together he also came over and listened to me once more." The evening concluded with Bastian and Virchow both giving him advice "about what I must still learn and declared themselves ready to give any help I might need."[16]

Eager to follow up on his introduction to Bastian, Boas visited him two days later, on Monday, at Berlin's Royal Museum of Ethnology: "Unfortunately I came on an inauspicious day since new things had come in which had to be unpacked, but Bastian graciously showed me the Eskimo objects and permitted me to work with them whenever I wanted." Bastian put Boas in touch with Professor Wilhelm Julius Foerster, the director of the Berlin Observatory, who would teach him "meteorological and magnetic observations and also skull measurements." Boas concluded, "Are you not also happy that I can learn everything that I want here?"[17] Once established in the circle of scientists, Boas continued to move in its orbit. At the invitation of Dr. Reiß, he attended the meeting of the geographical society and listened to talks by travelers who had just returned from "Northwest America (Alaska) and another from Madagascar." He attended "the obligatory dinner after the meeting to which Dr. Reiß invited me." He had met again with Professor Foerster and arranged a time to go to the observatory to "reckon and observe." Perhaps most important, he had gone to the museum to confer with Bastian, "where I had to report on my work and where he enlarged in a lengthy lecture on his ideas." Bastian, Boas observed, "is a very pleasant man who takes part most graciously in all my efforts but the most gracious is still Dr. Reiß who took so much trouble to introduce me everywhere that I cannot express my thanks to him enough."[18]

While enthusiasm was building in the German scientific community over Boas's promise and plans, bafflement, if not consternation, was mounting among his relatives. Salomon Meyer, affectionately called Uncle Mons, had written Boas's parents about Franz's overly ambitious "travel desires." In his letter to his parents, Boas referred to "Uncle Mons's foolish remark" and added, "Besides my travel desires [are] only to North America." Boas reiterated, "The only thing that matters is that I learn all that a thoroughly prepared geographer needs to know. That I strive to travel as soon as possible you already know."[19]

Jacobi wrote his parents a more serious critique of his plans on July 19, 1882. Boas had been participating in army maneuvers when the letter arrived, and then he was caught up in the delirium of release from the army and the details of his move to Berlin in October. He did not respond to Jacobi's letter until November 26. Point by point, in cool but combative prose, Boas addressed his uncle's letter: "First I must correct an error." He continued, "You thought that I had sought the fellowship in Baltimore because I thought I would get ahead better there than here. That was not the reason. I wanted to have the opportunity to continue my studies without being a burden on Papa, to learn things that I must know as a geographer, and which I absolutely need for my scientific goals." Driving directly to the heart of one of Jacobi's critiques, Boas asserted, "My dearest aim has always been, and still is, the achievement of a German professorship." He also addressed Jacobi's criticism that he had chosen not to take the state examination, a decision that Boas said was due "chiefly to the influence of his university professors, who regarded it as quite unnecessary." Boas anticipated that he would have to spend at the most "three or four years as Privatdozent," particularly if he selected geography. During this time, he anticipated becoming financially independent with the stipend he would receive from students who would pay to study with him. "In everything I do," Boas wrote, "the concern is chiefly with the years until I can become '*habilitiert*,'" the latter rank marking the successful completion of the dissertation, publication of articles, and public presentation and defense of his positions that would allow him to lecture at a German university. He continued, "Since, as you know, I wish to devote, if at all possible, a number of years to scientific journeys, I am advised by experienced persons to '*habilitieren*' myself next year and then get a leave of absence immediately, which I would spend in travel. Then, they tell me, if I have accomplished anything, I could count on an '*ausserordentlicher*' Professor at that university on my return."[20]

Boas's father, "with his usual good-heartedness," had agreed to support Franz for another year. In Berlin, Boas was currently studying precisely what he had intended to in Baltimore—"cartography, astronomical determination of places, and meteorological determinations." Then Boas addressed the same criticism that Uncle Mons had leveled against him: "Furthermore, I want to correct your misconception that I am dissipating myself over too wide a field." He continued, "If you remember my last letter and our conversation summer before last you will know that my study-plan has become quite fixed." Boas said that he was focusing on a topic linked directly to his "general train of thought" that he would use as his thesis for habilitation: "I am studying the wandering of the Eskimos, their knowledge of the country they live in and of adjacent lands, in the hope to prove a close connection between the number of persons in a tribe, the distribution of food supplies and the nature of the country." Boas said that he was publishing material on this topic in the *Gesellschaft für Erdkunde zu Berlin* during the winter. "Thus," Boas concluded, "I have specialized my work sufficiently and do not plan to jump from here to there in my studies."[21]

Boas continued, "My greatest desire is directed to the American polar region, and so far as it is at all possible I am very well equipped for it. I am completely at home in the literature of this region, as the small studies that will appear in the next months will show you. Furthermore, I am learning everything that is needed for scientific trips, and finally and most important I am learning the Eskimo language, and have already made good progress. If I should really succeed in getting there my chief field of work would be the wandering of the Eskimos." Informing Jacobi of his care with making contacts, Boas wrote, "I am taking great pains to interest the appropriate circles here in the matter. I have become acquainted with Virchow, Bastian and other important people, and am in communication with a gentleman in Bremen [Moritz von Lindeman] and in Copenhagen [Hinrich Johannes Rink] both of whom are authorities in the field, as well as with Scottish whalers." With great detail, Boas had worked out the plans for his travels. "I can tell it to you precisely," he wrote. "West of Davis Strait, opposite Greenland, Baffinland extends to about latitude 74 degrees north. On its west coast below 73-degree latitude lays Ponds Inlet and Eclipse Sound. Here there is an Eskimo settlement Kaproktolik." Annually these Eskimos traveled overland to trade at a settlement in the Fury and Hecla Strait. These latter Eskimos traveled "along the unknown eastern shore of the Fox Canal up to about 66 degrees N 75 degrees W," where Eskimos from the Cumberland Sound visit. "The chief problem," Boas wrote, "is cost. I have figured it out and find that everything can be done for five hundred or six hundred dollars." After itemizing his budget, he reviewed his ideas for seeking inexpensive or free transport aboard a whaler and soliciting sponsorship from the American Geographical Society. In sum, Boas wrote, "I hope to accomplish quite a lot through this trip. . . . I will be accepted among the geographers." Boas concluded, "Finally may I ask you not to tell my parents or sisters about my plans so as not to cause them unnecessary worry."[22]

Boas maintained that he wanted to shield his parents and his sisters from worry about his travels. In fact, he himself wrote to them frequently on this topic, as he did in the same month that he had written to Jacobi: "That I strive to travel as soon as possible you already know." In January 1883 he wrote, "Resign yourselves now to the thought that in any case, I shall go away." He continued, "For now I have turned to the German Polar Commission, in order possibly to contact directly the German station which I could use as a good starting point and support." Bastian, he said, was also attempting to get information for him, "and I shall hopefully get an answer soon regarding the time when the ship will sail." By the next week, Boas was making inquiries about when the whaler *Germania* would leave, "and whether I may possibly go along." Fischer, he wrote, "wants to put a notice of my trip in a journal."[23]

Boas had initially hoped to gain support from scientific societies. He had made an inquiry to the Humboldt and Ritter Foundations but to no avail. However, as he observed later, "I saw very soon that for a young and untried man, without personal connections, it was practically impossible to obtain funds for a journey from one of the scientific societies."[24] With resourcefulness, Boas presented a proposition to the owner of one of the Berlin daily papers. Clearly surprised himself that this plan had worked, Boas wrote his parents, "You are probably curious to know where I shall suddenly get the money. It happened this way. Last Friday I had the cheek to write to Mr. Rudolf Mosse, the owner of the *Berliner Tageblatt*, in the following vein. I outlined my plans and asked for 2500 Mark for the trip and promised to send him reports of the same. I called his attention to the fact that I was offering him the advantages that the *New York Herald Tribune* had obtained from Stanley at the sacrifice of much time and money, for a minimal sum (such impudence)." Boas stressed to the owner of the *Berliner Tageblatt* that his trip would garner "attention in many circles, first because it would determine the last of the unknown coastal regions of Arctic America and also that the method of travel would be unusual (still greater impudence)."[25]

In Heaven, in Love, and Separation

Boas received a letter of interest from editor-in-chief Dr. Arthur Levysohn, who had been directed by the owner of the newspaper to follow up on the proposition. "I just found out," Boas continued, "that Mr. Mosse is inclined to consider my proposition, only he would like to know my preparation and get to know my connections." Boas name-dropped liberally: "I spoke of everyone and used their titles, which apparently impressed him." Boas had come to the interview with a file of correspondence on his proposed trip, copies of his printed articles, and letters of recommendation, one of which was from a personal friend of Dr. Levysohn. "They still want a small paper in the form of an article," he enthused, "which I shall make as elegant and popular as possible. . . . I shall begin the essay this afternoon, 'Arrival of a ship at an Eskimo Village,' a highly colored account!" Very confident that he would receive the money, Boas had also spoken with the chair of the German Polar Commission, Georg von Schleinitz, about the possibility of obtaining passage on the *Germania*, whose captain was August F. B. Mahlstede. Schleinitz had said, encouragingly, "He could probably take me and a servant," for payment of one Reichsmark per day for food. Boas closed his letter, "Be happy together with me and write soon."[26]

The following day Boas presented his essay to the owner of the *Berliner Tageblatt* Mosse and to the editor-in-chief, Levysohn. Ecstatic with the positive response, Boas relayed Mosse's words—that "he would accept anything which was as well written" as Boas's sample article, and "that he had no further doubts about the matter." Boas said that before he left on his journey he would write an article on the "history of explorations in these regions and one on equipment and plans." Boas observed, "The Tageblatt will be in a position to publish direct news of the trip." He continued, "I pretended that the money needed would be considerable and that I was doing the Tageblatt a favor by letting them have my reports. I did not let them think that my trip in any way depended on their granting me the money." The contract would be finalized when Boas returned from Hamburg, where he was making arrangements for his trip. He would agree to produce "a certain number of articles," with the publication of these left to Mosse. "Furthermore," Boas continued, "I will bind myself to undertake the trip without asking for more funds." Boas would retain "free hand in regard to scientific publications," but the articles in the Tageblatt "must be published before those in [other] journals." In a postscript Boas wrote, "What makes me happiest is that I got the money through my own personal efforts." In the final agreement, Boas would receive three thousand Reichsmarks for a total of fifteen articles, to be published exclusively by the *Berliner Tageblatt,* with Boas's father providing bond for his son, making good on the agreement. The articles were to appear from August 1883 to April 1885. The agreement was mutually beneficial for both the *Berliner Tageblatt* and for Boas. As Müller-Wille notes, "With this contract the newspaper secured exclusive rights to first publication of any news that Boas would send from the Arctic," and this would be, as proudly proclaimed in the editorial introducing the series, for "the glory of *unser Vaterland,* our fatherland." Boas, in turn, gained through this agreement "a large readership throughout German-speaking Central Europe," and, as a result, he became quite well known "as a writer, traveller, and scientist."[27]

Boas traveled to Bremen to visit with Lindeman on February 1; to Hamburg to talk with Neumayer from February 2 to 3; to Kiel to consult with his professors from February 3 to 5; to Hamburg and Eimsbüttel on February 6; and then back to Berlin. Relating details about the longer-term strategies for his academic career, Boas wrote his parents about the counsel his professors had offered. Over dinner in Kiel, they had discussed Boas's plans for academic affiliation through the process of habilitation. As Boas related, Fischer and Erdmann and "several other men are of the opinion that I would be right to habilitate myself later."

In Hamburg, following Bastian's recommendation, Boas met with Georg von Neumayer, chairman of the German Polar Commission and director of the Imperial Seewarte (marine observatory), and with Austrian Carl Weyprecht, co-founder of the First International Polar Year (1882–83). Germany had joined with eleven other nations in an international effort to study climatological and physical factors in the Arctic and had sent a crew of eleven men to the northern end of Cumberland Sound to establish a research station. As Müller-Wille notes, Boas's choice of "location and research themes [were] certainly influenced by the contemporary scientific atmosphere that strongly encouraged research in polar regions."[28] Boas wrote his parents from Hamburg, "Neumayer unexpectedly received me most graciously and offered me much more than I had expected." Neumayer agreed that Boas could travel on the *Germania*—the two-masted schooner built in 1869 for Arctic waters—gave him "a number of maps and the inventory of the station out of which I should choose what I wanted," and "took over my entire equipment of instruments, guns, furs and a large part of the provisioning so that I shall have no cost in these matters." With astonishment, Boas noted, "This support is worth as much as an entire sum of 1500 Mark. The instruments alone are (according to how I want to supply myself) 830 Mark!" Boas was "twice as happy" that he had made the connection with the *Berliner Tageblatt*, and that this was "really the way I presented it to the people."[29]

Neumayer had invited Boas to give a lecture regarding his research plans to the Geographische Gesellschaft in Hamburg on February 2, 1883. To his parents, Boas wrote that his lecture "went off very well," though he initially "shook and trembled inordinately." At the conclusion of his lecture, Neumayer lavished so much praise on him that Boas said it made him "so uncomfortable" that he wanted "to run away." After the visit with Neumayer at the lighthouse in Hamburg, Boas went out to the borough of Eimsbüttel at the invitation of Captain Paul Friedrich August Hegemann, "an old, experienced Polar traveler," who had offered to order all of Boas's supplies. The next morning Boas and Hegemann went to the stores that "had supplied the earlier expeditions with provisions and clothing." The merchants in these stores would send Boas the "lists of necessities." Attempting to quiet their worries, Boas assured his parents, "I am well taken care of by advice and action."[30]

As Lehmann recalled, "My parents were very unhappy about the perilous trip, but also very proud. My father made only one condition. Franz should not travel alone." Boas's parents suggested Wilhelm Weike, the gardener and servant who had worked for the Boas family for four years. Just ten months younger than Boas, Weike had been born in the neighboring Westphalian farming village of Häverstädt. He attended the village elementary school from age six to fourteen, as required by Prussian law. By the age of nineteen, in January 1879, he had moved to Minden and by October 1, 1879, Weike was employed "as gardener and house servant" by the Boas family. Having earned their trust during his years of employment and being accustomed to hard work, Weike met the prerequisites of Boas's father.[31]

Boas warmed to the choice. In January he wrote his parents, "Ask Wilhelm seriously whether he would care to travel with me. Send me his last name so that I may write him myself." Boas continued, "Let him be examined once more to see whether he is healthy and strong enough" to make the trip. Meier Boas made all arrangements and assumed all the expenses so that Weike could accompany his son to the Arctic as his servant. In training for his trip, Weike was taught "to cook, to sole shoes, and to pour bullets" and to keep Boas's revolver and rifle in good working order. This young man of twenty-four would accompany the scientist-explorer son of his employer to the Arctic. Just four months later, Weike would write in his diary of the sights that were unfolding before him even prior to having sailed from Cuxhaven, Germany, "When one lives in a small town one has no concept of life in the big city . . . [of] all the rushing about and chasing in the streets with the horse trams and other conveyances, and . . . the commercial activity, and the trade and traffic from one house to another."[32]

Trying to quiet another concern of his parents, Boas wrote, "Incidentally regarding my trip, I can give you comforting information that where I am going there are Europeans, namely Scottish seal hunters, who live there all year round, so that I shall have them to fall back on." With his parents still worrying about their son's isolation during his time in the Arctic, Boas wrote the following month that he "would live together with 20 Scotsmen, among them one captain, and helmsman and a good spacious wooden house, and also about 5 tons . . . [of] coal, so that I could live in winter about as in civilized regions."[33]

Boas made little mention of Marie Krackowizer in his letters to his parents during the year of his military service and through the months he lived in Berlin. He did make reference to her, however, in notes to his sisters Hete and Toni, who were clearly his link to Marie. In May 1882, ten months after having met Marie, Franz wrote Hete on her birthday with a playful, parenthetical mention of Marie, "(Note: I wanted to see whether I could write one sentence which would fill an entire page. And you see that not only women, as Marie Krackowizer believes, but even your much loved brother can accomplish this.)" In a postcard to his parents, written while he was on military maneuvers, Franz added a note: "Have you, Hete, heard from Miss Krackowizer whether she passed her

In Heaven, in Love, and Separation

exams well?" Months later after their mutually professed love, Marie wrote to Franz that while he could solve many deep problems, he was slow to figure her out: "Toni was much quicker. She told me she saw a long time ago from my letters, that I loved you." Marie continued, "But I really did not want to betray it only I liked to write something about you because otherwise I would never find out anything about you." In candor, she said, "Hete was the most trusted in giving information about you."[34]

For Marie's mother, Emilie Krackowizer, the prospect of a match between Franz Boas and her daughter was fraught with challenges and worries. In February 1883 she wrote to Sophie Boas and to Toni that "Hete's letter to Marie yesterday . . . [fell] like a bomb upon us." She extended her "deep sympathy to the dear mother and gentle sister concerning the planned Eskimo explorations." Diplomatically, she countered, "If on the other hand you support the decision with pride then you must agree with your son and brother who follows the compulsion of his science so courageously." Emilie Krackowizer's letter was long and full of detailed news of Marie, who was "very busy with making clothes and will have finished the course the end of this month, and will be in a position to help herself in this, which in my opinion is of the greatest advantage in cramped pecuniary circumstances." Marie was taking French conversation, wanted to take flower painting, and was studying piano, though, candidly, her mother observed, "Her progress is not great!" The social life in Stuttgart was "quite limited and Marie is still waiting for her first ball." For Emilie Krackowizer, "time moves quickly enough and I think more than ever about the return trip." As they "move toward home in the fall," she said, they would like to stop in Minden, "if it is not inconvenient." Apologizing for her daughter who had not responded to Toni's letter, Mrs. Krackowizer wrote, "She is still in the 'Sturm und Drang' period and must clarify much in herself before she is all through." Finally, she observed of her daughter, "But she is good, honest, and true, I guarantee that."[35]

February and March 1883 involved the dizzying preparations for Boas's trip and the stark realization that he would be separated from his family for over a year. "Due to the long trip," Boas wrote his parents, "the days with you seem to lie almost like an eternity behind me." Boas had been invited to give a talk about his trip to the Gesellschaft für Erdkunde zu

Berlin in April. To his parents, he wrote, "You will then be able to see the lecture in print since the local papers always publish notices of the meetings and besides that they appear in detail in the records of the Society for Earth Sciences." Toni, who had moved to Berlin to be with her brother during the last few months prior to his departure, told Franz that his parents wanted him to give a lecture about his trip in Minden. He wrote them, "I do not think that would be right since it looks like bragging. If I were urgently asked to do it from *many* sides, then the matter could be considered. I or acquaintances of mine may not have anything to do with it." In tribute to Boas, his cousin Willy Meyer wrote, "Honest and sincere congratulations on your great scientific achievements!" Even as Boas was already "respected and celebrated," on his return, "lecture halls are open to you" and "your career is secured." In New York, "your name is on everyone's lips."[36]

Boas traveled to various cities at the end of March 1883 to make additional contacts for his trip. In his new capacity as a journalist for the *Berliner Tageblatt*, undertaking the writing of two trial articles, he reported on the Third Assembly of Geographers, held in Frankfurt from March 29 to 31, 1883. Here he met again with Neumayer, and he heard Friedrich Ratzel talk on "The Importance of Polar Research to Geography." With the assembly gathered during the period of the International Polar Year, Ratzel's speech focused on the shift in polar research from the expeditionary to the stationary approach, "to fixed stations where measurements and experiments agreed upon by an international scientific organization were conducted in a synchronized fashion." Ratzel's approach profoundly influenced Boas's conception and implementation of his research in Baffin Land and would, by extension, have profound implications for the future development of fieldwork in anthropology.[37]

Using the visit to Frankfurt as an excuse, Boas journeyed to nearby Stuttgart to visit the Krackowizer residence on April 1, 1883. On April 3 he wrote to his parents, "Luckily I knew the name of the street where the Krackowizers live and also soon found the house since I only knew it was between 4 and 10." Two months later, after Franz and Marie had exchanged many epistles of love, he wrote her about this visit to her home, "Do you believe that the 1st of April was an easy day for me? I had to collect myself entirely in front of your door in order not to betray all

In Heaven, in Love, and Separation

my thoughts and feelings immediately and I did not know how you felt towards me." Later Boas admitted that he had traveled to Frankfurt as an excuse to his parents and sisters for his visit to Stuttgart: "I had nothing whatsoever to do in Stuttgart but to see you. I could not leave Germany without having seen you once more, and now I am and remain your blissful Franz." He had written to Marie's mother in advance of arriving at their house, "so that he did not come," Marie wrote to Toni, "to a locked door which could easily have happened since we usually go for a walk on Sunday afternoon."[38]

In her letter to Toni with parenthetical remarks to Hete, Marie told of Franz's visit, "Do I need to tell you how happy we were to have him with us yesterday? I had not let myself dream of such a beautiful surprise, to see him once more and to be allowed to speak with him before his long," and then she inserted a black line, "trip." She continued, "I would like to have put between *long* and *trip* the words terrible and horrible but I may not do that anymore since he described it as not terrible at all." Through Franz's account, she came to understand "the whole thing much better," particularly that his travels would not be "'at random' over the entire northern planes." She would be able "to imagine sometimes at which of these very interesting tribes of Eskimos he happened to be." She admitted that she had shown him "Hete's map which I had admired and had already learned by heart . . . and he thought it was not quite accurate." Then, coyly, she asked, "Are you angry, Hete?" Picking up a pen, Franz had sketched a new map on the other side of the paper so she would "learn my lesson over again." Breathlessly moving on to the next topic, Marie effused, "I think it is very nice that Wilhelm will go with him. It must be a relief to know that a trustworthy person, whom you know, will be with him." Realizing that her words were tumbling forth on the page, she wrote, "I think I am writing a terrible jumble. Perhaps I did not sleep quite long enough." Marie concluded her letter, "Mama sends many greetings and tells you that she likes Franz very much and now understands why you are so proud of him and how difficult it will be to part with him." In a postscript, she added, "Please do not let anyone read this smear!"[39]

Under the pretense of telling about his voyage but really to convey his feelings about Marie, Boas wrote to Jacobi on May 2, 1883, that the "preparations for my trip are nearing their end." He told of his arrangement with the *Berliner Tageblatt* for the funding of his trip: "I like the connection with the newspaper. I attended as a correspondent for it the German Geographic meeting in Frankfurt am Maine." Boas segued into an account of his visit to the Krackowizers: "While I was there I could not forego the pleasure of going to Stuttgart to again see the Krackowizers before my departure, or if I should be honest, to see Marie." With great feeling, he wrote, "I could not bring myself to undertake this trip without having spoken to her once more." Boas remarked that Marie was "going back over there." He was hoping that "good fortune" would lead him to America where he might find "a steady position so that I may tell her what I feel for her." He continued, "I held it to be wrong at this time before the dangerous journey and considering my insecure future, to express myself even though my leaving becomes so very, very hard." In sharing "this extremely secret information," Boas found Jacobi to be the ideal confidante: he knew Boas "well enough to take part in my wishes," and he was "very friendly with the Krackowizers and will see Marie often." He concluded, "You must not think that because of this confession that I go from here very depressed. On the contrary, I know exactly what I want, scientifically and for my future life and go with a steady eye on that with confidence and hope."[40]

While clearly roiling beneath the surface with powerful emotions, Franz and Marie exchanged polite and restrained letters. "According to my promise," Boas wrote, "I am sending you today a map of the region where I shall travel and a short outline of the planned journey." While he might not be able to fulfill his promise "to send you a picture of myself in Eskimo costume," he said he would send a picture of himself as a "'European,'" but only if she would reciprocate with a picture of herself. Revealing the intensity of his emotions, he wrote that her picture "will keep alive the hope that I shall see you again." He told her of his prospect of meeting "an American whaler so that I could make my return trip by way of America." He concluded, "The remembrance of the few hours I spent with you in Stuttgart is a great pleasure to me, it is too bad that I had to leave so quickly."[41]

More artful in shielding her emotions, Marie responded to him playfully that, with such a long trip planned, he "will not reach the American whaler. We are planning to send one very early." In turn, Boas wrote, "It is very kind of you to send me a whaler real early." Then he added, "But seriously, I hear through Uncle Jacobi that [Emil] Bessels, a North Pole enthusiast in Washington, thinks in all probability that I shall be able to get free passage on an American whaler, all the more reason to go home that way." He told her that Jacobi had offered him "a large sum of money," in case he did not have enough for his trip. "Isn't that good of him?" he asked, observing, "I am also glad to know from the letter that he approves of my plans and wishes." Boas reflected, "Even though one ought to know what one has to do, there is satisfaction in knowing that a person whom one honors so highly, approves. I only hope that I shall have good luck among the Eskimo. The success of my trip depends on this." Continuing on the theme of luck, Boas reflected, "If one has luck one is known as 'the daring explorer,' if bad, as the 'adventurer.' It makes no difference. I know what I want and am looking hopefully into the future." Recognizing the fickle opinion of others, Boas expressed the desire that "the opinion of my friends does not depend on what others say."[42]

Taking pity on the two, Toni broke the juggernaut by writing to Marie about Franz's love for her. With effusive gratitude, Marie wrote to Toni, "If you knew what a period of uncertainty and despair I have lived through since April 1, you could then imagine how happy your letter . . . made me." With clarion honesty, Marie wrote, "The closer the time of Franz's departure draws near the more impossible it seems to me to have to stand his going away without my knowing whether he liked me just a little bit." Rhetorically she queried, "How could he otherwise be the center of my actions and thoughts if he had no interest in me." She continued, "Now I may think of him and all he does, what concerns him may make me happy or sad. Do you now believe that I love him, that I am happy and therefore will wait patiently without knowing anymore until he comes back, until I can see him again?" With agonizing self-doubt, she admitted, "But Toni, I cannot understand how Franz can like me because it seems to me that everything that is great and worth loving in him is lacking in me and I am afraid when he knows me better he may perhaps be disappointed. If this could happen then I would wish we had never seen each other, for I do not believe that anything could change my feeling for him." She acknowledged that Toni was right when she observed that Marie had "not yet seen many men." She countered forcefully, "But those that I have seen have made no impression on me and as much as I know there exists only one man, one who in the true sense of the word is *Man*, who can be honored and loved and he is Franz." Then, firmly, she said, "Now I believe I have told you enough and you must promise me that you will tell Franz no more than is necessary to give him quiet [so that he has] all his strength for his great work." "The rest," she wrote, "I want to tell him later if he really should ask me about it." She queried urgently, "But I may still write to him as before? I shall not even tell him that I like him. The poor man, that he should have so many problems just now in the last minute."[43]

Toni had no sooner received the letter from Marie than she shared it with Franz. In a letter written to Marie twelve days later, Franz told her with sweet honesty of his emotions on hearing this news: "I cannot comprehend the heavenly feeling that filled me that evening. It was in the arbor in front of our house where I first heard and saw it, and slowly, slowly I had to read it, word for word in order to believe this most wonderful happiness. I was not able to say a word, my heart beat so and I had to read your letter, which held all of my happiness, over and over alone." Immediately following his reading of Marie's letter to Toni, Franz wrote her, "Dear Marie! Now I may call you that." He continued, "I cannot believe it yet that only a few hours ago I had the most frightening doubts about telling you of my love." Before having read Marie's letter, Boas had written a declaration of his love, but he had not dared to send it. Of this first love epistle, he admitted, "The letter lies closed before me, now you may also read it." Boas had begun the first letter "Dear Fräulein, I cannot leave here without telling you how much I love you, how you are constantly in my thoughts, how you are the content of all my wishes and dreams. Now that the hour of parting nears, all of my resolutions to hide my love from you melt away; I must know whether you have a warm feeling for me, whether you love me in return." With profound and ecstatic relief after hearing from Toni, Franz queried, "Why did we both torment each other these long weeks when the knowledge of our love could have made us so happy?" He continued, "I do not know even now how I came out of Stuttgart, how I could leave you. Nothing has been so hard for me as to leave you without knowing whether you loved me."[44]

In another letter to Marie he wrote, "Do you know the last parting will always be printed in my memory." Franz continued, "How you sat with folded hands, half smiling, half fearful, [and] followed me with your look. At that time, I began to hope that you loved me. And I do not know even today how I found the door and the stairs. I only know I stood long in front of your house and later at night returned to tell you a silent farewell. I do not think I have ever felt such pain as on that evening when I left and had not told you what I felt." In her letter to Franz about his arrival in Stuttgart, Marie wrote, "And now I see you again so distinct and clearly before me as you stood in front of our door and greeted me. I thought I could not hide my joy at seeing you again after two long years." She continued, "And there I stood and what did I say?—nothing, I think—as I said nothing but foolishness the whole day long. . . . And then I see you at the piano. How you for the first time and last time played your "Nachtlied" (Night Song), my farewell. I wept in my bed that night." She recalled saying good-bye: "How I felt when I said adieu in our little hallway—how happy was my heart. I folded my hands forcefully so that I would not run after you and hold you back." Just days before his departure for the Canadian Arctic in 1883, Boas wrote Marie, "Music is for me a source of comfort in sorrow and music is often the first thing that enters my mind in sorrow or sudden joy." Referring to his visit with her and her family, he confessed, "For whom else did I play Schumann's 'Nachtstück' [night piece] but for you." He continued, "I have never thought of it without seeing you, beloved, before me, and on that evening I thought only of you. . . . This piece by Schumann shall also be the last which I shall play before I leave and I shall often hear its soft and quiet happiness in foreign lands."[45]

In the first love letter he had written to Marie, Boas stressed his firm intent of not binding her to him during his absence:

And if you do love me you must listen to this. I may not tie you to me today, and therefore would never be angry with you if during my long journey your heart spoke differently and you were to fol-low another man. I must leave you free as you are today. But when I return, may I then ask whether your heart still belongs to me. . . . I shall be back in the fall of 1884; if I should not come then I can still come in the fall of 1885. If then I have not returned, some misfortune has happened to me and you must no longer expect my return. But I go with a happy faith in my good fortune, and will you give me the hope that I may then come to you to ask whether you will be my Marie.

Resolutely he concluded his letter, "I have said what I had to say to you, and tremblingly await your verdict that will make me a happy mortal, or will rob me of the most joyful hope that has ever filled my soul." In both the first and the second letter that Boas wrote to Marie on May 28, 1883, he referred to the ease with which he would face difficulties if he were sure of her love for him. In the first letter, he queried whether she could give him "the right always to think of you when I am in snow and in ice, in the hope of a happy future." In the second, he declared, "If I may think of you and then see your eyes before me, I know that I shall not waver." He added, "And you also do not be afraid of the long separation. It is only a short time, which will hopefully smooth the way for my life's work. Onward!" As if sealing their new and sweet love, Boas declared, "Now I also know what to name my little boat that will take me on my journeys. Yours, the luckiest that I know. Formerly I wanted to call it *Vorwärts*, Onwards, but now your name, Marie, is a better *vorwärts*."[46]

The day after his declaration of love, Boas wrote to Marie's mother to explain his intentions. He enclosed a letter for Marie because he could not "send away the letter to your mother without sending you a few lines which tell you how happy I am." He continued, "I am in heaven since I know that you love me. I say it over and over to myself so often and I still cannot hear it often enough." True to his gift for focus, he added, "But with it all I continue to do my work." In the next sentence he shifted back to elation and disbelief and referred to her letter, which he had tucked in his shirt pocket over his heart: "Only sometimes I feel where your letter lies to see whether it is really, really true that you love me." Marie responded,

My Franz,

Are you really mine? Yes, you are that. I read that out of every word of your dear letters which I read over and over.

In Heaven, in Love, and Separation

Then she asked, "Why did you have to torture me so much? Why did you not tell me earlier that you loved me?" With a sweet truthfulness that struck to the heart, she confessed, "Do you know, I think I loved you before I saw you." She continued, "But I did not really know until your letter to mother came from Frankfurt. And then when I saw you again, when I again could look into your eyes, I thought I should have to throw my arms around your neck and always look into them to read whether you loved me. And you were so calm, so very calm that I had also to be calm but I hardly dared to look at you for fear that you might possibly read something in my eyes that you did not want to see."[47]

Marie said that she "always felt . . . quieted" in his presence so that her "inner self" felt that she had to see him again "in order to allay this terrible fear which sometimes overcomes me that we might perhaps never see each other again." She continued, "I am not as brave or strong as you and I am terribly afraid of the separation, I have only now won you over for myself and must already give you up." Marie asked Franz to write her "often for out of your written words speaks so much courage and confidence that I then can get rid of my foolish thoughts." As if she had coaxed herself through her worries, she confessed, "I could surely not love you as much if you could ever give up anything that you felt was right and necessary, or would only finish it part way because of a girl whom you loved." She continued, "Therefore go to your Eskimos, stay as long as you must and come back. And you shall come back! Yes, you shall. My heart tells me so."[48]

Marie's mother was not so charmed. Responding to Boas, she wrote,

Dear Mr. Boas,

I was not entirely unprepared for your letter since I surmised with the eyes and feelings of a loving mother, what on the one hand was beginning to stir in her heart and then that your visit did not seem as innocent as it was presented.

She continued, "Since you have however expressed yourself to Marie and have presented your plans for the future so openly to me, it would be wrong of me if I did not answer you honestly." With candor, she wrote,

What in the eyes of love seems like a small matter does not always seem so to the sterner view of the parents, therefore you must not be angry that I did not greet your love with absolute pleasure and would have wished that, considering the impending undertaking, the decisive word would have been suppressed, the word which ties the fate of my dear daughter to yours. For even though you say she should be free and not feel herself bound, this is only a figure of speech, since the heart of a girl who has promised herself to the man of her choice will still consider herself bound and her whole thinking and effort will be concentrated in that direction.

Emilie Krackowizer found his trip to the Arctic "and the whole project" as "less than safe." The future of her daughter's happiness depended on the success of Boas's trip, and even with success "the founding of a steady existence" would only be assured "in quite a distant future." For her daughter, "it will seem very hard that she suddenly must learn the seriousness of life when so few roses have bloomed for her. Marie is, or more accurately was always younger than her years in all of her nature and looked at life happily and ingenuously. She has only lately left the schoolroom and has enjoyed so few of the pleasures other girls her age usually have behind them." Emilie Krackowizer was sure that Boas would respond to her in the same way her daughter did: "But we love each other and with the knowledge that our love is mutual everything will become easy for us and we look hopefully to the future." Emilie counseled, "But we must not fool ourselves, that time still lies far off and that I therefore look to the near future with worry and sadness and could not accept your declaration with a happy heart."[49]

With Marie's mother unhappily resigned to this declaration of love and Franz's parents similarly concerned, Franz and Marie continued in their exuberant correspondence. From all but their family, Franz and Marie kept their newly declared love as "our sweet secret." "It is too nice," Boas wrote, "to have such a secret from the whole world." Marie responded, "I also say with you how wonderful it is to have such a secret from all people! What eyes the people here would make if they knew, if they knew!!" He asked her to make a small flag in black, white, and red, with her name embroidered on it, to fly from his boat and his sled: "This will flutter happily in the cold winds and keep my heart warm." She wrote about the lounging robe and pipe that she wanted to give him but all he wanted from her was her picture and the flag—he never owned a lounging robe and he didn't smoke a pipe. Marie and Franz wrote letters to each other at least once a day, if not twice. Franz's mother and sister Toni thought it unwise for him to write Marie so much, because the impending separation would be even harder for her after she had grown accustomed to frequent letters. "But I know they are mistaken," Franz wrote her. "The more we feel how much we are to each other the easier it will be for the bad time to pass." In another letter, Franz requested, "Write to me often as long as we can write. We must be nourished in the [next] 14 days for almost 1 ½ years [of separation]!" Then he promised, "While I am gone, I shall keep a separate diary for you, then you can later live that time through with me."[50]

On June 10, 1883, Boas left for Hamburg to make the final preparations for his Arctic voyage. He wrote Marie, "The departure from home this evening did not come lightly even though I shall come there once more." (Boas did return to Minden for one last time in mid-June.) Boas went directly to the observatory to meet with Neumayer, who was overseeing the preparations. "Here everything looks mixed up," he wrote. "They are still working on the Germania. Today she got new masts. My boxes stand around in the greatest disarray and await an organizing hand." Among this equipment, Boas had purchased "3 watches, a prism circle and horizont, a geodetic theodolite, apparatus to measure distance and smaller ones to measure angles, a large compass, barometer, thermometer, hygrometer, aneroid and a photographic apparatus. A small sled boat to carry provisions, guns and ammunition, food for 12 months, furs, woolen clothing." Through Jacobi's generous gift, Boas was able to purchase additional equipment. He also had the full support of the German Polar Commission and of the Scottish whaler that would take him to Kekerten in Baffin Land. Boas was feted at an estate near Hamburg by "a very large gathering of men and ladies . . . given by the man who equipped me." He was, as he wrote, "presented like a wonder-beast to be looked at closely, but not to be touched!" He continued, "I was allowed to live and had to give a toast during which I trembled quite a bit but I hope I did not seem ridiculous. We were back here at the lighthouse only at eleven-thirty. I practically fell asleep on the way back because I had not closed my eyes the night before on the train."[51]

Joined by his father and Wilhelm in Hamburg, Boas spent the afternoon of June 19 in a flurry of last-minute shopping for "knives and needles" that he planned to use in trade with the Eskimo. "Then I am finished with everything and we can sail away. . . . I must go on board right away to go with the captain," he wrote his family. He begged of them, "Please, please do not be sad. Just think how this trip should be the path to my happiness, to my future life and that you must accept the inevitable." To Marie he wrote, "Do not be sad tomorrow since the last day before my departure is here. . . . Now that the departure is so near I am completely at ease." Then he asked the question that would be repeated throughout their married life, "Can you be angry with me that my profession makes me go?"[52]

Meier Boas sailed with his son and with Weike as far as Cuxhaven where he said his farewell and returned home. Boas wrote, "Now Papa has also left me and soon we shall go out to sea. . . . We shall soon see each other again! Just realize that I must be completely responsible for Wilhelm and that this great responsibility must force me to take all precautions." Lehmann recalled the send-off for her brother: "When Franz finally left for Hamburg, he got a big escort from Neumayer, friends and professors and our father was also with him. He was with him as far as Cuxhaven, and then went the little sailboat to sea. It was too much for my father, the emotional stress, and he came back sick to Minden, [and had his] first heart attack."[53]

His family and Marie were left in sadness over his departure. Emilie Krackowizer wrote to Franz's mother, "Now the difficult farewell is behind you and your son has left in the service of science to undertake a difficult and dangerous trip, I can feel with you, my dear friend." She spoke of their children's "inspired love" and expressed the following wish: "And I say with you, may a lucky star shine for your son and therefore may it be decided that the two lovers shall have a happy future." She described the changes that she had observed in her daughter: "You would be astonished if you could see Marie. How her pleasures have changed. In this short time, she has become much thinner and it seems to me that the expression of her face has changed. The happy ingenuous girl has all at once become ripe and the seriousness of her position has drawn around her eyes lines that I would have preferred not to see so clearly for some time." Marie wrote to Franz's mother artfully and honestly about her love for her son. She queried, "And you are not angry with me that he has given me a part of the love that he has for all of you? He has so much that it will be enough for all of us and I shall honor it so well and become so worthy of it." Marie continued, "I shall do everything in my power to make your Franz happy in order to be worthy of all the happiness that blesses me." As a parting request of his family, Boas wrote, "Love her well, she belongs to us." In reference to Marie's planned visit to Minden, he said, "Let her stay a long time with you before she goes over there. Write to each other often then the separation will be easier for her."[54]

Marie visited with the Boas family in Minden for the three weeks prior to her October 14 departure with her family for the United States. In expectation of this visit, she wrote Franz, "I shall be in Minden in the same rooms where you are now, shall speak with the same dear persons with whom you now speak. Oh! And how much they will have to tell me about you." Playfully, she added, "Franz, there I shall find out all your wickedness. Are you not afraid of that? . . . And in your room! Shall I find everything there the way you left it?" On the eve of her departure from Bremerhaven aboard a passenger ship bound for New York, Marie wrote to the Boas family that she had "a very heavy heart" to be leaving them, "for you now belong to my people and I was so happy in my Franz's house. As long as I could, I looked out at dear old Minden and then I sat back in my corner and closed my eyes and everything that I had experienced with you passed before me."[55]

For Franz Boas, the love of his life, Marie, twined together with his passion for science. In the closing days of his preparation for his voyage, he expressed this sentiment in a letter to Marie: "Behind the pain of departure lies an unmeasured and immeasurable blissfulness which makes a new man of me. My head goes to the Eskimos, my heart stays always and forever with you!" His love for science had been a lifelong focus for him, from when he was a little boy who collected mosses and lichen for his herbarium and chipped away at fossils with his geologist's hammer, to when he was a promising young scientist about to step from Germany onto the world stage. His love for Marie had begun to blossom during their time in the Harz Mountains and opened to full-bloom two years later. Their romance had been conducted mainly through letters. Aside from the vacation days in the Harz Mountains, Franz and Marie had spent only one day together in Stuttgart on April 1, 1883. Never had they held each other in an embrace, nor had they kissed. In her birthday letter to Franz, Marie wrote, "When will the moment come when I may throw my arms around your neck for the first time?" Then she pondered, "I wonder how old you are? Just think I never thought of it before. I think it was said that you were 23 when you made your doctorate. So you must be 25 now. . . . Do you know that I shall be 22 next month?" For Boas, his love for Marie and hers for him gave compass to his life. He wrote, "In spite of all the pain I would not exchange for anything in the world the knowledge that you love me, that I love you. . . . If anything bothers me, I have only to think of you to feel my strength awakening, to endure everything." He continued, "Life is to live vigorously, to work and accomplish something in the tumult of the world, and the greatest happiness has he found who has a loving wife at his side with whom he shares all the hopes and disappointments, who fights for and endures his battles with him along with her hopes and wishes. May he succeed or not this most beautiful knowledge must enliven him. [Would that] such a fate be ours sometime."[56]

While preparing for the Arctic voyage, Boas was shifting from his graduate training as a physicist and the accompanying materialistic point of view to geography, with a more complex, nuanced consideration of the land, the people, and their migrations. In "From Physics to Ethnology," George Stocking links Boas's mentor Theobald Fischer to Carl Ritter, "who after [Alexander von] Humboldt was the leading German geographer of the first half of the nineteenth century." Ritter emphasized "the interaction of man and environment—the 'relation of all the phenomena and forces of nature to the human race.'" Fischer discerned in Boas's explanation of his research an influence from Ritter. "I am very pleased to see," Fischer wrote Boas, "that in addition to military service you still find time for scientific work. . . . The ideas and studies that you employ now . . . seem to be connected to Ritter's spirit." Four years later, Fischer again guided Boas to Ritter: "'I am glad that you seek to comprehend

In Heaven, in Love, and Separation

the significance of the historical factor in geography; this can come best through Ritter.'" Stocking points out that "his contact with the tradition of historical geography thus impelled Boas toward a holistic, affective understanding of the relationship of man and the natural world, which Fischer (and later Boas) regarded as very different from the approach of the physicist."[57]

Still, while Boas was shifting from physics to *"moderne Geographie,"* as this latter emerged in the 1880s in Germany, his intellectual approach was firmly grounded "in both the natural and social sciences, be it physics, geography, ethnology, and also philosophy." As he departed for Baffin Land, Boas was poised to begin his "one-year sojourn to conduct research into 'the elementary relationships between Inuit and their Arctic environment.'" Through his travels, Boas anticipated making his mark on geography, for, as he wrote, "I hope to accomplish quite a lot through this trip. . . . I will be accepted among the geographers." His scientific expedition to the Arctic would be his imprimatur on the academic world. As his mentors had told him, if he traveled and accomplished anything at all, his way would be eased for habilitation to any German university. Indeed, the scientific circle in Berlin was focused keenly on travel, exploration, and discovery. The mettle of a scientist—geographer, ethnologist, geologist, or anthropologist—was forged in travel, often, as with Bastian, the world over and throughout many years. The German scientists were not firmly situated in singular disciplines, nor were scientists elsewhere: an ethnologist such as Bastian could also be a geographer, while a pathologist such as Virchow could be an anthropologist. Trained as a physicist, and identifying increasingly as a geographer, Boas himself queried, "I am still debating whether I should let myself be accepted by the Anthropologists. It cannot be to my disadvantage in any case and I often come in contact with different persons." Of course, the anthropologists to whom Boas referred were physical anthropologists, since that was the designation used in Europe.[58]

When Boas left Cuxhaven aboard the *Germania,* bound for Kekerten in Baffin Land, he was still a physicist, laden with the complex equipment of his science that he put to immediate use. He wrote his parents, "I am already making scientific observations about the speed of waves, the transparency of water." He planned "some observations with an instrument which Neumayer sent with me." As he leaned into the "good wind" that was taking him to the Arctic with "air so quiet, so still [and] the heavens so blue," Boas was gently shifting to an expanded view, one that would embrace ethnology but would not abandon geography, though physics would slide ever so softly from his line of sight. He had all the ingredients for this gentle shift—language study, study of the people, and fieldwork, characterized at the time as travel.[59]

In a letter to his Uncle Jacobi, Boas conveyed his focus and intent. "I feel a strong working-power within me," he wrote, "and know for certain that I will make progress with my studies." In his diary entry for June 9, 1883, Boas penned his intentions: "It is my idea to make a name for myself so that when I return I can make connection with the *New York Herald*, under proper conditions, so that I can marry Marie in two years. It *must* go. Then I *must* go to Alaska for one-half year." Boas was indeed propelled ahead by his strong "working-power," but it would take him more than two years to find a job in New York, and then it would be with *Science* and not the *New York Herald Tribune*; and it would take him more than two years to be able to marry Marie. Before that time, he would find his way to the Northwest Coast of America, close to, but not quite in Alaska, and he would begin his lifelong study of the Kwakiutl.[60]

4

Creating a Future for Us

To Baffin Land and Back

The *Germania* had sailed away from the Scottish coast and past the Isle of Lewis. Boas wrote Marie a letter about his adventurous desires as a ten-year-old boy. It would not make its way back to her until the ship returned from the Arctic:

> Fifteen years ago . . . I dreamed of participating in a polar expedition; now I have attained this; I am on my way yet so differently from what I had dreamed of. I am not heading out under the orders of a friend, but am dependent on myself. Not simply inspired by geographical exploration, but with quite definite scientific goals! My thoughts are not always on my science; no, my love, my Marie, they are on you in my heart, and of creating a future around *us*, beloved. Can you believe that this is much better like this than when I first dreamed of an arctic expedition?

He concluded, "I cannot deny that I often used to think that I was unlucky, but now everything has come out so beautifully that often I am astonished."[1]

At three in the morning on June 22, 1883, Boas wrote to his family, "We are sailing away now. Take one more loving greeting from Wilhelm and me." In the middle of the night, the *Germania* had been towed out to sea by a tugboat and left to wait for a favorable wind. With the archipelago of Helgoland disappearing in the distance, the crew set course directly for Scotland. They sailed along its northeast coast in the North Sea past Moray Firth and Pentland Firth. With the powerful tidal currents of the passage through the Firth into the North Atlantic, the *Ger-*

mania was pitched and tossed on high waves and Boas was laid flat with seasickness while Weike helped the crew. In a letter to his parents, Boas noted, "So far Wilhelm is doing very well. He suffers very little from seasickness and helps on the ship where he can. . . . I especially let him help in the kitchen and help the carpenter." With calmer seas on June 28 and 29, Boas began his experiments on the transparency and color of seawater. He and Weike lowered a framed disc of white canvas over the side of the ship to test depth of visibility that in this instance extended to 6.5 fathoms. As they drew closer to Greenland on July 4 and 5, Boas remarked on the sea mammals that swam within sight of the *Germania*, the porpoises and the lone harp seal, and the birds that flew overhead, the fulmars and gulls.[2]

On June 23 Boas had begun his letter-diary for Marie that Carol Knötsch refers to as "this love-letter journal." Müller-Wille writes, "These private letters, which Boas wrote fairly regularly, also served as a field diary from mid-December 1883. For Boas these letters became the most important mental refuge during his arctic sojourn; he expressed his inner feelings in them." Referring to this as "a very peculiar document," Cole observes, "In a sense it is a single, 500-page letter composed over a fifteen-month period" that allowed for "amorous effusions," "escape" from tedious and challenging field situations and recording of fieldnotes. In addition to the letter-diary to Marie, Boas compiled, as Müller-Wille points out, "multi-layered and often parallel letters and journals," which he used in his subsequent publications. He wrote, "My dearest! Today I am starting to write my diary for you, and first of all I have to tell you how much I love you!" The diary, Boas wrote, "will remain for me the most precious memory of this journey."[3]

In one of his first entries Boas described his cabin on board the *Germania*: "Mine is on the lowest deck in the fore part of the ship. You have to descend a very steep stairway into a small ante-room." Boas continued, "The entrance to my cabin is to the left of the stairs. The cabin is quite large. In the center is a table which can easily seat four people on either side. . . . There is room enough for Wilhelm and me. We get air through the stairwell and two skylights." The room, however, smelled persistently of paint and tea no matter how diligently it was cleaned. Suffering already from seasickness, Boas moved into Captain Mahlstede's cabin on deck, where he had benefit of the sea breeze. "The seamen go about," Boas wrote, "in the most tattered clothing, torn coats, boots that are almost falling apart." Occasionally the sailors would rub the cracked leather of their shoes with bacon to render them at least partially waterproof. Attempts at hygiene were nominal. Everyone received a ration of water for bathing on Sunday; however, as Boas noted, "since the soap doesn't lather with salt water . . . one simply moves the dirt from one place to another." Boas continued, "Monday clothes are washed and dried on the rigging, but they are so covered with soot that they are almost blacker than before they were washed."[4]

Boas took his meals in the captain's cabin with the captain, the navigator, and the pilot, while Weike ate with the other four crew members. Boas described the kitchen and the cook: "It is a good thing that I do not look into the kitchen very often because what occurs there is anything but nice. The cook has to help with the rigging, rushes to his pots without thinking of washing his hands. . . . Water for washing dishes is available only in the direst need, so that you can imagine the mess." In pleasant weather, the sailors slept or read to pass the time. Weike was also able to rest, save for the English lessons that Boas insisted on giving him in the hopes that Weike would be able to communicate with the American and Scottish whalers and with the Inuit who used English as a lingua franca. Of these attempts, Boas wrote Marie, "I hope he will learn something before we reach the other side." Boas feigned a posture of repose in his description to Marie: "You must think of me now seated on a camp stool on one side of the ship, my back against the cabin, my feet against 'Bord.' This is how I am writing you, with an occasional look at the broad sea." Boas had Weike take a picture of him striking a similar stance: "I shall make a print of it for you. . . . I am standing in my most usual position and am watching an iceberg which is lying opposite me." In reality, if he was not seasick, Boas was writing articles for the *Berliner Tageblatt*; summarizing his "scientific plans and writing them out in detail;" conducting his experiments on sea water; or writing the detailed letter-diaries to Marie and to his family from which he would later extract information on his trip for publications.[5]

By July 8, in the early morning hours, they were sailing through "a severe gale" and, with the rising sun, had sighted the coast of Greenland, "35–40 miles away, through the fog." Weike wrote in his diary, "The gale became steadily stronger; one wave after another swept on board." Abandoning the effort to sleep, Weike got up, dressed, and delivered to Boas the birthday greetings and presents that his family and Marie had entrusted to him. In a seasick stupor, Boas lifted his head, checked his watch, found that it was three thirty in the morning, felt the raging storm tossing the ship, remarked feebly, "An early birthday gift," and collapsed back in bed. The *Germania* passed from the Atlantic Ocean into the Arctic Sea on July 9, and Boas noted, in the throes of intense seasickness, "I have lived a quarter of a century."[6]

Boas reflected on this experience of sailing into the Arctic Sea—of hearing the waves slap against the ice floes; the sailor's shout "Ice in sight!"; and of seeing the slice of iceberg rush past the ship. He wrote, "It has become clear to me now how necessary it is to see a thing in order to get a true living picture of it. I have seen many pictures of icebergs, but this small piece, roaring by in the fog has given me a better conception than any picture or any description. The surroundings, the sight and sound have left an indelible impression on me. The ship, the ocean alive with screaming birds, the thundering sound of the ice, the thick fog and the light of the ice create a background that cannot be reproduced in a picture." With the passing of the storm, Boas and Weike set to drying everything out. As Boas wrote, "Clothes are strung up, paper is spread out and we too let the sun shine on us."[7]

On July 31 Boas noted that they were "drifting near the land." However, for the next three weeks, with the shifting sheets of ice, Boas despaired of ever reaching land. They would draw near, it was within sight, and then, repeatedly: "Our progress has again ended . . . we have reached the edge of the ice and we can go no further." Boas could not sleep for worry. He wrote, "Just think of it if I have lost four months for nothing! . . . We are sailing further and further south to see whether there is an opening." On August 13 Boas noted, "Today there was no wind at all and we were in the midst of the ice, which lay in large floes . . . and smaller pieces all about us. There was some wind in the morning so that we ran into the ice with some force. I was awakened by such a crash at five this morning. I was tossed into the air while lying in bed." The ice grew thicker and thicker and "stretched so far . . . that it may be covering the entire Strait of Davis."[8]

Creating a Future for Us

On August 14 the wind died down, the fog lifted, "and suddenly we found ourselves quite close to Cape Mercy," located at the tip of the Cumberland Sound. Boas remarked, "I was completely overwhelmed with astonishment when the veil lifted and the high mountains appeared." With the "nearest point . . . only two miles away," they were so close but still thwarted by the ice. Fervently hoping to be able to round Cape Mercy, Boas wrote, "If only the stupid fog would disappear. We are now close enough to see the contours of the land—the steep cliffs, the snow in the deeply cleft mountaintops. I shall not sleep too well tonight for hoping that we shall sail around the cape. Onwards, only onwards!" On August 22 the *Germania* rounded Cape Mercy, sailed into the sound, and encountered more ice. On August 28 Boas wrote exuberantly, "Kikkerton in sight! The great news of the day! It is just appearing through the fog and we are sailing on under a favorable wind."[9]

With the sailor's shout of "Ship ahead!," those on board the *Germania* spotted a boat carrying Alexander Hall, a whaler from the Scottish station based in Kekerten, along with his crew of six Inuit sailors and a cook, who were returning from hunting walruses. In his article "In the Ice of the North—Kikkerton," published as part of his series for the *Berliner Tageblatt*, Boas recalled suddenly hearing a cry from across the water: "We expectantly looked for its source. . . . Then suddenly our captain, well known in these waters, called, 'Hello, Sandy!' The ship's mate also recognized his old friend from the whaling station, as their boat rapidly approached the ship. Soon it was alongside and Mr. Alexander Hall came aboard, warmly greeted by all of us. We learned that up until now no ship had entered the Sound, and that until a few days ago, the Sound had been packed with ice."[10]

Hall and the Inuit attached a rope to the *Germania* and rowed vigorously to guide it to shore. Another small boat came from shore with six Inuit women paddling and an old man steering. Together the two small boats and the crew's own small boat "pulled our old Germania into the harbor." Boas recounted, "We pushed slowly through the ice. We then saw the American station. They sighted us soon and raised their flag. We heard the dogs howling and saw snow tents of the natives. Then the Scottish station . . . soon raised their flag." Just before three in the afternoon, the *Germania* dropped anchor. Boas noted that they "had arrived safely in the harbor of Kikkerton," and "at 4:30 the captain and I went ashore in the Marie." In the story that he would later write for his children about his time in the Canadian Arctic, Boas described the Inuit women who had helped to pull the *Germania* to shore and who had come on board: "They wore long jackets made of sealskin, with enormous hoods in which they carried their little babies. They wore high boots made of sealskin, and short pants, which reached down to their knees. But they had put on their holiday dress to meet us, and [had] thrown gay petticoats over their fur dresses. They all brought little clay pipes, such as you use for making soap bubbles; and the first thing they did was to ask for tobacco."[11]

Boas's initial plan for the journey to Cumberland Sound had entailed traveling to K'ingua, where the seven scientists and four servants of the German Polar Commission would board the *Germania* for their trip back to Germany. Boas wrote, "There I shall take over the houses and inventory of the station and unpack my belongings." However, Boas came to realize the difficulties and expense of maintaining a facility with only Weike's help. Additionally, as Müller-Wille and Gieseking note, "he would have been isolated from the Inuit, who lived in dispersed settlements and around the whaling stations farther south in Cumberland Sound." A month prior to his departure, Boas had changed his plans: he wrote Crawford Noble in Aberdeen, Scotland, requesting that he and Weike be allowed to stay in his whaling station. Finding hospitality and friendship in Kekerten, Boas and Weike used the whaling station as their base from September 13, 1883, to May 6, 1884.[12]

The Scottish whaling station was made up of three storage buildings and living quarters in a "much-modified original house brought by William Penny in 1857." In his article of September 14, 1883, for the *Berliner Tageblatt*, Boas described his first view of Kekerten: "There were the tents of the natives. We saw the friendly home of Mr. Noble of Aberdeen and the Scottish station that stands next to its three supply sheds. Closer to the shoreline were the houses of members of the American station of Williams and Company of New London. On the beach there were lots of dogs, who now, during the summer, played around lazily." The ever-helpful James Mutch and Alexander Hall were in charge of the Scottish whaling station; and Captain Roach was in charge of the American whaling station.[13]

Creating a Future for Us

Aware that the *Germania* was to transport the staff from the station, Dr. Wilhelm Giese, leader of the German polar station, had sent a letter to the Scottish whaling station with Inuit who traveled by whaleboat, "asking whether the Germania had arrived and whether she could" reach K'ingua. Boas recorded in his letter-diary, "As the sound was blocked with ice I put myself at their disposal." He traveled to K'ingua with the crew of six Inuit in their whaleboat "as fast as possible." Before departing, however, Boas had "borrowed an Eskimo suit, as mine is not ready." In a letter that Boas sent to Marie via the Scottish ship, which was soon to depart, he wrote,

> You know that I travelled to Kingawa to bring news to the expedition there. But you do not know how beautiful parts of the trip were, how nights when I lay awake and the stars shone down upon me so bright and clear I thought of you and the glorious future when I shall hold you in my arms and your clear, true eyes will always tell me how much you love me. I shall always look to them for confidence and strength and all my happiness. And then when I looked at myself in my Eskimo costume, at the sleeping forms around me, at the drifting ice, it almost seemed as though I were dreaming.

Boas concluded, "Everything here is so strange and the joy in our love always new."[14]

After the rigorous three-day trip, battling heavy ice the whole way, they arrived at the opening to the K'ingua Fiord. There they found the *Lizzie P. Simmons*, the American whaling vessel commanded by Captain John Roach, that had last been seen in Kekerten two months before and was known to have "drifted northward with the ice." Captain Roach, the mate, the harpooner, and Boas sailed in a small craft and were followed by the six Inuit in the whaleboat to the station of the German Polar Commission. In his journal entry for September 7, 1883, Dr. Giese had noted the arrival of Captain Roach's boat. "To our amazement," he wrote, "it was followed by a second boat, in which, as it approached closer, we could distinguish only Eskimos." Dr. Giese approached the shore to greet Captain Roach, "but to his left another man unknown to me, pushed forward." Giese continued, "Outwardly he was dressed in native costume but by his walk he was immediately recognizable as a European. While still at a

distance he shouted to me, 'Greetings from Germania.' It was Dr. Boas."
With great relief, Dr. Giese determined "that tomorrow we would start
packing up." The *Lizzie P. Simmons* would carry the crew, the provisions,
and the instruments to the *Germania*. In a matter of days, they had closed
down the station and nailed the doors and windows shut. While Giese
had expressed his hopes that "Dr. Boas . . . will be in a position to make
use of the houses," Boas did not visit the station again during his time
in the Cumberland Sound.[15]

Boas's welcome in Kekerten had been facilitated by a letter of introduction from Noble, owner of the Scottish whaling station, who requested
that James Shepherd Mutch render all cooperation to Boas in his scientific
endeavors. Born in Scotland in 1847, and a servant in Noble's home, Mutch
had first come to the Canadian Arctic in 1865 on board a whaler and
returned to the Cumberland Sound two years later to assume the management of Noble's station. He was to remain in the Cumberland Sound for
seventeen years, only occasionally traveling back to Scotland in the spring
and returning to Kekerten in the fall. Married to an Inuk woman and fluent in Inuktitut, Mutch was to be "a most welcome and willing help" to
Boas in all matters. Boas acknowledged Mutch for his generous help "in
my long and tedious conversations with the Esquimaux, until I was myself
able to talk to them." He continued, "It was with his dogs and sledges that
I made a great number of my journeys; by his help I managed to get my
skin clothing ready in time to start the winter travelling."[16]

Settled into a comfortable dwelling that was "nice and warm," Boas
and Weike had a commodious living space and sleeping area with bunk
beds to accommodate four people. Of the station manager of the Scottish
whaling station, Boas wrote, "Jimmy Mutch is as friendly and cooperative
as possible and since we have combined our provisions we can eat very
well." "Wilhelm," Boas remarked, "is becoming a more perfect cook day
by day." Weike seemed both surprised and proud of his growing ability to
cook. "I was making an excellent bean soup," he wrote, "to which I added
barley and lentils; and then I cooked my rabbit. This made an excellent
meal." Boas had employed Ssigna as his Inuit guide after having witnessed
his skilled performance as the helmsman on the challenging three-day
voyage to K'ingua. Born in Davis Strait but having spent most of his fifty
years on the Cumberland Sound, Ssigna had been in the employ of the

American Station's Captain Roach, who had released him so that Boas could hire him for the year. Ssigna had knowledge, Boas noted, of "the coast of Cumberland Sound in almost all its extensions." Boas offered reassurance to his family: "I have hired an Eskimo [Ssigna], who understands English well and is very reliable, for the entire winter, and now have no further worries." In partial payment, Boas had given Ssigna the Mauser rifle in order to hunt for them. "In addition," Boas wrote, "he will receive a weekly ration of bread, molasses and tobacco."[17] Ssigna often brought Ocheitu (who had worked as resident servant at the German Polar Station in 1882–83), Utütiak (also called Yankee), Nachojaschi, and Shanguja on the land and sea travels, as he had done on that first trip to K'ingua. There were to be many excursions over treacherous waters and across frozen terrain that Boas and Weike would not have survived had it not been for the skill and attention of Ssigna, Ocheitu, Shanguja, and other Inuit who travelled with them. Boas was both cognizant of this and grateful for it.

Boas observed soberly, "At home I believed that I would have time for many things during the winter but that must have been an illusion because my time is always filled either with cartographic or ethnographic work." Boas reflected, "I have decided that I must limit myself to these two if I wish to accomplish anything—one year is too short a time." Boas began immediately to chart the terrain for his topographic surveys and, simultaneously, to learn Inuktitut vocabulary. After barely disembarking from the *Germania*, Boas visited an Inuit dwelling, a *tupik* (driftwood covered by caribou and seal skin to form a tent for use in summer) where he spent the morning collecting vocabulary: "I already have quite a number of words about furnishings of the *tupik* and parts of the human body." Boas never missed an opportunity to add to his vocabulary list. Just after noting that he had set sail with six Inuit for K'ingua in his first boat trip on the sound, Boas listed Inuktitut words and he added additional words the next day.[18]

Boas used Inuit place names on the maps he drafted. In his 1884 article "A Journey in Cumberland Sound and on the West Shore of Davis Strait," Boas stated succinctly, "I prefer to adopt the native names instead of the English ones." Expanding on this point, Boas wrote in 1885, "'It is truly to be deplored if indigenous names get lost, because, like the Eskimo ones, they are so fitting; I have experienced such considerable anger, annoyance and inconveniences from numerous English names and the absence of indigenous names, that the situation has prevented me from making use of the explorer's naming rights anywhere. It is certainly more valuable scientifically to preserve the indigenous names than to write names of all meritorious or not so meritorious friends à la Ross and Hall on bays and foothills.'"[19]

Boas came to realize with frustration "that all the information I had received in Europe was worth nothing." He expanded, "In Cumberland sound there was a very rough resemblance between the shores and the old chart, as some of the fjords, at least, were marked down, though in a wrong shape. The real shape of the gulf is very different from the one given to it up to this date." In his 1885 manuscript on "The Eskimos of Baffin Land," Boas wrote, "The coast that was rediscovered by Ross and Parry at the beginning of this century is seen by ships almost every year, but no traveler has ever disembarked on the rough shores, so that the topography of the land has remained quite unknown. Islands and long peninsulas hide fjords that cut deep into the land, so that the passing mariner gains the impression of a uniform un-indented coast."[20] Boas had planned to travel west from Cumberland Sound to Lake Kennedy, known by the Inuit as Lake Nettling. When he was finally able to do so in April 1884, he found that both "the shape and position" were wrong. Instead of one lake, there were two, Lakes Nettiling and Amakdjuak, and neither was located as indicated on the chart.[21]

Boas realized that the weather would perforce determine the pacing of his work. He wrote Marie, "My present plans are to travel about in the vicinity of Kikkerton, as I have done up to now, then when it begins to freeze to stay here until Christmas and to do ethnographical work." As the months passed, even when the weather should have precluded his travel, Boas journeyed "almost uninterruptedly around the southeastern coastal areas of Baffin Island to make observations of the terrain and carry out topographic surveys." Whether by small craft, larger vessel, dog sled, or on foot, Boas's travels were physically demanding and often breathtakingly beautiful. On October 19 he wrote, "And now when I look through the tent door and see the ice and snow, hear the sea roar, everything seems almost as if in a dream." From a point "seven miles inland from Kignait Fiord," Boas wrote Marie during a rest stop after a five-mile hike, "I am writing you while I am lying on a bank of moss. The sun is shining on my back. To the right is a huge snow-covered mountain, partially covered by clouds, to the left a high waterfall rushes and roars and directly below it, rises a high mountain. Signa has gone to hunt rabbits . . . and I am lying here thinking of my distant love." The next day from another camp, he wrote, "We hiked with full load, i.e. rifle and provisions, for 8 hours, but not on a level route; it was uphill and downhill through bogs and water, over rocks and stones. Moreover, we are now wearing genuine native Eskimo boots, . . . which do not have a firm sole, so our feet are still sore today."[22]

In appreciation for their knowledge of their own land, Boas asked the Inuit to draw maps of the area. He gave them lead pencils and thick carton paper. On November 5 Boas wrote Marie, "Almost the whole of Kikkerton is engaged in drawing maps for me, from which I hope to get on the track of my questions." James Mutch had identified for Boas a total of about ten to fifteen Inuit men and women whom he knew to be specialists in the configuration of the land and in place names. Boas had found that it was "better to question the Eskimos individually than several of them together, because it seems that they are shy in front of each other." He concluded, "One can never get as much out of them when there are several together as from one of them alone." So the Inuit would come to the station, singly or in small numbers. Boas noted, "In the morning Pakkak and his . . . [wife] were here, mapping [the areas of] Kignait and Padli for me. Since I am giving the natives tobacco for their maps, they are arriving on their own accord; thus in the evening Bob arrived with a [sketch] showing the Davis Strait coast from Padli to far to the north." Boas wrote in his diary for November 3, "The sketch maps are always valuable." Boas, Weike, and Mutch would open the table to its full extension, spread out an expanse of paper, and hoist themselves up on the table. Lying flat on their stomachs, they would begin sketching the outline of the maps that the Inuit had given them.[23]

In "Inuit Geographical Knowledge One Hundred Years Apart," Ludger Müller-Wille and Linna Weber Müller-Wille remark, "The working sessions with the Inuit experts were considerable linguistic and cross-cultural challenges for Boas. He was a native German speaker and had had training in classical languages and French in school. He had also learned English, the lingua franca of the whalers, and some smattering of Inuktitut (the Greenlandic variety) on his own before the arctic sojourn." Boas related that the conversation would be "seven-eighths in Eskimo and one-eighth in English." Mutch spoke with the Inuit in Inuktitut. Boas communicated with Mutch in English; with Wilhelm in German; with the Inuit, in the Pidgin English that the Inuit spoke, and Boas had acquired; and he made a valiant effort to use Inuktitut, which he resolutely attempted to learn. "The language," he admitted, "is quite abominably difficult!" Boas recounted how Pakkak had brought him a sketch map of the coast, on which Boas was asking him to identify the summer camps used for hunting caribou: "He is always greatly amused when I pronounce the local names." Boas also joked about the English he was learning at the whaling station: "'Oh well, Doctor, I will there go on land,' as they say here." Of his and Weike's acquisition of Pidgin English, Boas noted, "At first we could make ourselves understood only with the jargon that has gradually grown out of the intercourse between the whalers and the Eskimos. This is a colorful mixture of Eskimo and English words with some foreign admixtures, and with the most elementary grammatical structure."[24]

In the intensive interview sessions Boas continued his collection of place names and entered these on the maps following the directions of the Inuit. He combined this with his exacting and precise "geographic observations and geodetic surveys." From his eighth day in the Cumberland Sound, when he undertook the boat trip with the six Inuit north through the ice floes to the German Polar Station, Boas was resolute: "He would get to know the land, sea, and ice with the Inuit by acquiring skills in their language, learning their place names while traveling with them extensively throughout the area and seeing and experiencing all named spaces and places in situ." Boas had identified the key to slicing into the "complex relationships between Inuit and the arctic landscape," through recognizing the importance of the people's own place names for their land. In his *Erstlingsreise*, his first voyage, Boas had identified as primary the native terms of classification.[25] A worldview in anthropology would grow from this fertile point.

Shortly after Boas's arrival, many Inuit inhabitants of Kekerten were struck ill with diphtheria and pneumonia. In October Boas was called to assist a woman who was stricken with a high fever and who had severe difficulty in breathing. He gave her "turpentine for her chest, quinine to combat the fever, ammonia to relieve her respiration, and opium against her cough, but he could do nothing more." The woman died two days later. On November 18 Boas wrote, "This morning I sat in a tiny, tiny snow hut at the deathbed of a poor little Eskimo boy. The Eskimos are so confident that the *Doctorádluk*, as they call me, can help them when they are sick that I always go to them when they call me. And I always feel so unhappy when I am with those poor people and cannot help them." To Marie, he wrote, "This is the second deathbed I have attended here!" Boas continued, "I keep telling myself that I was not to blame for the child's death yet it weighs upon me like a reproach that I was unable to help." Another woman had had pneumonia but, though she had been deathly ill for three or four days, she had fortunately survived. "These poor people, man and wife," Boas continued, "lay sick together, and although the other Eskimos supplied them with meat, they would have been in a bad way if I had not brought them food and drink." On November 3 Boas had sent a stricken woman some hot cocoa and, to her and her husband, "some bread and meat because they had nothing to eat." Twelve days later, he wrote, "I am still having to feed Joe and his wife." To Marie, Boas wrote, "I shall never forget, in a small snow hut, seeing a mother beside her sick child, who scarcely showed a sign of life, and how she spoke most lovingly to him."[26]

Death continued to leave sadness and devastation in its icy path. In his diary he noted, "The Eskimos are very afraid of dealing with the dead, since they believe that their spirits would kill them." Boas explained the customs surrounding serious illness and portending death. According to the season the Inuit would build a small tupik or igloo and the stricken ones were "carried through an opening in the back. This opening is then closed, and subsequently a door is cut out." Boas continued, "A small quantity of food is placed in the hut, but the patient is left without attendants." However, if the Inuit did not feel that death was imminent, then "the relatives and friends may come to visit." The wrenching tragedy of losing a child was the same for the parents no matter the culture, nor the customs surrounding illness and death. On October 30 Boas wrote, "This morning Jiminie's child, who also had pneumonia, died. I saw him carry the box away, while his wife carried the dead child in her arms, sinking to her knees every few steps. The day before, Mutch had found the mother standing outside her house weeping over the loss of her child."[27]

On his initial arrival, when Boas had made it through the ice floes of the Davis Straits and had disembarked from the *Germania*, another devastating epidemic was plaguing the Inuit of Baffin Land: "I arrived just when many dogs had died from an illness that has flared up, now here now there, for a long time." In "A Journey in Cumberland Sound," Boas recalled, "In the fall of 1883 the dogs' disease, the horror of the Esquimaux of Cumberland sound and Greenland, spread at an awful rate over every settlement. No team was spared, and in December about one-half of all the dogs had died." Of Ssigna's ten dogs, two remained, and of Mutch's thirty dogs, eight remained. Boas wrote his parents that, with sea and land frozen, "these dogs represent the only mode of travel." He continued, "But it was precisely during this past winter that it raged especially virulently, so that at the time when I was able to start on my major trip [to Lake Nettiling], absolutely no dogs were to be had, and I could not stir from the spot."[28]

From October to mid-December 1883 Boas was tied close to Kekerten. He was unable to assemble a dog team for travel and, just as important, he and Weike did not have the skin clothing requisite for winter travel. The deaths of Inuit from diphtheria and pneumonia placed restrictions on the women who were working with the skins. Boas's sympathy and concern for the Inuit who were ill and dying warred with his desperate desire for the completion of the clothing. He had traded for furs and caribou skins in September and October. He wrote Marie, "I have bought furs and all I need now is a sleeping [bag]." He noted that he had traded for twelve caribou skins from the Inuit who had just returned from summer hunt. He added, "Now that I have them a weight has truly been taken off my mind, because for a long time I had been unable to buy any caribou skins, without which it is impossible to travel in winter." In the "Eskimo Story," Boas wrote, "As soon as they reached Kikkerten, and had unloaded their boats, I bought the necessary caribou-skins from them, paying them with tobacco, biscuits, molasses, caps for their guns, powder and lead. Then I secured the services of two Eskimo women, who were to work the caribou-skins into clothing for Wilhelm and myself."[29]

Boas did all he could to facilitate the completion of the work. By the end of October Boas wrote to his family, "I hope the women will soon start working so that I will get a complete new suit. They only begin when the ice has become firm, and they may not work for 3 days after somebody has died; so there is now no prospect of getting winter clothing custom-made." To Marie he wrote, "Unfortunately there are again two children very sick with diphtheria-like sickness, both died." The result, he said, was an "unpleasant interruption" in the sewing of his caribou clothing. After the three-day cessation of sewing on the caribou skins, the women would ask those in mourning for permission to take up the work again. Finally, at the beginning of December, the women were completing Boas's skin clothing: "My caribou pants are ready, as well as the boots which Betty [Ssigna's wife] has been adjusting." He was learning the nuances of the mortuary customs, "My bird slippers will be finished, although I was afraid that they would also not work on these, but it is only sealskin and caribou skin which they are forbidden to make into *new* clothing." He noted that the women could work on new European items and new clothing made from birds, or on old skin clothing.[30]

During the winter months, when Boas's travel was limited due to the decimated dog population, he perforce spent more time with the Inuit, either those at Kekerten or those in the areas to which his travels along the eastern shore of the Cumberland Sound took him. "Detained at Kik-kerton," as he characterized it, he began "in earnest" his ethnographic work. In "A Journey in Cumberland Sound," Boas wrote, "Every night I spent with the natives who told me about the configuration of the land, about their travels, etc. They related the old stories handed over to them by their ancestors, sang the old songs after the old monotonous tunes, and I saw them playing the old games, with which they shorten the long dark winter nights." By the end of December Boas noted that the language was coming easier to him, "Yesterday evening I again had a long conver-sation with an old woman who has come here from far to the north and whose knowledge extends as far as North Greenland! Gradually I can make myself understood somewhat with the Eskimos." He added the persistent refrain, "Their language is horribly difficult!"[31]

In November Boas and Weike had set up their tupik on the ice in the Kekerten harbor to make tidal observations by means of improvised techniques—by lowering a stone tied to a cord of specific length through the ice into the water, and then, when that didn't work, by lowering a twenty-five-foot mast from Mutch's boat. With the two of them alternating shifts to monitor the equipment and to record the tidal measurements, they also had to keep an eye on the ice. In his entry for November 8 Boas noted that "in half an hour the ice had moved out about 2'. . . . I considered it advisable to go ashore and take everything important with me. So I closed up the *tupik*, and at midnight headed home with some effort, against the raging storm." In his entry for the same day, Weike conveyed their swift departure from the tupik with more excitement: "It was almost high tide; travel across the fast ice was difficult, there were great cracks in it all over the place; we were constantly almost running into them." On Sunday, November 11, they were back on the ice, with Boas taking the watch from four to eight in the morning, during which time he spotted activity on shore, with people running about and shouting excitedly.[32]

Leaving Weike to tend to the tidal measurements, Boas went ashore to find the Inuit celebrating the "great festival" of Sedna. In his "Eskimo Story," he wrote, "I had not heard before about the festival, and was very much surprised when, one morning, I saw all the men running from hut to hut, screaming and jumping. They stop at the entrance of each hut, and when the woman of the house hears them, she steps out of the door, and throws a dish containing little gifts of meat and pieces of sealskin, among the yelling crowd, who scramble to get possession of the presents." After the distribution of the gifts, the people divided into two groups, those born in the summer and those born in the winter, for a tug-of-war. If those born in the summer win, "then it will be nice weather during the winter," but if those born in the winter win, "it will be a very cold winter." Boas continued with a detailed description of the subsequent events of the festival and offered an explanation of its purpose: to please the "old woman who is mother of the seals," and to insure good weather and good hunting for the people.[33]

For Boas the festival of Sedna and the narratives about her provided an increased understanding of the culture of the Inuit. As he wrote, "The belief in Sedna and her father is actually the foundation of Eskimo religion." As told in the narrative of Sedna, the mammals of the sea were created from the severed digits of her fingers. In an attempt to rescue his daughter from an abusive husband, who was a fulmar, the father placed her in his kayak and paddled swiftly away. Pursued by a flock of threatening fulmars, the father forced his daughter from the kayak. When she clung to the side, "The cruel father then took a knife and cut off the first joints of her fingers. Falling into the sea they were transformed into whales, the nails turning into whalebone. Sedna holding on to the boat more tightly, the second finger joints fell under the sharp knife and swam away as seals . . . . when the father cut off the stumps of the fingers they became ground seals." In agony and anger, Sedna sank to the bottom of the sea, where she took revenge on those who did not observe the proper customs of the hunt. She would not release the sea mammals from the pool at her side, in which they swam until she was placated by the attentions of the shaman and received the proper respect from the people: "As all sea animals have originated from her fingers the Eskimo must make atonement for every animal he kills." When the hunter brought the seal to his wife, she must stop all work until it had been butchered; when a walrus or a whale was taken, all must rest for three days. Boas continued, "Not all kinds of work, however, are forbidden, for they were allowed to mend articles, made of sealskin, but they must not make anything new. Working on new [caribou] skins is strictly prohibited. No skins of this kind obtained in summer may be prepared before the ice has formed and the first seal is caught with the harpoon." Boas wrote, "These regulations are observed very strictly and consequently the traveler who is not familiar with these customs is likely to meet the most unexpected difficulties in his undertakings in which he has to rely on the help of the natives."[34]

Boas had been subtly seduced into a pleasing relationship with the ethnographic, with the people. Patience was not an innate part of him. He strained in frustration against the customs that prevented the women from sewing his skin clothing even when he came to realize the significance of the restrictions. He was poised to be off on his voyages without quite realizing that a world was unfolding before him. Gone were the disciplined hours of study: "The amiable Eskimos come and go continually." Of the first few weeks in Kekerten, Boas remarked, "I hear continually—Herr Dr. here, Herr Dr. there!" Everyone was trying to show him "a kindness," as he wrote, "and I had no peace until the Germania sailed away on Sunday morning, the 16th. Now I am alone here in the Cumberland sound, but I have found such a kind and friendly welcome . . . that I feel quite at home here." Boas was soon to find that the "friendly welcome" meant that he was seldom alone. With no place to seek quiet refuge, Boas had lost control over his space: "When I am at Kikkerton I am in such great demand that I can't get on with anything." Returning from a cartographic trip, Boas wrote his parents, "I have now been living in the house again for some time, but my numerous conversations with the Eskimos don't allow me to rest."[35]

On one of his early trips in October that took him north of Pangnirtung Fjord, Boas watched a settlement spring up before his eyes in what had been an empty expanse: "We were busy unloading our things when we suddenly spotted a sail that was heading towards the same spot. Soon my people recognized the Eskimos in it; one of them, Yankee, spotted his brother; they then quickly ran down to help them unload." Unbeknownst to Boas, this site at the fjord entrance was used frequently as a stopping point for travelers due to its location on a well-frequented crossing point for various boat routes. The people were returning from the summer hunting season for caribou at Lake Nettiling and were traveling in "high-sided whale boats, 30 feet long, full of men, women and children." Boas continued, "Fore and aft they were piled high with skins. . . . In the middle lie the dogs which from time to time raise a dreadful music; astern tows a small kayak, the landing boat of the Eskimos. . . . Another boat arrived, which had been travelling with the first one, and now we were an entire village on the small headland where previously there had been nobody. 4 Eskimo tents and myself with 2 tents!" Boas visited the Inuit in their tupiks and gave them tobacco as a gift. Later, the Inuit visited Boas and "made themselves comfortable in my tent." Passing out a glass of rum and tobacco for all, Boas entertained until ten o'clock in the evening.[36]

On December 11, with the loan of Mutch's dogs, Boas, Weike, and Ssigna set out to survey the northeast portion of the Cumberland shore as far as Anarnitung. Equipped with "guns, lamps, provisions and sleeping bags" but minus the crucial kerosene stove that they had forgotten to pack, they traveled by dog sled, stopping each afternoon in time for Ssigna to hunt seal on the ice and to build a small igloo for the night. With the help of Weike, Boas took readings for the survey map. On December 14 the temperature began to rise and the snow to fall. Slowed by a two-foot accumulation of snow, the three could travel no more "than three miles a day." Having made such slight progress, they took refuge in their igloo. Waking in the morning, Weike and Boas "invented a lamp, that is almost our greatest necessity. To make it we used an old butter tin and cut three holes into the lid. We also made a pot out of an old tin can. Now we have glowing lamps and can quickly brew coffee and our igloo is also warmer." At this point neither Boas, Weike, nor Ssigna realized the precipice of danger on which they were poised. "Someday," Boas wrote, "when I shall relate this adventure it will sound terrible and dangerous." He continued, "Now we are laughing at our bad luck and the surprise of the people in Anarnitung when they see three men arrive from Kik-kerton on foot and with two dogs. . . . We have a long trek ahead, fifteen miles without a path or sign post!"[37]

As they settled into their igloo on the next night, December 20, with the temperature plummeting to minus 45°F, Boas took measure of their situation. The resupplies that Mutch was to have sent had not reached them due to the heavy snow. With food running low, no kerosene stove, little blubber for heating water and for cooking, a broken gun, and only one cartridge left for the other gun, Boas resolved "to leave everything and to travel to the next settlement, Anarnitung, which was distant about twenty miles." At five in the morning on December 20 they set off by the light of the moon shining brightly off the snow and kept trudging into the brief sunlight of the Arctic winter. At noon Anarnitung was within sight. Then, at twelve thirty, a dense fog settled, the sun went down, and they lost site of the settlement. Continuing in the dark, they scrambled over rough slabs of sea ice, jutting up to over six feet: "The holes between the pieces were filled up with soft snow, and we were obliged to crawl and stumble over the projecting points and edges of the slabs." By seven in the evening on December 20 they heard the howls of a dog team, changed course towards it, and came to land at ten o'clock at night. Totally ignorant as to where they were, Boas, Weike, and Ssigna spent the night moving about over a small space of ground, blessedly covered only lightly with snow, to try to keep warm. Boas recounted that Weike "had frozen his feet in the evening while crossing the rough ice, and could only walk with great difficulty." As the moon rose, they found sled tracks: "But our bad luck was not yet at an end; we took the wrong direction." Having gone too far north, they turned around, "and at last we arrived in the morning in Anarnitung after a walk of twenty-five hours, tired and hungry." Weike recorded for the December 21 entry, "As we entered Ocheitu's *iglu* the [Inuit] moved out from under their covers and we crawled under them. A young woman . . . even pulled the covers up over me. Ocheitu and his wife took care that we received dry clothes, and in due course his wife prepared our supper, so that we could first rest somewhat."[38]

For Weike the treacherous trek to Anarnitung resulted in third-degree frostbite of his feet. In his diary entry for December 13, Boas had noted, "I had almost gone alone with Ssigna because Wilhelm's suit was not finished, but Mr. Mutch took pity on me and lent him his outfit." However, the clothing did not fit—the pants were too large; the boots, too narrow—and thus Weike could stay neither warm nor dry. Unaware of the extent of Weike's injuries, Boas was up the next morning and off with Weike, Ssigna, and Ocheitu to survey the mouth of the K'ingua Fjord, "but I had to return to Anarnitung, as my servant's feet grew very bad and he only told me then that he had frozen his left foot." Weike recorded the details of his frostbite in very matter-of-fact prose. On December 23 he wrote, "This morning Ocheito and Singnak [Ssigna] went hunting. Herr Dr went with them. I had to stay in my sleeping bag with my blessed feet. During the night one of them had swollen so much that I had to cut the bandage away with my knife; everything inside my sleeping bag was covered with pus. When Ocheito bandaged me up again, he said that that foot was still frozen inside; on the other the frostbite was on the outside." Earlier, on the surveying trip with Boas, Weike had been incapacitated with pain and was taken back on a dog sled wrapped in his sleeping bag and tied to the sled. Weike noted that Ssigna and Ocheitu "derived great pleasure from tying up a 'gentleman,'" meaning a European. Weike continued, "I was tied up so tightly that I couldn't make the slightest movement; and this is how I was transported. When I reached Anarnitung three men grabbed my sleeping bag and carried me to the entrance to the *iglu* and then I was pulled inside." Weike's recovery from the third-degree frostbite was due to the initial emergency care by Ocheito and his wife. Without their expertise in treating frostbite in these crucial days, Weike might well have lost his toes if not part of his foot.[39]

With temperatures "too cold to transport him," Weike was left at Anarnitung in the care of Ocheitu and his wife, who fed him and tended to him with great care. Since Ocheitu had learned some basic German

Creating a Future for Us

from his employment at the German polar station (1882–83), Weike likely communicated with greater ease than he did when he was returned to Mutch's care in Kekerten to spend the months of January to May in recovery. At the station Weike spoke with Mutch "half in English, half in Eskimo." He wrote, "I string together the words that I know, so that he can understand; then he says it correctly in English. I can understand well enough, but can't compose a reply."[40]

Before Boas had started on his return trip to Kekerten, Ocheitu caught two seals, and the whole camp joined in "a great feast." Everyone came to Ocheitu's igloo to receive a piece of seal meat. In his December 23 diary entry Boas wrote, "Isn't it a fine custom among these 'savages' that they endure privations together, but all happily share in the eating and drinking communally when some game has been killed?" Boas continued,

> I often ask myself what advantages our "good society" possesses over the "savages" and the more I see of their customs, I find that we really have no grounds to look down on them contemptuously. Where among us is there such hospitality as here? Where are there people who carry out *any* task requested of them so willingly and without grumbling! We should not censure them for their conventions and superstitions, since we "highly educated" people are relatively much worse. The fear of the old traditions and the old conventions is truly deeply implanted in humankind, and just as it controls life here, it obstructs all progress with us. . . . The Eskimos are now sitting alert, their mouths full, eating raw seal liver and the blood stains on the other page will tell you how I was assisting them.

Boas continued with reflections on the import of this experience for him: "I believe if this trip has for me (as a thinking person) a valuable influence, it lies in the strengthening of the viewpoint of the relativity of all *cultivation* [*Bildung*] and that the evil as well as the value of a person lies in the cultivation of the heart [*Herzensbildung*]." Boas observed, "The quality is present or absent here among the Eskimo, just as among us. All that man can do for humanity is to further the *truth*, whether it be sweet or bitter. Such a man may truly say that he has not lived in vain."[41]

Throughout his time in Kekerten and in the Cumberland Sound, Boas had shifted to a realization that he liked ethnography—studying the people, their customs, and stories—better than he did the scientific tasks that accompanied his geographical work. As he wrote to his parents at the end of April during the preparations for departure from Kekerten for Davis Strait, "My work on the Eskimos has given me more satisfaction than my trips." In "Under the Arctic Circle," Boas reflected on how "by listening one becomes only half acquainted with the mode of life of a people." He continued,

> One must see and observe most of the habits and customs, and share in their activities. I learned about the secrets of their magicians, the Angekoks, when I was visiting an Eskimo whose wife suddenly became ill and soon died.... Similarly I learned the customs of the natives when we made journeys together by sled, and for days had to work and hunt together and share hunger as well as good times.... To learn intimately their character and their customs, to gain an understanding of their many curious customs, demands prolonged and faithful work, and paying the strictest attention to every manifestation of their living, no matter how seemingly unimportant. Every new observation provides new matter for thought, and is a link between other isolated observations, until the whole finally unfolds as a beautiful picture, in which we recognize, under the strange and foreign mode of life, the thinking and feeling human being, who resembles us in his character more than we could imagine from our first superficial impression.[42]

Boas had expressed this immersion into Inuit life by writing about his time in Anarnitung, when he journeyed there in February to hunt seals: "As you see, my Marie, I am now truly just like an Eskimo; I live like them, hunt with them, and count myself among the men of Anarnitung." He continued, "Moreover I scarcely eat any European foodstuffs any longer but am living entirely on seal meat and coffee." On the trip to Anarnitung, Boas had begun driving the dog sled by himself for the first time, though, as he said, he was "not managing it properly. The whip is quite long and my voice is not accustomed to the shouting and cursing." Boas went out seal hunting "exactly like an Eskimo with my harpoon and all the accessories." In these his first days of seal hunting, Boas stressed his patience: "I sat there just like the Eskimo at the water's edge behind my ice floe and waited patiently for a head to appear. You can't imagine what an impression it makes, to sit so near the water at this cold time of year, and to hear the roaring and rushing again." He was honest about the effect that two days of sitting on the ice had had on him: "I am heartily bored with seal hunting."[43]

While Boas had professed to Marie that he thought "nothing of the saying 'sacrifice for the sake of science,'" in fact the pursuit of science undergirded the drive in him that at times manifested itself as imperious and demanding. Boas lambasted the shaman who threatened to interfere with his work. In "A Journey in Cumberland Sound," Boas wrote about the conflict that arose as a result of the diphtheria epidemic. A shaman in the settlement of Imigen on the west coast of the Cumberland Sound had identified Boas as the cause of the disease and had told people that the only safeguard was to deny any help to him. "As soon as I heard this," Boas wrote, "I visited the settlement and told the men that every trade between myself and them would stop until they would invite me into their huts, even if I saw them in a starving condition I would not give them a piece of bread." Boas's message "had the desired effect, for one of them asked me to stop with him, and sometime afterwards the others came to Kikkerton to regain my goodwill by presenting me with a few sealskins."[44]

While outwardly there had been a resolution of the rift with the people of Imigen, Boas recognized the internal resistance. When he returned to the settlement in February, he found the diphtheria epidemic "affecting the children . . . raging terribly here." Boas continued, "I will suffer seriously from the sicknesses that are prevailing here, since I know that many Eskimos only reluctantly have any dealings with me, though they dare not express it to my face. Now none of them wanted to lend me any dogs, but when I asked for them, they did not dare refuse." As Knötsch expresses it, the Inuit "saw death following in his footsteps." With his persistent determination and with help from Mutch, Boas was able to put together two dog teams, with a total of fifteen dogs, for his week-long journey to Lake Nettiling. He left at the end of March, reached Lake Nettiling on April 1, and returned to Kekerten on April 7.[45]

Boas was balancing on a fulcrum that required the cooperation of the Inuit and, at the same time, that acknowledged the Inuit view of him as bringing disease to their families and to their dogs. He tipped decidedly toward insuring the success of his undertaking. Boas might have proclaimed to Marie that he did not support "the saying 'sacrifice for the sake of science,'" but he was in all his actions in Baffin Land focused on his science. He recognized fully that the Inuit associated him with death, but he adamantly insisted that they help him to meet his needs, whether this be for sled dogs or skin clothing. Of course, Boas knew that this relationship was predicated on cooperation, his goods in exchange for the Inuit assistance. Friedrich Pöhl remarks on this period in Boas's fieldwork, "When diphtheria was spreading and some Inuit suspected him to be the cause of the disease and would neither offer him to come into their tents nor loan or sell him their dogs, he worked with all his power to resist a change in role assignment. Boas played up his power." He faced off against the shaman Napekin whom Boas knew to be "the leader of the conspiracy against him." Napekin, as Pöhl notes, had "only a bad rifle and hardly any ammunition and was planning a longer journey, [and] Boas threatened to break off relations completely." Thus, while Boas recognized the connection that the Inuit made between his arrival and the onset of deadly diseases, he did not yield his position as a scientist on a mission, to garner the truth and to succeed. He did, however, exercise restraint when tempted to gather skulls from graves. "I went ashore," he wrote on October 10, 1883, on the journey to Pangnirtung Fiord, "and found traces of rabbits and three graves, which were very old. In two there were skulls overgrown with moss and lichens. . . . Unfortunately I cannot take away the skulls that were in the two graves, because of my Eskimos."[46]

On May 5, 1884, Boas and Weike left Kekerten for their journey to the Davis Strait. Boas wrote, "Since Mutch is willing to lend me dogs and a sledge, I shall take everything up and over the rocks in one haul." They departed on two sleds, piled high with supplies and pulled by twenty-five dogs. Three Inuit drove one sled; Boas and Weike, the other, with "flags flying from our sledge." Three days later, Boas wrote, "For the last time we saw Kikkerton, far in the distance, for the last time we saw the immense island Kikkertuktjiuk, which I drew for you, and we are now near the end of Kingait." In a strenuous journey, over hills, down flooded trails, with intermittent snow and blowing winds, they reached Davis Strait two weeks later, absent the crates they had left behind on the trail and with only "the *absolute* essentials" remaining. Nearly thirty years later, Boas would remark, "Most of my photographs were lost on my trip overland from Cumberland Sound to Davis Strait and on the broken ice of Davis Strait.[47]

Boas journeyed up the east coast of Baffin Land to make surveys from May 19 to July 20. Unhappy with the results, Boas wrote Marie, "It is really distressing that my great travel plans have been reduced to such a modest scale and yet I *must* be satisfied." Having charted the coast as far north as Cape Kater, Boas noted with resignation, "Even though my original plans have been distressingly foiled, at least I have travelled and mapped a substantial stretch of country here." Suffering from snow blindness, "bad weather and deep snow," and "dead tired from travelling," Boas thought incessantly of Marie, of family, of returning to his loved ones: "All my thoughts are of you and my family in Minden. My conversations with Wilhelm are always about home." As the time for departure drew near, Boas and Weike ceased to speak of "home and those at home" and instead spoke "only of the edge of the ice." Together, they imagined what their homecoming would be like: "Yesterday Wilhelm and I were picturing how it will be when we arrive; we have no clothes, because they are on top in Kignait [in boxes left behind]; for better or for worse we will have to go ashore in Eskimo clothing." Anxious beyond measure that he spot a ship in the Davis Strait, Boas said, "I promised one pound of tobacco to the first one to bring the news that a ship has arrived. Think of it, I shall be riding on a sled to the edge of the ice!"[48]

From July 20 to August 20 Boas and Weike stayed with the Inuit in the camp at K'ivitung, waiting and watching for whalers. On August 19 one of the Inuit had spotted a ship while he was out seal hunting, but then it was gone. Consumed with worry—would there be a ship? could they reach it over the ice?—Boas wrote, "I had been working until it grew dark, then played the concertina and sang, our usual activity when it got dark. I saw Wilhelm's face as his blood (like mine too) went to his heart. What news will I hear from home now? What things may have happened?" Then he added, "Wilhelm is coming now with the trunks, and then we will be off!" This letter to Marie, dated August 20, 1884, was the last entry in Boas's Arctic diary that he had begun on June 23, 1883. However, it was not until eight days later that they loaded the sleds and headed to the edge of the ice, only to encounter a gap of water thirty feet wide. Boas recounted, "The man in the crow's nest had, of course, seen us—6 sleds with many dogs. Three sailors came to meet us. . . . With their help we got across the rift. But do you think I could speak English? Without my volition Eskimo words [came from] me instead of English."[49]

Boas and Weike boarded the Jan Mayen, a whaler out of Dundee, Scotland, spent the night and moved the next day to the Wolf. Boas preferred the Wolf because it would sail to its home base, St. John's, Newfoundland, and from there he could sail on another vessel to New York. Captain Burnett told Boas that he had met Inuit "at Cape Roper with whom [Boas] had left a letter for the captains which he had read. As he had not heard that there was an explorer in that neighborhood he had thought the note a joke." Welcoming Boas and Weike aboard for the trip to Newfoundland, the captain said the ship would depart in the morning. Boas went ashore to make the final arrangements for his departure. "Hurray!" Boas wrote. "I have given all my things to the Eskimos." The next day the captain sailed to Exeter Sound to have some repairs made to his ship and to take on water for the voyage. Boas encountered two Inuit and their children, who recognized him in spite of the European clothing that Captain Burnett had let him borrow. Boas wrote, "As I expected the Eskimos whom I had seen at Cape Mercy during the winter were here." Boas served as interpreter between the Inuit and the captain, who was hoping to trade for furs. "The Eskimos," Boas continued, "were very much surprised that I could speak Eskimo so much better now and we conversed about old acquaintances and about everything that had happened in Cumberland Sound since that time." With generosity and, undoubtedly, good sense, Boas had given his Inuk friend Aranin the two puppies that he had taken on board the Wolf to bring with him to New York and to Marie. In June when his sled dog, Pegbing, whelped, Boas had written to Marie in his letter diary, "My pups are now giving me a lot of fun; they can see now and are crawling around very amusingly. Perhaps I will bring one home with me." At three months, the puppies would have been a handful for Boas, or more likely a handful for Weike on board ship, but would prove invaluable to Aranin, whose own dogs had run off.[50]

On August 31 the Wolf weighed anchor and set a southern course for St. John's, Newfoundland, where they arrived on September 7, 1884. Boas rushed to the telegraph office to send telegrams to his family in Minden, to Marie and Jacobi in New York, and to the *Berliner Tageblatt* in Berlin, all with essentially the same message about his safe arrival in St. John's. In her response, Marie telegraphed, "Am well and happy at Bolton, Lake George. Awaiting you." With the kind monetary assistance of the owner of the Wolf, Boas was able to purchase clothes for both Weike and himself and the two of them took a room in the Atlantic Hotel. Because of his exclusive contract with the *Berliner Tageblatt*, Boas had to dodge the reporters who had heard about the European explorer who was returning from the Arctic. He wrote his parents, "How much I wish I had you all here instead of all the strange faces, could see you and hear your dear voices. Instead I am surrounded by newspaper reporters, who wish to suck me dry. But I send them all away."[51]

Boas and Weike boarded the passenger steamer, the Ardandhu, on September 10 for a stop first in Halifax, Nova Scotia, and then on to New York Harbor, where they arrived on September 21, 1884. Just before weighing anchor for Halifax, Boas noted, "How strange do I feel here now among the many people and with my poor English-Scotch-German-Eskimo language." Once in Halifax, Boas wrote Marie, "I would have liked nothing better than to board a train immediately and hurry to you, but I must take Wilhelm and my belongings to New York." To his parents, he wrote, "All my thoughts are now centered on my reunion with Marie, as you may well imagine. I am so glad that she knows that I am back and that I can write her. How happy I will be when I shall have her again!" Then, as if remembering the longing of his parents to see him, Boas added, "And you dear parents must also be happy although I cannot come to you immediately. As soon as I shall have put my belongings into some sort of order I shall send you my diary which however is often incomplete." As he drew nearer to New York, Boas grew more agitated. As if trying to calm himself, he wrote to Marie, "Patience, a few days more and I shall be with you and may kiss your lips for the first time." Then he confessed that he should have been writing to his parents rather than to her: "This sheet of paper should really have gone home, but before I knew it, it was addressed to you and I am talking to you instead of to my parents and sisters." Boas concluded, "It seems more difficult for me to wait the few days until at last, I shall see you than it was the long time in the cold north."[52]

The third week after he had arrived in New York, Boas wrote to his parents describing his trip from Halifax that went "quite quickly." He continued, "On the evening of the 19th we saw the lights from Cape Cod and docked in Martha's Vineyard. They were glorious days; we made fast progress and on the 20th in the evening we saw the lights of New York lighting up the sky. We had to anchor at Hell's Gate and the next morning at 5 o'clock we moved on by daylight. Naturally I had hardly slept at night and was astonished by the wonderfully beautiful display as we passed by this Giant City under the enormous Brooklyn Bridge and rode into the wharf at 6:30." Boas said he had left everything on board the ship and along with Wilhelm: "I took the ferry across to New York. In a drugstore I looked up Meyer's address and rode up with the horse car. They were just at the point of sitting down to breakfast as I rang and came in."[53]

Anticipating the arrival of her nephew and of Wilhelm, Aunt Phips had roused everybody in her household from bed at 6 a.m. on Sunday, September 21. In her letter to Boas's mother, Aunt Phips wrote, "At 9:30 when we were just sitting down to breakfast, the bell rang and they are here! To begin with I took at least 6 kisses and want to tell you right away Franz and Wilhelm look *very* well." She continued, "I had imagined they would have come back starved!" Aunt Phips pulled them in, sat them down, and fed them breakfast. Then Boas read through his stack of letters while poor Weike sat dejectedly with no news from home. The friends and relatives began to stream into the house. As Boas wrote to his parents, "A terrible lot of company was here in the afternoon and I was really completely dazed. Almost everything I saw and heard confounded me." After dinner, they walked over to see Jacobi. Aunt Phips wrote, "We came back at 9:30 and I sent Franz to bed soon. He wanted to re-read his letters and I thought it would be good if he were alone." She added, "You cannot believe how excited he is. Everything seems so new and different." First thing Monday morning, at seven, Boas sat down at the piano to play. His cousin Lizzie, who was in the next room, heard him play and said he played very well, but Boas insisted "his fingers are like wood and more used to direct the whip than the keys." At ten o'clock, his uncle took Boas and Weike shopping for clothes. Aunt Phips wrote, "He wanted to go to Lake George at 6 o'clock. His longing is tremendous. I think he has no plans yet for the next weeks. He

Creating a Future for Us

wants to have some good days with his beloved." Then she concluded, "Wilhelm just came back and says Franz had gone. You know, Sophie, I would not say it to anyone, I am . . . heartsick that he has gone again. How all of you must feel!"[54]

Arriving at Bolton Landing, Boas had hired a carriage to take him to Alma Farm. Marie, however, had gone to Caldwell, Boas wrote, "below Bolton and had naturally not found me. In the meantime, I was at the farm and . . . horrified not to find Marie again. I had to be patient for 4 more hours before she finally, finally came." Boas continued, "Do you believe that we are now happy? And what painful happiness it was when I could hold Marie for the first time alone in my arms. Let me pass over these hours that belong only to us. Happy days we had at the lake, especially before Mr. Meyer came up. When we were all alone with the mother and Helene [Marie's sister]—those two days after we came. This place will always be unforgettable."[55]

Soon after his arrival at Alma Farm, Boas and Marie both wrote letters to the Boas family in Minden. He explained, "Marie ran into the other room to write to you also, since the carriage which will take the letters along leaves in 10 minutes and when we are together we do not write." In her letter, Marie wrote with unrestrained exuberance,

My dear Franzenmenschen [Franz's people]

He is here, finally, finally I have him! . . . Oh! how can one find words to describe our happiness. It is hardly to be believed. It still seems to me often that I am dreaming when he is not actually with me, when I cannot see his eyes, kiss his mouth and pull his black, black locks. I cannot believe it. How does he look? So healthy and brown and wonderful as never before! His curls are not yet long enough. He had to cut them very short but I am pulling on them so much so that they may have a nice length shortly.

Marie wished they could all be together, that Franz and she could "quickly come together to you!" Admitting that she hardly knew what she was writing, she said, "I only know that I feel he is here, he is mine. He has been given back to all of us." She sends them "a thousand kisses," and tells them that she will "take good care of him, our Franz. Oh so good that he shall forget his worries and his hardships. I believe this long year is already almost forgotten. In my happiness it is to me as though I had never cried about him, never worried and fretted! He is now with me and I want nothing more now, and I know nothing more and I feel nothing else!" In his letter to his parents, Boas wrote, "Oh how joyful, how happy I am now after all these long, long torments. You must now make our engagement known right away." He said he would send a list of addresses and asked that they date the engagement "as of May 30, 1883." In a letter sent to his parents in October, Boas noted, "We want to wear rings but I must earn the money myself." To this end he applied his fifty-dollar honorarium for his talk in November before the Deutscher Gesellig-Wissenschaftlicher Verein von New York (German Social and Scientific Association of New York).[56]

On July 11, 1883, just off the coast of Greenland on his way to Cumberland Sound, Boas had written to Marie, "This afternoon I read my birthday letters again. It is too funny how everyone firmly believes that I have gone out to attain fame and honour." He continued, "Not true; they don't know me at all, and I would stand very low in my own estimation if that was the *purpose* for which I was investing trouble and effort. You know that I am aiming for something higher than this and that this trip is only a means . . . to that goal." It was true, Boas said, that perhaps he wanted "*recognition* for my achievements," and acknowledgment as "a man of action." He concluded, "Empty fame is worth nothing to me." Wasn't it natural for him, he queried, "to wish to plan for our future and to hope that what I am doing will help." In another letter to Marie on the same theme, Boas wrote, "The only measure of one's accomplishment is the knowledge to have done one's duty, whether the success is great or small. Believe me, Marie, flattery will never turn my head. I have no doubt as to my goal. I know what I have to do and the value of my work." Each person who "goes out to make a discovery" does so for his own reasons. Boas continued, "You know what my reasons were—a desire to build a foundation for an independent existence and scientific interests, and this even before I knew that my beloved loved me."[57]

As Boas was preparing to depart Kekerten, he had written his parents on April 30, 1884, of his own harsh critique, "Not one of the expectations

Creating a Future for Us

with which I came here has been realized. Luck was not very favorable." In 2016 Igor Krupnik offers a different evaluation: "The very pattern of scientific anthropological research among the Inuit originated with Boas's yearlong fieldwork on Baffin Island in 1883–1884." Trained as a geographer and "proficient in the use of maps," Boas broke with previous researchers of Inuit culture, who focused on natural history. Instead, Boas studied "the human-culture-environment relations" and scribed "a more modern type of research." Krupnik continues, "He acted as a true pioneer by creating a focused research niche for himself and thus opened the path to the next cohort of Eskimo scholars."[58]

In "Franz Boas' Expedition to Baffin Island, 1883–1884," Cole and Müller-Wille have appraised this undertaking one hundred years later: "This plan was extraordinary for its time, breaking with almost all practices of previous polar expeditions in its emphasis upon a detailed study of a limited region over an entire year and in its reliance upon a small, virtually one-man expedition living in large measure off the land." Cole and Müller-Wille note, "Boas did not shut himself up in Mutch's whaling station, a well-equipped compound with most of Cumberland Sound's Inuit population close by." During the 364 days that Boas was on Baffin Land, he spent 209 days in tupiks or igloos, frequently travelling to other settlements. While at Kekerten, Boas "spent a full 30% of his nights away from the station or ships." From August 29, 1883, to May 6, 1884, Boas completed "five boat trips to the northern and southeastern reaches of the sound, into Pangnirtung and Kingnait fiords and close-by islands during September and October, and twelve extended sled journeys between December and April covering practically the complete coastline of Cumberland Sound and the route to Lake Nettilling to the west."[59]

Boas charted a course for others to follow in the use of native place names, that would, for anthropologists, expand to a focus on the native terms of classification and to a people's own view of their world. In 1883–84, as Müller-Wille remarks, Boas "carried out the first extensive survey of place names among the Inuit of Baffin Island." He engaged the Inuit in drawing maps of *their own land*, which would show the people's graphic view of their lived-in spaces. Boas combined the maps drawn by the Inuit with the extensive and precise data that he collected on the configuration of the land and "on the weather and the sun's position, on tidal fluctuations, and on ice conditions." He drew this complex mass of information together into "the first map of this area that was based on exact geodetic measurements, and its validity endured well into the twentieth century." There were, as Müller-Wille and Weber Müller-Wille note, "no better maps produced" for the area he surveyed until the 1920s and 1930s, at which time the Canadian government published new maps of Baffin Land "using Boas' map of 1883–84 . . . as the baseline."[60]

Boas's work resulted in "a collection of 930 toponyms fully documented on his surveyed maps, covering both [Cumberland Sound] and the eastern coast." Müller-Wille writes, "The topographic surveys, which led to Boas's cartographic masterpiece, printed by the renowned Justus Perthes publishing house in Gotha . . . , and the documentation of place names from oral tradition . . . , which he began right from the beginning and carried out consistently and in detail with the Inuit, are the expression of his research initiative at grasping human environmental relations in the arctic habitat of the Inuit."[61]

In 1984 one hundred years after Boas's Baffin Land work, Ludger Müller-Wille and Linna Weber Müller-Wille presented to the people of Pangnirtung the collection of 930 Inuit place names and the maps that Boas had created with the Inuit.[62] They write, "Among the Inuit experts Aksayuk Etuangat, the oldest person in Pangnirtung at that time, stood out and was the link between distant past and present. Reviewing the names . . . triggered his recall of his parents' and grandparents' stories of Inuit knowledge, including place names as well as tales about Boas and his sojourn among the Inuit in Pangnirtung." Recognized as the expert with "encyclopedic local knowledge," Etuangat "easily knew and confirmed" from 35 to 40 percent of the place names listed by Boas; he "remembered another 30 percent when they were mentioned or shown to him on the map." The rest of the place names from Boas's collection were not part of the current "repertoire of Inuit toponyms . . . and thus remained as part of the historic record of Inuit life of over a hundred years before."[63]

Müller-Wille and Weber Müller-Wille presented Boas's maps, lists of place names, and notes to the five men, who had been selected by the community for their expertise. Ranging in age from fifty-one to eighty-three, the Inuit experts of Pangnirtung "expressed astonishment that Inuit place names known to their parents and grandparents existed on maps published in Germany in the 1880s which they had never seen." As Allan Angmarlik and Josephie Keenainak remarked on viewing the Boas material, "Why is it that Germans had Inuit maps already in 1885 and till today Canada still has none with Inuit place names on it?"[64]

From this first fieldwork in Baffin Land to his later research in the Northwest Coast, Boas recognized the importance of cartography and the people's own place names as a way of encapsulating the lived and visualized spaces. As Müller-Wille notes, "Boas used cartography as a means to convey the importance of geographical dimension and interpretation. In many publications over the span of his career he included maps, which in almost all cases he had either surveyed, drawn, or designed himself. The visualization of space and spatial organization of both physical and human elements were an integral part of his presentations." The geographical grounding that lay solidly at his intellectual core escaped many who knew him well. Student and longtime colleague Robert Lowie remarked in *Biographical Memoir of Franz Boas, 1858–1942* that, because of Boas's critique of simplistic environmentalism, "for years I failed to grasp how carefully he took cognizance of geographical factors."[65]

In his work on Baffin Land, as Müller-Wille explains, Boas positioned himself "between the prevalent approach of spatial *Entdeckung* or discovery of *unchartered lands* carried out by expedition, and the novel application of stationary *Feldforschung*, field research as it was being conducted in polar sciences." Boas, fortuitously for those who followed him, elected for field research, referring to his work "among the Inuit a *Forschungsreise* a research journey, not an expedition." Müller-Wille notes that Boas was likely influenced by the International Polar Year (IPY, 1882–83), as "planned and designed as of 1875 made the first major step to get away from the itinerant expeditions that only produced measurements and data for many places for short, mainly summer periods. The new approach was to conduct observations and collect data in one place (stations) over a fixed period and collect data simultaneously in fixed locations at the same time." This was the model for the IPY and was reflected in the work at the Kingua station. Müller-Wille continues, "Still the IPY activities were called expeditions." The stationary approach "was widely discussed in the 1870s in the natural sciences as well as in geography and 'social sciences.' Clearly, Boas derived from this approach that a one-year period was essential" with respect to "topographical, environmental, and logistical" factors.[66]

Boas had recognized the opportunity to augment his fieldwork by having Wilhelm Weike keep a diary that would provide a way of checking his own record. As Müller-Wille and Gieseking note,

> In various respects Franz Boas was a pioneer in his perceptions and ideas. Thus he was unusual in that as a young scientist he wanted to ensure that he had a second observing voice, by asking Wilhelm Weike, who accompanied him as his servant, to keep a regular journal. And Wilhelm Weike fulfilled this duty faithfully; he thus created and bequeathed a first-hand vision of the everyday affairs of an arctic expedition, of his relationship with Boas, of the social interaction of the whalers of widely differing nations, living in the Arctic and of his encounters with the numerous Inuit.

Written in a refreshingly natural style, Weike's journal is a counterpoint to Boas's own diary and journals. While Boas's records, save for his family letters and his love letters to Marie, had the disciplined focus so characteristic of his work, Weike's entries were full of humorous accounts, notes on his activities, and records of the meals he had cooked. Boas could not have anticipated the tone and flavor of Weike's diary entries when he required that Weike begin a record, and likely the freshness of Weike's accounts was not of importance to Boas. Nonetheless, by having Wilhelm Weike keep a diary, Boas ensured that the year on Baffin Land would be recorded from two perspectives: that of himself as scientist, and that of Weike, as assistant.[67]

While Weike was Boas's servant, he was also so much more. He was the cook, challenged to prepare a leg of caribou, a couple of ducks, seal meat, caribou tongues, or anything that was brought into the kitchen at the station or into the tupik or igloo. He was the research assistant who helped to stack the rocks for the cairn, to position the theodolite, to put up the tupik, to harness the dog team, and to drive the sled. Cole and Müller-Wille remark on the "invaluable" contributions of Weike to Boas's research: "At the station he worked at odds and ends and cooked meals for 'Herr Doktor' (his diary refers to Boas in no other way . . .). He cleaned, washed clothes, sewed and boiled coffee, their beloved and indispensable 'arctic beverage.' In the field Weike helped with all duties. He enjoyed fishing and hunting, especially for rabbits, ptarmigan and, later on, caribou with the Inuit companions." Weike helped to make "observations and surveys," and he usually carried Boas's "expeditionary flag," which Marie had made for her fiancé. In short, a world apart from his accustomed employment as gardener and servant for the Boas family in Minden, Weike was there to assist Boas in all his work in a setting that called on Weike to be creative in ways he could never have anticipated.[68]

Almost simultaneous with his landing in Kekerten, Boas recognized in James Mutch a generous man who would help him in every way. Clearly a people person, Mutch had the same effect on others as he had on Boas: he inspired trust and respect because he extended these to others. Mutch became the person who made all things possible for Boas. He served as Boas's "mentor and mediator for negotiating among cultures, languages, and people." When Boas needed dogs for his travel, Mutch let him borrow his; when Weike needed winter clothing for their near-disastrous December trip, Mutch loaned him his; when Boas needed Inuit to draw maps for him, Mutch identified Inuit especially gifted in their knowledge of the land; when Boas needed help understanding Inuktitut, Mutch translated; when Boas had to abandon crates on the strenuous trip to Davis Strait, Mutch had Ssigna retrieve them, and Mutch sent them on by ship to their destination.[69]

This cooperative and collaborative relationship between Boas and Mutch continued after Boas left Cumberland Sound. Over the years, from 1885 to 1922, Boas and Mutch exchanged letters. Among other forms of assistance, Boas engaged Mutch in the purchase of a collection of six hundred material culture items for the American Museum of Natural History; Mutch sent Boas the requested information about "the floe edges for all the years since 1894"; and, perhaps most important, he made a collection of "Notes and Stories," which was published by Boas in *Second Report on the Eskimo of Baffin Land and Hudson Bay*, with James S. Mutch listed as one of the contributors. Thus, in this initial fieldwork experience, with Boas having just gotten his feet wet in the Arctic, he seized the positive advantage by working with James Mutch and subsequently continued this relationship for years to come, as he would with other collaborators in other fieldwork settings. Harper notes that Boas would continue in future fieldwork to develop "a relationship with untutored men in the field, men who could assist him, collect for him, provide him with the raw material to interpret in popular and scientific journals, texts and lectures." For Mutch, the collaboration must have been rewarding: he had found someone who was vitally interested in hearing about his years of experience with the Inuit of Baffin Land.[70]

The young Boas, on his *Erstlingsreise*, his first voyage, recognized the importance of learning the language of the people and of living with the people to learn from them. As he wrote in 1885 in "Under the Arctic Circle,"

> Without an intimate knowledge of the language, without an understanding of the thinking and feeling, of the religious concepts and traditions, all patterns of life of native peoples, who live completely beyond the pale of the manner of our thinking and living, must seem absurd and unworthy of human society. The appellation of "savages" for many aboriginal peoples has found such wide acceptance only because the traveler observed the life and activity of the natives from the viewpoint of his European social background. The investigator who lives completely as a member of the tribe which he is studying learns to recognize, under strange and foreign mode of life, the thinking and feeling human being, who resembles us in his character more than we could imagine from our first superficial impression.

Requiring "years of hard work and unselfish devotion," the ethnographer, poised between two cultures, "must try his best to translate himself into the views and modes of thought of the people." In addition to "living completely as a member" of the people, the ethnographer must record "the raw material . . . in a scientific manner," by employing "methods of observation appropriate to the particular circumstances." In *The Central Eskimo* (1888), Boas presented his expansive approach of including detailed aspects of the life of the Inuit that he had recorded and material that others had compiled. One hundred years later, resident of Pangnirtung Allan Angmarlik (1957–2000) had happened upon a copy of Boas's *The Central Eskimo* and "devoured it, finding through it a link with the disconnected past."[71]

While not recognizing it himself, Franz Boas had realized a large measure of his goals for his voyage to Baffin Land. Admittedly, he had not succeeded in charting all of the vast territory as he had planned: life and death in Cumberland Sound intervened. His firm plans yielded to requisite flexibility—not a trait that came easily to Boas. Knötsch remarks on his adaptation to "external circumstances" that necessitated change of plans, "Boas was constantly obliged to function within the limited breathing-space left to him." And Herskovits notes, "We have here a valuable lesson in the importance of flexibility in the field situation, and of recognizing and following new leads, whenever they may appear and whatever reorientation in objective they may necessitate." Serendipitously, while he waited less than patiently for the completion of his skin clothing and for the acquisition of a dog team, Boas settled into life with the Inuit of Kekerten. In so doing, he found that the ethnographic profoundly augmented cultural geography. Boas did not abandon modern geography: it remained present in his work as a firm and formative layer. The Inuit of Baffin Land showed Boas graphically in their sketch maps, and ethnographically in their daily lives, what he had known intellectually at the Christian-Albrecht-Universität in Kiel and in his study in Minden: that to understand a people, one must understand their lived relationship with the land. Boas had infused Ratzel's interplay between "*Mensch* and *Erde/Umwelt*, humanity and earth/environment," with the essence of the lived experiences of the peoples of Baffin Land. Boas left the Canadian Arctic in 1884, never to return, but marked forever by his experiences.[72]

5

Divided Desires

Pulled between New York and Germany

Boas wrote to his parents from New York, "Is it not terrible to have one's heart in two places?" He wanted to stay in New York, to find a job in the United States, to marry and make a home with Marie, yet he yearned to see his family in Germany. Emotionally, he was pulled in two directions. "My desires are divided," he admitted to his parents. "I would so much like to be with you but cannot leave yet." Boas was also going through, as he described it, "an uncomfortable transition" of having to adjust to all that had happened during his absence. Foremost, he was trying to meet people who could help him find a position, to publish articles, to write his "big book" on the Eskimo, and to make his name known in a new country. With ever-mounting pressure coming from his family in Minden—particularly from his mother and his sister Toni—Boas countered that it would be irresponsible to leave the United States so soon after his arrival before he had attempted to establish himself.[1]

The question "What now?" pressed, as he wrote to his parents, "with irresistible force and the uncertainty in which I float does not let me rest." The dilemma reverberated in his head: "I wish I knew how, where and *when* our future will show itself." On his arrival from the Arctic, he had scarcely found Marie and embraced her when he began to worry: "Already when I was still at Lake George I became restless, to sit there doing nothing and mainly because of that I came back so quickly to start working for I must soon publish something." After eight days at Alma Farm with Marie, Boas had returned to New York City on October 1, and the next day he went to see Jacobi "to discuss the future with him." Boas wrote Marie, "Oh, I wish a position could be found for me very,

very quickly and I could lead you home." He added, "I am still hopeful, why should it not be possible for me?"[2]

In his room at Aunt Phips and Uncle Kobus's house, Boas set about trying to make sense of his papers and notes that had gotten so "terribly mixed up towards the end." He arranged his materials on a big wooden desk, "which once was Uncle Jacobi's office table." He requested that his parents send him *right away* the book about the polar regions and his excerpts from the books. Unsure of how many reports he had sent to the *Berliner Tageblatt*, Boas enumerated what he thought he had completed and expressed the desire to be "finished very soon in order to work on the scientific material undisturbed." In his own estimation, he had, as he wrote to his parents, "not done much, 3 reports to Berlin, an English article. Now I am [occupied] with the maps and a lecture, which I shall give on the 5th of Nov. for $50"—the lecture to be for the Deutscher Gesellig-Wissenschaftlicher Verein von New York, the German Social-Scientific Association of New York. He concluded, "Today and tomorrow I shall really write in detail."[3]

Paying heed to Jacobi's suggestions, Boas left as soon as possible for his first trip to Washington DC. On October 14 he met with the Arctic explorer Emil Bessels and Otis T. Mason, the curator of the department of ethnology at the U.S. National Museum, who were both affiliated with the Smithsonian Institution. Of Bessels, Boas wrote Marie, "I told him during the conversation that I wanted to stay here but we really did not discuss anything," though Bessels proposed that the next day they would "create a 'battle plan.'" Boas went to the Smithsonian Institution, "where I 'hunted up' the director of the Ethnographical division, Prof. Mason, who was very friendly and cordial. He asked me right away whether I would like to have my things published by the [Smithsonian], which I neither rejected nor accepted." Because he was so frequently in Washington, Boas took a room in a boardinghouse for eight dollars a week, the same residence where Bessels rented an entire floor. "We two polar people," Boas wrote his parents, "preside at both ends of the table."[4]

Otis T. Mason aimed so eagerly to please Boas, but he was unable to do so. He had been hired as curator of the department of ethnology of the U.S. National Museum at the Smithsonian in 1884 to bring order to "the great collections piled in confusion in its halls." Having only been on the job a few months by the time he met Boas, Mason had no idea where to find anything. Boas wrote Marie of his impatience with "the slowness that everything happens here, the wretched mix up in the museum." Boas had hoped to gain access to the "Cumberland material." He wrote Marie, "To look for [Charles Francis] Hall's collections remained but a noble promise." To his parents he remarked that Mason and he "ran around all morning unpacking crates." To Marie he wrote, in utter frustration, "To hunt through the collection is hair-raising work since everything is distributed around."[5]

Boas tried repeatedly to approach John Wesley Powell, director of the Bureau of American Ethnology (BAE) of the Smithsonian Institution, about a position. Bessels advised, "Powell cannot make an offer until he knows his appropriation" from Congress, and he suggested that Boas should accept a low salary and thus not necessitate much of a reduction in Powell's budget. On one occasion when Bessels took Boas to see Powell, Bessels turned to Boas just before entering the office and said that it would be better not to talk about a position because Powell had much on his mind. In addition to a job, Boas was also hoping that the BAE would publish the book he was writing on the Eskimo. Bessels asked Boas about his strategy: Would he talk with Powell only about the publication of his work, or would he also ask about a position? "I said I did not see any reason," Boas replied, "why one should play hide and seek for any length of time, since I don't care [for slithering] . . . about something like a serpent."[6]

While Boas was gaining facility in his written English, his spoken English caused him challenges and, ultimately, embarrassment. In fact, he avoided speaking in English at public presentations, if at all possible. At the Anthropological Society of Washington, Boas had the secretary read his paper: "I do not want to lecture in English myself. There will probably be a lot of discussion of which I am a little afraid because of my lack of knowledge of the English language. But I cannot avoid taking part." For his first lecture to the Deutscher Gesellig-Wissenschaftlicher Verein von New York, Boas spoke in German. He wrote his parents, "Now you want to know how my lecture came off." He continued, "The hall was very large and quite full, about 300 people, men and women. Unfortunately, much too large for my voice so that those listeners further away did not understand me." Following the lecture, he said, "I had to defend my skin against various questions, which I succeeded in doing pretty well." In sum, he said, "I cannot really praise myself for the way it turned out because I spoke too quietly. I wish I had the opportunity to speak here another time in order possibly to correct my mistake."[7]

Boas had strategized carefully about arranging for lectures to give him exposure to those who might be able to offer him a position. "I want to suggest to Uncle Jacobi," Boas wrote Marie, as to "whether he could perhaps get me an invitation to a good University, perhaps Columbia College, to give a *series* of lectures about general earth science." He added, "But only if at the same time the possibility existed to interest the administration." With trepidation, he concluded, "Probably a big discussion will evolve, about which I am a little afraid since I know only so little English." He met with Jacobi and Carl Schurz over lunch to plan for what "I should do about the Columbia lectures." Jacobi, in turn, enlisted the assistance of Ogden N. Rood, chair of the physics department at Columbia. With the synopsis of Boas's proposed lectures in hand, Rood solicited approval from Columbia College President Frederick Barnard. Rood wrote Jacobi, "Dr. Barnard was so pleased with the analysis of these lectures" that he hoped to gain the trustees' consent to open the lecture series to the public for the first time. If the trustees refused, "the lectures will simply be under the auspices of the Engineering Society." Marie and Aunt Phips helped him prepare. Marie found "the speech sounds a little stiff still, but quite readable," but Aunt Phips said, "It does not sound stiff." However, Boas did not trust his aunt's judgment since she was "not unprejudiced."[8]

Sadly, the first lecture was such a disaster that barely anyone came to the second. Months later, after he had returned to Germany, Boas wrote Marie, "Do you know why I was so hurt because my second lecture at Columbia College was so empty? Because it hurt my vanity, and I know that I cannot speak well. If I had known that my performance had been a good one, I *believe* it would not have mattered." With a boost to his pride following a successful lecture in Berlin before the Gesellschaft für Erdkunde zu Berlin (Geographical Society of Berlin) on May 2, 1885, Boas conveyed to Marie that in this instance he had "spoken really effectively." He had "ignored" his notes and had guided himself "by the mood of my audience." During his forty-five-minute presentation, "people listened to me attentively . . .

and no one left." In candor, he admitted, "I was terribly frightened at first, but quietly told of my trip, and brought in the results only now and then." To his parents he wrote, "I am gradually learning to judge the feeling of the audience, whether they are listening attentively or not. The crackling of paper which people have in their hands is an indication of their feelings. On the other hand, if the eyes are suddenly turned to the lecturer and everyone sits up a bit indicates that they have become more attentive." Boas admitted that he was still "frightened" of getting "stuck in the middle of a sentence and not [being] able to find the right words."[9]

Making every effort to find employment in the United States, Boas shuttled back and forth between New York and Washington. Jacobi used his considerable influence to press Powell hard and Boas met with Powell repeatedly. Still, nothing was forthcoming other than opportunities for Boas to be published by the BAE. New York yielded only the disappointment of the two lectures at Columbia College. Through Jacobi's connections, President of Johns Hopkins University Daniel Coit Gilman expressed an interest in helping Boas to "advance." Boas traveled to Baltimore, where Gilman greeted him in "very friendly" fashion and showed him around, but nothing came of this either.[10]

Boas grew fatigued with the "visits [that] take so terribly much time," and his family grew utterly impatient. They feared that he would take "a second-grade position" that would allow for "no opportunity to work," and that the "deciding factor" for their son would be that "Marie lives here." To his parents, Boas countered, "But I may not let your wish decide. It is completely taken for granted that I shall not make a decision without finding out what the conditions are in Germany. . . . You should not give yourselves over to illusions about the German conditions. Three years is the minimum that I see to reach Professorship." Each letter from Minden brought more pressure and more demands that he come home. In sadness, he wrote, "You cannot imagine how heavy my heart feels when your letters arrive. . . . I am almost afraid to open them because I know only too clearly that your longing for me speaks out of them." Boas was grateful to his father for his understanding: "I thank you dear father heartily for your words about the shape of my future. I am really happy that I am acting entirely according to your opinion and feel much less oppressed because of it."[11]

Without Boas's knowledge, his sister Toni had enlisted the aid of Boas's mentor, Theobald Fischer, in persuading him to come back to Germany. She had sent copies of her brother's letters so Fischer would know Boas's thoughts. Sympathetic to Toni's longing for her brother's return, Fischer had responded to her first note that he had "urgently" advised Boas "to have a long stay in Washington to complement his studies." By December Fischer apparently thought Boas's stay in America had been quite long enough. He wrote Toni that he had advised Boas to return to Germany. Fischer remarked, "Your brother wrote me all sorts of rubbish, which he could only have gotten out of a Yankee newspaper or else from a progressive or social-democratic German one—namely that in Prussia under such a minister of education, he could not freely speak his thoughts and convictions, that he would not be hired because he is an Israelite." Fischer regretted hearing such views from Boas: "Ideas so contrary to the truth, being spread by our lying press and hence the misled foreign press." He was adamant Boas should return to see for himself "that the conditions are far different from the ones the anti-German side fools him into believing; that they are endlessly better than in the rotten Yankee Republic where the ruthless and unconscionable get the best of the bargain." Fischer had invited Boas to attend the German geography conference in Hamburg, to "make himself known," and to see for himself if he has cause "to judge our circumstances so unfavorably." Then, if he was not able to find a position, Fischer continued, "there is still time to Yankeeize himself." He concluded, "You are quite right, in the United States it's all about the money bag, not the knowledge and intellectual ability."[12]

Fischer wrote Boas that he had begun "to see our German relations through Yankee-glasses," and that perhaps Boas had been deriving his opinions from "progressive newspapers." He referred to a discussion they had had in Kiel concerning "the question of your conversion to Christianity, and I told you that I would consider such a move quite superfluous." Fischer assured Boas that his being "an Israelite in relation to progress in an academic career will not for a moment be a hindrance." With Boas's "knowledge and talent," Fischer stressed, he would succeed, "if you are a Jew or a Christian, no matter." After providing a few examples of Jewish scholars who had been promoted to prestigious positions, Fischer continued, "If an Israelite performs accordingly and is pleasant as a person and as a colleague, for this is much appreciated by the departments . . . , no one cares about it if he's an Israelite. . . . If Israelites complain of not getting ahead, then this is because of their personality, not their confession, neither would a Christian get ahead in such case."[13]

While he condemned anti-Semitism, Fischer suggested that Boas look "soberly" at the behavior of the majority of his fellow believers. He continued, "You must arrive at the opinion that they indeed manage to offend even calm and level-headed people." It would, however, take a long time to progress from a Privatdozent to a full professor since all the chairs were filled, save for in Berlin. Boas, he said, would certainly "be a professor . . . , but when will that be?" If Boas desired to marry soon and did not want "to wait for a number of years," he should follow a different career path and attempt to find a job in an institute, such as the Justus Perthes Institute. Fischer concluded on a positive note: "When you are back, we will talk in detail about your plans. I think you will be astonished to see what progress we have made in almost 2 years of your absence."[14]

Fischer's opinion was squarely in accord with that of his mother and his sister. He wrote Toni, "You see my dear Miss, it would be best according to my feeling if your brother came back here." Boas did not read Fischer's views in this way. He wrote Jacobi, "I received the enclosed letter from Fischer today. You can see from it what the prospects in Germany are, and that not much is to be expected. When you have finished it please give it to Marie who will send it to Minden." Jacobi urged Boas's mother to have patience. Her son should be allowed a few months in the United States to write, publish, and make connections. Jacobi continued, "Franz is working industriously, of what success remains to be seen." Jacobi said that Boas feared displeasing his family. He went on, "But I have encouraged him not to take this into consideration. I look at the issue matter-of-factly from the point of view that he ought to ensure a way to earn his living." Jacobi noted, "Before Franz can achieve anything, he must make himself known," and to accomplish this, he had to publish his work. "Some things are in print," Jacobi said, "a large work will be printed by the government. Publications are his passport; without them he is between heaven and earth, he is nothing at all." Pointedly, he stated, "This winter is important and should not be disrupted." He should be allowed to take his time, to do his work, to try to find something in the United States, and if he doesn't, then to look for his position in Germany. Clearly having discerned a mother's jealousy for her son's affections, Jacobi concluded, "He is still yours and will remain yours."[15] Sophie Boas admitted the family's real anxiety: "The fear that he might want to establish his future altogether in America." She characterized this possibility as a fate so hard that she could neither express her feelings, nor "know how I could stand it." In a straightforward assessment of her son's character, she wrote, "We would have to bear it for he has a stubborn head and does what he wishes."[16]

Boas admitted to Jacobi that when he read "such a letter from home" about his "stubborn head," he became even firmer "in the decision that I have reached." He concluded, "Of course I do not deny that the desire to marry is another moving force in my actions, but not to such a degree that everything else depends on it."[17] In reply Jacobi counseled that, if one had money and wanted "to marry quickly, a delay of 24 hours is too long. But if he first needs to obtain a position . . . it just takes time." Jacobi continued, "To be honest, I *used* to believe that you'd prefer a professorship" in Germany. He added, "If I were Franz Boas and had the prospect of a German professorship, I'd work for it. The fact that the German political situation was not congenial to me would not be sufficient reason to not want to take part in enduring and improving it. I don't like everything here either."[18]

Jacobi maintained that the time Boas spent in America was an investment in his future: "Even if the time would be 'lost,' i.e. lost from the standpoint of money, it pays for itself many times over by new experiences and viewpoints." One needed experience to find a position in America. He continued, "To land in America [and] to embark again, would have been a folly. It takes months to learn the prospects and views." Boas was making every effort to find a position in the United States and would not have to "reproach" himself later. Jacobi reflected, "What you are doing here, is also not lost on the other side. What you have in print, . . . you can now judge as well as your future readers." Jacobi counseled, "As a fact, I would repeat what I have said to you and your mother, that one or two months here would not have made sense, 4 months allowed you to look around better. . . . And when you appear at the Geographical Congress, without having first been in Germany, you will be a novelty and moreover be able to debut with materials written in a foreign language." Jacobi added a final suggestion: "And when you have made a decision, do not let yourself be browbeaten by each of the numerous incoming letters, and enjoy the humor, and the love of work."[19]

His family in Minden continued to write unrelenting pleas for him to return home. In frustration, Boas responded, "I wish for an end to this American uncertainty." Boas told his parents of his emotional turmoil over the "uncertain future and the longing for you." He said, "I know quite certainly that when I am a half hour from here I shall have just as strong a longing for here, but right now I want to be with you." To Marie, he wrote, "If I just did not have to hurry so to go to Germany. I cannot help it that it is so, and you know how I am drawn to my parents and sisters." Pulled toward Minden, still Boas wandered the streets of Washington and looked longingly at "the little houses in which we may perhaps live." In the next sentence, Boas recognized the "castles in the sky" that he might be building based on the "deceptive possibilities" of a job with the BAE.[20]

Finally, in January 1885, Boas resolved that he had to return to Minden by March. To Marie, he wrote, "I want and must be gone by March. . . . I had a letter from Toni today; I am almost desperate about the conditions that my efforts to stay here bring about at home." Boas was torn asunder by his dual loyalties to his family in Germany and to his fiancée in New York, and by his desire for challenging and fulfilling work. In his letter to Marie, Boas continued, "It is quite possible that I might find a sufficient position in Europe but should I sacrifice all of my plans for work to this wish of my parents? It is more that I am their only son and the decision becomes more difficult for my parents who, as it now seems, never thought seriously that I would want to come here. But it would be just as hard for you—your mother and sisters and brothers—, if you go with me to Europe." Boas fell back on the accepted notion that "it is the custom with us that the wife follows the husband; therefore, it would not be so bad with yours because it is expected."[21]

If the employment opportunities were equal, Boas conceded, "I would surely decide on Europe." However, he saw before him in America "a large field of work" and "a small one over there." Boas continued, "You must feel how these thoughts fill my head, day and night and really leave me no quiet moment. I have stated it and shall hold by it, that I shall not bind myself here before I have seen the German conditions. But I cannot and do not wish to promise more. No matter how much it hurts, if I see that I am right in this, and I believe I am, I shall not go back to Germany unless I see that I cannot find a footing here from which I can build." While his family insisted that he was swayed entirely from his desire to marry, Boas explained,

> Marie, do you understand that I do not want to act *only* from that point of view, to be united with you soon? . . . You know how all my hopes are aimed at the time when I can finally lead you home. . . . I believe I am not conceited but I know what I am worth and what I can accomplish and therefore I also feel the duty to produce what I can even though the duty is hard. . . . I know what I want and shall do everything to accomplish what I want.

With combined anguish and determination, Boas concluded his letter, "The last two years have taught me a great deal, the last few months, even more! You do not know how it hurts me to cause hurtful hours for my dearest relatives, my parents and sisters, but I cannot change it."[22]

To his parents, Boas wrote, "The few months since my return have really been the most upsetting of my whole life and unfortunately this unhappy time is not yet over." Boas felt torn asunder by the emotional tensions and Marie often blamed herself. She felt that she was "the reason for these opposing struggles." Boas hoped that his letter to his parents would convey "very clearly and directly what I want and on what principles I am handling" the decisions. Boas stressed the benefits of having the BAE publish his manuscript: "Having my ethnographic material published here is from the scientific point of view very good since I would not have it presented so well or with so many illustrations. I shall probably have more than 200 illustrations pertaining to ethnographic matters. 140 are already photographed and will then be drawn."[23]

In despair, Boas wrote Marie, "You cannot imagine how terrible I feel about the many warnings from home, not to stay here. . . . I almost do not know whether I have lost all feeling for what is right and proper for children in relation to their parents." Now with his father also pressuring him, he felt that, aside from Marie, no one supported his hope of finding employment in the United States. Boas continued, "I have told you and everyone so often that the work of a German professor does not satisfy my vision. I must have work in practical life in order to feel satisfied. . . . The way I see it, I am locked out of that possibility in Germany. Here it is presented to me. If I could only succeed in selecting a Geographical Science and places where it would be nurtured I would consider myself happy and I consider that in itself a worthwhile task." Boas maintained that it would be "incomparably more difficult and in a smaller dimension" to find a position in Germany. He continued, "Here everything in our science lies in raw material. Therefore, there is much effort to be expended." Boas concluded, "And finally I must always also point out my political convictions which simply cannot come to terms with the German situation. Does not this conviction, to be able to work and accomplish things to a very different degree, justify my right to try to lay the foundation for the future here? Tell me, dear love, whether I am right or not."[24]

Boas wrote Jacobi, in the same vein, "Our science does not exist in this country as yet; it must be created, as you yourself have said. I recognize this as a worthwhile task, and I can envisage none of equal importance in Germany. I have long known that there is much to do along these lines here, I have just learned how much is to be done." Boas continued, "My field is the Polar Regions, as a result of my last and only studies. Polar explorations at present have no future here as far as government support is concerned; I would try to get them sensibly under way. You may believe that this is too difficult for me, but I know how to use my resources and believe I could get it going. Under the assumption that I stay here, I have made the first trial steps; I have gotten after Bessels who has written a letter that I have prepared." He asserted, "I am pretty tough, and carry out what I have developed in my head if it is at all possible. My aim would be to establish a society that would sponsor systematic arctic explorations and studies, that could be carried out with relatively small means, and would be truly scientifically planned." Additionally, he would "study the geographical instruction in schools, and emphasize the lack of proper preparatory education of the teachers." Boas had managed to interest Bessels in the project, but, he noted, "one can rely on him only if one is constantly driving him," and, he reflected, "although Bessels is interested—after all polar exploration in moderation is the aim of his life—he will never achieve anything because he lacks decision and firmness." Additionally, Boas said, "We do not see eye to eye"; therefore he could not count on Bessels to institute that which "I wish. He just complains about the impossibility to organize new expeditions but does not seek out new possibilities unless someone makes life miserable for him."[25]

Boas contrasted his hopes for establishing a field for himself in the United States with the constraints that would be placed on him in Germany. "That is work that I desire," he wrote, "and which I could not develop in such breadth as a German professor." He continued with a critique of German academia and the political situation:

> You do not know the snobbish aristocracy of the leading circles in Germany, and the great difficulties that are created for the young docents who wish to do more than to teach. And the problems here are incomparably greater and more worthwhile. These things prejudice me against a German professorship. And then there is the old reason that I have so often spoken to you about. I do not wish to keep my mouth shut about political matters and be damned to absolute subservience. I have often told you that scientific work alone does not satisfy me; I must be alive and creative.

Boas reflected, "I believe I have demonstrated by the preparations for my voyage that I am resolute enough to stick to my plans in order to accomplish something." He admitted a fierce attachment to his ideas: "Such brain children as I have just described are naturally dear to the originator, and you can imagine that it would be a hard and costly decision to give them up." In the penultimate paragraph of his January 18, 1885, letter to Jacobi, Boas wrote, "I have purposely said nothing so far about Marie. I need not state that to marry is my dearest desire. . . . It is true I had not formerly thought that waiting would be so difficult. But I state to you with certainty in Marie's name and in mine that we will not sacrifice everything to an early marriage." He framed his desire to marry within the scope of his desire to find a professional position: "I do not believe that I am conceited, but I feel that I can accomplish something; whether I have the capacity to organize something remains to be seen, but I hope so. Just because of my judgment of my own capacities I feel it a duty to accomplish something and will not let my deepest yearnings prevent their consummation." He admitted that he would "prefer a poorly paid position here, that would give me opportunity to function according to my ideas to a better position in Germany."[26]

The "unhappy theme [of] America-Europe" continued in the communications between Boas and his parents during his remaining weeks in the United States. On January 20, 1885, Boas wrote his parents, "There are no such positions which you designate as 'First Class.' They can only be a first step to other positions." Boas continued, "I do not agree with you that a Professor, a German Professor is the most desirable of all because the circle of work of a Professor does not lie in the direction in which I want to work." He concurred that the position of professor was most prestigious, but, he added, "I do not have the ambition to prefer a purely prestigious position over one which opens the way to a greater sphere of influence." Yet again, Boas laid out his position: "If I could have in Germany, for instance, the directorship of an organization like [Justus] Perthes, I would take hold of it with both hands." He continued, "Here I would accept a position at Johns Hopkins or Harvard University. Now you surely ask why I would take such a position here, which I would not consider my ideal in Germany. Because the conditions here are entirely different. Here geography is still in the making. With us it is finished or practically finished." Because the field was still open, as Boas represented it, in the United States, "an American professor can accomplish more than a German." This was, Boas said, the standpoint from which he was appraising "the conditions here and also the practical possibilities."[27]

Boas spent most of February 1885 in Washington DC. He wrote his parents that he had "started an argument with a Mr. [George] Melville" in an article in the February 6, 1885, issue of the *New York Evening Post*. Melville had proposed an expedition to the North Pole, and Boas opposed the plans. Boas's published opposition to Melville's proposed expedition had to do both with Boas's assessment of the weakness of Melville's plans and with Boas's need to establish his scholarly and expeditionary credentials. Melville responded to Boas's letter in the February 17 issue of the *New York Evening Post*. Of this Boas wrote, "Melville's reply is scandalously weak, and I want to give him a piece of my mind. I hope Science will accept it. How I must work hard these days to compose an article spiced with citations." *Science* did accept Boas's reply, in which he wrote, "In short, Mr. Melville's theory cannot uphold itself, and a plan founded upon it cannot prove successful. We wish Mr. Melville might confine himself to the principle that every plan of advance towards the pole should be made according to former experiences, not vague theories."[28]

Boas hoped in particular for openings in the Smithsonian and the U.S. Army Signal Office, the latter of which documented weather patterns and provided military information to the army in the time of war. Schurz was putting in "a good word for him at the [U.S.] Signal Office." Boas had received an offer from the Smithsonian and the Signal Office to go to the McKenzie Delta for two to three years. In addition, the Signal Office was proposing to establish "an observation station in Davis Straits and may perhaps ask me to do it." Boas wrote Jacobi, "The Signal Office has its civilian scientific staff, and I am competent to do the work, and should like to do it, if the matter with Powell falls through." He added, "Of course I would not regard either position as permanent but would keep in mind the possibility of a university appointment." With appropriations scheduled for March 4, Boas was still waiting to hear from Powell; and Boas was hoping that something would come of his discussion with Otis Mason about "the gaps" in the ethnological collection of the BAE. As his time in the United States was drawing to a close, Boas wrote Marie, "If I only knew some way out of this unhappy dilemma." Boas was faced squarely with another period of separation from Marie. "Complaining," he told her, "does not help. We must bite into the sour apple once more."[29]

To his parents, he wrote, "You can really not realize how painful this winter has been for me. I am happy that it is coming to an end and that our constant longing can be satisfied." In preparation for his trip to Germany, Boas was completing his work in Washington and anticipating the two lectures at Columbia College. He placed great weight on the lectures: "I shall know whether any chance exists to stay here or not." He continued, "You can be quite easy about it. Your 'stocks' are very high, the ones for staying here are very low." Boas delivered his lectures at Columbia College on March 2 and 3. Sadly, they were poorly delivered and poorly received. He departed for Germany March 10, 1885, on board the ss Donau. His mother met him at Bremerhaven and accompanied him home, where they arrived in the middle of the night. Four months earlier Boas had encouraged his family, "Be patient for a short time longer, then take the rope that pulls the ship into strong hands and in no time I shall be with you to tell you all my 'heroic actions,' which consisted mainly of eating seal. I hope in the meantime Minden will be quieted down concerning the 'Historia Boasiana' so that I can let myself be seen on the streets without danger." His family had not been patient, but they had indeed pulled and pulled on the emotional ties that bound Boas to them until he relented and returned.[30]

Back in Minden he felt simultaneously at home and as if he had to relearn everything: "Sometimes it seems as though I had hardly been away, and again as though decades had elapsed." The day after his return, Boas wrote Marie of his father's arrival from Paris, "Oh, Marie if you had seen how the dear old father threw himself on me and cried like a child, and just could not quiet himself again. I thought my heart would burst from joy and sorrow." The Marienstrasse house had been festooned with floral wreaths and garlands. Everyone in Minden was eager to greet him: "The day after my arrival all kinds of people, many of whom I do not know, sent flowers and wreaths as greeting." In astonishment he wrote, "I receive letters of greeting from all over, and I am having trouble answering them." The "Historia Boasiana" that he had referred in his letter to his parents in November had not died down. "I hesitate to go out in the street," he wrote Marie. "People gape after me so and all kinds of strangers greet me."[31]

Fischer invited Boas to Marburg to welcome him home. The next week Boas traveled to Marburg to talk with Fischer about his prospects for employment in Germany. He reported to Marie, "The academic career is even under the most favorable circumstances a lottery." On April 11, 1885, Boas was in Hamburg attending the Fifth *Deutscher Geographentag*, the gathering of German geographers where Fischer had arranged for Boas to speak. He successfully delivered his paper "The Eskimos of Baffin Island" to rousing applause. Astounded by the welcome, Boas contrasted his reception in Germany to what he had experienced in the United States: "I have an altogether different position here than over there. There no one knew me, here I am well known. It is true I see no adequate reason for that but accept the fact with thankfulness. All the geographers of any significance come to me to be introduced, to wish me luck, and particularly to talk with me about my scientific plans." He

Divided Desires

was ecstatic about the contacts he had made and wrote Marie that he had discussed his work over beer for more than an hour with the "chief methodologist among German geographers," whom he identified as Hermann Wagner in a letter to his parents. He received invitations to speak at Halle, Frankfurt, Berlin, and Strasburg, and he received "support from all sides." Boas wrote Marie, "I tell you all this because I know it will give you joy and because in a certain sense it can give us some confidence in the development of our future." Exuberantly he added, "Dearest, you cannot imagine how much good this has done me after the vain efforts in America, and how it strengthens me. It is very hard if one finds no understanding of one's whole strivings."[32]

With pride and satisfaction, Sophie Boas wrote Jacobi of her son's many successes during his month in Germany. He had returned from his trip to Berlin "very satisfied" and was "looking into the future with more courage and energy." She wrote of his initial days in Minden, "When he arrived here . . . he was so downhearted and discouraged after all of his failures over there, that my heart bled for him." She exuded, "Oh, my dear friend, I am so happy with this dear wonderful son. . . . His pleasant childlike temperament wins everyone's heart. You must not laugh at me that I am taken in by him." Boas spent his time in his study with the door firmly shut against distractions, she said: "He is working very hard all with brief interruptions, and we see him only at mealtime."[33]

On April 20, 1885, Boas also sent a letter to Jacobi along with his mother's, but while hers was jubilant, his was resigned and despairing. "It is a bitter thought for me," he wrote, "that nothing has come of all the plans for reaching my scientific goals, and that I shall have to construct a new work for myself here. I do not believe that there is any chance to plan a future for myself in America from here. You know what drew me over there. Here I must live with my theoretical plans and confine myself to them exclusively." From a political perspective, Boas observed, "I found conditions just as I had expected. All of Germany lies in the dust of Bismarck's brutal power, and through him we have come to the point that we can proclaim: thank God that we have conquered all of our idealism and are now working for practical goals." Boas was pleased in one respect: "I can be satisfied with my reception here in Germany." He continued, "I do not know to whom I owe it that I am so well known in learned circles. Certainly not to myself for I have not written anything worthwhile. Probably Neumayer, Bastian, Virchow, and Fischer have spoken about me, and their interest has made me known. In this respect my path is smoother than over there, since I am well-known and my name has a good reputation. I must confess that recognition by scientists has been very encouraging after the many failures in America." He concluded, "Even though one should have one's own estimate of one's accomplishments, the complete lack of success of all of one's efforts is dispiriting."[34]

Boas adopted the same strategy in Germany as he had in the United States: to give lectures to as many professional organizations as possible, to make contacts with as many people in positions to assist him as he could find, to write without respite articles and books, and to follow every possible lead for potential employment. On April 15 he spoke about the folklore of the Eskimos of Baffin Land before the Berliner Gesellschaft für Anthropologie, Ethnologie und Urgeschichte (Berlin Society for Anthropology, Ethnology and Prehistory), and his presentation was well received by Virchow and Bastian. On May 2 he lectured also in Berlin before an audience of four hundred at the Gesellschaft für Erdkunde and met two days later with the society's vice president, Dr. Johann Wilhelm Reiß, who was "particularly friendly" to him and "was pushing" Boas for the position as secretary of the society.[35]

Boas wrote Jacobi, "I can be well satisfied with the outward honors that I received in Hamburg and now in Berlin, but I find it very inconvenient to be a well-known traveler." He continued, "I have received an urgent invitation to become a Privatdozent in Halle, and they would like to have me in Berlin too. But after a quiet and factual discussion no one will guarantee me the probability [of] a position for many years to come." As he said, "Some professors" had put Boas "in touch with a large Viennese geographical institute which is seeking an editor": the Hölzel Institute. Boas was also able to talk at length with Bastian, as he wrote to Marie, "about the plans I had had for America, and he was very taken with them and would have wished that I had stayed over there." In similar fashion, Boas wrote Jacobi that Bastian was "very sad that I do not wish to travel anymore," but he added that he "wants to ship me off 'with wife' by main force." Boas concluded, "If I do not have bad luck (although I seem to specialize in it) I may hope soon to have an adequate and secure position."[36]

Divided Desires

Boas traveled to Copenhagen to work with Hinrich [Heinrich] Rink on the translations of Eskimo folktales. Always straining to complete his projects quickly, he found the work with Rink "very strenuous." As he wrote Marie, "I see with horror how slowly we progress." Candidly Boas observed, "Actually I find old Rink rather dull. He can become enthusiastic about some things, just like a young man, but in general he is quite indifferent." Just sixty-five years old, Rink, with his trembling hands and sunken face, gave "the impression of great age." Boas wrote, "The poor devil said to me today, 'Hurry and get your folk tales printed, I wish to live to see them.'" Six months later Boas wrote Marie, "The mythology of the Eskimo is finished, and the tales are almost all written out." This was published in 1885 as "Die Sagen der Baffin-Land-Eskimos." Simultaneously Boas was working on the manuscript on Baffin Land for Justus Perthes in Gotha. He told Marie, "The manuscript of the book for Perthes is beginning to grow. I am working very hard. I hope to be finished with all, including maps, by the end of June." *Baffin-Land* was published in December 1885, by Petermanns Mitteilungen, and would serve as his *Habilitationsschrift*, or the formal document presented for his *Habilitation*.[37]

Surrounded by his family but nonetheless working alone in his study in Minden, Boas grew impatient with "the nature of my activities at present." He wrote Marie, "This work is so unsatisfying. What does one accomplish sitting in a room all day and writing a book that at best four or five people will read? For me to work like this without being useful and without taking part in some *actual* activity I cannot stand. Of course, I must finish this old junk and I will have accomplished something worthwhile if I write a tolerable book. Then a few persons will leaf through it, two will read it with interest, a few with criticism and cursing because they have to report on it." Nearing the completion of his book, Boas experienced "the same kind of stage fright as at a lecture, only in exaggerated form." Boas was also meeting defeat in his efforts to find employment. "My hopes in Berlin [Geographical Society] are also shattered," Boas wrote Marie, "and I do not know what I shall do next." He bemoaned that all he could give her was "one disappointment after another."[38]

In June 1885 Fischer found it "incomprehensible" that Boas hadn't heard back from Vienna, particularly after the letter Fischer had written in support of Boas. By September Boas had heard that this position, at the Hölzel Institute, had also come to naught. Fischer reiterated his recommendation that Boas pursue the Habilitation, a process whereby one endeavored to prove that one was *habilis*, or "fit" to be a member of the faculty. Fischer continued, "The academic career is always some kind of lottery and causes quite a few qualms for someone who like you wants to get married and also isn't in the position to make any large material sacrifices." Fischer counseled Boas on how to pave the way to Habilitation with a specific university and stressed the importance of establishing rapport with faculty early on. It was important, Fischer remarked, to experience life at one's university of choice for a while to get a feel for the place and to get to know potential colleagues. Referring to Alfred Kirchhoff of the University of Halle, who had offered to work with Boas, Fischer wrote that he would be "an exceptional teacher and mentor." Also important, as Fischer stressed, Boas would find at the University of Halle a well-developed teaching environment for geography.[39]

Boas decided to take Fischer's advice and to undergo the process for Habilitation in geography. He had been searching for months in both the United States and in Germany for a job, and he faced the stark realization that, at twenty-seven years of age, he was still dependent on his father to pay his expenses. As he wrote Marie, "Even if I don't stay here it is better to come over there with some kind of title than just as a private person." An individual who successfully completed this post-doctoral degree would advance, as Müller-Wille writes, to "*Privatdozent*, a prerequisite to get a *Ruf*, a call to a chair in a discipline as *Ordinarius / Ordentlicher Professor* or full professor at a German university." The candidate for Habilitation was required to submit the Habilitationsschrift, the major published treatise, and several other publications for "internal or external evaluation by several assessors." Müller-Wille continues, "Once accepted, the *Habilitand* presents a lecture at the *Habilitationskolloquium* before all professorial members of the faculty, who all vote on the outcome passing or failing the candidate. If successful the candidate is invited to hold the public *Antrittsvorlesung* or *Praelectio*, the inaugural lecture, to obtain the *venia legendi*, the authorization to lecture as a *Privatdozent*, usually an unpaid position."[40]

Initially Fischer had counseled Boas to habilitate with Kirchhoff at the University of Halle and even suggested that Boas consider habilitating under Fischer himself at the University of Marburg. However, Fischer, along with Hermann Wagner at Göttingen and Alfred Kirchhoff at Halle, decided it was best to use Boas's placement to strengthen the discipline of geography in Germany. All three advised Boas to habilitate at the Friedrich-Wilhelms-Universität in Berlin. As Cole notes, "Preeminent in so many areas of learning, the senior Prussian university had only one professor of geography, the sixty-seven-year-old Heinrich Kiepert. . . . Aside from a strong cartographic concern, his interests never went beyond the lands of classical antiquity, and he remained unaffected, even disapproving, of new trends within the field. Notoriously unpleasant, he attracted few students." When Boas settled on Berlin, Fischer wrote him, "I am happy that you have resolved to habilitate in Berlin. . . . It is the best prospect for you." He added, "Failure seems to me absolutely inconceivable."[41]

In his first meeting with Kiepert, Boas discovered his unpleasant nature: "I called on Kiepert and was unable to write for two days because I was so furious." Boas continued, "The stupid ass appears to wish to take a completely negative stand. He declared that he would not be in a position to criticize my work, since he is a historical geographer and does not wish to have anything to do with the modern (*naturwissen-schaftlichen*) [natural science methodology] environmental tendency. I should go to Helmholtz and Bastian. And he said it all in such a manner that I wanted to throw a fat volume, like the dictionary which lay under my nose, at his head." Responding "in soft flute-like tones," Boas expressed his confidence that Kiepert would be able to judge his works. "As he had no other excuse," Boas remarked, "he said he would have no time before November and dismissed me until after October!" With an almost audible groan, Boas said, "If no one speaks for me, I certainly have no chance here."[42]

Boas had many supporters who urged him on. "I have had a letter from Prof. Wagner in Göttingen," Boas wrote Marie, "in which he urgently advises me to stick it out here." Prof. Kirchhoff in Halle commiserated with Boas about Kiepert: "I understand your anger very well." Sagely he advised, "Once you *are qualified* as a professor in Berlin, the old man will no longer be able to put difficulties in your way." Fischer tried to soothe his edgy student by assuring him that if Kiepert tried to harm Boas, he would "only be hurting himself." As a further balm to the nerves, Fischer suggested, "You needn't waste your time about cramming on his whims; it's completely useless." Feeling like a sacrifice on the altar of the improvement of geography at Berlin, Boas wrote Marie, "Of course they are all glad if someone here squabbles with Kiepert in the interest of geography, but it does not please me to be the victim."[43]

Boas had asked an assistant to find out what Kiepert said about him. He wrote Marie that Kiepert responded, "'Bah, he just traveled about a bit with one family and imagines that he has done wonders. If that represents ethnological work a fine ethnography will come of it. And now he wants to write a fat book about it.'" As Boas progressed further in the process of Habilitation, Kiepert's remarks, as reported to Boas, became more extreme. Boas reported to Marie that Kiepert said that "I did nothing on my trip but prove my incompetence, that I brought back no ethnographic material, that I made no observations about language, customs, and usages. But he knows that I have brought back much material in each of these fields. About my book he says that there is nothing scientific in it, nothing but gossip about seals, and that the last part in particular is worthless." Boas said, "If no way can be found to throw Kiepert off the commission for my habilitation, I shall probably leave here in a hurry."[44]

Saner minds prevailed. Fischer advised, "An important discipline at the country's largest university . . . could not be left to drift because it suited one old man." The distinguished geographers and allied scientists strategized to minimize Kiepert's influence: "Bastian, Reiß, and Förster promised their support, and Neumayer introduced him to Wilhelm von Bezold, the university's new meteorologist who reacted sympathetically. Since he would not formally apply for the Habilitation until the appearance of his Perthes book, his major qualifying piece, there was time to let these influences work in his favor." Kiepert effectively disqualified himself from judging Boas's work by writing, "I can only repeat what I have already imparted orally that over the whole subject to which your work belongs, I have absolutely no judgment to inspect your habilitation." If the faculty assigned him this "task," he would "reject" it, and they would have to refer Boas "to a real expert in this case . . . to our new meteorologist Prof. Betzold [sic] and the ethnographic part to Prof. Bastian." At a February faculty meeting, von Bezold was named as Boas's chief examiner; Kiepert, as "a subsidiary examiner." Puzzling from afar, Marie asked what Kiepert had against Boas. "The chief thing," Boas replied, "is common envy." Boas was not alone: Kiepert had treated others who had tried to become *habilitiert* in the same way. Additionally, Kiepert had "very bad relations with the rest of the faculty with whom I am on good terms, so that he wants to get even with them through me. The chief thing though is that he fears I might take from him his few students." Boas concluded, "The faculty knows the facts but has not the gumption to oppose Kiepert vigorously."[45]

In the midst of this unpleasant academic wrangling, Boas was employed by Adolph Bastian at the Ethnological Museum in Berlin. From mid-September to mid-December 1885, Boas helped to prepare for the move to the new museum building the following year and to catalogue and display the newly acquired "extensive collections made by Captain Adrian Jacobsen in British Columbia and Alaska." Boas wrote Marie, "I am glad that I can at least support myself." Perhaps with premature optimism, he added, "It is true that Papa still has to advance me money." Working with a senior staff member "who changes his mind every day because the work bores him," Boas despaired that the exhibit would be any good. He wrote Marie, "If only the exhibit will not again be changed (one seems here to have a predilection for unnecessary work) the public will be able to enjoy my tasteful work." Bastian was able to find additional funds to hire Boas again in mid-January to continue work on the exhibit for the Northwest Coast Indians. Assigned "exclusively [to] Americana" artifacts, Boas held out hope that Bastian intended to keep him on permanently. However, by mid-March, Boas was frustrated with Bastian's indecisiveness as to how long he would be employed at the museum.[46]

Boas began work at the museum in January 1886 with nine Bella Coola Indians. The Jacobsen brothers, Johan Adrian Jacobsen and Bernard Fillip Jacobsen, brought the Bella Coola to Germany and to Berlin at the behest of Carl Hagenbeck, the promoter of touring shows, or *Völkerschauen* (exotic peoples shows). Adrian Jacobsen had begun working for Hagenbeck, owner of an animal shop and zoo in Hamburg in 1878, when he brought a group of Sámi along with an ethnographic collection to Germany as a touring show. Subsequently Jacobsen brought three Patagonians, and in 1880 he brought eight Labrador Inuit, all of whom died of smallpox within the month of their arrival in Europe. After three of the Inuit died, "Jacobsen arranged for the others to be vaccinated against smallpox, but preventive measures proved to be too late. Between January 7th and 16th, all of the remaining Inuit died in Paris." This experience cooled Hagenbeck and Jacobsen's ardor for *Völkerschauen*. However, on his return from the Northwest Coast collecting expedition, Adrian Jacobsen told Hagenbeck of the "'Longheads' of Quatsino Inlet," and Hagenbeck was enticed to undertake another touring show.[47]

Adrian Jacobsen had already signed a contract for a voyage to Siberia. His younger brother Fillip traveled to the Northwest Coast in British Columbia but was unable to complete an agreement with the Indians. Receiving news of his brother's trouble, Adrian Jacobsen left Russia for the Northwest Coast, to help negotiate a travel agreement with nine Bella Coola men. In Victoria the Jacobsen brothers had met the Bella Coola, who had been traveling away from their home territory to find employment harvesting hops. The Bella Coola signed a contract with Adrian Jacobsen as the representative of Hagenbeck to perform in cities throughout Germany. Arriving in Bremen in mid-August 1885, the Bella Coola appeared first in Leipzig at Pinkert's Zoological Garden in the third week of September. In their travels to thirteen cities throughout Germany, they put on shows for the general public, schoolchildren, and scientific societies for one year, seven days a week and at least eight hours a day, before they returned to the Northwest Coast. In addition to zoological gardens, the Bella Coola performed in a variety of venues, including "hotels, occasionally in exhibition rooms such as Castan's Panopticum in Cologne, and Berlin's Kroll'sche Etablissement." In Halle they made an appearance before the *Verein für Erdkunde*, where "Carl Stumpf spent four sessions with the singer Nuskilusta recording his songs." In Berlin, Virchow, Bastian, and Krause introduced the group to the Berliner Gesellschaft für Anthropologie, Ethnologie, und Urgeschichte. At this meeting, as Boas wrote Marie, "I shall say a few words at the anthropological society about the language of the Bella Coola Indians, just to make myself heard again."[48]

Boas "spent two strenuous weeks with the Indians" working on their language when they were in residence at the Kroll'sche Etablissement. While collecting "a lot of material" with the intent of making "quite a good study out of it," Boas was at the mercy of their touring schedule. "Of course nothing is complete," Boas wrote Marie, "and just now as I begin to perceive the soul of the language they are leaving." After his initial meeting with the Bella Coola, Boas published an article, "Captain Jacobsen's Bella Coola Indians," in the January 25, 1886, issue of the *Berliner Tageblatt*. In a successful bit of archival sleuthing, Douglas Cole found this previously overlooked piece in the J. A. Jacobsen papers on file at the *Museum für Völkerkunde* in Hamburg. Significantly, Boas began his article by raising an ethical question about exhibiting foreign people, the concomitant health hazards for those exhibited, and the exhibitionism inherent in the displays: "'It has long been the fashion for representatives of foreign tribes to be brought to Europe in order for us, as far as it is possible, to be shown their lives and customs. A friend of humanity might well reflect upon the admissibility of such exhibitions, when he sees the wretched Australian or the vigorous Eskimo waste away under the influence of a foreign climate—when some individuals are gazed at more in wonderment for their striking bodies than because they represent a vivid representation of the manners and customs of their people.'" As Cole clarifies in an endnote, Boas's reference to "'the wretched Australian or the vigorous Eskimo'" wasting away "is probably to the death of seven of eleven Terre del Fuegians"—not Australians—"shortly after one of Jacobsen's Labrador Eskimos succumbed at Paris, all in 1881."[49]

In his article on the Bella Coola, Boas discussed "'a wonderful technique in the use of the carver's knife and paintbrush and a finely developed artistic sense'" and the graceful moves of the dancers who transport the audience "'into a foreign world whose outlook, whose customs, have taken a quite different course from ours, but which we must acknowledge as a high culture state.'" As if in anticipation of his research focus for decades to come, Boas wrote, "'The performances are remarkably rich and give an admirable demonstration of how the religious and artistic element reaches everywhere into the social life of this remarkable tribe and is especially noticeable in the numerous festivals.'" Referring to the article on the language of the Bella Coola that he was preparing for *Science* (1886), Boas wrote Marie, "I must confess that it was not a *pure* scientific interest that enabled me to work with such energy with this people. I wanted more to present the Americans with something Indian, and possibly my work can become very useful to me." He admitted that he had placed the article in *Science* to annoy Powell, whom Boas thought had done very little to assist him, and "to remind the Canadians of my existence."[50]

In May 1886 Boas's work for the Habilitation was "accepted by the faculty" at the University of Berlin, and he was "assigned a subject for a lecture, 'About the Ice Conditions in the Arctic Ocean.'" At the end of May, he delivered his lecture:

> In the Senate Hall of the university there were about 30 professors. I saw [Theodor] Mommsen, [Hermann von] Helmholtz, [Emil du Bois-]Roymond and other big shots. Then I was told to begin. I had previously hung up my map and spoke briskly for three quarters of an hour. When I was finished I was allowed to sit down between the men who had reviewed my work, Bezold and Kiepert. The dean opened the discussion and von Bezold asked for more detailed information on icebergs. Following that we discussed the interior of Greenland, rain and wind conditions in North America, the paths of storms over the Atlantic Ocean and Europe and with that Bezold was satisfied.

Expressing his displeasure, Kiepert remarked that Boas barely "touched on the field of geography," and that for this reason, "he understood nothing of my lecture." He asked "how the rivers of Siberia could melt so much ice." Boas answered him and then was excused by the faculty: "Then after 2 minutes the dean sent me his calling card in which he asked me to visit him today and told me that I had been accepted." To Marie he wrote, "So your dearest becomes Privatdocent." With one more lecture for students on the canyons of Colorado, Boas completed the requirements for Habilitation. To please Marie, Boas sent her the printed invitation to the lecture. "The silly newspapers," he related, "printed everything." He continued, "I feel so free and light since the matter is over, it has oppressed me all winter. Particularly that I no longer hear the word, Kiepert." On the same evening, the geographical society of Berlin met and Boas "was overwhelmed with congratulations, as though I had achieved some great success." To his father he wrote, "All Berlin knew of my new title."[51]

Boas had been worn down by his ceaseless efforts to gain recognition for his work and to find employment. He wrote Marie, "It seems to me as though I had become 5 years older in this year of my return." He continued, "The constant disappointments and the sad experiences with so many persons don't pass over one without leaving an imprint." With all of his efforts "to get ahead . . . nowhere is there a sign of success." As the culmination of all his challenging experiences, Boas remarked, "the unforgivable behavior of the tribe of professors has just strengthened my feelings and burning desire to get away from here." He no longer knew "where all my beautiful and brave plans have gone to."[52]

Marie began to feel that Franz was succumbing to the pressures from his family to remain in Germany. "You are wrong, my dearest," Boas wrote Marie, "if you believe that the wishes of my family have any weight in my decisions, and when you believe that I let myself be influenced by them to reach any particular decision." He pleaded with her not to say "that you must give up even the slightest part of your rights in me to anyone." In a mirror image of his reasoned pleas to his family when he was in the United States, Boas wrote Marie that he could not leave right away: "In short I would throw away eight months here if I went over there now." In an effort to ease the strain of Boas and Marie's separation, Boas's father had offered to send money for Marie's passage in order, as he said, to have the pleasure of seeing them both together in Germany and to present them to their friends. Boas's mother and sisters continued in the attempts to bring Marie to Berlin. Since Hete did not have room for Marie in her apartment, Boas's mother proposed to rent a room in Berlin for herself and Marie in the early summer. In response to Marie's letter, Boas wrote, "I too did not like the idea that Mama and you should rent a room and live here [in Berlin]."[53]

Boas wrote his parents, "I believe it would be useful for me to take advantage of the university vacation and go abroad, unless I should beforehand find a suitable connection or a beginning of a permanent position." The pressures did not let up in Minden. Trying to explain to his family why he felt his place was not in Germany, he wrote to them, "I think from my experiences this year, you will see that I was correct in my judgment of conditions here." Boas traveled to Minden over the Easter holiday and tried in person to convince his parents that he should go to America, rather than having Marie come to Germany. To Marie he wrote, "Believe me, the discussion this morning was difficult, but I could not give in and jeopardize our prospects, and so as things are here now, my coming over is the only sensible move. It is so difficult for my folks for they fear that which we desire, but they cannot say that I am wrong. It hurts me so to destroy their hopes to see us together here, but it cannot be otherwise. . . . They do not understand what draws me over there, what persuades me to prefer work in America to a German professorship." He ended by saying, "Only Papa agrees with me."[54]

The emotional crisis continued. "I was most unpleasantly surprised," Boas wrote Marie, "that the old quarrel about America started again when I was in Minden." In despair, Boas gave "up all hope of explaining to people," either in Minden or Berlin, "why it is that I wish to go abroad and that it is possible to accomplish over there that which cannot be done here." The response was always the same: "'Yes, but when you are once a professor you will have enough free time to do what you wish.'" With clarity of purpose and tenacity of intent Boas wrote,

> They cannot understand that I have other ideals than to have a lot of free time for myself. I want to accomplish something with my labors and it won't help very much to give birth to many or few fat books or to let the students sleep in my classes or in someone else's. On the other hand, I see in America the possibility of being able to bring it about that many will work for the sake of science, and also many other ways in which one can be much more useful. Oh, dearest, that must be joy-giving labor to watch how through one's efforts and worries, the germs one has planted develop, and to have accomplished useful work, which has originated from one's own spirit and labors. On this road, no labor is too great, no unpleasantness too repellent.

He concluded, "This kind of activity is virtually closed to me here, abroad there is opportunity, and that is why I am trying so hard to go to you."[55]

During this time of his "divided desires"—from Baffin Land to St. John's, Newfoundland, and then to New York in September 1884, to Germany in March 1885, and back to New York in July 1886—Boas had spent twenty-two months and twenty days in intense work. He had lived in constant frustration at not being able to realize his goal of obtaining a position. He wrote and published continuously. His articles appeared in the popular press and in scientific journals and transactions. His first book, *Baffin-Land: Geographische Ergebnisse einer in den Jahren 1883 und 1884 ausgeführten Forschungreise* (1885), was published in German by the prestigious Justus Perthes in Gotha. He completed his second book, *The Central Eskimo*, in 1885 and dedicated it to Bessels; it was published in English by the equally prestigious *Annual Report of the* BAE in Washington DC, in 1888.

During his isolated angst, Boas had despaired of spending time writing a massive tome that few people would read. Over a century after its publication, Müller-Wille assessed the importance of *The Central Eskimo*: "The 1888 monograph has been quoted over and over again and is often referred to as one of the major starting points of scientific endeavors regarding the peoples in the North American Arctic." From September 1884 to July 1886, while in New York and Germany, Boas published twenty-nine works, five of them in English. Examining all of Boas's works on the Arctic, Müller-Wille remarks, "There has been a neglected dimension of the considerable and important scientific opus that Boas had already published in German during the 1880s. In those publications he had already presented the origin and foundation of his own scientific approach to studying the relationship between Inuit and the Arctic environment." Müller-Wille continues, "After his interlude in the United States in 1884–1885 Boas would pass the *Habilitation* in Berlin in June 1886. With that success Boas became very much embedded in and influenced by the concepts of *modern geography*, as it was understood in Germany at that time. This was more noticeable in his expanding research, publications, and evolving academic networks than has been generally understood by non-German reading scholars, mainly anthropologists, in North America, including those who analyzed Boas' academic and scientific career extensively."[56]

While Boas embraced modern geography, he did not feel that the established German geographers would grant him the intellectual breadth to develop his ideas. As he expressed it to Marie, "When I begin my scientific work in Germany I only get enemies and opposition since they stand in such contrast to the modern directions and direct their derision against certain leaders of today's Ethnography and Geography." While working on his publication for Perthes on *Baffin-Land*, he wrote Marie, "I wonder how the methodological paper will turn out; I myself find it very important, since it represents considerations that are very real to me."

However, he felt himself on new terrain and was unsure of the significance of his writing: "When one like me comes from exact science to a half historical field, one easily doubts whether the new work is at all worthwhile, whether scientifically it does not occupy a lower position than the physical striving to establish laws." As he progressed in his work on *Baffin-Land*, Boas lamented even more about his position with respect to established science. He wrote Marie of "the unbearable yoke that burdens the young scientist here." While the geographers were, as he said, "very encouraging to me," he found that he did not "fit in their company." The geographers with whom he spoke conveyed to him that he was too young to propound new works on the methodology of geography. Boas maintained that "the right to express his opinion must be given to the youngest when he believes that his views have matured." Boas acknowledged, "Of course one must know what is going on in the whole field, to be modern one must steep oneself in the field, and that I do, but not for the sake of recognition from the fancy specialists. It is undoubtedly wrong that the carrying out of scientific work, here, is almost exclusively the privilege of the professors. My God, what nonsense that often brings to light!"[57]

On Christmas day Boas wrote Marie, "I no longer wish to compare to today the high hopes and plans with which I returned from the North, and with which I even came to Germany." None of his dreams had been realized. He continued, "I now feel like the youngest in an order, who must sit out a time before he may open his mouth in the chorus of general wisdom. I shall now do nothing further than go along with the rest of my young colleagues along the old paths; in that way I shall probably best get ahead. I have gotten nothing for all my plans and works but a sympathetic shrug of the shoulders, and even for scientific problems that are close to my heart the quieting assurance that I am still too young." He feared that he might one day become like the established geographers, that he would "be a member of the order founded on mutual admiration." As he wrote, "The fault is in part mine. I do not have to have aims that lie outside of the usual fields, and no one can understand why I do not find a professorship the ideal of all activity." When he had returned to Germany, he had spoken with his family about his plans and goals, but he had grown gradually more and more despondent: "I really only now notice when my parents and sisters ask me about details that I have given up almost everything." On occasion Boas could ride a crest and hope again, "but the time will come when I can carry out my ideas and aims." However, he kept his dreams to himself: "I no longer talk about it here." He remarked upon his brother-in-law Rudolf Lehmann, who could "not understand in the least that I cannot be satisfied merely by working at my desk, but that I desire to share in the work of mankind." Boas reflected, "It is only a matter of feeling and one can quarrel with no one about the value of one's own activities."[58]

On July 10, 1886, Boas departed for New York, after a brief stop in London, where he sought out the director of the Geological Survey of Canada, Alfred Selwyn. In June Boas had received a clipping from a Montreal newspaper that had raised his hopes about the possibility of his plans to continue ethnographic work in Canada: the Royal Society of Canada had recommended assisting "'Dr. Boas of Berlin . . . in his further work on the ethnography of Canada.'" To his parents, Boas wrote, "At last I have found Selwyn and you may look forward in peace to the winter as I think the matter with Canada is hopeless." Knowing nothing of the resolution of the Royal Society of Canada, Selwyn showed no regard for "the ethnographic work I am interested in and in which the society is interested." Boas added, "Since he is chief, I suppose it is hopeless. . . . I am sure you are glad about this news; I, not at all."[59]

In agonized anticipation he wrote Marie, telling her not to meet the steamer: "I must first see you alone. I guess we shall be able to bear those few hours." Boas sailed into New York Harbor on July 27, 1886. He had come back to Marie, accompanied by his sister Toni, who had joined him on the ss Eider in Southampton. Just prior to his departure from London, Boas had written to his parents, "So farewell and my best greetings. Only three months and I shall be back." But Boas was not to return ever again to live permanently in Germany. His family's fears were realized as his and Marie's dreams were fulfilled. Franz Boas found an expansive field of engagement and opportunities for work in the United States, but not without first making his way across the North American continent to the Northwest Coast, where he would meet two of the Bella Coola Indians, Alkinous and Itlkakuani, whom he had first encountered in Berlin. From Berlin to the Bella Coola and on to the Kwakiutl, Boas had found the rich field for his years of work to come.[60]

6

West to the Indians

Northwest Coast Fieldwork, Employment by Science, and Marriage

On the train somewhere between St. Paul and Brainerd, Minnesota, Boas wrote Marie, "First to the North, when I went to the Eskimo, then to the East to Europe, now to the West to the Indians. I no longer desire to go to the South!" Armed with introductions to "all kinds of possible and impossible people," Boas had boarded the train at Penn Station in New York, bound for somewhere "in or near Victoria." Carl Schurz had obtained for him a free railroad pass on the Northern Pacific Railroad, and Jacobi had loaned him five hundred dollars. Boas planned to conduct three months of fieldwork, from September to December 1886, among Indian groups of the Northwest Coast, and to gather ethnographic artifacts to sell when he returned east, in order to repay Jacobi and to cover his additional expenses. As Boas explained to his parents, he had decided to go because Jacobi, Schurz, and others thought it was a good professional move. "Please join me," he wrote, "in my wishes that I will be successful." He concluded, "Now my name will again appear in some newspapers, and people will at least know my name."[1]

Before leaving for the Northwest, Boas travelled to the Smithsonian to work on the editing of *The Central Eskimo* manuscript, about which he was "very unhappy." He wrote Marie, "They are making so many changes. What I feel worse about is the fact that even if it were written in German, the same changes would be made." He related that he always wrote "very briefly and directly," but that the editor was "adding a lot of 'stuffing.'" At Jacobi's encouragement, Boas attended the American Association for the Advancement of Science meeting in Buffalo. "I have been asked by many to read a paper," Boas wrote Marie, "but I do not wish to, as my English is too poor and I have decided that the next time I speak I will do it well." With reference to the failure of his lectures at Columbia in spring of 1885, Boas remarked with finality, "Until that time, I shall keep my mouth shut." To his parents he wrote, pleasantly surprised, "I was glad to discover that due to my journey and my publications I am also very well known here."[2]

Boas described what he saw when he stepped down from the Northern Pacific Railroad car at the end of the line in Tacoma, Washington, on September 17, 1886: "Other new cities may appear strange to one, but this one seemed still stranger. Burnt down forests extend into the city. Part of a street is built-up; next to it stand sad remnants of tall trees. The entire region between Helena and here, as a result of the senseless burning down of the woods looks unspeakably sad. The endless smoke indicates that fires must be raging more fiercely in other parts." On board the small steamer North Pacific, he made his way from Tacoma to Victoria. On his first excursion in the city, as he wrote his parents, "I discovered pictures of my Bella Coola everywhere and soon found their source—an Indian trader who had had them re-photographed" from those taken the year before in Germany by Carl Günther. Boas located the trader and "immediately asked about the Bella Coola and heard that two were still here but intended to leave for home that evening." Boas enlisted the help of two Bella Coola women (who had just been passing in the street) in finding these men: "I went with them, and after searching for a while I found my good friend Alkinous in a small house of a Bella Coola woman. He was of course very much surprised when he recognized me and said I must be a 'smart man.' It amused me to see the astonishment of the women when they heard me speak their language." After searching a bit more, Boas found his other Bella Coola friend, Itlkakuani. Boas "gave him a letter for Captain Jacobson," who had returned with the Bella Coola from Germany. Then Boas said, "Good-bye, after giving him greetings for his fellow tribesmen."[3]

Boas went frequently to the outskirts of town in Victoria where the Indians lived. As he wrote Marie, "Tonight I was down in the settlement again." In his 1889 article "Reisen in Britisch-Columbien," Boas wrote, "'The Indians who live close together here belong to the various language groups of the coast. And since they do not speak any English, they use a mixed language, the Chinook (Jargon), in which the conversation goes along easily.'" Boas found the Indians "reserved at first," but, in their impoverished situation, they welcomed payment and worked with him. "I began to ask about the language," he wrote. "In the beginning it is always hard work. But I soon found the pronouns and a few verbs. That is usually sufficient to break the ice." Boas's "old friend from Berlin, Itlkakuani," was still in Victoria. "So I went to his tent," Boas continued, "and began talking at once; I showed him my drawings from various museums, and it was soon apparent that they will be very useful." In Victoria, "the kindest man I have ever met" took Boas in his wagon to talk with an Indian woman who was married to a white man. Boas gained her help "because of the manner of my introduction," through the assistance of this gentle and "highly respected" man. "I asked only one question," Boas related, "and the entire myth of the origin of the world descended upon me." Of his collection of tales, Boas wrote, "This mass of stories is gradually beginning to bear fruit because I can now discover certain traits characteristic of different groups of people. I think I am on the right track in considering mythology a useful tool for differentiating and judging the relationship of tribes."[4]

In Victoria Boas left behind items he wouldn't need, boarded the Barbara Boskowitz on October 5, 1886, and sailed to Nawiti with "a colorful group" of Indians. Passing between towering mountains along the narrow waterway where pine forests reached down to the sea, the steamship docked at the small Indian village with seven houses. "The steamer whistle blew," Boas wrote, "and before long we saw forms who, wrapped in brightly colored blankets, had been sitting idly in front of their houses jump up and run to the boats. Two boats were quickly launched and the men, wrapped in woolen blankets, rowed toward the steamer. The boats were loaded and we rowed to shore, while the steamer continued on her way." As they came to shore, Boas overheard the Indians talking about him: "Since I looked relatively respectable they took me for a missionary. But I explained to them that I was no priest."[5]

The day after his arrival, Boas attended "a great potlatch festival in the neighboring house." The people received him in friendly fashion:

In the center of the room was a huge fire; on it stood a large kettle in which fish oil and halibut were being cooked. . . . The men and a few women sat on the platform, which encircled the room. A man sat on the left holding a large drum on which the sun, the crest of the host, was painted. . . . The Indians were all crouching with their backs against the plank. . . . They were packed closely together and sang to the beat of the drum. . . . The host stood alone in the middle and clapped his hands and sang.

While the host was singing, tending the fire, and minding the food, the chief stood and delivered "a long speech with raised voice and animated gesticulation." The chief praised the host, who had given away two hundred dollars worth of goods at the potlatch. Soon Boas became aware that he had become "the subject of their speeches." A young man who spoke English interpreted for Boas. Confused about the purpose of Boas's visit, the people were worried that Boas "might be a government agent come to put a stop to the festival." Previously an agent had told them that "he would send a gunboat if they did not obey" his orders and give up their festivals. Boas realized that he had to explain his presence: "So I arose and said: 'My country is far from yours; much further even than that of the Queen.'" He didn't care about the Indian agents, nor did he want to interfere with their festivals. He continued, "My people live far away and would like to know what people in distant lands do, and so I set out." Boas's speech was received well, for, he related, "all the chiefs have been coming to see me to tell me that the 'hearts' of all their people were glad when they heard my speech."[6]

After sketching totem poles and dwellings, collecting tales, purchasing masks, and hosting a feast for the village, Boas departed Nawiti for Alert Bay with others by boat on October 17. Through intermittent stormy weather and frothy seas, the group was forced ashore one and one-half miles from Fort Rupert, where his traveling companions chose to stay. Boas traveled on with an Indian guide, who paddled the canoe and managed the sail. "More quickly than was to be expected," Boas wrote, "the wind rose to storm's height. All my life long . . . I shall remember this canoe trip. First we had to pass through heavy seas, after which we reached calm waters under the protection of land."[7]

At Alert Bay the people on shore saw the boat approaching and jumped into the water to pull them to dry land. Boas recounted, "My Indian friend and I laughed about our trip, and he said to me: . . . 'You were just like a deer, so quickly you jumped on shore!'" Boas lost no time getting to work. The afternoon of his arrival, he sketched houses and totem poles, and in the evening began collecting stories "like mad." At the end of the day, as he recounted, "I slept like a log." Over the next several days, Boas collected Kwakiutl family histories, learned about the cannibal figure in their mythology, purchased "a rattle belonging to a long story," acquired more masks, began work on the distribution of the Indian groups, and wrote until, as he said, his fingers were lame.[8]

On October 26 Boas returned to Victoria to continue work with the Bella Coola. He wrote Marie, "I now know the Bella Coola language quite well and understand it." With the help of a "dear Catholic priest," Boas worked with a Tlingit woman and then spent time in his hotel room transcribing his growing collection of tales—by October 31 he had a total of 119 tales. In preparation for his trip to the village of Cowichan, Boas borrowed a camera from a photographer: "I hope the pictures will be better than the ones I took when I was among the Eskimo." Likely the photographer was Oregon Columbus Hastings, who owned a studio in Victoria and who, in subsequent years, would work with Boas on photo documentation of northwest coast Indian groups. Departing from Victoria Station on the evening of November 3 Boas observed, "The railway journey, which took about two hours, is almost more beautiful than anything I have seen yet. The train passed through wonderful forests, along steep mountain slopes, over deep black canyons, and through lonely mountain scenery." Arriving in Duncan at ten thirty in the evening, Boas found "no station house or anything resembling one." Two men showed up to retrieve the mailbag, loaded Boas and his six pieces of luggage along with the mail into the wagon, and headed for Cowichan.[9]

The residents of Cowichan were suspicious of Boas and of his interest in photographing their totem poles and homes. With a commanding manner, he refused to pay for taking pictures: "This morning I had quite a scene in the upper village. I had my camera with me and photographed a handsome totem pole in front of a house. Shortly afterward the owner, a young man, appeared and demanded that I pay him, which naturally

I refused to do, so that I should not deprive myself of the possibility of photographing whatever I might wish." As Boas continued through the village, the young man offered to serve as his interpreter. "The whites look upon the Indians not as humans but as dogs," Boas wrote, "and he did not wish anyone to laugh at things that were their laws, such as painted houses and articles used for celebrating their festivals." Imperious in his manner, Boas showed no compunction in taking "two especially well-preserved skulls" from the old cemetery on the hill. He did the same in Comox, where he traveled next.[10]

Arriving in Comox on November 11, Boas found himself in "the saddest-looking village of any I have seen so far." He concluded, "It is apparent that the inhabitants are dying out rapidly. There are ruins everywhere, and beautifully carved totem poles stand in front of empty shells." Trying to puzzle out the complexity of the languages, Boas found that the Lekwiltok, who lived in the first village, spoke "the same language as the inhabitants of Alert Bay." Boas located the Comox, who kept themselves apart, in "the last houses of the settlement," besieged and enslaved, as they had been in the past by the Lekwiltok. Of the Pentlatch, he wrote, "There is only one family of these left, the last of the tribe." Boas added, "I immediately made friends with them and am now learning this newly discovered language." After five days he noted, "I now have about four hundred words in both the Comox and [Pentlatch] languages. I still have no texts but hope to get some soon. It is always quite difficult to get started in a language, but I shall be very happy if I can get one thousand words and a few texts in both." Of his work with the Comox and the Pentlatch, Boas remarked to Marie, "I then will have covered all tribes of the seashore between Vancouver Island and the continent." On his last Saturday in Comox, at the sound of the whistle announcing the arrival of the Barbara Boskowitz, Boas made his way to the pier: "Since I had a number of acquaintances on board, I wandered down to the boat. To my very great surprise, I met Jacobsen, the Bella Coola man from Berlin, who is on his way home. We were both delighted to meet and spent several hours in conversation. I was very glad to speak German again. It is nice to meet unexpectedly an old acquaintance in another corner of the world. Above all it is refreshing to meet someone who is glad to see you." They spoke about Berlin and about Jacobsen's time in British

Columbia, where he lived, as Boas related, "all alone among the Bella Coola and has started a fishery and animal breeding station."[11]

On December 2, Boas traveled by steamer to the copper-mining town of Nanaimo, where he continued work on languages. Finally, he returned to Victoria by train on December 10, and began preparations for his trip back to New York. From his initial days in Victoria, Boas felt certain that he was uncovering important information: "I am now convinced that this trip will have the results I desire. Today I have made many notes about masks and such things. A few spirits have wandered into my diaries." However, he was struck repeatedly by a concern that would torment him throughout his decades of work on the Northwest Coast. He wrote Marie, "I don't feel too happy because I know that my work here will remain unfinished since I have so little time." In his letter-diary to his parents, Boas reflected that the "geographical part of my work has been about the most difficult. The names of the tribes were unknown, and, after I had found seventy tribes with the greatest difficulty, I had to arrange them according to language and dialect and determine their locations." Toward the end of his time in British Columbia, Boas reflected positively, "Looking back on the whole trip I may say that I am satisfied. The ethnographic conditions of this province are now completely clear while before not much was known about them." In his last letter to his parents from Victoria, Boas related that he was winding up his work, writing a few last letters, packing his ethnographic collection and his baggage. "It is a strange feeling," he wrote, "to have again completed this type of work. Now for a year or longer I shall have to live on the memory of this quarter of a year."[12]

Still uncertain as to whether he would be returning to Berlin, Boas told Marie, "In view of Germany, I have emphasized the geographical questions more than I needed to otherwise, and soon I shall publish a paper which my Herren Kollegen (colleagues) will like." In addition to keeping "geographical questions" in the forefront, Boas had also taken the practical steps of sending off the schedule of his lectures for the next summer by steamer from Comox on November 18: "I shall announce the lecture as Ethnography of Northwestern America."[13]

In a last letter to Marie before his return, Boas wrote that he would return to New York on December 27. He continued, "I am feeling awfully funny. The big job is finished and if I have forgotten something or done something wrong, it cannot be corrected any more. All in all, I can look back to these past months with great satisfaction, but I am glad that they are over." He added, "Marie, I don't want to think about having to go back to Germany!" Boas admitted that, in some moments of quiet reflection, he imagined a future in Germany. "To be frank with you," he wrote, "it would only mean satisfaction of a petty vanity. I don't want to deny that I sometimes thought how nice it would be if my colleagues over there would recognize my achievements, which would be better than those of many of them." These thoughts were "fortunately" fleeting. He reflected, "I prefer to picture myself working here to bring scattered efforts into focus scientifically and above all, in my small way, thus to work for the German idealism, which I possess and which is my driving force." With determination, he said, "Darling, I don't want to give up all hope until everything is over. I believe it is the better part of my soul, which wants me to do this work. I remember as if it were yesterday that I said once that it was not an urge for adventure which drove me to the Eskimos but the urge to gain so much recognition that I would be able in due time to contribute to the world, *my way*." He would achieve this goal, Boas asserted, "however hard it may go."[14]

Delighted to be back in New York and ecstatic at seeing Marie, Boas set to work in his room at Jacobi's house, with frequent visits to libraries for research. By the end of the first seven days, he had sent "a paper with a large map to *Petermanns* [*Mitteilungen*] on which I have been working the whole week."[15] He was focusing next on an article for *Science*, "which must be finished this week." As he had told Marie in August 1886, "I am writing a paper on 'The Study of Geography,' at which I have been laboring for 1 ½ years." Completing it in the next two days, Boas delivered it personally on Friday, January 7, to the office of *Science*, into the hands of the editor, N. D. C. Hodges. Keen to gain a correspondent in Berlin, Hodges invited Boas to dinner to discuss a proposition. This was the break for which Boas had been waiting for so many years. He wrote Marie, "Dear Love! The dinner last night had an unexpected result. Mr. Hodges, editor of *Science*, wished to engage me as Berlin Correspondent. I said I could not accept without further thought as I am attempting to remain here. He then asked whether I knew how to draw maps and I told him of my work. He then asked me whether I would consider taking over the geographical part of *Science* and how much pay I would want." Boas told him that he was unable to gauge the expenses in New York and thus could not immediately tell him the salary he would need. Hodges told Boas that he needed an "assistant editor and *Science* wanted to stress geography and finally asked me to present a plan for geographical papers." Boas concluded, "Oh, Marie, will we succeed at last? Just think of it, my love. That would be in large measure what I had hoped for . . . here."[16]

Boas left on his trip to the University of Pennsylvania, where he met Professor of Linguistics and Archaeology Daniel Garrison Brinton, who had invited Boas to dine with him. To his parents he wrote, "I should be very happy to get the position on *Science* because it would be the beginning of a geographical journal, which is absolutely necessary here." He then went on to Washington and wrote Marie that he was investigating "the possibilities of printing maps and the prices at the Bureau of Ethnology and Hydrographic Office." He was also checking into the financial viability of *Science*. The next two weeks were a whirlwind of activity. Hodges and Boas drafted a contract for this newly created position of assistant editor of *Science*. The formal contract, signed on February 1, 1887, stipulated that Boas was to prepare and supervise "the printing of maps in such manner as shall be a credit to the journals" and to provide "abstracts, translation, reviews of the journals and books in your departments and by your own writings, furnish for publication with such an accord as we shall from time to time deem desirable." Boas would be paid $150 per month, and the agreement would extend for two years, after which "either party [was] to give the other six months' notice of his unwillingness to continue it after February 1, 1889."[17]

Boas wrote his parents, "Is it not strange that through a stroke of luck, I found the work I have wanted?" With enthusiasm he continued, "My position will give me an opportunity to arouse interest for my subject and to work for a study of it. If I have the ability, I can become the American Petermann." He went on, "My task will be to use my section to interest Americans in Geography and further to make the journal as useful as possible for Europe, by printing new maps of America." Indeed, he received many congratulatory notes. Albert Gatschet, a linguist at the BAE, wrote, "I am very happy to hear that you have gained a firm position at *Science*."

Robert Bell, assistant director of the Geological Survey of Canada, who had attempted unsuccessfully in 1886 to assist Boas in finding support for his ethnographic work in the North, wrote, "I am glad to hear you are to remain in America and to occupy such a useful post as assistant editor of *Science.*" George Mercer Dawson of the Geological Survey of Canada, who had also been very helpful to Boas, sent his congratulations when he saw the announcement in *Science.*[18]

Boas sent his formal request for emigration and urged his parents in a letter three days later that they not delay in helping with his emigration papers. The danger of war in Germany under Bismarck was great, and Boas could conceivably be called back for the draft. He wrote, "I am trying to get rid of my collection so that I can at least pay my travel expenses and have a little over. I am not thinking of getting married before I have repaid uncle [Jacobi] my travel expenses." The night before, there had been "a big party," where Boas's collection was exhibited. One of the founders of the American Museum of Natural History, Albert S. Bickmore, was present, along with "the family Schurz [and] the family Putnam." Boas continued, "I lectured for about two hours and I think the people were interested." He added, "I was very proud of the compliment paid me by Schurz that I had learned a great deal of English but I am in no way satisfied with myself."[19]

In another letter Boas wrote his parents, "I can scarcely believe that this continual struggle shall have come to an end and above all if you agree to my request that we shall be able to marry very soon." He and Marie wanted to plan their wedding for the middle of March. Marie's mother also wrote to Franz's mother, "'Franz loves Marie so much, and she belongs to him with all of her heart that it would have been a serious blow to them if they'd have to separate again and suffer through an uncertain, bitter period of separation!'" While she had viewed the early engagement as "'a bit hasty,'" all was "'secure and now both of them shall be rewarded with each other for the sacrifices made.'" She continued with a description of the flurry of activities in preparation for the marriage: "'Last week, we were running about almost constantly to find an apartment and to buy Marie's trousseau.'" Finding a suitable place for them to live was a challenge "'since housing is the major expense.'"[20]

Boas's sister Toni was not, however, in a celebratory mood about Franz's having accepted "an inferior position in an inferior country."

Douglas Cole notes, "Toni had been the single sour note at the wedding." She had remained with relatives in New York while Boas traveled to the Northwest Coast, and she had not had an easy time during her stay. While the trip had been intended as a vacation to help pull her "from her dejection," it was instead a time of sadness for her. She was in New York when Aunt Phips died in January and for the marriage of her only brother in March. Toni "disliked America, both for what it was and for stealing her brother and his talents." While Boas worried that her dyspeptic view would influence his parents' opinion, his own enthusiasm was not dampened.[21]

On March 10, 1887, Franz and Marie were married in a simple ceremony conducted by a judge at the New York apartment of Marie's mother. Boas immediately sent a telegram to his family in Minden: "Greetings from myself and wife." Uncle Jacobi toasted the newlyweds at the reception for family and friends held immediately following the ceremony. For the next two days, Boas and Marie spent their honeymoon at the Krackowizer family home on the Hudson River, in the community of Sing Sing. On their return to New York City, Boas and Marie took up residence in a third-floor walk-up: a two-bedroom apartment on 196 Third Avenue, with a rent of $35 a month. Jacobi and Uncle Kobus had given them a $700 wedding gift to purchase furniture; and Boas's father and Uncle Mons had given them $1,000, which went directly into the bank.[22]

Years later, in 1919, Boas wrote his eldest child Helene of these early years of marriage and of the economic challenges. Helene had communicated to her mother that she "ought not to have children until heaven knows when." Boas queried, "Are not the duties to children, whom we love, the strongest incentives for us to use all our powers for their good?" He continued,

> I do not like always to speak of our youth, but I have to, to explain to you how we lived. We married on the strength of two-year contract, with the yearly income of $1,800. I was in a foreign land without any assurance of finding a permanent position. When you were born [in 1888], I knew that my contract would expire in half a year and I would have to arrange my life in an entirely new fashion. When Ernst was born [in 1891] I had a regular income of $1500; when

West to the Indians

Hete was born [in 1893] I only had a temporary job at the World's Fair. When Trudel was born [in 1897] I had a yearly contract with Columbia. If I had not felt my duty towards you all and Mama, I might have sometimes become discouraged. Without the courage to conquer, no one can make his way. I wish you had spoken to me about this so that we could have talked and I could have made my views clearer in talking to you than in writing.[23]

By November 1887 the new letterhead for *Science* declaimed in capital letters, "Map-Making in All Its Branches, Under the Supervision of Our Geographical Editor." Boas worked energetically to connect *Science* with scholars in Germany and in Canada and to strengthen the ties with those in the United States. Fischer wrote, "I can certainly understand that you are pleased to have now found a permanent position, a sphere that suits you and that you are now in the position to take the second step, ... to be married. Who knows if you will not come back to the Fatherland sooner than you think and then I can meet your wife." Fischer wrote that he would be glad to submit articles: "If I understand you correctly, you would support contributions by German geographers?" He said that he would "gladly provide occasional posts" and that he would tell others at the next meeting of geographers when he would have "the opportunity to speak with experts about your business." Hermann Wagner from Göttingen reflected, "I had no idea that you wanted to permanently settle in America," but he guessed at the reasons since prospects for employment were dismal in Germany. He continued, "In your position as ... co-editor of Science, you have ample means at hand to fulfill the promise which you gave me on departure, which concerns the takeover of our Geographical Yearbook." Thus, Boas became editor of the North American section of the *Geographisches Jahrbuch*. Even Kiepert, his erstwhile nemesis at the Friedrich-Wilhelms-Universität of Berlin, wrote in his capacity as editor of *Globus* that he would encourage the publisher to establish an exchange with *Science*.[24]

Working five and a half days a week at the office of *Science*, Boas was also trying to reorganize the American Ethnological Society (AES), founded by Albert Gallatin and John Russell Bartlett in 1842. In its initial years the AES served as the "center of anthropological interest in

New York City" but had rapidly deteriorated following Gallatin's death in 1849. Writing under the title of Geographical Editor of *Science*, Boas contacted many people, some of whom had been associated with the remnants of the original American Ethnological Society. Alexander Cotheal, who was president of the American Ethnological Society, responded, "I should rejoice to see the Ethnological Society restored to activity and at the next meeting will bring your communication to its notice." Boas was initially unsuccessful in reviving a nearly moribund society whose members were still trying to put flesh on its bones, but he continued in his efforts through the next two decades, when he became editor of the new publication series of the AES in 1906. Boas was, as Marian Smith noted, "the moving force behind the society's rejuvenation."[25]

Boas became widely known through his position at *Science* and his attempt to revive the American Ethnological Society. He was invited to participate in the founding of the American Folklore Society and the launching of the *Journal of American Folklore*. In December 1887 William Wells Newell, the central force in the organizational effort, wrote Boas, "Your name does not appear on the list of membership of the proposed Folklore Society. I wish the Society might have the benefit of your support and advice, and take the liberty of enclosing a circular." Boas was not in attendance at the January 4, 1888, meeting in Cambridge, where the American Folklore Society was founded, but Newell informed him by letter that he had been appointed to "a Committee to arrange for a Journal." Newell observed, "I suppose that our plans are understood, and that the Committee will be the Editors." Newell served as editor of the *Journal of American Folklore*, and Francis James Child (of Harvard), Thomas Frederick Crane (of Cornell), and Boas served as assistant editors. Proud of this appointment, Boas wrote his parents that the next day the American Folklore Society was to be founded in Cambridge: "I shall have the honor to be proposed as an editor."[26]

In December 1887 Horatio Hale wrote Boas to ask if he could "undertake a piece of scientific work on behalf of the British Committee for the Advancement of Science." Hale continued, "At the Montreal meeting of this association, four years ago, a Committee of the Section of Anthropology was appointed to collect information concerning the aboriginal tribes of Canada, and a small appropriation was made to defray the expenses of the work." While E. B. Tylor in England was titular chair of the committee until its dissolution in 1898, the Canadian members of the committee carried out the majority of the work. As secretary and research director, Hale worked closely with the chair, Sir Daniel Wilson, president of Toronto University; Robert Bell, assistant director of the Geological Survey of Canada; and with the director of the Geological Survey, Dr. George Mercer Dawson.[27]

In his letter to Boas, Hale stipulated that the committee was interested in "a full report respecting the tribes of British Columbia." With "the large amount of information" that Boas had already amassed, Hale surmised, "two or three months might be sufficient for this work." Hale expected Boas to provide "an account of each of the eleven or twelve linguistic stocks in that region." He anticipated that Boas would compile the following: "an outline of the grammar with a . . . vocabulary—and a description of the physical traits, character, traditions social and tribal organization, customs and arts of the people of each stock—and of course an ethnographic map." The members of the committee expected Boas to compile a report for the British Association for the Advancement of Science (BAAS) meeting to be held the following August, though Boas was free to defer the full report for a year and submit only a précis.[28]

Undaunted by Hale's ambitious plans for two to three months of intensive survey work, Boas replied, "I feel honored by the confidence you place in my knowledge of the ethnology of British Columbia, and thank you for suggesting my name for carrying out the work requested by the British Association for the Advancement of Science." He would "be delighted to take up the work," but he first needed to speak with his employer to ascertain "whether I can get away from here for so long a time." By the end of February Boas wrote Hale of his acceptance. "I have asked Mr. Hodges whether he can let me go for two months," Boas related, "and I am glad to say that he has no objection." He would leave for British Columbia on May 25, 1888. To his parents he wrote, "I am really looking forward to get into the 'field' again for a short time."[29]

In the early months of 1888, Boas was working intensely with Newell on the creation of the first volume of the *Journal of American Folklore* and negotiating with Hale for the field trip to the Northwest Coast. Growing dissatisfied with his position at *Science*, he wrote several drafts of a letter to the publisher, Charles Scribner's Sons. He began one draft with startling candor: "Gentlemen, I intend to discontinue my connection with *Science*.... My reason for doing so is this. When I became connected with 'Science' it was understood that we were to develop a map department, but I find that Mr. Hodges, the publisher of 'Science,' cannot carry out my plans, and therefore I look about for a more satisfactory occupation." In another iteration of this letter, Boas removed the reference to *Science* and to his disappointment with Mr. Hodges and instead pitched his idea for developing a journal about travel and exploration, "similar to the French *Le Tour du Monde* and the German, *Globus*." He requested "a personal interview" in order to explain his plans more fully.[30]

In receipt of Scribner's February 3 polite rejection letter, Boas nonetheless persisted. He detailed the practical nature of his plan so that they might "revise" their decision. Boas envisioned providing illustrations and maps for the journal that could then be used in Scribner's other publications. He pointed to the revenue that Charles Scribner's could garner from the advertisements placed in his "journal of travels"—for "sporting goods, outfits for parties, surveying and drawing instruments, watches, saddles, ... photographic outfits, books of travel, provisions, certain classes of dry goods, medicine, etc." Scribner's turned Boas down again, politely but firmly.[31]

Marie was pregnant with their first child. Boas felt great pressure to find purchase for his plans to develop mapmaking and geography in the United States, broadly conceived, including a commercial venue, and to do it profitably. It was for naught: Scribner's had rejected him, and Mr. Hodges of *Science* would not or could not accommodate Boas's plans. Nonetheless, no matter how frustrated Boas was, his position as geographical editor at *Science* was important as a mark of his professional status to those in Canada who were sponsoring his fieldtrip to the Northwest coast. Robert Bell wrote Boas, "I was glad to hear you are to have an opportunity of making ethnological investigations so congenial to your tastes and at the same time to enjoy a holiday. I presume you will retain your connection with *Science*."[32]

Boas dug into his work at *Science* so he would be prepared in advance for his time away during the summer months in British Columbia. He was also working on some of the languages of Vancouver Island, with Marie

West to the Indians

helping him by arranging words written on slips of paper in alphabetical order. He wrote his parents that he had been focusing "during the last weeks . . . only on Indian language," because he needed "to know about it for his next field trip."[33] While he didn't identify the "Indian language" in his letter to his parents, Boas was gathering vocabulary on the Salish, Kootenay, and Kwakiutl. Henry W. Henshaw of the BAE had sent him Salish names—"nothing more than geographical terms attached to bands or isolated settlements." Dawson wrote about the connection between Kwakiutl and Salish and sent the map he had created with native geographical designations on it. "The Indians," he wrote, "became quite interested in giving me all names they knew as we went along shores in canoe."[34]

With trepidation about leaving Marie, who was six months pregnant, Boas departed from New York, bound for Ottawa, on May 25, 1888. He visited with Robert Bell and then boarded the Canadian Pacific Railroad with a pass from the BAAS for travel to Vancouver. Boas wrote to his parents of his frustration, "At the last moment I had to change my plans completely," in order to make "a survey of all tribes." He disdained this approach, because "it must of necessity be very superficial." Boas had intended to focus on the Kootenay and to meet the objectives of the BAAS by obtaining "information regarding the distribution of the tribes" with a visit to "the Salish people of the interior." At the end of April Hale had reiterated the committee's interest in "a general outline or 'synopsis' of the ethnology of the whole Province." In May Hale was even more emphatic about what he did not want to receive from Boas—that being "a minute account of two or three tribes or languages." Hale continued, "We wish to have from you *a general synopsis of the ethnology of the whole of British Columbia, according to the linguistic stocks.* We do not expect you to visit every part of the Province; but we think that with what you have already seen of it, and what you can learn from the natives and white residents and from books, you should be able to give an ethnological description of the whole region, from north to south, *without omitting any stock.*" He also wanted "fuller" information on the "physical traits of the natives." In addition to recording anthropometric measurements by following "Virchow's scientific formula," Hale advised, "it would be well to describe the complexion, features, and general appearance of the natives of the various tribes in ordinary language, noting their difference if any, which of the 'European natives' . . . do they resemble, and in what aspect?" The committee was not "expecting too much," Hale opined, "in asking for a general report from you in the ethnology of the whole Province."[35]

Hale had set the rules of engagement in his first letter to Boas on December 30, 1887, where he stipulated the interest of the committee in "a full report respecting the tribes of British Columbia." In his eagerness for both employment and a return to the Northwest Coast, Boas had accepted these terms. Still, he had clearly shaped the objectives according to his own expectations, grounded in his experiences from his previous work in the region. Hale was stubborn; Boas was also stubborn, or, as he said of himself, of "persistent will." Their clashes emitted sparks of anger and frustration in equal measure during the 1888 and 1889 fieldwork. The conflict started with the initial agreement for the time to be spent in the field. While Boas had arranged to take a two-month leave from *Science*, Hale complained that his proposal had been for "two or three months' work, not including the time in transit." The conflict continued to more substantive matters. After detailing the approach that Boas was to follow, Hale added, "You must not think me over-particular in these suggestions. They are the result of considerable experience; and I think I have a pretty good idea of what the Committee will desire." The latter point was the trump card: Hale was the research director for the committee of the BAAS. He was the piper calling the tune; Boas had no choice but to follow his directions, complain as he might in his letters home.[36]

The tension reached its peak in the 1889 fieldwork. Boas told his parents about Hale's "lack of consistency." He wrote, "I am afraid the results of this trip will be pretty pathetic because I have to follow such senseless instructions." In scarcely controlled anger Hale wrote Boas in the midst of the 1889 field season, "I cannot understand why you should persist in causing me an immense amount of useless trouble, as well as much annoyance, by objecting to my instructions which you are expressly engaged to carry out. Kindly go on, hereafter, with your usual energy and ability, in the course which, after much experience and careful consideration, I have marked out for you."[37]

Hale did loosen his grip on the reins, but only after Boas had secured his standing. After the first two summers in the Northwest Coast, Boas had firmly established his fieldwork reputation in British Columbia, been employed by Clark University beginning in November 1889, impressed E. B. Tylor with his work, and gained financial support from the BAE. In a striking change of tone, Hale wrote Boas in May 1890, "I will not hamper you with specific instructions. You will consider yourself entirely at liberty to act on your own judgment." Jacob Gruber writes of the conflict between Hale and Boas, "In these exchanges, of course, one must remember that [Hale] was a man of seventy-two, with some fair distinction in the field, addressing a Boas of thirty whose work had not yet found him a position in the establishment." Hale likely regretted that, but for his age and the state of his health, he would have taken up the research in British Columbia. This would have been a continuation of the work he had done in the territory of Oregon, where he had mapped "the ethnic and linguistic diversity of the native peoples on the west coast from California to British Columbia" in 1842. In sum, Boas-the-Younger was able to engage in the research that Hale-the-Elder wanted to do. In frustration, Hale aspired to control and to direct Boas, and to claim at least part of the results of Boas's work. "The comprehensive character of Dr. Boas's report," Hale wrote to Dawson, "was due to my suggestion." He continued, "I recommended that his *first* report should be a general one, covering the whole Province, and illustrated by an ethnographic map. The understanding is that his future reports will be devoted to distinct and, as far as possible, exhaustive monographs on the several tribes, taking them in the usual convenient order. I am glad that this plan has your approval."[38]

Hale tried to exercise control and Boas reacted as he always did to external constraints that thwarted his wishes, with red-hot anger. Boas remarked on "another letter from Hale" that he had received toward the end of July 1889: "I pondered long after reading it, about what I should do." He decided to write letters to Hale, Dawson, and Tylor, and then thought better of it and tore up the letters, "because I thought it would not be the right thing to do to write them while I am here." Five days later, he again wrote to Marie, "You cannot imagine how angry I am with Hale's instructions. Apparently he is not familiar with the existing literature on the coastal tribes, otherwise he would not state that the tribes of the west coast are the least known." Boas continued, "The opposite is the fact. The outcome of this trip will be very meager, I am afraid, just because I have to follow useless instructions."[39]

During the first field trip funded by BAAS in 1888, Boas had made frequent reference to his hope "that Professor Hale will be satisfied with my work." With resignation, Boas added, "If not, I cannot help it." Clearly pleased about his study of the languages, Boas wrote Marie from Vancouver, "Up to now I am quite satisfied with my results. I . . . am studying the Tsimshian language frantically. Tomorrow morning, I hope to find a Kwakiutl and a Haida; and then I will be 'fixed' all right." Still in Vancouver the following week, Boas had worked with a "Tlingit lady" for three hours, "but then she began to mutter." He had hoped to begin work with "my Kwakiutl, George Hunt"; however, in his capacity as interpreter, Hunt had been called to "a court sitting." In this first mention of the man with whom Boas would work for over four decades, Boas expressed frustration: George Hunt had not shown up after the court closed, and Boas went in search of him. "After much trouble," Boas wrote, "I finally succeeded in getting Mr. Hunt for a morning and obtained all kinds of worthwhile information from him."[40]

From the place where he was staying in Port Essington, Boas wrote, "Tsimshian is about the only language spoken in this house. . . . I have never had a better opportunity to learn a language; I learned more yesterday than in a week elsewhere." Traveling back to Vancouver on board the Cariboo Fly, Boas found a Bella Bella "who is willing to tell me things, so that my days are not entirely wasted." In mid-July Boas went to Windemere on the Columbia River, where he "found a few Kootenay" and "engaged an interpreter." Succumbing to the stereotype of appearance and dress, Boas wrote in his letter-diary, "These are the first real Indians that I have seen: red skin, eagle noses, the famous blanket, moccasins, . . . and deer skin jacket, with hair hanging loose or braided."[41]

Boas went to the provincial prison, where, with the permission of the mayor of Victoria, he measured Indians. In addition, he brought "the Indians to the photographer," O. C. Hastings, to have portraits made of them "nude to the waist." Two weeks later, in Port Essington, Boas "discovered a photographer [Mr. Brooks] as I was wandering about in the evening. He had come from Victoria to photograph all the sawmills and salmon fisheries." Boas continued, "I got hold of him right away and had him photograph five beautifully tattooed Haidas," in both front and back views. The anthropometric work, the portrait photographs, and the measurement and classification of crania and skeletons were all part of what was then designated as anthropology, separate from ethnology, which comprised the study of languages, folklore, and customs. Of this focus on anthropometrics, Boas wrote his parents that he was "with all my heart at my work, which turns out to be very successful." From his last week's work, he added, "the anthropological results were the best so far."[42]

In Victoria, Hastings, the photographer who had photographed the prisoners, took Boas by boat to an island in the harbor just outside of the city, "where there are Indian skulls." Other grave robbers had beaten them to it: "We discovered that someone had stolen all the skulls, but we found a complete skeleton without [a] head. I hope to get another one either today or tomorrow." Boas continued, "It is most unpleasant work to steal bones from a grave, but what is the use, someone has to do it." Boas "locked the skeleton into" his trunk until he could "pack it away." The grave robbing haunted him: "I dreamed of skulls and bones all last night. I dislike very much working with this stuff; i.e., collecting it, not having it. I shall of course defer all measurements on dead material until sometime later. I am as well known here in Victoria as a mongrel dog." While he had intended to wait on measuring "the dead material," Boas couldn't resist removing the skulls—"which I had stolen"—from his trunk and measuring them.[43]

In Cowichan, Boas had made contact with William Sutton and his younger brother James, both of whom robbed graves and sold the ill-begotten skulls and skeletons to the ready market of North American scientists. Knowing that Boas was a potential customer, William Sutton made his collection available. Boas wrote, "I . . . measured frantically all day long—about seventy-five skulls. . . . I hope I shall receive an affirmative answer from Washington so that I can buy it." On his return to Victoria from a two-week stay in Port Essington, Boas took advantage of the stop in Comox to walk across a muddy expanse, exposed in the low tide, to a small village. He had persuaded the photographer, Brooks, to accompany him so that he could "photograph the village while I tried to get a skull." Boas continued, "I wanted him to do this in order to distract their attention. . . . Of course I did not tell the photographer (a stuttering idiot) what I wanted until we were there. I took a skull and the entire lower portion of the man."[44]

Boas had written to the BAE to see if "they would consider buying skulls this winter for $600; if they will, I shall collect assiduously." Otherwise, Boas wrote, he "would not do it." From her vantage point at Alma Farm, Marie "worried that all the skulls Franz has collected will be lying about in their home until Franz has had time to measure them." With a positive response from the BAE, Boas purchased the entire collection of crania and skeletons from the Suttons. In preparation for his departure home, Boas packed the crania, skeletons, and ethnographic collections in twelve large boxes, registered them with customs, and sent them to the AMNH for storage until he could determine the disposition. With what he had collected himself and had purchased from the Suttons, Boas had in total "85 crania and 14 complete skeletons."[45]

Before his departure from Vancouver, Boas had arranged to have William Sutton organize further looting of skeletons. Sutton wrote Boas about the dangers and travails that his two brothers and another party had faced "in procuring native remains." Sutton noted that there were very few remains in the places that Boas had identified. They had to pay "some of the Indians . . . a dollar apiece" to lead them to the burials in "caves and such out of the way places." Sutton continued, "Some half-breeds at Fort Rupert started quite a disturbance and tried to incite the Indians to shoot them. Mr. Spencer of Alert Bay [brother-in-law of George Hunt] laid complaint before [the] Superintendent of Provincial Police, and I have had quite a lively time to prevent an investigation." In total his two brothers and the other party had "managed to get together (49) skeletons including crania (excepting one), and seventy-four crania including a number of pelvis bones; making in all one hundred and twenty-three individuals." He assured Boas of the care taken in packaging: "Every skeleton is in a box by itself, having made boxes especially for them." Sutton continued, "We have been at a great deal more trouble and expense than I anticipated, but the collection is no doubt well worth the trouble as there are some most extraordinary heads. I would like to get them off my hands as soon as possible as I am afraid of the authorities confiscating them, there has been such a disturbance over them, they may be compelled to take action." For the "forty-nine skeletons with heads," he asked twenty dollars apiece, for a total of "$980 and seventy heads including some pelvic bones @ $5 would amount to $370 making in all $1350." Sutton wrote that Boas would have "a complete collection from one end of the island to the other." Eager to be free of these stolen remains, Sutton asked Boas to let him know if he "can arrange to take them right away."[46]

Indeed, Sutton had reason to be concerned. In January 1889 he wrote, "The Indians of Cowichan lately discovered that some of their graves have been molested and have been raising quite a rumpus. Information was laid and a search warrant obtained to search the mill premises for the bodies, but nothing was found." Incensed by the desecration of their burial sites, the Indians hired a lawyer to represent them: "Action has been taken against my brothers, and I expect to have a good deal of trouble, as the Indians have employed a lawyer to work up the case." Sutton did ship the collection of crania and skeletons at his own expense to Boas and awaited payment, which he received in installments over the next twenty-two months. While expecting to interest the BAE or the AMNH in the collection, Boas did not sell the crania and skeletons until 1894, when the Chicago's Columbian Museum—later known as the Field Museum of Natural History—purchased them for $2,800. Boas's "collection of crania," as it was designated, was of minimal use, due to missing labels and uncertain provenance. George Dorsey, who had moved from his position at Harvard, where he had taught anthropology, to the Field Museum in 1896, wrote Boas, "Your collections of skulls and skeletons in their present condition, while perhaps 'useful' are not valuable as ethnic specimens. Several skulls have no labels and no 'locality' is assigned. The bones are *not* numbered." Dorsey appealed to Boas for "anything and everything which will make perfect the data of your collection—with such data it is a most valuable collection of rare skulls and skeletons; without, a collection of bones."[47]

Boas returned from his 1888 fieldwork in the Northwest Coast to Alma Farm on August 1. Happily, he was received by Marie, who was eight months pregnant. Less happily, he received a termination letter from *Science*. In six months he would have no job. Hodges wrote, "You chance to come back on the very day that our contract comes for a written notice if either wishes it discontinued on the 1st of February." To limit the expenses of *Science*, Hodges was compelled to let Boas go. "You will understand," Hodges continued, "that I take this course with no account of any dissatisfaction [with] you, for my respect for your labors constantly" has grown.[48] Continuing with his work at *Science* for the next six months, Boas grew increasingly disillusioned. In November he wrote that it was "deteriorating from week to week." By December, Boas remarked in a letter to his parents, "*Science* has become almost exclusively a trade journal." He would be very happy "to sever connections with it," but with no other source of income and with Marie and three-month-old Helene to support, he could not do so.[49]

Boas bent his efforts toward trying to find employment. He wrote Powell about his British Columbia fieldwork, "The material I collected among the Tsimshian is very good, as I happened to meet a good interpreter, a woman who knew English perfectly." He continued, "Besides this I have now material of all Salish dialects of British Columbia and of the [Kootenay] inland." He added, "Besides linguistics I paid attention to the study of religion, sociology, etc., and collected 85 crania and 14 complete skeletons." In mid-August 1888 Boas traveled to Cleveland for the AAAS meetings, where he gave a paper. This was his first talk in English at a professional meeting since the disastrous lectures at Columbia College in 1885. Adept at networking, Boas "met many old acquaintances and made new ones from all over the country." In a chance encounter on the train to Cleveland, Boas met G. Stanley Hall, who had just a few months before assumed the presidency of the newly established Clark University in Worcester, Massachusetts. Intent on developing an American university on a German model, Hall took note of this young scientist with superb German educational credentials. One year later Hall would write Boas offering him a position at Clark University; Boas would receive this letter when he was again in the field in Northwest Coast British Columbia.[50]

While at the AAAS meetings, Boas wrote several drafts of a letter to Tylor, to propose a multiyear program of research and collection in the Northwest Coast. In one draft he wrote, "It happens that my present contract with *Science* ends next spring. I should gladly avail myself of this opportunity to devote my time more fully than I have done so far to ethnology and to carry on my researches on the Canadian tribes in a systematical way." Boas opined, "About 3 years would be sufficient to study the ethnology of B.C. in reasonable detail." In another draft of this same letter, Boas stressed, "You will undoubtedly be aware that the inquiry, if to be done at all, must be done at the earliest possible date, as what little there is left of native culture is disappearing rapidly." He proposed compiling a collection of "the arts and industries of the various tribes and the style peculiar to each," as well as continuing with "ethnological, linguistic and anthropological work." Boas concluded, "I think three months or so, for each [linguistic] stock would be sufficient to reach satisfactory results. The actual cost of collecting such material I estimate at from 700 to 900 dollars per annum." Tylor responded tentatively, yet positively, to Boas's proposal: "There is some prospect of the British Association Committee being able to go on with the exploration of British Columbia." Tylor said that Boas's letter would prove useful to him "in the negotiations at the British Association."[51] Boas succeeded in gaining funding for additional work in the Northwest Coast. Hale wrote, "From the renewal of the grant, and from what Mr. Bloxam and Dr. Tylor write, it is evident that your report has given good satisfaction." The committee, Hale conveyed, was "desirous of securing your services for another year (at least) and will do it so far as the means in their control will allow." Clearly Boas had gained the support of Tylor and of "others on the committee," who wanted him to continue "your researches in British Columbia until the ethnology of that region has been thoroughly studied."[52]

Boas spent the fall months of 1888 and the early months of 1889 piecing together work to support his family. As the time approached for his job to end at *Science*, he and Hodges reached an agreement for Boas to contribute "three columns of geographical and ethnological matter and notes on various subjects" each week, and a sketch map "every third week," for which he would receive a monthly salary of fifty dollars. Boas also successfully reached an agreement with Powell, for temporary employment at the BAE at a salary of one hundred and fifty dollars a month, to work "up my Indian material for him." Additionally, Boas was elected as secretary to the Deutscher Gesellig-Wissenschaftlicher Verein von New York at an annual salary of four hundred dollars.[53]

Boas also made plans to bring Marie and baby Helene home to his parents and sisters in May. Overcome with excitement, Boas's mother wrote, "Such a glorious surprise. Such rejoicing has not been in the family for years. You want to come here and we are to see you and your child!" Boas's mother planned for every detail of their visit with particular attention to her granddaughter. She wrote, "You will see that I shall be the most sensible and not spoil the child. I was always very strict with you children. But Toni, Hete and Anna will be quite foolish and try to outdo one another. And Papa—he of course will let her dance all the time." On May 2, 1889, Boas, Marie, and baby Helene, accompanied by Marie's younger sister, Alice, boarded the ss Rugia for their trip to Germany. Midway through their voyage a fire broke out in the after-hold and resulted in a terrifying night and an uncomfortable forty-eight hours on deck for the passengers. With all the excitement of the Atlantic transit, they arrived happily and safely at the Berlin apartment of Boas's parents.[54]

While Boas could stay only until the end of June, Marie, Helene, and Alice remained until August 1889. Leaving the baby in the care of her grandparents, Marie accompanied Boas to Hannover on June 24, where he traveled to England to visit with Tylor in Oxford. On the evening of Boas's departure, his mother wrote the two of them, "My dear children, I have just bathed your sweet baby and now she is asleep, having finished her bottle to the last drop. We have been following you on your journey all day long. You are probably eating your mid-day meal in Hannover now. We will see you again tomorrow night, Marie. I wish you a good journey, my dear boy, and hope all your plans will succeed." Boas arrived in New York just long enough to collect his mail and then was off for the Northwest Coast for fieldwork from July to September.[55]

Boas had gone "West to the Indians" for the first time in September 1886, with independent funding, full of hope for finding his place in America, and full of dread that he wouldn't find employment and would have to leave Marie for a return to Germany. In 1888, newly married, and in 1889, with Marie expecting their first child, he traveled back to the Northwest Coast with BAAS support. In all three field trips and in those to come, as with his time in Baffin Land in 1883–84, Boas suffered from being separated from his family. At the same time, he relished in the challenges of fieldwork. It was not at all, as some have maintained, that Boas did not like fieldwork. In June 1888 he wrote his parents from Victoria about how hard it was to be apart "from one's wife." He continued, "But I am with all my heart at my work, which turns out to be very successful."[56]

In 1889 he wrote Marie from Victoria, referencing his fieldtrip the previous year, "Do you know that [next week] will have been one year since

I came back? Darling, I am so tired of all this traveling and wish I could stay at home with you next year." He missed being with baby Helene, seeing her first tooth come through her sore gums, being together with Marie on their baby's first birthday. Using two terms of endearment for Helene, "Bublichen" and "little worm," Boas wrote Marie, "Darling, Friday I received your letter of July 16 with a lock of Bublichen's hair. Oh how happy I was! So the little worm says 'tik tok' and has two teeth! How she must have changed." Trying to visualize his daughter, he asked, "Darling, does Bubli still hold her arms back when she runs?" With the anxiety of a parent absent from his baby, he pondered, "I wonder if Bubli will remember me when I come back?" Over and over in his letters to Marie from the field, he counted the days until they would be reunited. From Alert Bay, he wrote, "After today there are still thirty-three days to go, just one-third of the period I shall have been gone. Sweet wife, if I only could be with you; I am sick and tired of traveling." Using the name they had chosen for a boy, he rejoiced at the news that Marie was pregnant with their second child, "I am so glad that you *finally* wrote about Ernst." To his sister, he reflected on his aspirations to be a good father. He hoped "to have time to devote to my children, and not be a stranger to them as is so often the case with fathers."[57]

From 1886 to 1889, while he struggled to find or to create a position that would support his work in geography—specifically in cartography—he was pulled inexorably toward ethnology and anthropology because there was funding to support his work. In a proposal to Hale in 1889 that was ultimately not funded, Boas suggested a means to combine his interest and training in cartography with his ethnographic work, particularly "in making characteristic maps of mountainous regions from reconnaissance work, as will necessarily form a great part of Geographical work in B.C." Boas proposed working May through September on both ethnologic work among "various tribes," and on geographic work. "This work can be successfully combined," Boas continued, "with geographic work and I should suggest to you to make a proposal to the Geological Survey to that effect, that 4 months in summer be devoted to geographic work."[58]

While Boas continued to hope that his "map business" would succeed, it did not. It was his "Indian material" that garnered attention. As if moving pieces on a chessboard, Boas was claiming a territory for himself. This was comprised of fieldwork in the Northwest Coast of British Columbia, a focus on the study of languages, of mythology and folktales, of art styles in architecture and crafts, and of meticulous anthropometric work. All this was to show how one group of Indians was connected to or distinct from another. Cartography would not be a central part of this undertaking, as he was beginning to realize: "I only wish my map business were also under way, so that I could drop *Science* altogether, but at present I cannot do this."[59]

Boas's mother asked him "whether the uncertainty of my financial prospects does not make me feel uncomfortable and whether I would not prefer a permanent position." Boas responded with resignation, "This cannot be helped." He continued,

> Two years that I have been here is a short time, and one cannot accomplish much in that time. But I have succeeded in being known and accepted as an expert in my field here, I have not lost contact with the scientific world in Germany, as a matter of fact I have strengthened it, and I have accomplished more than I could have accomplished over there. . . . But it is due only to my work on *Science* and in the West, that I became connected with the Folklore Journal, the [*Internationales Archiv für Ethnographie*] and presumably also with the Canadians.

Johannes Dietrich Eduard Schmeltz, conservator of the National Museum of Ethnology in Leiden, had invited Boas to serve as the North American editor for the *Internationales Archiv für Ethnographie*. The first volume was published in 1888 in Leiden, Leipzig, London, New York, and Paris. Boas's affiliation was listed in the table of contents as "American Folklore Publication Society." Under "Notes and Correspondence," Boas published a short entry on "The Game of Cat's Cradle," as played by the Eskimo of Baffin Land, who "pass many an hour" twisting a looped thong of sealskin about six feet long into a multitude of shapes.[60]

In place of the security of a government position, Boas was prepared to take "the risk." He desired to change his contract with *Science* in order to give himself more time for his scientific endeavors. He wanted to work with Powell on his Northwest Coast materials, but he wanted to be in control of his own time. "It is very satisfactory to me," he wrote, "to be in the midst of scientific work, to work where I wish and use my ability in ways that I consider useful and to know that I owe this to my good luck and to my knowledge and activities." Forever wanting to convince his parents, and perhaps also himself, he added, "The best position in Germany could not make up for this. You see, I was right. What I sought here I have found, a broader sphere of activity than I could have found [elsewhere]."[61]

While Boas was happy to have found a rich field of work in the United States, he remained a German scientist to the core of his identity. To his parents he wrote, "With respect to science, I still feel like a German. It is strange how different American scientists are from German scientists. They are more dilettantes and one notices immediately that the foundation is not the same." He concluded, "There are, of course, also excellent people." With a firm grounding in the German approach to science, and, more specifically, to geography, Boas was also shaping his approach to the study of ethnography. As if placing stepping stones on the path that would help lead him toward the central place he would occupy years later in American anthropology, Boas was crafting innovative fieldwork techniques; developing approaches to the study of languages; establishing the importance of the collection of texts, and crucially, the collection of myths and folktales in the native languages; and emphasizing the relationship between the groups that he referred to as "tribes." In just the first few days of his 1886 field trip, when he had arrived in Victoria, Boas used to great benefit the drawings he had had made of ethnographic artifacts from museums in Berlin, New York, and Ottawa. He showed these drawings to his "old friend, Itlkakuani," one of the Bella Coola whom he had met in Berlin the previous year. Of the use of the drawings Boas said, "It was soon apparent that they will be very useful." Ira Jacknis writes, "The method Boas devised, now called 'photo-elicitation,' though relatively radical at the time, has since become one of the standard techniques of material culture research."[62]

The essence of Boas's approach to the study of languages, cultures, folklore, race, and diffusion of culture traits took shape in the first three field trips to the Northwest Coast of British Columbia in 1886, 1888, and 1889, and of course had foundation in his earlier work in Baffin Land. In a letter to Powell Boas detailed "the method to which I have heretofore adhered in field work." He continued, "I endeavor to obtain vocabularies and grammatical notes and at once proceed to collect texts principally on ethnological subjects, which I make on the basis of further ethnologic and linguistic researches. I attempt to study the customs and traditions of each tribe in the greatest detail and later to proceed to make a card catalogue of all characteristic peculiarities of a tribe, which are finally tabulated. Then it appears that certain phenomena are always coexistent. These must originally have belonged together while newly developed or introduced phenomena appear in various combinations or [are] isolated." In his first Northwest Coast fieldtrip in 1886 Boas had identified, "with the greatest difficulty," seventy tribes; and had arranged them according to language, dialect, and location. In his study of languages, Boas began by eliciting pronouns and verbs, compiling lists of vocabularies, and recording texts phonetically in the native language. As Boas explained to Powell, concerning his study of the Chinook, "I propose to treat the language separately and to give a series of texts, a grammar and a dictionary of the same."[63]

In his collection of tales and myths in the native languages, Boas had planted himself on fertile intellectual ground. He wrote his parents, "This mass of stories is gradually beginning to bear fruit because I can now discover certain traits characteristic of different groups of people. I think I am on the right track in considering mythology a useful tool for differentiating and judging the relationship of tribes." Boas recognized the complexity in the study of narrative and linked this complexity to material culture and to ritual. In Alert Bay in 1886 he collected Kwakiutl family histories, purchased a rattle and collected the story that went with it, purchased masks and undoubtedly learned the stories associated with each, and worked on understanding the connections between the native groups.[64]

From Alert Bay, Boas had written to Marie about the offer he had received from Hall for a position at Clark University. He told her he would probably know before her return to New York from Germany "whether the Worcester matter will materialize." Hall had not written to Boas "if he wants me as anthropologist or as geographer." He advised Marie that, if he accepted the position, she would need to find, "a boarding house in New York where we could live until October." He asked that she be sure "that I have a study because I shall have very much to do before we leave." From Kamloops, the last stop of his fieldtrip, Boas wrote, "What do you say to my accepting Hall's offer? I wish I could have talked the matter over with you! But there was nothing I could do about it." He expressed the hope that she would "like it there and soon make friends," and that "they will be satisfied with me and that the position will become a permanent one."[65]

To his parents, Boas wrote about the practical aspects of moving, how they needed to buy new carpets, and how their furnishings were shabby. More important, he wrote about his anxieties and his hopes: "*If* I shall succeed in Worcester, i.e. if I will be able to lecture and teach well, of which I am not at all certain, I promise myself a great deal from the position, so it could become the center of my scientific activity." Cautiously he added, "But that remains to be seen. For the present, I shall continue my association with Canada, as my reports are not yet finished."[66]

In Washington Boas visited Powell, who congratulated him on the position in Worcester and inquired how much he would be paid. Boas wrote his parents, "When I said $1000, he said that is not enough on which to live." Powell assured Boas that "as long as you are not getting more, you may count on getting $600 a year from us." He added, "'For a year or two I had in mind to have you here at the Bureau. I like your way of working and I can make use of you.'" Powell told Boas that "in a year or two he would be able to offer me a position." In characteristic fashion, Boas added, "I said nothing but I know that I would prefer to work independently in Worcester."[67]

Boas had decided on the topic for his lecture class: "The Anthropology of America." Finally, in November 1889, Franz Boas would step into the classroom to teach his first students of anthropology at Clark University.[68]

7

All Our Hopes Came to Such a Disgrace

Boas at Clark University

On October 4, 1889, Boas and Marie traveled to Worcester to visit with Clark University President G. Stanley Hall. They walked through the town and campus and found a rental home. Just two days prior, on October 2, Clark University had begun its first fall term. Toward the end of August, while still doing fieldwork in British Columbia, Boas had received the offer letter from Hall, and he had negotiated the later start date of November 1. Less than one month prior to the beginning of his employment, Boas was still trying to elicit from President Hall the parameters of his appointment. As he recounted to his parents, his "first and chief question was, 'What is the Anthropology Department to be, an independent department or a branch of Psychology?'" Hall responded, "'This is a question we wish to answer through experiment. Make of it what you can.'" Boas then inquired as to who his students would be, to which Hall responded, "None under 25 years of age, mostly professors and docents of the university, for example, himself, the psychologists Donaldson and Sanford and others." Befuddled by the lack of structure, Boas admitted, "I must say that I am not starting this work very hopefully, as it is a very difficult problem and I am doubtful whether I am equipped at this time to do what is required of me."[1]

Boas thought that Hall didn't really know what he wanted. Hall, however, was clear about his goal: he wanted to establish the first exclusively graduate university in the United States. The focus would be on natural sciences, with departments of psychology, biology, chemistry, physics, and mathematics. Hall had been recruited to the presidency of Clark University in spring 1888 from his position as professor of psychology and pedagogy at Johns Hopkins University. He had convinced Jonas Clark, the university's founder and benefactor, to delay the opening for one year and to finance Hall's eight-month "pedagogic trip" to Europe to visit universities. Through his connections in Europe and the United States, Hall recruited an outstanding faculty. As Dorothy Ross writes in her biography, *G. Stanley Hall*, "The university opened with eighteen members of faculty grade and thirty-four students. Of this group . . . fifteen had studied or taught at Johns Hopkins University, nineteen had done graduate work at European universities, and twelve scholars not on the faculty already held PhD degrees. As a group, they were uniquely well trained for and dedicated to scientific research." Having come from the faculty, Hall knew how to recruit faculty. Although he wasn't in the position to offer them high salaries, he could offer them "minimal teaching obligations, maximum time free for research, and all the research equipment they needed." Proud of the results of his recruitment, Hall recalled, "We had brought together a teaching force . . . nowhere equaled in the country." In his memoirs Donaldson echoed Hall's observations on the faculty: "The years at Worcester were splendid. I never had such choice colleagues—Michelson in Physics; Nef in Chemistry; Boas in Anthropology; Bauer in Paleontology; Bolza and Tabor in Mathematics; Whitman in Zoology; Sanford in Psychology; Lombard in Physiology; Mall in Anatomy and Hall himself. It was an unusual group and we were mutually beneficial."[2]

With the beneficence of Jonas Clark and the vision of G. Stanley Hall, Clark University rose from the fields on the outskirts of Worcester, Massachusetts. Arthur G. Webster recalled his arrival, fresh from his four years of study at the Friedrich-Wilhelms-Universität of Berlin with Hermann von Helmholtz, at the nascent Clark University: "I remember perfectly the day on which I first saw the university, and the rather unpleasant shock I had as I stepped off the horse-cart in response to the direction of the conductor. The grounds were then surrounded by a simple picket fence, the yard was grown up to tall grass, and the now familiar architecture of the main building, which with the laboratory building, was all there was on the lot, did not arouse my enthusiasm." Still, while the setting and the exterior of the buildings were absent grace and charm, the interior had "rooms of very ample dimensions and . . . finishing of the highest quality."[3]

In laying out the campus that would bear his name, Clark was hoping to rival Johns Hopkins and to overtake Harvard. The intent was to give the faculty what they needed so that they could focus on their research and their work with graduate students. "Surrounded by a provincial city," Ross writes, "they centered their lives during the day and far into the night on their research and study." Years after the founding of the university, Hall hearkened back to this early vision: "It was nothing less than the conviction that we represented—small, weak, and unworthy as we were—the very highest vocation of man—research. We felt that we belonged to the larger university not made by hands, eternal in the world of science and learning; that we were not so much an institution as a state of mind and that wherever and to what extent the ideals that inspired us reigned we were at home; that research is nothing less than a religion."[4]

Hall convinced the trustees to establish positions for docents, who would be paid a salary considerably less than that of the professors. While he had modeled these positions on the German university system of *Privatdozenten*, the salaried position of docents at Clark University was a departure from that in Germany, where the students who studied with the docents paid them.[5] As instituted at Clark University, the docent position allowed Hall to hire highly trained academics and to pay them a scant salary.

Hall had explained to Boas, "Our Trustees have established a few Docentships intended primarily as honors but yielding an income larger than that of Fellow. Docents will be fitted out with rooms, books & apparatus & expected to give a limited number of lectures & reside here during the academic year." Hall continued, "These appointments are annual & are intended to give a few men, deserving & awaiting more permanent & more lucrative positions, opportunity to spend a profitable year in qualifying themselves more fully for academic advancement here or elsewhere. The pay is $1000." Boas had accepted the position on the condition that he could have his summers free to continue his work in the Northwest Coast in order to augment his salary. Hall responded that he had no problem with Boas having "as early a summer as you wish & I am glad to hear that you propose to keep up your connection where you are."[6]

Hall explained, "We have carefully considered the department you so well represent in connection with the plans of this University." He con-

tinued, "It is an experiment not yet tried in this country as you know &
we cannot launch out too largely at first but must proceed tentatively."
To Boas's query about "the approximate limits of the field you wish me
to cover and what you think its relation should be to the plan of the University," Hall replied that Boas needed to determine "the ground you wish
in instruction & by the methods you wish." He went on:

> If I have myself any preference intelligent enough to be considered,
> it would be to touch upon the whole field in the broadest possible
> way by a hasty preliminary survey, citing a few standard works &
> then to work your way to those special problems & parts of the field
> in which you have yourself done most. I have a general concep-
> tion that Myth, Custom & Belief or the Psychological side, are on
> the whole of greater import & interest at present than craniology,
> pre-historic remains or even industries, important as these are &
> desirable as it is that something be said of them.

Hall asked Boas to send him a "list of your chief publications & account
of your work," as well as a list of books and journals for first-year students.
He also asked for "a description of the field you intend to cover, methods
& such other things as students might desire to know." Hall concluded
with the following advice: "By all means do not burden yourself with
lectures or instruction. Condense the matter & save yourself time here
for your own work."[7]

Paying no heed to Hall's assessment of craniology as having lesser
import than other aspect of anthropology, Boas wrote asking for "a set
of anthropometric instruments." He asked, "May I be allowed to send
my collection of crania and skeletons (about 150) to the University?"
He added, "I am afraid of the danger of its being destroyed by fire in a
wooden house," in the event that he had to store the collection at home.
Boas sent Hall his complete list of books for the first-year students and
requested a small budget for "books on South America & Central America. Much of the literature on South America is not trustworthy and I
have written to . . . men in Caracas, Venezuela, and Cordova, Argentina
Rep. for information."[8]

In his first year at Clark University, Boas taught two yearlong lecture
courses—Anthropology of North America and Methods of Anthropo-

logical Investigation—and two laboratory courses. As described in the *Clark University Register and Second Official Announcement*, Anthropology of North America covered the following: "The distribution, physical characters, languages, inventions, customs and beliefs of the various tribes . . . beginning in Arctic America and proceeding southward along the Pacific Coast" and then moving "east of the Rocky Mountains." Particular stress was placed on "the diffusion of cultural elements all through North America." The course on Methods of Anthropological Investigation was divided into two parts: "The methods of describing and measuring skeletons and living individuals formed the subject of the lectures until Christmas. . . . [and] the use of anthropological apparatus was explained." The second half focused on "the subjects of language, social institutions, religion, and customs." The laboratory courses consisted of "two courses, each of two hours weekly." The first covered "the methods of field investigation," and the second, "Anthropometry." The catalog described Boas's courses for the second year (1890–91) as follows:

> 1. Physical Anthropology, Osteology, particularly craniology. Physical character in the living subject. Anatomy of races. In connection with the course of lectures, practical work on methods of studying the anatomy of races will be conducted in the anthropological laboratory.
>
> 2. Anthropology of Africa. Geographical distribution, physical characters, languages and culture of the native tribes of Africa.

In the spring, Boas offered "a special course of lectures" on American Myths.[9]

By the third year Boas had reduced the number of lecture courses he offered to be commensurate with his position as docent. The catalog entry for 1891–92 reflected this with a bare three lines devoted to "DR. BOAS.–ANTHROPOLOGY. The work of next year will be: 1. Lectures and laboratory work on Physical Anthropology. 2. A course of lectures on the Application of Statistics to Anthropology." Boas obtained a fellowship in 1891–92 for Alexander Chamberlain, who in turn offered "a course of lectures on the Relation of Linguistics to Anthropology and Psychology."[10]

Boas's work with Chamberlain reflected the focus on graduate education at Clark University, tailored specifically to "the needs of those

All Our Hopes Came to Disgrace

students who present themselves." Chamberlain arrived at Worcester from his position as a fellow in modern languages at the University of Toronto. Delighted with the prospect of coming to Clark University to study under Boas, Chamberlain had written, "I beg to thank you for the interest you have taken in regard to my appointment as Fellow in Anthropology, notice of which I have duly received." Boas had intended that Chamberlain arrive for the 1890–91 term. This was contingent on Chamberlain being able to join Boas for the BAAS-sponsored summer fieldwork in British Columbia in 1890, the substance of which would provide the basis for his work as a fellow at Clark University. Sir Daniel Wilson, president of the University of Toronto, had stipulated that Chamberlain must be on hand to assist Boas in the Northwest Coast no later than the end of June or he would have to defer the trip for the following year. Due to previous obligations, Chamberlain could not depart before the end of July. He wrote Boas that he would "devote the whole of next summer to anthropological work." He planned to work with the Mississagas, "to collect some more material & shall try if possible to get some anthropological specimens." Chamberlain joined Boas for the 1891 summer fieldwork in the Northwest Coast, came to Clark University as a fellow in anthropology under Boas's tutelage, and completed the first PhD dissertation in anthropology in the United States: "The Language of the Mississaga Indians of Skūgog: A Contribution to the Linguistics of the Algonkian Tribes of Canada" (1892).[11]

Even though Hall expected him to teach only "a limited number of lectures," Boas aimed during his first two years at Clark University to become indispensable to the president. With the number of lecture and laboratory courses he offered, Boas had equaled or exceeded the work of the professors who had been hired at three times his salary. When the time came for him to sign his reappointment letter for his third year, Boas sought clarification about his employers' expectations. As he wrote, he had accepted the reappointment "to my present position on the old basis only with the clear understanding, that under such conditions I am not willing to devote myself so exclusively to the development of the Department, as I have done heretofore." Boas wanted to perform "the duties of a docent, that is to deliver lectures at regular intervals" and to continue the "independent researches by students in the laboratory." Apparently, Hall, who had previously expressed a lack of interest in physical anthropology, had suggested that Boas set aside his work in the laboratory. Boas asserted that "a discontinuation of the laboratory and of independent researches by students in the laboratory would be almost equivalent to a loss of all that has been accomplished during the past two years."[12]

Boas's salary remained low in spite of his own efforts to garner a raise and Hall's promises to give him a salary commensurate with his performance. The strain was clear in Marie's letter to her in-laws: "Today I am furious at the old misers at the University! What are they thinking? That we can live on $1,500 in this nest when everything is as dear here as in New York!" She had hoped that the university would provide a salary of at least a $2,000, so "that Franz would not necessarily have to take on extra work again." With each annual reappointment, Boas had to negotiate permission to assume responsibilities external to Clark University in order to augment his meager salary. The BAE supported Boas's 1890 summer fieldwork in the Northwest Coast for a total of $1,100, with a salary of $150 per month for 3 months and $650 travel expenses, the latter covering payment for the assistance of the Indians. Boas's work focused on "the coast Salish and the Chinook of the lower Columbia River." Powell advised, "The first of June is considered a favorable time for the trip, and it is deemed best that you should first visit the Chinook of the lower Columbia. After obtaining a good vocabulary of this language, the Salish tribes may be visited in such order as you may deem best." While working on the Siletz Reservation in Oregon, Boas remarked, "The Chinook spoken here is very different from that in British Columbia, and therefore I experience difficulty in talking with them." Boas also received $300 in support from the BAAS for purchase of ethnographic specimens and as payment for anthropometric work. Of his work with the BAAS, Boas had written Hale from New Westminster, BC, that he couldn't work "satisfactorily here" because the people were occupied "too long in the canneries." He was "almost desperate and thinking whether it would not" be better "to give up the work for the present and not to spend your funds in such unsatisfactory way." With great embarrassment, he admitted that he had missed his boat to Victoria; it had left one day ahead of schedule. Replying sympathetically, Hale wrote that Boas had "done the best" he could after the steamer left unexpectedly. He assured Boas that he had written to the BAAS committee that Boas would pay "special attention to anthropological measurements, and I am glad to know that you have an opportunity of doing so."[13]

In Boas's 1891 appointment letter, Hall had written, "The Trustees are disposed to look with favor upon your proposition . . . to cooperate with Professor Putnam in preparing physical charts of Indians for the [Chicago Columbian] exposition, provided it does not interfere with your regular work in Lectures & Laboratory in this University." Additionally, the trustees would allow Boas to give a series of "eight lectures at the Peabody Museum at Cambridge next year provided it is understood that the course is given by the courtesy of this Institution." During the 1891 summer field season, funded in part by the BAAS, Boas worked with Chamberlain on linguistic matters. In his cool appraisal of Chamberlain, Daniel Wilson had written, "He is studious, shy, and thus far has shown more aptitude for the closet than the field. But possibly, if once he overcomes his reserve, his quiet manner might not be unacceptable to the natives." Reiterating this point of view the next year, when Chamberlain joined Boas for fieldwork in the Northwest Coast, Wilson expressed a desire to see Chamberlain work with Boas and not by himself.[14]

In 1890–91, Clark University's second year of operation, Hall tightened the budget but still maintained high expectations for research on the part of the faculty. He wrote Boas (and, undoubtedly, other faculty members) that he was preparing a "private printed Report to our Trustees" on the research work carried out at the university. He asked for "a brief and not too technical description of what you attempted & accomplished here in the way of research," to be accompanied by a list of publications with the number of pages, "if the work is far enough along [and] done since you joined [Clark University]."[15]

The élan of the first two years ended for Boas and for other members of the faculty when it became clear that the budget challenges were a result of Hall's opaque decision-making. From late December 1891 through the winter of 1892, there was froth and turbulence between the faculty and the president, which resulted in a vote of no confidence in the president by the faculty and a raid on the faculty by the new president of the University of Chicago, William Rainey Harper, in April 1892.

The turf war of the group of faculty members and docents against the president would draw in the board of trustees. Ultimately this resulted in an exodus of teaching staff and students that would threaten the very existence of the university. Through a combination of serendipitous and predictable factors, the stage was set for this perfect storm between the president and the faculty.

Hall was stricken with a personal tragedy that sapped him of the energy needed to direct the university. While he was away from home recuperating from diphtheria, his wife and eight-year-old daughter were asphyxiated on May 15, 1890, by gas that escaped from a faulty furnace. Unrelated to this, but nonetheless simultaneous, Jonas Clark's enthusiasm for the university he had founded began to wane. He grew disappointed and disillusioned with what he had intended as a gift to the community, and with the reactions of the citizens of Worcester to the university that he had established, above all, "*in & for Worcester.*" Instead of appreciating the center of elevated learning, many of the townspeople resented Clark University and all that it represented. What emerged was the classic tension between town and gown, a divide between the residents of the community and the denizens of the campus.[16]

The *Worcester Telegram* enthusiastically inserted itself into this divide with inflammatory articles describing and decrying the vivisection of cats and dogs that took place in laboratories on campus. Albert B. Southwick, editor of the editorial page for the *Telegram & Gazette* from 1952 to 1986, characterized the founder of the *Worcester Telegram* Austin P. Cristy as "a firebrand, remembered for his antagonisms." Cristy, a man of strong emotions, "was a Republican on steroids who despised his competitors." He detested Democrats, the Irish, and those who drank alcohol, in equal measure. With his rigid, xenophobic views and his insistence on journalism with popular appeal, Cristy undoubtedly encouraged his reporters in their aggressive and incendiary reporting about the university.[17]

The title of a March 9, 1890, column set the dramatic and unsettling tone—"Dogs Vivisected, Scientific Torture at Clark University, Helpless Animals Are Killed By Inches, Cruelty that is Reduced to a Fine Art. Dumb Victims writhe under the Cruel Knife, Afraid the Matter Would Reach the People, Detailed Description of Docents' Doings." The divide between the town and the gown was clearly drawn: "Ever since the erec-

All Our Hopes Came to Disgrace

tion of the big brick buildings out toward New Worcester not much in the line of results has been seen by Worcester people save the big word CLARK on the front." The reporter of the *Worcester Telegram* used aggressive investigative techniques; asserting that the "newspaper representatives of Worcester have been excluded from the . . . institution and reporters have been furnished with no news," the reporter of the *Telegram* simply "went in" and searched the building— the basement, the boiler room, the classrooms, and the laboratories—described a harrowing scene of dogs kept in unsanitary pens in the basement. Since much of the article was written in a sensationalist manner, it is difficult to assess its veracity. Certainly, the following description was false, since the animals were not operated on without first being anaesthetized. Eliding science with an allusion to the magical reading of entrails, the reporter linked all this to the docents, who themselves were an unknown category of academics to some readers of the *Worcester Telegram*, and, therefore, imminently suspect: "It must be a great pleasure to the dog when he is led out for vivisection to know that he is being cut to pieces scientifically, and that he is being slowly put to death in order that he may be honored by having his quivering entrails gazed upon by a learned docent of anthropology, biology or some other ology."[18] The reporter sought out Jonas Clark, whom he described as "the millionaire founder of the institution," at his home. Clark acknowledged that vivisection was undertaken at the university, as it was "at every university in the world." Stepping arrogantly into the divide, Clark maintained that the people of the town "'don't understand high scientific researches and their prejudices can be worked upon.'" When the reporter posited again, "'The people don't know what is going on there and they want to,'" Clark retorted, "'Well, it's none of their business. They can't understand it, and so there is no way they can know anything about it.'" Suffering from diphtheria, President Hall was spared the intrusion of the reporter into his home on this instance, but not the reporter's disparagement: "Prof. G. Stanley Hall, president of the institution, is sick with diphtheria, and there is evidence that his disease may have been contracted from filthy conditions that directly result from vivisection." In his autobiography Hall recalled the unrelenting attack on Clark University by the "leading daily paper of the city," which published articles "several times a week for about six months." Hall continued, "I had personally to answer scores of calls by day and by night from those who had lost pet cats and dogs."[19]

The reporter linked vivisection to "Jonas G. Clark's pet hobby ... to have his university like the German universities."[20] Appealing to xenophobic sentiment, the reporter continued, "There the docents and the students, after they go through a course on vivisection on animals, get up high enough to vivisect each other in sword duels. They cut each other up." Making "a trip to interview ... docents," the reporter selected two who had been educated at German universities. He went first to the home of "Dr. Oskar Bolzar [*sic*], whom he found to be a mathematical calculator of remote degree," and then to the home of "Dr., or, rather, Docent Franz Boas, who lives at No. 210 Beacon street." Identifying Docent Boas as a lecturer in anthropology, who "has been vivisected to quite an extent and bears the marks," the reporter sketched a physical description of Boas in sensationalist detail: "He is a German, a student at one of the German universities, and has evidently studied human vivisection with a rapier, or has had it practiced upon himself, as numerous scars on his face show. He is a battle scarred veteran, though still a young man." The reporter continued, "On the left side of his forehead near the temple two scars convene and cross. A scar ornaments also the left side. His nose was at one time nearly severed and the left side of his face from the angle of the lips to the ear shows a long scar." With heavy sarcasm, the reporter concluded, "He is a very learned man."[21]

Undeterred by the sensationalist reporting, Boas undertook a project to measure children at the Boys Club in Worcester. In January 1891 Boas applied to the Worcester school board for permission to expand his project to the city schools and gained approval "to go among any of the public schools and take such measurements of the boys and girls as he desires for statistical purposes."[22] The *Worcester Telegram* made every effort to whip its readership into a frenzy of indignation. Schoolchildren were having "'their anatomies felt of and the various portions of their bodies measured for no reason established in science, and by a man unknown to Worcester, either personally or by established reputation, except as the representative of an institution UNDER A BLOOD RED CLOUD.'" Attempting to smear Boas with innuendo, the reporter accused him of having "'fooled around with the top knot of medicine men and

All Our Hopes Came to Disgrace

toyed with THE WAR PAINT of bloodthirsty Indians.'" This man, with a scarred visage that would "'make a jailbird turn green with envy,'" would be touching their children's bodies.[23]

Apparently recognizing scurrilous reporting for what it was, the school board maintained its support of Boas's project. Boas was also able to secure permission for his research from 80 percent of the parents. By minimizing the number of measurements, the five-person team—led by a fellow in anthropology, Gerald West, who worked with four assistants— proceeded with efficiency. Every three minutes, they completed the measurements on one child. Before he had even begun measuring the schoolchildren, Boas had conveyed to his parents that he was "'fed up with the whole thing.'" Marie wrote Boas's mother of her own concerns, that the newspaper reports might "'cripple Franz's work' even though all the educated people of Worcester are on Franz's side." Hall equivocated. At first, yielding to the fiery rhetoric of the newspaper, he withdrew his support of Boas's project, and then, when the school board reconfirmed its support, Hall offered his full endorsement.[24]

Unwilling and perhaps unable to communicate with the plain-speaking residents of Worcester, Hall failed to assuage the townspeople and to make them feel that they were part of the adventures of building a new university. Clark faded from the scene: he took his fortune and dreams away from Worcester and from Clark University in May 1891. Hall reflected on Jonas Clark: "During the third year he had entirely withdrawn from the board and never afterward attended its meetings," and gave the university no more financial support. President Hall was challenged on all sides—from the town, from the benefactor of the university, from the faculty, and from the students—and he was found wanting. He lacked the crucial negotiating style and the transparent honesty needed to handle a crisis with a highly intelligent and highly energized faculty. With his obdurate personality, his resistance to compromise, and his predilection for masking the unpleasant, Hall was in the tight spot where no university president ever desires to be—squared off against an angry faculty.[25]

The spark that set fire to faculty resentment sprang from a seemingly minor, though callously handled, matter. In fall 1891 President Hall withheld the twenty-five-dollar monthly stipend for a fellow who had missed the start of school because he had been caring for his ill mother. Of this incident, Donaldson recalled that "Mead was a Fellow in Whitman's department [of zoology] and Whitman was for resigning." From October 1891 to January 1892, the "general indignation" over the treatment of the fellows intensified when "several men were about to seriously consider offers elsewhere," and the teaching staff shared the view that "the University was in very great danger." By mid-January, from morning to evening the days were filled with meetings—meetings in the homes of faculty members and of docents, with the president, and with the entire faculty. As Donaldson recounted, "A half-dozen of us came together to see what could be done in order to put matters straight. We made suggestions but Hall resisted and was uncompromising. We had many meetings, mainly at my house and the conferences seemed to bring out a number of instances of trickiness and sharp practice on Hall's part that were distinctly unpleasant." It was unlikely that anything else could be accomplished during this time, save for the endless meetings.[26]

One week later, on January 21, 1892, after day-long meetings, the group comprised of Donaldson, Michelson, Whitman, Nef, Mall, Lombard, Boas, Bolza, and Baur met in Donaldson's house at seven thirty in the evening. The men had invited President Hall, who, in a poor decision, declined to attend. All concurred that "the attempt to save the university from the impending danger by openness and frankness" had failed due to the willful actions of the president. In what must have been a somber, almost ritualistic, procedure, each voiced his position: "Prof. Michelson could see no other course than to resign. Lombard said he had told the President that if things didn't change he would leave. Donaldson said, 'I shall resign.' Mall said that under existing circumstances he could not remain here after this year and he should resign. Whitman and Nef said [they would resign]. Bolza said, 'I am ready to resign.' Boas and Baur [each] said, 'I shall resign.'" Together they drafted a letter of no confidence in the president and tendered their resignation effective September 1, 1892.[27]

In subsequent negotiations, the president agreed that a committee would be established to meet with him and to discuss the points of discord. "The concerned faculty," as they were called, met with the president, agreed to put aside their disagreements, and requested "that the paper containing their resignations be destroyed." However, two days later, President Hall had changed his mind, and the faculty felt betrayed. At this point the trustees had been drawn into the dispute. They saw "no recourse but to accept the resignations tendered" and concomitantly, stated their support of President Hall. The crux of the disagreement between the faculty and docents and the president involved questions about who should be responsible for making decisions about faculty governance—the faculty, or the president. As Ross remarks, this conflict occurred prior to the "development of processes and procedures for dealing with shared governance."[28]

William Rainey Harper, president of the newly established University of Chicago, saw ripe pickings at Clark University. Throughout the tumultuous winter months, Whitman and Mall had been in secret negotiations with Harper. Informed about the dissension and resignations at Clark University, Harper came to Worcester on April 16, 1892, "settled down in Whitman's house and began to gather a scientific faculty." As Ross recounts, "Within a few hours of his arrival, Harper formally engaged five men in biology." Among these were Whitman and Mall, who "wanted Harper to take seven faculty members, including Boas; he left with eight," but did not take Boas.[29]

With a lasting sense of betrayal, G. Stanley Hall recounted the events of this day in his autobiography, which he wrote three decades later, toward the end of his life. Unbeknownst to him, he said, Harper had met with the dissident faculty in the home of Whitman, where he had "engaged one morning the majority of our staff. . . . Those to whom we paid $4,000, he gave $7,000; to those we paid $2,000, he offered $4,000, etc., taking even instructors, docents, and fellows." As Hall described, "When this was done he called on me, inviting me also to join the hegira at a salary larger than I was receiving—which of course I refused—and then told me what he had done." Likening Harper's methods to those of a "Standard-Oil institution"—in reference to the source of wealth of the benefactor of the University of Chicago, John D. Rockefeller—, Hall continued, "I finally threatened . . . to make a formal appeal to the public and to Mr. Rockefeller himself to see if this trust magnate (who was at that time about at the height of his unpopularity and censure and who was said to have driven many smaller competing firms out of existence by slow strangling methods of competition) would justify such an assassination of an institution as had that day been attempted here." For one who had brought faculty, docents, and graduate students with him when he had left Johns Hopkins University, Hall's indignation seemed slightly overblown. Hall had, of course, merely poked holes in departments at Johns Hopkins, while Harper had devastated every department save for Hall's own, that of psychology.[30]

With the philanthropic backing of John D. Rockefeller, Harper was in position to stress "the larger opportunities offered at Chicago, opportunities for advancement, for research, for developing great departments of knowledge, for enlarged usefulness." As Hall had been, so Harper was skilled at the recruitment of high-powered faculty, though there were instances in which he had to offer considerable enticements. Such was the case with C. O. Whitman of Clark University, who, as Goodspeed wrote in *The History of the University of Chicago*, "drove a hard bargain." Whitman had wired President Harper, "'I can accept on following terms, salaries and running expenses [for the Department of Biology] thirty thousand dollars, equipment twenty-five thousand, building one hundred and fifty thousand.'" Whitman "did not get his building for biology, and Mr. Michelson [of Clark University, who did not negotiate] did get the great Ryerson Physical Laboratory." Five years later, in 1897, Whitman got his building as a gift from Helen Culver.[31]

As Jonathan Cole notes in *The Great American University*, fierce competition in recruiting outstanding scholars was standard among American research universities at the end of the nineteenth century. "The University of Chicago," Cole writes, "is perhaps the quintessential example of how a new research university could achieve high standards in very little time." In *To Advance Knowledge: The Growth of American Research Universities, 1900–1940*, Robert Geiger remarks that the University of Chicago had caused "turbulence in the academic marketplace," by beginning its first year "in 1892 with a faculty of 120, including 5 teachers enticed from Yale and 15 drawn from Clark." Ross summarizes the exodus from Clark: "In the end, two-thirds of all those of faculty rank and 70 percent of the student body left Clark in the spring of 1892. Half of those leaving went directly to the University of Chicago. Out of the ruins of Clark, Chicago had the foundation of distinguished departments in physics, chemistry, biology, and mathematics."[32]

Nine faculty members had signed the letter of no confidence in President Hall and had tendered their resignations. Of these, seven went to the University of Chicago, with the following appointments:

Albert A. Michelson, Head Professor of Physics
C. O. Whitman, Head Professor of Biology and Professor of
    Animal Morphology
Henry H. Donaldson, Professor of Neurology
John Ulric Nef, Professor of Chemistry
Franklin P. Mall, Professor of Anatomy
Oskar Bolza, Associate Professor of Mathematics
Georg Baur, Assistant Professor of Comparative Osteology
    and Paleontology

Warren P. Lombard went to the University of Michigan as a professor of physiology. Only Boas was left without an academic position. Possibly Harper decided not to offer Boas a position because, as Browman and Williams suggest, "Boas lacked any national visibility" in 1892. Or perhaps Harper left the decision as to whether or not to hire Boas to Albion W. Small, who was head professor of social science and dean of the college of liberal arts. With respect to the latter point, Harper had given responsibility to the heads of departments to identify potential faculty and then to consult with the president. Albion Small headed the department of two, joined as he was by Frederick Starr, assistant professor of anthropology. As the first professor of sociology in the United States, Professor Small would not have relished being outnumbered by two anthropologists and thus was likely in hearty agreement with Harper's decision not to hire Boas. Finally, there was the possibility that Harper simply did not warm to Boas when he met him in Worcester. Goodspeed remarked that Harper followed an intensive process for identifying potential faculty, but, ultimately, he relied on his own judgment when he met with the potential faculty in person. In sum, there is simply no definitive answer as to why Harper did not hire Boas.[33]

Boas and Marie had passed a full life as a family during their three years in Worcester. In February 1891 "'the shrieking Ernst'" had been born. Boas joked in his letter to his parents that his son was the reincarnation of the Raven in the folk narratives that he had collected in British Columbia.

The following year, in February 1892, Boas had become a naturalized United States citizen. Boas and Marie had made enduring friends with the Baurs, the Donaldsons, and with Oskar Bolza. Marie wrote to her in-laws about "the custom in the small towns" to have new comers over for dinner. "We really have more company with us here than in New York. It is easier to get people together and it's all simple here." With the gift of money from Franz's parents, they rented a piano: "We really are spoiled children. . . . Franz plays every day now." Marie wrote of the friends who gathered to play "something from Mozart" and other selections, "On Sunday Prof. Michelson, a physicist, played the violin; and Herr Loeb, the viola; and Franz the piano. . . . I am so happy for Franz that he now and then has some music." In June 1892 Boas and Marie, with their little girl, Helene, who would be four years old in September, and baby Ernst, at sixteen months, departed Worcester for Germany.[34]

Boas would return to Worcester in September 1909 from his position as professor of anthropology at Columbia University for the twentieth-anniversary celebration of the founding of Clark University. Professor of Psychology E. C. Sanford had extended the invitation to Boas: "It would give us all the greatest pleasure if you would consent to be present and to give one of these lectures in the psychological program. We wish to emphasize the research idea for which the university has stood so far as it has been able from the first, which you have so fully exemplified." As a participant in the conference on psychology and pedagogy—the highlight of the gathering, as Hall called it—Boas delivered a lecture on "Psychological Problems in Anthropology." With pride, Hall listed the participants in his autobiography: "In psychology we were fortunate in inducing Sigmund Freud of Vienna, W. Stern of Breslau, C. G. Jung of Zurich, E. B. Titchener of Cornell, F. Boas of Columbia, Adolph Meyer of Johns Hopkins (both the latter formerly at Clark), H. S. Jennings of Hopkins, H. Ferenzi of Prague [sic; this was Sándor Ferenczi], Ernest Jones of Toronto, and William James." Hall recalled, "Nearly every day was spent in listening either to formal lectures and demonstrations by these and other eminent experts or in more informal conferences, which were facilitated by provisions by which all could take their meals with those of their own group."[35]

Hall treated both Freud and Jung as his honored guests. He scheduled the conference around Freud's availability in the fall, rather than with the first conference in July on Child Welfare and Research. In his letter to his wife, Jung wrote that Hall's wife "promptly took over Freud and me as 'her boys' and plied us with delicious nourishment and noble wine." Freud and Jung moved into the Hall's home, where they were "beautifully taken care of." Hall had extended the courtesy to both Freud and Jung to speak as they chose, either in German or English. Of his experience Freud wrote, "In 1909 G. Stanley Hall invited Jung and me to America to go to the Clark University, Worcester, Mass., of which he was President, and to spend a week giving lectures (in German) at the celebration of the twentieth anniversary of that body's foundation. Hall was justly esteemed as a psychologist and educationalist and had introduced psychoanalysis into his courses some years before; there was a touch of the 'king-maker' about him, a pleasure in setting up authorities and in then deposing them." Buoyed by the reception in America, Freud reflected, "In Europe I felt as though I were despised; but over there I found myself received by the foremost men as an equal. As I stepped on to the platform at Worcester to deliver my *Five Lectures upon Psycho-Analysis* it seemed like the realization of some incredible day-dream: psycho-analysis was no longer a product of delusion, it has become a valuable part of reality." Jung referred to Freud's speeches at Clark University as his "'American triumph.'"[36]

As Hall noted, at the conclusion of the conference "the University departed from its custom of being very chary in the conferring of honorary degrees and bestowed thirty doctorates of no less than nine kinds. . . . This was more than three times as many honorary degrees as we had given in the preceding twenty years." In his letter to Boas in advance of the conference, Hall wrote that the faculty had voted to award him an honorary degree because he ranked "supreme" in his achievements in anthropology.[37]

On Hall's retirement, Boas wrote, "At this time when you lay down the burdens that you have carried so long, permit me to express to you my thanks for your serious attempt to develop the highest ideals of scientific achievement in our university life. Even if circumstances did not permit the realization of your great plans to their fullest extent, I feel certain that your work has given a stimulus to research that is even now bearing fruit." Hall responded, "I cannot forbear telling you how very

deeply I appreciate your kind phrases and your courtesy in writing at all."
He went on, "The great cloud on my life, which will never entirely lift,
was the situation here at the end of 1893." After reviewing the record of
the debacle, Hall concluded, "But I will not expatiate on these, the most
painful memories of my life, but I must express my profound appreciation of the fact that you are the only one of those who left us at the close
of the third year who has had a kind word for me. I can only hope that
with the years all those who survive will have a little of the same feeling
and insight that you do." Thus, the relationship between Franz Boas and
G. Stanley Hall resolved in friendship and reconciliation.[38]

Nonetheless, when Boas left in 1892, he had only profound regret
for the squandered potential of Clark University. Writing to his father
from Cambridge, where he was working with Putnam in preparation for
the anthropological exhibit at the World's Columbian Exposition, Boas
reflected, "After having lived so long there and having had such relationships . . . I feel a great affection for Worcester. I will, whenever I think
about it, always be angry that all our hopes came to such a disgrace.'"
Boas, Marie, and the children had returned early from their family visit
to Germany because an epidemic of cholera had broken out in Hamburg.
When they disembarked in Baltimore, Boas bade farewell to his family,
who traveled on to New York, arriving there on September 17, 1892. Boas
headed straight to Cambridge, where he and Putnam worked in frantic
preparation for the Columbia World's Exposition in Chicago, scheduled
to open in less than eight months.[39]

Fig. 1. Franz Boas, about age four, 1862. Franz Boas Papers, American Philosophical Society

Fig. 2. Franz Boas, about age twelve, school group portrait, ca. 1870. Top row, right-hand side. Franz Boas Papers, American Philosophical Society

Fig. 3. Franz, *standing*; Hete and Anne, *seated*, 1873. Franz Boas Papers, American Philosophical Society

Fig. 4. (*top*) Boas family, seated around table (*left to right*): Franz, Sophie, Meier, Toni, and Anne. 1881. Franz Boas Papers, American Philosophical Society

Fig. 5. (*bottom*) Boas's fraternity, Burschenschaft Alemannia Bonn, with Boas (*second from lower left*), 1878. Franz Boas Papers, American Philosophical Society

Fig. 6. Franz Boas as a soldier, ca. 1881. Franz Boas Papers,
American Philosophical Society

Fig. 7. Franz Boas with three other soldiers, ca. 1881. Franz Boas Papers, American Philosophical Society

Fig. 8. Franz Boas on board the *Germania* en route to Baffin Land, 1883.
Franz Boas Papers, American Philosophical Society

Fig. 9. Franz Boas in Inuit clothing, ready for sealing.
Studio portrait recreated in Minden, 1885. Franz Boas Papers,
American Philosophical Society

Fig. 10. Franz and Marie Boas, wedding portrait, 1887. Franz Boas Papers, American Philosophical Society

Fig. 11. Franz, Helene, and Marie, Worcester, Massachusetts, 1890.
Franz Boas Papers, American Philosophical Society

Fig. 12. Franz Boas at World's Columbian Exposition, 1893.
Franz Boas Papers, American Philosophical Society

Fig. 13. (*left*) Franz Boas with baby Gertrude Marianne "Trudel," ca. 1898, New York. Franz Boas Papers, American Philosophical Society

Fig. 14. (*below*) Franz Boas with wife, Marie, in study, 1900. Franz Boas Papers, American Philosophical Society

Fig. 15. Franz Boas with George Hunt and family at Fort Rupert, ca. 1894.
Franz Boas Papers, American Philosophical Society

Fig. 16. (*top*) Fort Rupert, 1894. Smithsonian Institution Archives

Fig. 17. (*bottom*) Franz Boas and George Hunt holding blanket and
Kwakiutl woman weaving cedar bark, Fort Rupert, ca. 1894.
American Museum of Natural History

Fig. 18. (*opposite top*) George Hunt in front of grizzly bear carving at
Kwakiutl cedar plank house, with Leather and Shoe Trade
Building in background, World's Columbian Exposition, 1893.
American Museum of Natural History

Fig. 19. (*opposite bottom*) Kwakiutl Indians at World's Columbian
Exposition, 1893. American Museum of Natural History

Fig. 20. (*above*) Kwakiutl Indians in front of cedar plank house,
World's Columbian Exposition, 1893; George Hunt, seventh from right.
American Museum of Natural History

Fig. 21. Clark University Psychology Conference, 1909.
First row: Boas (*far left*), William James (*third from left*),
G. Stanley Hall (*center*), Sigmund Freud (*seventh left*), and
Carl Jung (*eighth left*). Clark University Archives

8

The World's Columbian Exposition

Boas and Frederic Ward Putnam

In the 1906 *Boas Anniversary Volume*, Frederic Ward Putnam wrote, "When I was appointed Chief of the Department of Ethnology of the World's Columbian Exposition, Dr. Boas . . . was appointed Chief Assistant of the Department. During that time of untold trials and difficulties in making the first scientific anthropological exhibit in this country, . . . to none did I owe so much as to Dr. Boas for the final success that attended our efforts." Elsewhere Putnam described his experiences in Chicago as being squeezed dry like an orange and thrown away. "The Trustees and the head official of the Columbian Museum," he asserted, had treated him with utter "ingratitude." President of the World's Columbian Exposition Harlow A. Higinbotham was "unsympathetic toward Putnam and his plans. . . . and even admitted to Putnam during one of their disputes that he never entered the Anthropological Building during the Exposition." As Putnam's assistant, Boas was on the receiving end of institutional "intrigues" and dismissive treatment by the same people who had so insulted Putnam. Putnam had hoped to become the director of the new Chicago museum that would grow out of the exhibits gathered for the world's fair, just as Boas had hoped to become director of the anthropological department.[1]

The denouement of disappointments for Putnam and Boas played out against the phantasmagorical backdrop of the 1893 World's Columbian Exposition. Ultimately, their exhaustive and frantic work to fill the Anthropological Building with exhibits, and to transform the grounds outside the building into Mayan ruins and Northwest Coast living villages, yielded an important contribution to the development of anthropology as a science and to the creation of the core collection for a new museum. "The collections in the Anthropological Building," Ralph Dexter comments, "became the nucleus for the departments of zoology and anthropology in the Field Columbian Museum organized immediately following the Fair." The collections of Northwest Coast Indian cultures displayed in the exhibits and explained by the Kwakiutl Indians in their village settlement marked the World's Columbian Exposition as "the single event" from which "all subsequent work" on the Northwest Coast would be measured.[2]

Putnam and Boas's exhibits were not the only presentations of anthropology at the World's Columbian Exposition. With multiple anthropology exhibits and little coordination between the organizers, the theme seemed to be "more is better." Anthropology exhibits were included in state buildings—for instance, the living exhibit of the Penobscot Village sponsored by New York State, and Canada's display, which included a representation of Cree Indians. Of the two major anthropology exhibits, Nancy Fagin writes, "One was the combined exhibit of the Smithsonian Institution, the Bureau of Ethnology, and the United States National Museum. The other was an exhibit by independent, newly formed Department of Ethnology. The two exhibits had only a superficial resemblance; they were conceived, organized, and developed along very different lines." As the principal organizer of the U.S. government exhibit, Otis T. Mason from the United States National Museum (usnm) arranged the ethnological exhibits around John Wesley Powell's linguistic map of North America. Mason had a 16 ft. x 12 ft. linguistic map mounted at the center of the exhibit and created separate alcoves with "typical inhabitants" of the areas represented. As Mason explained, "I have arranged the costumes and art productions of these families in separate alcoves, so that the student taking his position in one of them may have before his eye practical solution of some of the theoretical questions which have recently arisen concerning the connection between race and language and industries and philosophies." With his extensive artistic training, William Henry Holmes of the Smithsonian Institution created the life-sized figures that were arranged in dioramas along the exhibit's central aisle.[3]

The U.S. Government Anthropology Exhibit drew from "closed collections," as well as from the collections of the Smithsonian, the Bureau of Ethnology, and the USNM. The challenge for those mounting the exhibit—Powell, Mason, Holmes, and others—was the time pressure of bringing together the artifacts for the exhibits from the copious collections in Washington DC. In contrast, Putnam and Boas were gathering the artifacts for their exhibit through "open appeals." From the beginning of their preparations for the exposition, Putnam, Boas, and approximately one hundred assistants worked fervidly to bring together an extensive exhibit. At the same time, the whole organization of the exposition was wildly scrambling to construct "the White City" and to gather materials from around the world to fill the exhibit halls.[4]

Plans for the World's Columbian Exposition had begun in 1889, at the time of the Exposition Universelle in Paris that commemorated the French Revolution. Curtis Hinsley notes that "the winter of 1889–90 saw a fierce competition arise among Chicago, New York, St. Louis, and Washington, DC for congressional approval to hold the Columbian Exposition." Despite the prevailing East Coast view that Chicago would never be selected as the site for the World's Fair, over two hundred Chicago businessmen successfully lobbied Congress. Money and organized power yielded positive results. The U.S. Congress in April 1890 selected Chicago. Intended as the celebration of the four hundredth anniversary of Christopher Columbus's arrival in the New World, the exposition opened in 1893, rather than in 1892, with the additional year for planning and construction.[5]

The organizers of the exposition desired to create "an American fair, the grandeur of which would prove that American culture was not only equal to, but had surpassed European culture." To accomplish this, they planned to make everything bigger and better. If the Paris World's Fair had 72 acres, Chicago's would have 686 acres, or, as sometimes claimed, over 1,000 acres. If Paris's fair was situated on a portion of the Seine, Chicago's would be built on Lake Michigan and have canals, lagoons, and basins carved out of the swampy land. If Paris had Jules-Alexis Coutan's fountain with the figure representing the City of Paris cutting through the waves, Chicago would have William MacMonnies's fountain of Columbia, borne aloft on a throne in a ship of state paddled by allegorical figures representing "the arts, sciences and industries," as the symbol of America. There was also to be *more* of everything. In "Electrifying Expositions: 1880–1939,"

David Nye remarks, "Many visitors saw more artificial light in a single night there than they had previously seen in their entire lives. . . . Mobile jets of the outdoor electric fountains at either end of the Court of Honor shot water high into the air and wove complex patterns against the night sky. Spotlights underneath the fountains were fitted with colored filters, which permitted operators to create symphonies of color as they spewed forty-four thousand gallons of water a minute in kaleidoscopic variation."[6]

These same planners of the fair allowed for the decorative backdrop of the Native populations. Indians in native dress paddled birch bark canoes in the lagoons, along with, as landscape architect Frederick Law Olmsted wrote, "'Malay proas, catamarans, Arab dhows, Chinese sanpans, Japanese pilot boats, Turkish caiques, Esquimaux kiacks, Alaskan war canoes, [and] the hooded boats of the Swiss lakes.'" Most displays of living people—classified as primitive, or savage—were relegated to the mile-long Midway Plaisance, where the people lived in villages and encampments, made crafts, cooked food, and danced and sang for the crowds.[7] In "Rituals of Representation," Burton Benedict notes, "At both the Chicago fair of 1893 and the St. Louis fair of 1904 'villages' of living peoples were placed in the fairgrounds in what were supposed to be evolutionary sequences from the most 'primitive' . . . to the most 'advanced,' who approximated Euro-American physical type and culture." Thus, the Bedouin Encampment was located at the end of the Midway Plaisance, opposite the Military Encampment; just up the Midway was the Dahomey Village, opposite the Captive Balloon. Then, in order as one moved up the Midway Plaisance toward the heart of the fair, among other displays of living peoples, were the following: Chinese Village, Indian Bazaar, Algerian and Tunisian Villages, Cairo Street, Persian Concession, Moorish Palace, German Village, Turkish Village, Javanese Settlement, South Sea Islanders, Samoan Islanders, Japanese Bazaar, and Irish Village. Right in the middle of the Midway's panoply of excitement was Chicago's answer to the emblematic Eiffel Tower of the Paris World's Fair: "The Ferris Wheel was designed by G. W. G. Ferris. It was a vertical revolving wheel . . . capable of carrying at each revolution 2,160 passengers to a height of two hundred and fifty feet."[8]

The anthropology building was located in the far southeast corner of the fair. About the constant delays in the completion of the building, Boas wrote his parents, "'The construction department *always* leaves us in the lurch.'" Originally planned to be part of the centrally located Manufacturer and Liberal Arts Building, anthropology was squeezed out when more space was needed to display national and international exhibits focusing on manufacturing and industry and, indeed, also when Putnam needed more space for the anthropological exhibits. In December 1892 the board of directors decided that a separate building, "unpretentious and devoid of all ornamentation," would be constructed for anthropology. Putnam had early stated his vision for the architectural style of the anthropology building at the world's fair. In an interview on May 31, 1890, with the *Chicago Daily Tribune*, Putnam had opined, "'The building to contain such an exhibition should be . . . of a style of architecture corresponding in some degree to one of the types of great stone structures in Mexico, Central America, and Peru in pre-historic times, of which the ruins in several cases are fairly preserved.'" Putnam hoped that this would be a permanent building, to form the center of a "'great ethnological museum.'" Putnam did not get this, however. Instead he got a big, plain box of a building, but it was solely devoted to anthropology. He wrote his daughter Alice about his challenges, "'I am driven to death now with plans for interior of my building which is now called the Anthropological Building. It was first called Educational Building, and then Liberal Arts, but I have now got it officially named the Anthropological Building.'"[9]

Marginal in placement and set apart from the palatial and watery white city, the Anthropological Building was adjacent to the cab shops, near the greenhouse and the dairy barns, and just opposite the Forestry Building. A *New York Times* article, "Prof. Putnam's Hard Luck, His Difficulties with the Anthropological Exhibit," remarked on "one very important section of the World's Fair, which because of its inaccessibility and distance from the main buildings, is likely to be overlooked by nine out of every ten visitors." The author asserted that "the long and tedious tramp in sand ankle deep" was worth the effort. In this area—"what might be called the kitchen and the back yard of the exposition"—the anthropology building was set back, "the furthest in the rear, the most forlorn in its exterior and interior, and pre-eminently the one with the most promise of being a failure." As if the marginal location were not insult enough, there was also the interminable "clacking of the elevated railway," about which Putnam complained well in advance of the opening of the fair.[10]

If the Anthropological Building suffered by comparison to the elegance of the White City, so did Putnam suffer by comparison to the central planners of the World's Columbian Exposition. The *New York Times* article described Putnam as a quaint academic, who had a deficiency of good sense. In particular, the article noted that Putnam seemed "to be a sufferer from that great drawback of scientific and professional persons—lack of practicability." With a singular focus on "his ethnological research," Putnam apparently had "none left for the everyday affairs of life which require policy and executive capacity." The reporter continued, "Consequently he has got into snarls and imbroglios and has been buffeted about by more worldly and self-assertive chiefs of departments, who got things done while Mr. Putnam had to wait, and as a consequence his building at this date is unfinished, his ethnological exhibits, many of them, are between here and Patagonia, and the poor scientist has to carry a load of detraction, criticism, and denunciation." The article concluded on a positive note: "One thing he still takes a special pride in, despite his troublesome critics, is physical anthropology." While failing to note that Franz Boas was head of this department, the reporter continued, "The sciences of anthropometry, psychology, and neurology will here be practically illustrated, and the visitor may have his measurements taken and learn his place on the charts demonstrating the physical characteristics of man."[11]

Putnam's feelings must have been assuaged by knowing that he was supported in his home press. In September 1890 the *Boston Herald* had represented his work in glowing terms: "'One of the most interesting features of the World's Fair . . . at Chicago will probably be the American ethnographical exhibit under the direction of Prof. F. W. Putnam of Harvard. The general plan of the exhibit has been approved by the Fair commissioners at large and by the local board of directors and is now under the consideration of a special committee.'" A proud and accomplished academic, Putnam was curator of the Peabody Museum of American Archaeology and Ethnology, professor of American archaeology and ethnology at Harvard, and permanent secretary of the AAAS from 1873 to 1898. From his position at Harvard, Putnam was a leader in American archaeology and ethnology. However, Putnam was out of his element in Chicago, working neither in the museum nor the university, but rather in the setting of a world's fair with "more worldly and self-assertive chiefs of departments, who got things done," as the *New York Times* article represented it.[12]

Still, while not central in location, nor ornate of exterior, the Anthropological Building was spacious—255 x 415 feet, with floor space when the gallery was included of 158,234 square feet. In his 1893 article "Ethnology, Anthropology, Archaeology," Putnam explained his plan "for a department which should illustrate early life in America from remote ages before historic times down to the period of Columbus." Putnam continued, "The legend over the main entrance, 'Anthropological Building, Man and his Works,' is very comprehensive and indicates the scope of the department, which not only treats of the moral, mental and physical characteristics of man, but also shows the beginnings of his great achievements in art, in architecture and in manufactures."[13]

The Department of Ethnology and Archaeology, designated as Department M, continued to expand. The area of physical anthropology was added, with "its subdivisions of psychology and neurology." History, prehistory, and natural history—the latter because the organizers of that branch objected to the original intent, to include it with the Department of Livestock—were also added, as were "the sections of Sanitation and Hygiene and Charities and Corrections of the Liberal Arts Department." Putnam distinguished between "departmental exhibits," under the purview of the Department of Ethnology and Archaeology, and the "isolated and collective exhibits," the latter of "which included the Midway Plaisance, the state buildings, the Viking ship, and the special concession exhibits, such as the Eskimo Village and the Cliff Dwellers." Many anthropological concerns were only nominally under Putnam's purview. As Gertrude Scott notes, Putnam, in all likelihood, "was not directly responsible for any Midway enterprise," and thus he was probably not involved "with the village concessions." J. W. Skiles and Co. of Spokane, Washington, owned the Eskimo Village concession and had sent "an expedition to Labrador to collect ethnological material and to bring a number of Eastern Eskimo" families, along with their dogs, to live "in twelve bark-covered huts very much as they live at home."[14]

Boas was officially appointed as chief assistant in charge of physical anthropology on May 11, 1891. Putnam was enthusiastic about Boas's suggestion for "'a series of charts which would represent the bodily form of Indians.'" Boas worked with two populations: American Indians and American schoolchildren. During the summer fieldwork seasons of 1891–93, "over 70 volunteers, mostly students from universities, were sent out to measure native peoples of America." By the time of the opening of the anthropological exhibits at the fair, 17,000 Indians and 90,000 school children had been measured. The display included the following: "Charts, diagrams, photographs, scientific instruments used in the work, and collections of skulls and skeletons of the native peoples." Visitors to the exhibit on physical anthropology had the opportunity to have "specially trained assistants . . . take measurements and give tests of sight, perception, touch, etc."[15]

Boas wrote of his work at the World's Columbian Exposition, "'It was my general plan to illustrate the culture of the tribes of Fort Rupert most fully, because they have exerted an influence over all the tribes on the North Pacific coast.'" This was demonstrated, Boas maintained, by the fact that the names for the ceremonies all derived from the Kwakiutl language. In "Northwest Coast Indian Culture and the World's Columbian Exposition," Ira Jacknis notes that Boas was incorrect on this point, that, rather, the "terms and the ceremonial complex" had spread from the northern Kwakiutl Haisla-speakers and had been adopted by the Kwakiutl of Fort Rupert and other coastal peoples. Nonetheless, based on his premise developed during his fieldwork in the Northwest Coast, Boas desired to have a large, thorough display of Kwakiutl lifeways from Fort Rupert.[16]

As Jacknis recounts, Boas commissioned Hunt in August 1891 "to 'obtain a large house and the model of a whole village, buy canoes and a complete outfit to show the daily life of the Indians, and everything that is necessary to the performance of their religious ceremonies.'" With the consent of officials at the Canadian Indian Affairs and under the escort of James Deans, George Hunt served "as manager and interpreter" and had brought "nine men, five women, and two children (a 5-year old girl and an 18-month-old boy)" from Fort Rupert to Chicago. Arriving on April 12, 1893—two weeks before the World's Columbian Exposition officially opened and three months before the Anthropological Building would be ready—the Indians from Vancouver Island "were all housed temporarily in three small rooms in the stock pavilion . . . until they moved into the traditional beam and plank houses on the ethnological grounds." Unfortunately, storms in Fort Rupert and Alert Bay had delayed the shipment of their house and the 365 ethnographic items that focused mainly on the winter ceremonials. Hunt had assembled an expansive Northwest Coast collection: "Hamatsa, Grizzly Bear, Nutlamatla—virtually every Kwakiutl (and some Bella Coola) secret society—were represented."[17]

When the shipment arrived in May, the Kwakiutl erected the forty-five-square-foot, cedar-plank dwelling on the shore of South Pond. They leveled the beach in order to launch their canoes. In his report, Johnson quoted Boas's description of the dwelling:

> The front of the house was painted. Over the door was the thunderbird, and on each side the moon, both crests of the owner. The posts were carved. The house that was represented at the Exposition belongs to the clan Ne-ens-sha of the Nakanigyilisala tribe, and represents the houses of their mythical ancestor, Kanigyilak, the creator of the salmon, the great transformer, who transformed the semi-human animals of his time into men and animals. He was conceived by a woman who was exposed to the rays of the sun. He built the house for himself and his brother Nomokwis, and his descendants have built the same kind of house ever since.

The smaller, approximately twenty-nine-square-foot Haida house that Deans had shipped from Skidegate was erected right next to the Kwakiutl cedar-plank dwelling. Boas had commissioned James Deans, the Scotsman—sometimes Hudson Bay Company employee, farmer, and coal worker—to make a collection of Haida material culture, which he did with gusto. He brought three boxcars of items, including an entire Haida house with long cedar beams and carved columns and a forty-two-foot pole. As Deans reflected, it was "'a rather poor specimen of a Haida house but then, as so few of the old houses were left . . . I could do no better.'" Jacknis describes the setting: "In addition to a 40-foot totem pole outside the Haida house, the Northwest Coast village included a Tsimshian heraldic column, Bella Coola memorial columns, Salish house posts, and two Tlingit poles . . . . To complete the scene, several canoes were drawn up on the pond's edge." With the elevated train tracks, the Leather and Shoe Trades Building, and Lake Michigan as backdrops, the Northwest Coast settlement was tucked between the Dairy Building and the Indian School, the latter an exhibit by the U.S. government intended to illustrate the modern education of the Indians.[18]

Before entering what would be their homes for the duration of the fair, the Kwakiutl performed "'the first of a series of ceremonials.'" On the day prior to the opening of the fair, "a requisition went in . . . for 39 yards of blue and scarlet flannel, 232-dozen pearl buttons, and other material needed at once to complete the outfit of the Fort Rupert Indians." One week later the blue and scarlet flannel had been crafted into ceremonial garb bedecked with pearl buttons for the Kwakiutl. As Jacknis recounts, "On the afternoon of May 6 . . . the Kwakiutl marched in procession from their temporary quarters to their plank house, where they dedicated the house and totem poles with dancing." One of the women, of noble lineage, "sponsored a formal feast, complete with orators for the host and guests." While living in this village on the fairgrounds, the Kwakiutl provided demonstrations of their lifeways to visitors, "'whatever is asked of them in relation to their customs and mode of life, particularly the ceremonies connected with their secret religious societies.'"[19]

Both Putnam and Boas were swamped with crushing, overwhelming work. Throughout his career, Putnam added responsibilities without ever giving anything up. As Dexter notes, in the early days of the World's Columbian Exposition "Putnam kept on with his work at the Peabody Museum in Cambridge and fulfilled his duties as permanent secretary of the American Association for the Advancement of Science. Even though he was given a leave of absence from the [Peabody] Museum in 1892, he maintained close touch with matters at home; and his work arranging the meetings and editing the proceedings of the American Association for the Advancement of Science continued unabated throughout the Fair period." While in the thick of organizing the exhibition, Putnam wrote to beg forgiveness from Alice Fletcher, who was serving as the assistant for the Indians of the Western United States for the Department of Archaeology and Ethnology, for the five unanswered letters. There were, Putnam confessed, five hundred unanswered letters on his desk: "'Well,

I am simply overworked and driven to death. This World's Fair business has become a perfect mountain. I am directing parties all over North, South, and Central America and as I have to keep all in funds and report to Chicago monthly and ask for money all the time that doesn't come as fast as it ought to—it is no small job.'" With equal candor, though two years following Putnam's expression of fatigue, Boas wrote his parents, "'I do not have very good remembrances of 1893. A rushing rat-race, great uneasiness, and unsatisfactory work have been its watchwords.'"[20]

While Boas judged his work to be "unsatisfactory," amid the fair's frantic activity he accomplished tasks that had lasting impact. On top of unrelenting responsibilities, Boas taught George Hunt to write texts phonetically in the Kwakiutl language. The foundation for the Boas-Hunt collaboration in collecting and transcribing texts, which lasted from 1893 until Hunt died in 1933, was put in place at the World's Columbian Exposition when Boas sat with Hunt in the Kwakiutl settlement teaching his orthography for the Kwak'wala language. In "The Kwakiutl of Vancouver Island," Boas referred briefly to this time at the World's Columbian Exposition: "We had a number of Kwakiutl there, in charge of my former interpreter, George Hunt; but, being overburdened with administrative duties, the summer passed without any possibility of an adequate exploitation of the rare opportunity except in so far as I succeeded in finding time to interest Mr. Hunt in methods of recording and collecting, which have yielded valuable results in later years." In her assessment of George Hunt's contributions to Kwakiutl ethnography, Berman remarks on the "large, documented museum collections" he had made for Boas over the years, and his work as "a linguistic consultant and researcher." Berman writes, "What he will perhaps be best remembered for, however, are the tens of thousands of pages he composed in the Kwak'wala language on ethnographic and folkloric subjects. These materials make up all but a small portion of the eleven volumes of Kwak'wala text and translation published by Boas."[21]

Boas facilitated the research of two other scholars in the village settlements: he encouraged Harlan Smith to work with the Eskimo from Labrador, and J. Comfort Fillmore to record Kwakiutl ceremonial music for the winter dances. Smith, assistant to the Department of Archaeology and Ethnology for Ohio and Michigan Archaeology, sent Boas a manuscript of the "Eskimo Stories . . . I collected, under your direction, at the Eskimo Village of the W[orld's] C[olumbian] Exposition, together with some further remarks and comments derived both from observations there and subsequent reading." He explained his approach and asked for Boas's guidance: "I have given an account, it seems to me, of about all I learned of the Eskimo and so perhaps have given too much detail & too popular for a scientific publication." He requested that Boas "cut out such unimportant parts or you may indicate them & suggest any changes which you think best & return ms. to me to change." He added, "I fear many things were misunderstood by me and were it not that you were to inspect it before publication I would not dare to send it to an editor."[22]

While there is no copy of Smith's original manuscript, likely Boas changed very little, since the points in Smith's letter appeared in print just as he listed them. The value and charm of the article is in the detail of the account and in the personal reflections on the performance of the narratives, precisely the points about which Smith was concerned. Boas's retention of the "detail & . . . popular" showed that he valued these aspects of Smith's work. In the first narrative, "Olŭngwa," Smith referenced both Boas's *The Central Eskimo*, which Boas had let him borrow, and Rink's *Tales and Traditions of the Eskimo*. "This story seemed to be made up of several short parts, some of which are apparently incomplete and show but little relation to each other." Smith continued, "Collected October 2, 1893. Olŭngwa . . . was a medicine woman, perhaps an angakok, or possibly a pivdlerortok, 'a mad or delirious person,' able to fore-tell events, unfold the thoughts of others, and 'even gifted with a faculty of walking upon the water, besides the highest perfection in divining, but was at the same time greatly feared.'" Smith had substituted the name "Sedna," following Boas's discussion of the sea goddess by that name in *The Central Eskimo*, for "'the woman whose fingers had been cut off,'" as she was continually referenced by the narrator and his wife. Smith continued with a description of the performance that revealed the meaning of the designation for this character: "When telling of Sedna, Conieossuck and his wife would clutch the top of the table, from the side, then letting go the right hand would draw it edgewise over the fingers of the left: or she would hold both hands while he struck them with the edge of his: thus representing the cutting off of Sedna's fingers."[23]

Boas sent Smith's manuscript to Newell for publication in the *Journal of American Folklore* and then sent his own contribution with the following explanation: "I happened to fall in with a party of Eskimos here a few days ago, and obtained some information from them which fitted in nicely with the paper I sent you a few days ago." In "Notes on the Eskimo of Port Clarence, Alaska," Boas explained that a "party of Eskimo from Port Clarence . . . stopped in Chicago on their way to Washington." He was able to ascertain whether "certain traditions, which are of great importance in the mythology of the eastern Eskimo, are found also in Alaska, and if the peculiar secret language of the Angakut is known to tribes of the extreme West."[24]

Boas also encouraged musicologist John Comfort Fillmore "to study a large number of Kwakiutl and other songs of the northwest" from Indians at the World's Columbian Exposition. As Fillmore wrote, "I also recorded songs of the Navaho, besides making some valuable collections on the Midway Plaisance." Using a gramophone, Fillmore collected "more than a hundred" Kwakiutl songs. Before he used this new form of technology, Fillmore had expressed a preference for transcribing music without the use of a phonograph. Recounting his "own methods" for recording Indian music, Fillmore wrote, "First, to listen to the singer attentively without trying to note down what he sings. This gives me a good general idea of the song. The next step is to note down the song phrase by phrase. Then I sing with him, and afterwards by myself, asking him to correct any errors in my version, of course noting down carefully all variations." After having recorded the Kwakiutl music, however, Fillmore wrote Boas about the challenges of puzzling out the stick-beats: "The one advantage of the cylinders, as to the rhythm, has been that, by reducing the speed very low, I could count the beats, which I found impossible when I heard the songs at Chicago."[25]

In "A Woman's Song of the Kwakiutl Indians," Fillmore recounted, "A little before noon on the 3rd of September of . . . 1893, I sat in the lodge of the Kwakiutl Indians, from Vancouver Island, on the Columbian Fair Grounds, Chicago." Fillmore continued, "Close at my right knee sat Duquayis, chieftainess of the tribe, a bright-looking, cheerful responsive young woman of about twenty-two years of age. She was nursing her baby, a strong healthy-looking child. On the other side of me sat another young woman, whom she had called to sing with her a woman's song of the tribe, for my especial benefit." Fillmore related that Duquayis had not believed "any white man could sing the songs of the tribe correctly; but after I had taken her and her husband, with the interpreter, to a room in Music Hall where there was a piano, and had played and sung with the Indians for an hour some half dozen or more of the songs I had been collecting," she apparently acknowledged that "the white man could master the Indian songs." With Boas observing, Fillmore recorded the songs "as fast as I could; but, as they sang faster than I could write, I soon had to ask them to repeat a portion of it." With good-natured self-effacement Fillmore recalled, "Then I sang it with them, which seemed to afford them a good deal of amusement, whether because of the phenomenally unpleasant quality of my voice, or because of my peculiar pronunciation of the words, I could not determine. However, I was determined to get the song, so I did not mind their fun, or, rather, I smiled and laughed good-naturedly with them and sang away." The two women became "extremely interested in what we were doing and eagerly corrected all my errors of pronunciation, clapping their hands and laughing gleefully when I had done it to their satisfaction." James Deans, who was serving as interpreter, told Fillmore, "'You must know, sir, that Duquayis has just done you the greatest honor in her power. She has not only given you a woman's song; she has given you her own particular song . . . which she alone sings at the potlatch.'"[26]

Fillmore returned to Milwaukee, where he was director of his own music school, to work on the transcription of the Kwakiutl music and to puzzle over "the relation of those stick-beats to the song [which] . . . still baffles me." Fillmore concluded that this was "the really serious problem in this Kwakiutl music." He wrote Boas, "I understood you to say that these cylinders belong to the Exposition Association. Will that corporation pay me anything for all this hard work?" While interested in the project, Fillmore admitted that he didn't want to carry the whole load himself without recompense: "I am at recent indebted to Mr. Goodwin's generosity for the use of a phonograph and a battery. I cannot afford either to buy or to rent one." He held out hope that "the Exposition Association" would enable him "to buy such an outfit." Boas wrote Fillmore that Professor Putnam would pay him fifty dollars, and an additional fifty dollars "on receipt of your report on primitive music at the World's Fair." He concluded, "This was the best I was able to get for you." Fillmore replied, "Of course, $100 is no pay for the work I put on these cylinders; but I should do it anyhow, *aus Liebe zur Sache* [from love of it], & I am glad to get anything." Boas planned a trip to Milwaukee to work with Fillmore on adding "the words to the tunes." He hoped that Fillmore would be able to transcribe "as many songs as possible by that time so that I may finish the text of all of them." Boas added, "You know most of the songs belonging to the winter dance ceremonial and I wish to place them in their proper places in the description of the ceremonial."[27]

In 1896 Boas published "Songs of the Kwakiutl Indians." In it he noted that he and Fillmore had recorded the music separately for these eleven songs: "Mr. Fillmore's records were obtained from phonographic cylinders while mine were written down from the singing of the Indians themselves." He continued, "On the whole our renderings of the music agree closely." In "The Social Organization and the Secret Societies of the Kwakiutl Indians," Boas remarked on this "series of phonographic records of songs belonging to ceremonials" that he and Fillmore had transcribed. He noted that he had been able "to verify many of the phonographic records by letting the Indians repeat the songs two years after the records had been taken." While in his publications Boas had remarked on the congruence between Fillmore's transcription of songs and his own, he was more candid in his letter to Marie from Fort Rupert in 1894: "Today I corrected a few of the songs Fillmore wrote down in Chicago. Either the Indians sang very differently into the phonograph, or he could not hear them well. I am positive that I have written them down correctly now, and the difference between my rendering and his is immense." He added, "I have now had enough practice to write it easily." Thomas Ross Miller writes about the disposition of these recordings, "There are even restrictions imposed after the fact on the songs Boas and Fillmore recorded for demonstration purposes in 1893 at the World's Columbian Exposition in Chicago. These wax cylinders of Kwakiutl songs were willingly made by the singers. Some of them were composed, apparently on the spot, by Boas' lifelong partner George Hunt, yet the songs remain individually inherited property." Miller concludes, "Several were 'returned' to their owners by artist Bill Holm in the early 1960s. Even if they were made by singers expressly for reproduction and transcription, songs remain the hereditary property of individuals."[28]

With the explosion of energy invested in the development of the World's Columbian Exposition, the evanescent dream city came to a sudden end on October 30, 1893. In "Memory and the White City," Neil Harris writes, "And then, not unexpectedly but abruptly nonetheless, the fair was over. Not only did it end, but fires, vandalism, and systematic disassembly quickly dismantled almost every physical vestige of its existence." The power and personality struggles that had marked the planning of the fair continued through to its closing. The *Chicago Evening Post* had remarked on this conflict more than two years before the fair opened: "'Fighting the fair seems to be a favorite diversion. The pathway of the Columbian exposition is strewn with mementos of conflict.'" As it turned out, Putnam and Boas figured as "'mementos of conflict.'"[29]

The "split authority structure" of the World's Columbian Exposition obfuscated the person who was really in power. Director-General George R. Davis represented the national organizational structure; president of the Chicago Exposition Company Harlow Niles Higinbotham oversaw the local organizational structure. Higinbotham held the purse strings. Prominent and wealthy Chicago businessmen had formed a corporation, the World's Columbian Exposition in 1889, and had "raised more than $5,000,000 by subscription." As the financial challenges mounted for both the fair and the country, these same businessmen found more resources, often by reaching into their own pockets. Money is power, and thus originated the overarching sway of Higinbotham as president of the World's Columbian Exposition, Inc. As a partner in Marshall Field & Co. of Chicago, Higinbotham was in business with Marshall Field, the man who was to give the seed gift of one million dollars to insure the success of what would become the Field Museum of Natural History. Davis was a senior colonel in the Illinois National Guard and Republican Representative to the U.S. Congress. He struggled in his capacity as director-general of the World Columbian's Exposition to hold his own against the well-heeled businessmen of the World's Columbian Exposition, but his tenacity usually turned to frustration. As Dexter notes, "Putnam became an innocent victim of the animosity between Higinbotham and Davis. Putnam remained loyal to Davis and avoided as much as possible any contact with Higinbotham."[30]

Putnam never quite realized that H. A. Higinbotham, as president of the World's Columbian Exposition, Inc., held ultimate power, and not Director-General Davis, who had hired Putnam and who was charged with planning and producing the fair. Nor did Putnam realize that he was sandwiched between these two opposing foes. Higinbotham clearly understood the source of the conflict with Putnam: "'The whole trouble seems to have arisen from the fact that Prof. Putnam understood instructions from the Director-General of the World's Columbian Commission as binding on the World's Columbian Exposition. The dual organizations of the World's Columbian Exposition and the World's Columbian Commission somewhat complicated the business of the position which he occupied as Chief of the Department of Ethnology, and I can readily understand how he understood that the Director-General had a right and also power to issue instructions.'" While Higinbotham explained the confusion in the "dual organizations" in a dispassionate manner, he was known to treat Putnam with callous disregard. In one instance Higinbotham ordered workmen to create a larger office for himself. Without consulting Putnam, the workers removed the partitions to Putnam's temporary office on a Sunday when no one was around. Dexter quotes Putnam in a letter to Davis:

Upon arriving at my office this morning, I found it in a state of confusion and nastiness that is disgraceful to all who had anything to do with it—without my knowledge or notice from anyone, a force of workmen was put into my office during my absence since Saturday; and partitions have been torn down and plastering removed without any care being taken of all the records and valuable property belonging to my department of the exposition. This office was given to me for my use until another could be provided for me and to be treated in this disgraceful and arbitrary manner is a deep insult to me personally as well as to the position which I hold in the Exposition.

Higinbotham had claimed the working space right out from under Putnam and had in one disruptive move insulted both Putnam and Davis. As Hinsley notes, within eight months "Putnam was forced to move his office nine times."[31]

The Chicago business magnates were playing a high-stakes game, and they did not view Putnam or Boas as part of their team. At the close of the fair, Putnam returned home and left Boas in charge of overseeing the monumental task, which lasted for nine months, of returning the items on loan, or cataloging and transferring them to the Columbian Museum. Back in Cambridge, Putnam responded to a letter from Samuel A. Crawford, assistant secretary to the board of directors of the World's Columbian Exposition, who had asked Putnam to urge the Columbian Museum to purchase the Gunning collection of idols and the library that went with it. Putnam replied, "I am sorry to say that I feel that suggestions of mine are no longer desired by the Trustees and the head official of the Columbian Museum." With uncharacteristic animus Putnam continued, "Since I left Chicago it has been clearly indicated to me, . . . that my advice is no longer desired."[32]

The tidal wave of exhaustion and disappointment engulfed both Putnam and Boas at the end of the World's Columbian Exposition. Each handled it in his own distinctive way: Putnam with patrician grace, Boas with pugnacious missives. Putnam had hoped to be appointed to the position of director of the Columbian Museum of Chicago. He was passed over for Frederick J. V. Skiff, who had worked directly under President Higinbotham as deputy director-general of the World's Columbian Exposition. From his office at the Peabody Museum, Putnam wrote, "I am now getting settled in my old routine in Cambridge, and after the wear and tear of the Exposition I can assure you that the quiet and comfort of my office is a blessing which I fully appreciate." Putnam didn't remain long in the "quiet and comfort of his office." As an "institutional entrepreneur," he seized the next opportunity to shape anthropology in a museum setting. In 1894 he "took charge of the Department of Anthropology of the American Museum of Natural History" on a part-time basis. Putnam wrote Boas, "The Trustees of the American Museum have placed the Anthropological Department of the Museum under my charge, and for the present I am to go there one week in four." Putnam was offered "the position of Curator of the department of Anthropology . . . at the rate of $3,500 per annum."[33]

Boas and Putnam had both anticipated that Boas would be appointed director of the Anthropological Department of the Columbian Museum in Chicago. However, since Putnam's critics saw Boas as Putnam's man, he was tarred with the same brush. Just as Putnam had been accused of being a poor administrator, so was Boas. He wrote Putnam, "The delays in the completion of the Anthropological building were used to best advantage against you and your administrative ability was assailed in every way. . . . I have learned that . . . I was charged with lack of administrative ability again on account of the delay in getting the Anthropological Building into shape." Boas reflected on Putnam's early efforts to introduce the idea of a Columbian Museum, and how Putnam had run headlong into the objections of the President William Rainey Harper, "as he wanted the Museum for the University of Chicago." A keen administrator who was aware of the potential for conflicts of interest, Rainey "viewed the new Field Museum as a potential rival that might 'affect us very severely' unless aligned with the university." Thus, in this "political tangle between the museum, university, and government science," the forces of Chicago businessmen elided with the academic power structure of the University of Chicago, the latter financed by the Rockefeller fortune, and linking right back to business.[34]

While Harper was involved in shaping decisions with respect to the museum, as Boas said, "he left the management of the campaign for the University in the hands of Prof. Chamberlin who has proved to be a most shrewd politician." The University of Chicago Professor of Geology Thomas C. Chamberlin had in his previous position as president of the University of Wisconsin worked with the U.S. Geological Survey in 1881, and he had been affiliated with Powell, Holmes, and Walcott. Chamberlin saw an opportunity to build a scientific center at the University of Chicago, to be directed by "his former colleagues in the Survey, Charles D. Walcott in geology and Holmes in anthropology." In Chamberlin's own words, they would make a "'glorious team' to lead Chicago science to 'the highest and best things.'" Boas conveyed to Putnam that "Chamberlin has two ends in view, one to make the Museum subservient to the University, the second to strengthen the Geological Survey." After securing the support of the trustees, Chamberlin, in Boas's words, sought out the "man whom he could influence the most," for the position of the director of anthropological exhibits, and this was Holmes.[35]

With outrage, Boas conveyed to Putnam Chamberlin's plan to create a position for Walcott and to entice him away from the U.S. Geological

Survey. "In order to further his plans regarding Walcott," Boas wrote, "he is trying to divide the Department of Paleontology which is now in charge of Baur and to make invertebrate Paleontology while vertebrate Zoology is to be part of Zoology." He concluded, "The division . . . is made only to make room for Walcott at the University." Certainly, Chamberlin did not want Boas, for, as Boas had written his parents in February 1894, "'I am a thorn in Chamberlin's eye because he regards me as one of Putnam's men.'" Boas summarized in the opening to his four-page letter of February 18, 1894, "Mr. Holmes has been practically appointed director of the anthropological Department and the Museum authorities are willing to let me step down and [let me] take the ethnology under him which he does not want." He added, "This information comes from Harper." Boas did not garner this directly from a conversation with President Harper, but, rather, "indirectly and from certain remarks which have been made in my presence in the Museum."[36]

Boas fought with a war of words. He told Putnam of his plan to write Director Skiff to ask if anyone "besides myself is being or has been considered for the position of Director of the Anthropological Department, since I have been in charge of the Department." If Skiff equivocated or answered in the affirmative, Boas wrote, "I shall discontinue my present relation with the Museum at once. You will see that I shall have to go now [in February] or in May. These people simply want to take advantage of my knowledge of the collections and break off after I have made the installation." Recognizing the precariousness of his situation, Boas acknowledged that "I may be willing to make a new bargain with them to finish the installation for a decent pay and this I should do only because I must try to make money." Boas had been working exhaustively and unceasingly to transfer the collections of the World's Columbian Exposition to the new Columbian Museum to be housed in the Palace of Fine Arts, one of two buildings to remain as the fair's legacy to the city. As he noted, "Unfortunately the greater part of the work has been accomplished already; else I should stand a much better fighting chance." Once more facing uncertain employment, Boas ended his letter to Putnam, "You spoke several times of recommending to President Elliott to appoint me at Harvard University. I beg to ask you now most urgently to use your influence in that direction."[37]

Boas and Skiff exchanged numerous curt and acrimonious missives during the winter and spring of 1894. They were able to reach an agreement by mid-February. Skiff proposed that Boas stay "until the period of installation is over, providing you are paid a greater salary than you are at present receiving." Boas had responded, "I am ready to continue in charge of the Anthropological Department of the Columbian Museum until the first of May 1894, provided I am paid the sum of eleven hundred dollars for my services during that period." In an effort to ferret out the details of the offer made to Holmes, Boas also exchanged letters with Holmes and W J McGee at the BAE. Holmes tried to shut down Boas's questions by responding that the communications had been confidential. McGee wrote that Holmes was not "a party to any arrangements prejudicial to you." McGee also attempted to calm Boas and to support his colleague at the BAE: "There was undoubtedly, a small group of men, including Prof. Chamberlin, . . . who desired to have Prof. Holmes go to Chicago." McGee posited, "This desire doubtless grew out of appreciation of Prof. Holmes' experience and ability in museum work, an experience and ability which in my judgment place him in the front rank of museum men in this country, and indeed in the world; and the technical skill and knowledge are combined with genius in original research." Assuring Boas that Holmes had initially "hesitated" because he was troubled by "the confidential nature" of the offer, McGee stressed that Holmes was much concerned "as to how you would be affected should he accept." McGee assured Boas that Holmes did not "accept until he had made the provisional condition that you should, if you desired, be retained in the museum in an important capacity." McGee wrote that he was providing Boas with extensive details in order to show how far Holmes was "from engaging in any arrangement which might be deemed injurious to you."[38]

Holmes wrote Skiff about his concerns: "'Boas's antagonistic position with respect to my coming has given me a good deal of discomfort.'" At the same time, he thought that "Boas's departure would be a calamity." Holmes suggested that Boas be put "in charge of physical anthropology and made 'agent of the Museum for all the great northern regions of the globe,'" with his time divided equally between the field and the museum. In the end, Holmes's effort to create a position came to naught. While Boas was willing to accept "a curatorship of overseas anthropology," he wanted this to be at an equal salary to other curators. When Holmes arrived in Chicago on May 7, Skiff took him uptown to a meeting of the executive committee of the trustees of the museum. Boas, it appeared, had overplayed his hand. The trustees were not willing to encumber an additional eight thousand dollars to hire him, an amount that would have made Boas's salary equivalent to Holmes's. On this point of equity Boas was most adamant. Boas was put out of his office, or, as he wrote his parents, "'I was chucked out.'"[39]

Neither Putnam nor Boas ever stood a "fighting chance" for what they hoped to realize in Chicago—Putnam as head of the Columbian Museum and Boas as director of the Anthropological Department of the Columbian Museum. The monumental work that both had invested in the fair and the confusion over its organizational structure overlay the ground rock of the World's Columbian Exposition: the city of Chicago. From the battle in 1890 over choosing the site of the world's fair to the challenge in financing it, as well as to the selection of those in charge of the exposition, this was enduringly about Chicago and the future of the city. The struggle along "'the pathway of the Columbian exposition'" was fundamentally a struggle between Chicago and the East Coast. In 1890, when Chicago was selected as the site for the Columbian World's Exposition, the city was widely known for its stockyards and for the 1871 fire that had entirely consumed it. Chicago was dismissed by those on the East Coast as a place to slaughter livestock and to make money. Following his appointment to chief of the Department of Ethnology and Archaeology, Putnam had warned Davis about the views of "'the eastern people.'" Davis typified this disparagement by Easterners as an attempt to "'roast'" Chicago. Those in charge of the exposition wanted to forge a new image of their city, one of creative achievement and of expansive wealth.[40]

The powerful forces in control of the exposition were guided by an implicit agenda, that all things from the Columbian World's Exposition should benefit Chicago and those based in Chicago or allied to it. The selection of Skiff as director of the Columbian Museum and the passing over of Putnam fit snugly with this agenda: Skiff was an ally and crony of Higinbotham and the other leaders of the World's Columbian Exposition, Inc. The appointment of the director of the anthropological exhibits at the Columbian Museum was carried out with subterfuge. As Douglas Cole notes, "Holmes appointment was intended to be secret—secret, Boas thought, only from him." Boas was kept dangling *and* working. While he clearly suspected that he was not going to be appointed to the position he so desired, and that he felt was his, he could not find the definitive answer to his question: Who was going to be the new director of the anthropological exhibits? All the while that Boas was writing letter after letter to Skiff, confidential negotiations were underway to recruit William Henry Holmes to the position.[41]

From the start, Holmes did not really want the position, and he certainly had no desire to move to Chicago. He was born, as he liked to reflect, in 1846, the same year that the Smithsonian Institution was founded. He had established himself in Washington as "the leader of 'Washington anthropology.'" Nonetheless, he allowed himself to be recruited to the position in Chicago, where he was in charge of the exhibit that had been assembled by Putnam and Boas. Never acclimating to his new position or to Chicago, Holmes disliked the administrative work at the Columbian Museum. Further, he "found when he got to Chicago that his appointment was considered tentative, and he was kept 'on the ragged edge of uncertainty.'" In three years Holmes had left his position in Chicago to return to Washington DC, where he headed "the Department of Anthropology in the reorganized National Museum."[42]

Aggrieved at the way he was treated, Putnam wrote Boas from Cambridge that he was "very much disgusted" with matters at the Columbian Museum. He continued, "I feel that I have been very shabbily treated by Mr. Skiff and the Trustees, after . . . all the work I did for the Museum, the conception of which was mine and would never have been accomplished had I not worked for it as I did." Putnam concluded with indignation, "Such ingratitude I have never heard of before and I am very much disappointed." The following week Putnam sent Boas a check to cover the expenses for the loan of exhibits from Europe and referenced "the Columbian Museum and your position." Putnam referred to the "humbuggery" of it all:

> I have wiped my hands of the whole Columbian Museum business, which has been a dirty piece of work on the part of many, and I

am glad that I got out of it before Chamberlin began his intriguing and Skiff began playing his double game. We know that such things cannot succeed in the end, but unfortunately science must suffer in the meantime. I did hope that the Columbian Museum would start on a good honorable scientific basis, but I suppose that was too much to expect. I am very sorry for the Museum that it has lost your services.

Skiff didn't want anyone at the museum, Putnam insisted, who was associated with him. Additionally, both Putnam and Boas were too bruised and insulted to recognize one salient point: W. H. Holmes was a distinguished and recognized anthropologist. As Cole notes, his "stature could justly rank second to none." Being considered also for a position at the AMNH, Holmes had been characterized as "'at the head of his profession.'" Thus, while Boas and Putnam declared Boas the best suited for the job, others recognized the achievements of a quiet scholar of erudition whose career had been so entwined with the Smithsonian and Washington as to render him ultimately inextricable. He stayed in Chicago only three years before moving back to Washington.[43]

Putnam wrote Boas, "I have told all hands that I have come in contact with that you are the best man for the place, and should have been retained." Indeed, the word did spread about Skiff's treatment of Boas. Just one week following Boas being "chucked out" of his office, Newell wrote him after having spoken with Putnam that he could not fully "express my disgust at your own personal news." The following week Daniel Brinton wrote Boas, "The action of the Managers of the Col. Mus. was most shabby. I cannot believe that Mr. Holmes was a party to it." In June Georg Baur remarked, "I just learned from Donaldson about the dirty trick the Museum people played on you, and am again furious." He asked, "What can be behind it," and then, with an indirect reference to Chamberlin, "Is our common friend still intriguing?" Baur concluded, "It again shows the absolute ignorance of the administration." Hale also wrote Boas in June that "the actions of the authorities in charge of the Columbian Museum was most disgraceful." He continued, "It will, I believe, prove in the end more injurious to them than to yourself." He hoped that the "results should be to place you ultimately in a much better position than you would have held with them." Hale ended, "Your proper place is a professorship in a first-class University."[44]

During this time of uncertainty in Chicago, Boas never relented in pursuing other venues for permanent employment. He wrote McGee at the BAE about the possibilities for his doing anthropometric work: "Perhaps you can make an arrangement so that I devote a few months to the organization of that work taking it up in Indian schools." Boas reminded him that, with some fieldwork, he could "complete the work on the Chinookan language, part of which is now being prepared for the printer in your office." There was a brief glimmer of hope that the University of Pennsylvania would create a position for Boas through joint funding with the Wistar Institute of Anatomy and Biology. This prospect fizzled because the deed of trust for the Wistar Institute forbade joint appointments. Harrison Allen, anatomist and physician at the University of Pennsylvania, wrote Boas, "I need hardly tell you of my profound disappointment that our efforts to secure you for our University have failed. We did everything in our power, but the Fates appeared to be against us."[45]

Boas's friend and colleague Henry Donaldson tried repeatedly to sound out President Harper about the possibility of employing Boas. On August 18, 1894, Donaldson wrote Boas that he had met with the president, who "is a very much exhausted man, and by reason of that fact does not take a very cheerful view of life." Undoubtedly, after the tumult over the appointment of Holmes as Director of Anthropological Exhibits, Harper was not inclined to entertain the thought of employing Boas at the University of Chicago. Harper opined after Boas's time at the World's Columbian Exposition that "Boas did not 'take direction' well."[46]

Boas was poised on the knife's edge, not knowing where he would find employment, not knowing how he would be able to support his family. The only certainty for him was uncertainty, in his awareness that he was totally dependent on the decisions of others. In May 1894 Boas had written his parents, "'All our Chicago ships have gone aground.'" Chicago had been for Boas and Marie a time of despair and grievous loss. He and Marie had rented an apartment on Stewart Avenue, approximately three miles from the World's Columbian Exposition. With only two positive points in its favor—it was located across the street from Marie's sister, Alice, and it was affordable—the flat was small and hard to heat. Under pressure of work, Boas left early in the morning and rarely returned home in time to be with his children. On March 24, 1893, Marie had given birth to their third child, Hedwig. The nurse did not come and Marie's mother, who was to arrive five days later, had been delayed due to a broken wrist. Boas assisted the doctor in the home delivery. When she did arrive, Marie's mother and her sister Alice helped enormously with caring for Marie, the new baby, two-year-old Ernst, and three-and-a-half-year-old Helene. By April Helene came down with the measles and passed them on to Ernst. By May baby Hedwig, affectionately called "Hete," was so ill that she was unable to keep food down, and by July she was still underweight by about three pounds. As Cole recounts, "In August all three children had fevers; in December it was flu, followed by whooping cough." Alternating nights, Boas and Marie sat up with the children. The baby's cough worsened, her fever rose, and she developed bronchitis. On January 11, 1894, as Boas cradled ten-month-old Hete in his arms, she struggled for breath and then died. Later, when Boas was in the Northwest Coast, he wrote Marie, "I think again so much of our poor little child. I don't know why. I saw before my eyes . . . how she hit around with her little hands, and how I held her in my arms—the poor, poor little thing."[47]

Boas and Marie's dear friends, who had moved from Clark University to Chicago, stood by them in their time of tragedy. Georg Baur made arrangements for the burial. A tiny coffin was delivered to the family's apartment and baby Hedwig was laid inside. The next day, Franz, holding the coffin in his lap, and Marie rode together in a wagon to Oakwood Cemetery. Baur, Donaldson, and Bolza met them there. In freezing weather, they gathered around the small and barren plot to lay the baby to rest. Cole recounts, "The cemetery was detestable—a barren, treeless field bordered by swamps and manure fields. The grave site was too small for plantings, so they bought a new, family-size grave and themselves moved the baby to it on Saturday." Sunk in unrelenting sadness over the loss of his baby Hedwig, Boas was also inundated with the medical bills that had been accumulating with each childhood illness in the fall and then were compounded by the two doctors who attended Hedwig in her last week of life. Both Putnam and his father had lent him money. On the heels of this family tragedy and economic hardship, Boas saw his job hopes evaporate.[48]

The lease for the Stewart Avenue apartment ended in April. Marie left with Helene and Ernst to stay with her mother in New York, and Boas accepted Donaldson's invitation to stay with him. When Boas left toward the end of May, Donaldson wrote him that "the house seems quite lonely again now that you have departed." While Dawson had asked Boas to return to the Northwest Coast to conduct additional fieldwork for the BAAS, Marie queried, "'How much richer does it make us?'" She reasoned that he would just have another report to write, which would interfere with any job that might come his way: "'Don't go west. I can't let you go.'" Boas listened to Marie and returned to New York.[49]

Joan Mark identifies the three major centers for anthropology in the nineteenth century, all on the East Coast: Harvard was first, Washington second, and Philadelphia third. Initially the two centers of Harvard and Washington "were nearly equal in resources and prestige." Mark continues, "They were competitive, but generally in a friendly way, and individuals moved back and forth between them." From these East Coast institutions, Mark recounts, "Putnam, Fletcher, Cushing, and Holmes all knew one another, and they knew John Wesley Powell and Franz Boas. Together they made up a complex and interlocking scientific community. They worked with an eye on one another." There was, however, a new force at play, with the emergence of the power brokers in Chicago. The scientists at the World's Columbian Exposition, at the Columbian Museum, and at the University of Chicago were not so genial and polite to others. They were playing for keeps. There was in this battle between the East Coast and the Midwest the genesis of grit that emerged most clearly in the treatment of Putnam at the Chicago World's Fair. The Columbian Exposition coincided with, and likely provided impetus to, the founding of the University of Chicago, which was emerging rapidly as a new center of power and influence.[50]

While Putnam and Boas left Chicago with battered egos and deflated spirits, their combined work yielded lasting results that lay much farther out on the horizon than they could see. Ironically, Putnam's success at the Chicago World's Fair also made him vulnerable to the expansive criticism to which he had been subjected. He became so conspicuous to Higinbotham and others of the World's Columbian Exposition, Inc., and to members of the press precisely because of his grand vision for the anthropology exhibit. As Dexter notes, "For two years he planned the greatest exhibit of its kind ever assembled and sent out field workers all over the New World to collect specimens and data for the grand exhibition." When Putnam's collections outgrew the space allotted to him in the Manufacturers and Liberal Arts Building, he needed a separate building. The delay in its construction was laid at Putnam's feet. In a sense, he was blamed for his vision and his success. Putnam's massive collections formed the core of the departments of zoology and anthropology in the Field Columbian Museum. Putnam's and Boas's work lived on, long after the Anthropological Building and the other buildings of the Columbian World's Fair lay smoldering in ruins.[51]

As the World's Columbian Exposition prepared to close its doors, the same press that had pilloried Putnam now praised him. On October 8, 1893, the *Chicago Sunday Herald*, as quoted in Dexter, called Putnam's anthropological exhibits "'one of the marvels of the Fair'":

> To collect this has been the work of three active years by Prof. Putnam and his corps of assistants. Nearly every quarter of the globe was explored in search of material to illustrate the development of mankind. Nearly every museum in the country has also contributed its share, to say nothing of the exhibits sent by archaeologists in foreign countries. From ancient Greece to modern Mexico the world has been ransacked. From the very hour of his appointment as department chief he set about the difficult problem. He started expeditions to Peru, Chile, Bolivia, to North Greenland, and Labrador, to the British Northwest Territory, and to nearly every country of Europe in search of material for his great work.

The praise was too late to give balm to Putnam's wounded spirit.[52]

Boas's lasting contributions to the World's Columbian Exposition remain in iconic representation in the Kwakiutl *hamatsa*. Jacknis writes, "Franz Boas first witnessed the return of the Kwakiutl *hamatsa* (or cannibal dancer) initiate in a dramatized version at the fair." He used this as an inspiration for his work for the U.S. National Museum, when he constructed the life figure groups. Additionally, the Smithsonian modeled their creation of the cedar-plank screen after the one created at Chicago's fair. Jacknis continues, "Boas's display, in turn, was copied by George Dorsey and Charles Newcombe at the Field Columbian Museum in 1901 . . . [that] remains on view to this day. Thus, a performance at Chicago in the summer of 1893 has continued to serve as a key image of Kwakiutl culture." George Hunt and the other Kwakiutl from Fort Rupert constructed a village on the shores of Lake Michigan, which would live on in Boas's, Smith's, and Fillmore's recordings of songs, and in Boas's and Hunt's collections of linguistic texts. For Boas, the work with the Kwakiutl in Chicago would reverberate for years in his Northwest Coast fieldwork.[53]

Boas's accomplishments elicited boundless pride within the family circle. Sophie Boas wrote her son, "According to a recent letter from Jacobi you are known in the U. S. A. as 'erster Anthropologe' [the first anthropologist] and you need not fear that your work at the Fair was in vain." Sophie continued, quoting Jacobi, "'The work he did in Chicago was prodigious and has received recognition. Even his old tormentor President Hall at Clark University calls him the most prominent American anthropologist. He is a fine fellow and already very famous.'" She advised, "So my dear boy, keep up your courage and do not allow yourself to be depressed. Everything must turn out well in the end." Knowing clearly her son's reaction to adversity, she reflected, "Of course you are right, dear Franz, to try everything to assert yourself. If you would only not allow yourself to become so angry and upset. You use up your strength too soon and will be old too early in life." She concluded, "I love you dearly the way you are but for your own good I wish you were different."[54]

9

Your Orphan Boy

Struggling to Find a Place

Boas returned from Chicago to his family in New York City in the latter part of May 1894 and stayed in the city for one month. Just prior to his departure for Alma Farm, Boas wrote Georg Baur, with a candid reference to his severe depression, "I have long wanted to write, but am so lazy and dispirited that I hardly do anything. I had intended to go to Germany, but had a breakdown as a result of all the excitements of the past year. The doctor forbade me to go and demands that I rest in the country." To Franz's parents Marie wrote, "After all the stress and excitement, poor Franz is completely kaput.'" Serving as his doctor, Jacobi ordered Boas to sleep ten hours a day, to work only moderately, to eat well, and to nap in the afternoon. The trip to Germany to visit his father, who had been ill, was canceled. Following Jacobi's instructions, as Boas had written to his parents, "'I will let my nerves run down and I will await my future in peace.'"[1]

For Boas, working moderately meant three hours in the morning and three in the afternoon. While he expressed pleasure that he was able to sit in the park in the afternoon and "'do some scientific work again,'" he was still spurred on by his competitive edge and his desire for vindication. "'When all my things in press appear,'" Boas wrote, "'enough people will see and understand that no one here has accomplished as much as I have.'" Defiantly, he had told Skiff in Chicago that "'I am both here and abroad, one of the first in my field and . . . in about two years I will be uncontestably the first.'" Boas's insistence to Skiff that he would be first in his field was undoubtedly a protestation of rage at having been excluded from what he had regarded as his rightful job as director of the anthropology department of the Columbian Museum in Chicago. Highly regarded in the United States and abroad, nonetheless Boas was without a position. He was, as Douglas Cole characterizes him, "a loose fish in part because he had willed it." In his relentless efforts to find the perfect position and to avoid compromising his principles, Boas ended up, as Curtis Hinsley and Bill Holm explain, "excluded from the networks of personal and institutional loyalties that largely controlled entrance and advancement in American anthropology in the last years of the century." Boas did, however, have the support of his two guardian angels, Putnam and Jacobi, and the wind beneath their wings would eventually carry him to joint positions at the AMNH and at Columbia University.[2]

Donaldson wrote Boas with sympathy, "It does seem that your moves are checked on all sides but I trust that we shall get daylight through the difficulty before too long a time. I am glad that Dr. Jacobi told you what to do and that you are doing it." He added, "It seems quite remarkable to me that you have been able to hold out the way you have and I do not believe that anything short of training in the Arctic regions would have fitted you for it." By mid-June Boas was emerging from his depression. He wrote Baur that he was "beginning to feel better." Boas had traveled to visit AMNH President Morris K. Jesup in his Lenox home. Wealthy banker and philanthropist Jesup was typified by a friend for his "'ability to make money and the disposition to dispose of it in unostentatious benevolence.'" Jesup expressed his concern to Boas about his health: "It seemed to me last evening that you looked tired and worn. Had you not better take a week off now?" At about the same time, Donaldson had written to Boas, "I trust that your forced leisure will accomplish its purpose and that you will find Lake George as beautiful as ever." Four days later he wrote, "I was glad to get your letter, but it did not give me the impression that you are resting to any great extent." Indeed, as Donaldson had surmised, Boas was back at work. In fact, he had not ceased working. From mid-May through June 1894, Boas had written his report for the World's Columbian Exposition, though he had been convinced for months that those in charge had little interest in the significance of his work.[3]

Through the influence of Putnam as permanent secretary of the AAAS, Boas had been elected vice president of Section H, the anthropology subsection, for 1893–94. Thus, while in the midst of his challenge to find permanent employment, Boas could take satisfaction in knowing, as

George Stocking points out, that "the first eight years of his work in this country had just won him recognition as the presiding officer of what was then the only national organization in his profession—Section H of the American Association for the Advancement of Science—an honor that pleased Boas all the more because some still thought of him as a 'foreigner.'" By mid-May 1894 Putnam had written Boas to inquire about the title for his address to the annual meeting of the AAAS, to be held in Brooklyn in August 1894. Boas set about writing his talk, "Human Faculty as Determined by Race," while at Alma Farm with Marie and the children. Boas felt devoid of a "'special gift for popular presentations,'" and he was frustrated by having to take such a broad and sweeping approach to race. Nonetheless, he was pleased with the reception of his talk, which he delivered on August 21. Cole reports, "Marie and many other friends and relatives were in the audience; he was particularly gratified when Mrs. Jacobi complimented his English."[4]

Boas's 1894 address was an early statement of his approach to the study of race. With logical precision, he dissected assumptions about the supposed superiority of the white race, assumptions based on "the inference . . . that the white race represents the highest type of perfection." Boas posited, "Furthermore, as the white race is the civilized race, every deviation from the white type is considered a characteristic feature of a lower type." He continued, "First of all, we must bear in mind that none of these civilizations was the product of the genius of a single people. Ideas and inventions were carried from one to the other; and, although intercommunication was slow, each people which participated in the ancient civilization added to the culture of the others. . . . Ideas have been disseminated as long as people have come into contact with each other and . . . neither race nor language nor distance limits their diffusion."[5]

Stocking remarks on the "limits of Boas' critique in 1894." Boas anticipated that "some mental differences between races would be found to exist; he accepted the inference his friend, the neurologist Henry Donaldson, made from apparent differences in 'the capacity for education' to the cessation of brain growth in the 'lower races.'" Stocking continues, "In short, he had not achieved a fully developed notion of the cultural determination of behavior as an alternative to the prevailing racial determinism." However, the seeds to his approach to race were present in 1894;

they were logically packaged and promised future development. Here were the shackles of tradition that Boas himself aspired to cast off: "The power with which society holds us and does not give us a chance to step out of its limits cannot have acted as strongly upon them as upon us. On the other hand, the station obtained by many negroes in our civilization seems to me to have just as much weight as the few cases of relapse which have been collected with much care and diligence." W. E. B. DuBois and other leaders of the black intelligentsia responded with alacrity to Boas's "Human Faculty as Determined by Race." Undoubtedly Boas had posited points perilously close to the offensive assumptions about the inferiority of "the races not equally gifted"; at the same time, he put forth the proposition that "many individuals of all races" could be equally gifted.[6]

Putnam offered encouragement to Boas during the months of his unemployment and then during the even longer months of his temporary employment. In his new position as curator of the Department of Anthropology at the AMNH, Putnam hoped that he might be able to do "something for you by and by." Putnam continued, "As soon as their new wing is completed, which will be some time this year, there will be a good deal of arranging to be done, and . . . I shall hope to have you with me in New York for some special work which may lead to something more." Putnam concluded, "Of course my great wish is to have you here in Cambridge, but I see no chance of bringing that about at least for some time. We are all so poor that it is difficult to get a living salary for anyone." He closed the letter, "However, keep me posted, and believe me, / Ever your sincere friend, / F. W. Putnam." By mid-May 1894 Putnam was still explaining his new position at the AMNH. "Now as to the New York Museum," he began, "I have had no 'plans' about New York." Clearly Putnam felt the need to repeat his rationale for taking a second job as curator when Boas had left Chicago unemployed and without the position he thought would be his: "I have taken the position because I believe that I can do much in guiding anthropological research by having the direction of two great institutions. I think much good will come out of cooperation in this way, and I believe it will give me the means of placing some good men in good positions by and by. Unfortunately, at this moment neither the New York Museum nor the Peabody Museum has funds for the employment of additional workers and we are forced to wait for a while." Putnam held out the tantalizing prospect, that he had "some projects ahead which I hope to work out, and I believe if I do that they will also be to your benefit." About these projects, he could say no more, but he assured Boas "that you must always think of me as your sincere friend, and one who will help you in any way in his power, and that with the many things I am connected with, something may turn up for your benefit." In a handwritten postscript, Putnam added, "Of course I shall be pleased to have you make the Museum your scientific headquarters and I can give you a place to work in but unfortunately no salary."[7]

Toward the end of June 1894 Putnam wrote Boas that he would be seeing Jesup in July to talk about "the whole question of anthropology at the New York Museum and how it shall be represented." By July Putnam was hoping that he had "a wedge for you with respect to the New York Museum." Finally, Putnam had settled on a project, and he had spoken with Jesup about having as complete a collection as possible made of "models illustrating the different tribes of America." Putnam continued, "These models to be in every respect correct and dressed in the garments of the people, and arranged in groups so as to represent the life history of each tribe represented. I told Mr. Jesup that there was no one better prepared to do this work than you and I thought as you were going to the north-west coast this fall, and as we had so many garments and objects of various kinds from that region, it would be the best region for us to begin with in the preparation of the ethnological groups." Jesup was enthusiastic about the idea; Putnam asked Boas, "How much of this can you undertake this coming fall?" Putnam continued, "I believe if you could make some models of the people, or if that is impossible, take very accurate measurements, photographs, drawings, etc., so as to have a set of models made illustrating the people and some of their industries, and some phase of their home life with its proper surroundings, that would be a first rate thing for you; and you would then be employed to set up the groups, and in that way you would have your wedge started for a position in the Museum."[8]

In November 1894 Putnam wrote his first "brief report upon the Department of Anthropology" for Jesup. He stressed the importance of creating life "groups made of models taken from life among living peoples. . . . Each of these groups should show a family or several members of a tribe, dressed in their native costume and engaged in some characteristic work or art illustrative of their life and particular art or industry." While Putnam envisioned the life group models "made of all the peoples of the Earth," he maintained that the initial focus should be on "the native peoples of America, from the Eskimo of the extreme north to the inhabitants of Tierra del Fuego." Skillfully, Putnam maneuvered his discussion from the more general life group models to Boas's work in the Northwest Coast. He wrote Jesup, "I am glad to be able to report that material for the construction of two such groups as I have described is now being secured for the Museum by Dr. Franz Boas from the tribes living on the Island of Vancouver."[9]

Putnam extended messages of hope and Boas's family despaired. Of the ethnographic work in preparation for the World's Columbian Exposition, Boas's brother-in-law Rudolph Lehmann had opined that Boas "had arranged the whole thing; it was all your work and Putnam had pocketed the honors." While relaying Lehmann's remarks, it was clear that Boas's mother, Sophie, was in accord. With her practical and no-nonsense manner, Marie was thoroughly impatient with what she viewed as Putnam's never-ending promises that yielded few positive results. Boas, however, remained "Your Orphan Boy," as he had signed his letter to Putnam on January 4, 1893, and held onto Putnam's optimistic predictions of a positive future. Boas appreciated Putnam's gifts, for, as Joan Mark writes, "Putnam was an organizer, an energetic and genial man who did not dominate others, for he preferred to work alongside them." Mark continues, "He gave advice and friendly counsel to nearly everyone who entered the field" of anthropology. This advice and counsel eventually did pay off for Boas.[10]

Over the summer months and into the following year, Boas began bundling short engagements together, or, as he called it, "'doing jobs,'" so that with the sum total of payments he might earn enough to support his family. With funding from the BAAS, Boas carried out three months of fieldwork in British Columbia from September to December 1894. Putnam encouraged Boas to submit a grant application directly to him for funding by the AAAS for the restudy of the California Indians at the missions of San Luis Rey and San Juan Capistrano. The anthropometric work, including casts and photographs, needed to be redone because the researchers who had undertaken them for the WCE had made mistakes.

By August Putnam had sent Boas two hundred dollars from the AAAS for the California Indian project. Boas was also engaged in another anthropometry project, this one with the Department of the Interior's Department of Education for two hundred dollars, to write a monograph on "the measurement of children with a view to growth and development in the School period."[11]

Putnam was able to obtain three hundred dollars from the AMNH for Boas to prepare northwest coast life model exhibits. Jesup had authorized, as Putnam wrote Boas, "not over $300" for material for the groups. Putnam continued, "While your employment at the museum is held in abeyance, there is little doubt in my mind that you will be employed at the compensation you have stated in order to prepare the groups." He closed, "So I do not see, my dear fellow, but what things look bright for you ahead, and that after the cloudy days the sunshine is coming." For a similar but distinct project, Otis Mason had offered Boas a salary of three hundred dollars a month, for the approximately two months that Boas would work at the U.S. National Museum (USNM) on the life figure models of Northwest Coast Indian dancers. When completed, these models would first be displayed at the 1895 Cotton States and International Exposition in Atlanta, Georgia, and then would become part of the permanent collection at the Smithsonian's USNM. Before he departed for the Northwest Coast, Boas visited Mason in Washington DC to discuss this work. Boas was also engaged to conduct a survey of the collections on Northwest Coast artifacts in European museums and to compile a descriptive catalogue of the collection in the USNM.[12]

Boas suggested the following life groups for the AMNH: "1) woman making a mat or a hat and continually rocking a baby; 2) woodcarving, and painting; 3) the hamatsa returns from the woods." In these three groupings Boas had, even prior to his 1894 fieldwork in Fort Rupert, identified the life models he wanted to create. Indeed, he had described what would become emblematic of his fieldwork in the Northwest Coast, through the photographs compiled for the construction of the models. Ultimately these photographs would become, as Aaron Glass remarks, "preeminently mobile, traveling between scholars as well as back to indigenous subjects, they [would] . . . play a central role in recursive representation and the creation of generalized cultural emblems."[13]

Your Orphan Boy

By September 1894 Boas was back in the Northwest Coast. His energy and his exasperation had returned. From North Bend, British Columbia, he wrote his parents, "I could tear my hair that nothing came of the Chicago business. When I think of the $7,000, how nicely I could have helped them, instead of having to count every penny." He concluded, "Well, something better will come up soon. One cannot always have bad luck in everything one touches." He worked with a resolve that his research would lead to a job. From Victoria he wrote Marie, "Yesterday afternoon I went with equipment and a photographer to the prison and got photos and one [plaster] cast of an Indian. I hope to get more tomorrow and the day after so that I will have good things for the Museum, so they will hire me to make their groups in case there is nothing better." He concluded, "At present I am so hopeful, as if all our troubles had been solved. I am so tired of this kind of wandering life I lead." Gradually Boas adopted a new attitude about his research, one that was less frenetic and obsessive than his approach in previous visits to the Northwest Coast. He wrote Marie, "I am slowly getting into the mood for 'field work' again. I don't let myself worry and just do what I can. If there is no work to be found, I don't mind and take it easy. You will see how fat and healthy I will return."[14]

Boas's new attitude was directly linked to the expectations of those funding and directing his work. While his first Northwest Coast field trip in 1886 had been self- and family-funded, the research trips of 1888 and 1889 were funded exclusively by the BAAS Committee for the Study of the Northwestern Tribes of Canada. Secretary of the Committee and Research Director Horatio Hale had been emphatic in his instructions about where Boas was to go, what he was to study, and how he was to report it. Boas bridled under Hale's control, broke loose from the exclusive funding of the BAAS, and obtained support from the BAE for his 1890 and 1891 research, much to the disappointment of members of the BAAS. Committee Chair Sir Daniel Wilson wrote Boas in 1890, "I learn from Mr. Hale, with much regret that we shall not be able to secure your valuable services to the extent that we desire." In the fall of 1891 Hale quoted Wilson's remark in his letter to Boas: "'I note your information about Dr. Franz Boas. . . . I wish it were possible to secure the entire services of the doctor in our Canadian field of research; but it is vain to hope for such good fortune.'" Boas had achieved the autonomy he desired.

In 1890 he received support from the BAE for "a trip to Puget Sound for the purpose of conducting linguistic investigations among the Coast Salish and the Chinook of the lower Columbia River" and in 1891 for a field trip to the "Columbia and the Yakima Reservation." BAE ethnologist Henry W. Henshaw extended only minimal direction as evident in his "hasty word" in response to Boas's letter of July 1, 1890: "By all means, if possible, obtain a vocabulary of the Cayuse. It will probably be the last opportunity a linguist will ever have. If possible also secure some account of their tribal history, where they formerly lived, the reason for their rupture with their relations to the east."[15]

Boas did accept a small amount of funding from the BAAS to collect ethnographic artifacts and to compile anthropometric measurements. Chagrined at the loss of Boas's full attention to fieldwork for the BAAS, Wilson wrote, "I have full confidence in your judgment, and shall feel much obliged by your formulating a plan of work for yourself—as far as you can give us your valuable services." Boas's acceptance of the three-month BAAS support in 1894 hinged on two factors: Boas's financial need, and Hale's withdrawal from the Committee for the Study of the Northwestern Tribes of Canada. Boas and Hale ended their tumultuous relationship with gracious words, long in coming for both of them. Hale wrote Boas, "I have thought myself fortunate in being able to assist in carrying forward our investigations. . . . I hope these services to science will be long continued, and that the friendly relations and personal regard between us will be maintained while I live." With affection and respect, Boas wrote Hale, "Anthropologists are certainly very much indebted to you for your devotion to this work, and it must be a great gratification to you to have helped to continue the work which you inaugurated so excellently during the Wilkes expedition."[16]

In 1894 Boas was returning to familiar places and familiar people. In his letter to Marie, written from Glacier, BC, he described his vigorous three-hour hike "up the mountain without a trail." When he arrived at the top, "I went straight to the glacier, which I knew from my first trip." The next day, Boas wrote Marie about "the old owner of the Hotel." He continued, "I recognized him right away." From Victoria Boas related, "Yesterday I saw the [Indian] woman and the little child who were in Chicago. She had lost her husband, whom you may remember. He was the one with

Your Orphan Boy

the side whiskers. He suffered from the heat in Chicago." As he entered the harbor of Fort Rupert on board the Barbara Boskowitz, Boas told Marie, "a few Indians came out in one canoe. Among them was my old friend . . . who had been head of the Chicago group." Boas described the voyage north: "I stayed on deck the whole time because I was so interested in the country in which I spent some time eight years ago. I know every promontory, every bay, and the legends connected with them. After about two hours the village of Nawette [Nawiti] appeared, and two boats with Indians approached. Among them was Tom, my old . . . interpreter, who was one of those who had been in Chicago. The village is as primitive as it was before. The people still wear nothing but woolen blankets. Their faces are still painted. Everything invoked old memories."[17]

Boas described his arrival in Fort Rupert on November 13, 1894: "I was coming down the coast in a small steamer which, as it approached the village in the middle of the night, blew its whistle until a canoe came alongside." George Hunt was in the canoe and likely had been waiting on shore the whole day for the arrival of the steamer. Hunt took Boas to his one-room house. "Considering the fact that he has six children," Boas wrote Marie, "two of whom are married and also living there, you can imagine that the house was very crowded." Hunt was "having another little house" built right next to his place where Boas stayed. Boas continued, "The first morning we discussed what I planned to do, and I invited all the Indians to a feast, which took place in the afternoon. That was a sight! There were about 250 Indians in the house—men, women, and children. They were painted red and black and wore jewelry; each was dressed in his cedar bark cloak." People crammed into the small, unfinished house where Boas was staying and spilled outside. After the arrival of "members of the secret societies," when everything went "dead silent," there were the welcoming speeches, the singing, and the "'feast'" that Boas provided of "hard tack and molasses." He explained, "Before we ate I made my speech. I said that I had wanted to come for a long time and that I was glad to be here now." In "The Indians of British Columbia," Boas gave a synopsis of his speech and the formulaic response of the Kwakiutl:

Before the biscuits were distributed I had to make the formal speech deprecating my small feast and asking my guests to be happy and to eat to their hearts' desire. In return I was told that no feast like mine had ever been given and that I was a great chief. The figurative speech of the Kwakiutl Indians has it about like this: "You are the loaded canoe that has anchored in front of our village and is unloading its riches; you are the precipice of a mountain from which wealth is rolling down upon all the people of the whole world; you are the pillar supporting our world." And all this for a treat of hard tack and molasses.

Boas concluded, "But the gross flattery of this speech must not be taken too seriously, as it is simply a stereotype formula used for expressing the thanks for a feast." As he wrote to Marie, "Then I spoke to the people who had been in Chicago and gave them their pictures," which had been taken at the WCE.[18]

Not only was Boas returning to familiar places and seeing people he had met before, but he was also more relaxed in his work and more patient with the expectation that he attend all the feasts. "I am going to these feasts in a blanket and head ring," Boas wrote Marie, "and am on very friendly terms with the people." Of his good fortune he observed, "I am much better off here [in Fort Rupert] than in Alert Bay because there are no white people here." He wrote Marie, "The salmon were all cooked and placed on platters. These were long flat platters as one can see in the museums. Olachen [fish] oil was poured over them and we started eating. You really should see me in my blanket eating with a spoon out of a platter together with four Indians!" Boas concluded his time in Fort Rupert with an apple feast for the people and went several nights without sleep because the people "will be dancing to bring back the new Hamatsa," the cannibal spirit.[19]

Boas took the Barbara Boskowitz to Victoria. From there, as he wrote his parents, "I am on my way again to the interior where I hope to make a few hundred more measurements if possible . . . and then I return via San Francisco to New York." He added, "The thing I look forward to most in 1895 is the 'Wiedersehn' in Berlin." From South Bend, Washington, Boas wrote his friend Baur, "I must still spend a week at the mouth of the Columbia River, and then go to southern California." He added, "The results of my trip are fairly good, but not exceptionally so." At the end of his three months in the Northwest Coast, Boas yearned for home. As he wrote his parents, "The last weeks of work out here are very sour for me." All that kept him in place was "despicable money." At the end of his fieldwork, he didn't remember the positive feelings he had had at the beginning when he had written Marie that "the disagreeable feeling I had that I don't get along with the Indians is slowly wearing off now, and I am hopeful that I will get good results."[20]

Completing his fieldwork, Boas traveled to Southern California to conduct anthropometric work on the Mission Indians. He went to San Francisco on January 13, 1895, and gave a lecture on January 16 to students and professors of Stanford University. Intent on using his time well, Boas was making contact with people at both Stanford and the University of California, for, as he wrote his parents, "'I must make myself personally known as widely as I can.'"[21]

Boas returned to his despair about his lack of a permanent job. From Bay Center, Washington, he wrote, "'What good is the consciousness that I am among the best in my field here in America if I cannot use my ability, but am forced to work, here and there, to earn our living.'" Boas revealed his soul's torment in his letter to Marie from San Francisco on December 30, 1894. He reflected, "'It is the second time that I have looked into hell.'" Douglas Cole reflects, "The first had been Baffin Island during the winter of 1884–85." He continues, quoting Boas, "'And I hardly know which is worse.'" Boas knew well "'how to be silent with dignity,'" but he needed at this time "'for once to cry out before you.'" The mood of despair lifted somewhat when he met with people from Stanford and Berkeley. As he wrote his parents, "'After almost 5 months of loneliness, human contact did me a lot of good.'"[22]

While Boas was completing his work in California, Putnam was attempting to gain permission from Jesup to hire Boas. On December 8, 1894, Putnam summarized his conversation with Jesup: "I respectfully make the following suggestions. First—that I be authorized to propose to Dr. Franz Boas that he shall so arrange his plans as to be able to accept a position in the Department as early as possible next Fall, at such a salary as may be agreed upon, but not to exceed the amount stated in our conversation." A notation, penciled in the margin, read "$3,600 to $4,000 a year."[23]

Reaching New York on January 29, 1895—after having travelled through "the villain blizzard"—Boas wrote his parents, "'Oh, how happy I am to be back with my family!'" He had resolved not to be separated from his family again, "Wherever I go after this, you will go with me. In the event that I have to stay in Washington for two months, you will go with me; or if I should have lectures in Cambridge for four weeks, then we would go there." True to his word, Boas, Marie, Helene, and Ernst traveled by train from New York to Washington in mid-February 1895. They took up residence in first one boarding house, then another, when the landlady of the first proved to be an alcoholic.[24]

Boas found the Washington anthropologists "surprisingly sympathetic" to him. He suspected that Mason and McGee felt bad about his situation following the unpleasantness over the Chicago Columbian Museum, when Holmes had been hired and Boas had been fired. In June 1894, one month after Boas had returned home from Chicago, emotionally and mentally exhausted, McGee had written Boas about the prospect of the BAE publishing his anthropometric work. McGee closed the letter, "Trusting that you are rapidly regaining your wonted health and intellectual vigor." Boas wrote Putnam, "'The Washington people felt uncomfortable.'" He surmised, "They had 'participated in the performance,' but did not anticipate the final outcome. 'Therefore I know, they will be willing to do for me a good deal that they might otherwise not do.'" Assistant Secretary of the USNM J. Brown Goode had written Boas about the construction of the life models, "We are desirous of having the group (for which you have the materials) mounted, and shall probably wish to exhibit it in Atlanta [at the Cotton States Exposition], and I hope that we may be able to make a satisfactory arrangement with you in regard to superintending its construction and proper labeling." Goode also wanted to engage Boas for "doing some work upon the collections" of the Northwest Coast material in the USNM, specifically to "identify every object with reference to is geographical and ethnological source, and its use." Goode continued, "This information, together with the material which I am sure you would be able to supply from your own experience as to the industrial life of these peoples in connection with these objects, would be a valuable contribution to ethnology, and would no doubt serve not only as a basis for the full labeling of this collection,

Your Orphan Boy

but also for a bulletin which we might well print." Goode concluded, with emphasis, "The main object after all . . . is to bring under control *the collection* which we now have."[25]

In his initial meeting with Mason at the USNM in July 1894, Boas had agreed that he would "set up a figure of some kind representing a dancer" on his return from the Northwest Coast. Boas explained to Putnam that he would create separate life models for the USNM and the AMNH: "I should select another subject, of course, for Washington and there would be no trouble in finding still another or others for groups to be set up in New York." Putnam was nonetheless concerned:

> Now a word about your present work: I trust the groups you are making will not be anything like those you have planned for the New York Museum, as that would not be at all advisable. Please let me know about this. I trust you will have as little as possible in common in the groups. You can readily see what my trouble would be if after all I have said about my plans for the New York Museum, I should have anything that would look like a copy of what you had done for Washington. It would be bad for both of us.[26]

Because of his anxiety that Boas's life groups at the USNM and the AMNH would duplicate themes, Putnam insisted that Boas abandon his plan for the AMNH, to create one of the models of "the hamatsa returns from the woods." Aaron Glass writes, "This initial suggestion for a Hamat'sa group in New York had the possessed initiate emerging from the woods, a ritual stage prior to that illustrated in Washington." The model for the USNM was based on the exhibit created for the 1893 WCE—"Chicago Jim as a Hamat'sa" emerging through the mouth of the cannibal spirit that was an opening in a painted ceremonial screen. Instead Boas created models for the AMNH that focused on the technologies of working with cedar bark. Of these life groups, Boas wrote in the 1900 catalogue for the AMNH North Pacific Coast collection, "'The importance of the yellow and red cedar is illustrated in the group case in the center of the hall. A woman is seen making a cedar-bark mat, rocking her infant, which is bedded in cedar-bark, the cradle being moved by means of a cedar-bark rope attached to her toe. Another woman is shredding cedar-bark, to be used for making aprons.'"[27]

Boas completed the life group model and his study of the collection. He gave Goode "the result of my examination of the collections from the North Pacific Coast in the United States National Museum." He had organized the material into "eight groups: Yakutat, Tlingit, Northern British Columbia, Kwakiutl, Nootka, Coast Salish, Chinook, Salish of the Interior," and he included "an evaluation of the collection and what needs to be done to it." With the work on the life group models and the catalog completed, Boas, Marie, and the children left for Europe on board the Dania of the Hamburg-America line. Finally, they were able to make the trip to see his father, who had been in ill health. Boas and Marie had had to postpone the trip for ten months, first due to Boas's mental exhaustion on his return home from Chicago in May 1894, and then to the numerous short-term jobs he had had to complete.[28]

USNM Curator of Anthropology Otis T. Mason wrote Boas about the preparation of the life group figures for the 1895 Cotton States and International Exposition in Atlanta, "I think our painter has succeeded pretty well in getting the color of faces." Mason added, "You must be having a good time in Berlin with all the great ethnologists. I hope you will present my kind regards to Dr. [Adolph Bastian], Dr. [Eduard] Seler, Dr. [Albert] Voss, Dr. [Fedor] Jagor and others who may inquire about me." Boas grew impatient with the view that he was "having a good time." In a letter to McGee, who was the ethnologist in charge of the BAE, Boas conveyed what he had written to Powell: "It seems to me that you think I am having engagements here in Europe, but all the work I am doing is literary work for American institutions."[29]

With the confluence of forces, the two leaders of American anthropology—Putnam of the Peabody Museum and of the AMNH, and Powell of the BAE—began a tug-of-war for Boas. In a letter dated June 7, 1895, Powell had offered Boas a position as editor for the BAE Department of Ethnology. Boas acknowledged receipt of the offer for a position at the BAE in editorial work, with "the remaining part of my time and energies to be expended, continuing my scientific researches, the pay to be $1800 for the coming fiscal year." McGee wrote Boas of the offer, "Congratulating you on the continued success of your work." Putnam realized that Powell threatened his plans for bringing Boas to the AMNH. He sent a telegram of "calculated exaggeration" to Boas in

Berlin: "jesup joins Columbia to secure you hold Washington off = Putnam." Suddenly Boas held in his hands one offer and the possibility of another. He had to decide which would be the most beneficial for him and his family. Following Putnam's advice, Boas maneuvered for time in his response to Powell and attempted to postpone his decision for six months. "I should accept your offer without hesitation," Boas wrote Powell, "if I had not undertaken a series of obligations which I cannot settle in the short period between now and the first of July. . . . I am unable to withdraw from any portion of the work, which will keep me occupied until the middle of December. If you should be able to keep the position open for me until that time I should be inclined to accept your offer." Powell responded with regret that Boas couldn't assume the position immediately. There was, Powell emphasized, "a large amount of proofreading and other editorial work" to be done by August, but, he added, he would "endeavor to hold the position for you until the literary work on which you are now engaged is completed."[30]

Putnam was clearly put off his game. In a long letter to Boas, Putnam began, "Your cablegram has put me into a very unhappy state of mind." He continued, "I wrote to President Low about getting you for Columbia College, after a consultation with Mr. Jesup. Mr. Jesup thought if we could manage to keep you in New York through the winter somehow or other, that next year would open better for us in many ways, and between Columbia College and the Museum we could be pretty sure of giving you a satisfactory position." Boas read the tentative nature of what Putnam had dressed up as a conditional offer, one which depended on "managing to keep you in New York," and "somehow or other" having something open up. Depending on the viewpoint, this might well be the pivotal point. Boas's family thought Putnam had been offering hope but stringing him along, but Putnam maintained he had been trying to open a "wedge" for Boas. The stakes were high: there could be a job in New York, but there was a job in Washington. How could Boas keep both options and maximize his choices? Putnam continued his effort at suasion by quoting President Low, who at that time was in Europe: "'If Dr. Boas is available in the autumn I shall be glad to do everything in my power to bring about such cooperation as you suggest, but until my return it is impossible for me to say more.'" Marie was exasperated.

"'Putnam is a beast!'" she exclaimed. "'I know what the delay means—that he has nothing definite and thinks he can regularize things when you go back.'"[31]

Putnam envisioned having Boas join with William Z. Ripley, "who has been appointed Professor in the Institute of Technology, but who also holds the position of Lecturer in Columbia," and with Livingston Farrand at Columbia. Putnam added, "If we can keep you in New York we shall have a very strong team there; and I believe that both Mr. Jesup and Mr. Low will be very anxious to see this brought about." He continued, "I am getting considerable hold on the people in New York, and I think if we can all pull together there we can build up a great anthropological institution which will be worthy of our efforts. Now while I feel very confident that you will be all right and will have a good position in New York next year, if you can manage to take some temporary position for the winter, that is two or three months at the Museum in connection with some good position in the university, and that all will come out well." Putnam appealed to what he knew to be Boas's desire for freedom from constraints: "I should hate to have you go to Washington, where I do not believe you would be either as happy or as free as you would be in New York." Then in a reasonable tone, he queried, "Now is it not possible for you to postpone the consideration of Powell's offer until you return to this country?" By that time, Putnam thought, "we could determine matters pretty well." He added, "At the same time, I cannot ask you to give up a certainty for a strong probability." Finally, he advised Boas how to approach Powell: he should say that he would like to wait to decide until he returned to the United States so that he would be able to talk with him in person, and that he shouldn't say anything about the New York possibilities because "that would at once make him say 'now or never' to you."[32]

Boas responded to Putnam, "Your NY scheme suits me in every respect," he wrote, "and I am indebted to you for broaching it." He told Putnam, as background, "My name has been suggested to Pres. Low as long as 3 years ago by my friend Dr. A. Jacobi of NY, Professor of Diseases of Children at Col[umbia] College who has also sent him my bibliography." Boas reflected on the plans for Ripley and Farrand to take on work as anthropologists. He opined that Ripley was "unknown as an Anthropologist," and that Farrand's knowledge of anthropology was limited. "These

Your Orphan Boy

two young men," Boas acknowledged, might become "good Anthropologists and . . . may build a Dept., and such a gradual development may suit President Low best." Nonetheless, while Boas considered "the outcome of the plan in regard to Columbia College doubtful," he was "willing to run the risk, if you can offer me anything definite in connection with the Museum." Boas followed Putnam's advice. He had written Powell that he was endeavoring to bring all of his "present engagements to a close as rapidly as possible." Fulfilling part of his obligations to the BAE from his fieldwork conducted "in the summers of 1890 and 1891 and in December 1894," Boas enclosed "the first half of *Kathlamet Texts*," which would be published by the BAE in 1901.[33]

In a loquacious, seven-page letter, Putnam cajoled Boas not to give up hope: "You may be sure that it is not any falling off of interest in you or in the great work I wish to accomplish with your assistance that has delayed my writing to you." He told Boas about his two-day visit "with Mr. Jesup at his country place in Lenox where I had a splendid opportunity to talk to him about the great scheme I wish to carry out for the New York Museum." Jesup was "thoroughly interested," Putnam conveyed, and was "pretty confident" that arrangements could be made with Columbia College so that Boas could split his time between the museum and the college. Jesup "seems to think," Putnam opined, "that President Low's letter to me was favorable and that we could bring about that connection." Putnam couched the tenuous nature of the possible joint employment with the AMNH and Columbia College with the certainty of the museum work in the fall on the life group models for three hundred dollars. Appealing to what he knew was Boas's sensitivity about status and position, Putnam explained that Boas would be "Assistant in charge of the divisions of Ethnography and Physical Anthropology." Then he described the plans to construct the wing of the museum to be devoted to the anthropology department with a half-million-dollar appropriation. Concluding the overview of his plans, Putnam admonished, "You also must have faith enough in me to believe that I will probably succeed in what I have undertaken to do." Putnam had also "passed a few hours with Professor Goode," and they had spoken about Boas. Goode related that the BAE was trying to hire Boas and that he hoped to have Boas's services through this connection with the National Museum. "Then he asked," Putnam wrote, "if I was trying to get you for New York and suggested the idea of a division of time between New York and Washington." With characteristic optimism, Putnam surmised, "So I think you have the reins decidedly in your own hands, and if you postpone Powell's offer until you get over in the fall and can look your ground over, everything will come out to your satisfaction. The result will be, I believe, that you will settle in New York." Putnam concluded, "Now my dear friend I cannot urge you to give up a sure thing for a position that you feel may be uncertain. I can only reiterate that I think you would make a great mistake to bind yourself irrevocably to Washington while there [are] so much better prospects ahead for you in New York; and I believe you can hold Washington in abeyance until you return and see how things are to be in New York."[34]

While Putnam thought Boas had the reins in his hands, Boas felt in a quandary. "I am at a loss to know what to do," he admitted to Putnam. While he could understand that Jesup wanted to delay a decision until the work on the life groups had been completed, Boas would have "to give Powell a definite answer" on his return. He hoped that Jesup and Low would have "at least a first statement . . . as to what they are willing to do." Boas received a less-than-patient communication from Washington. McGee requested that Boas "report in this office at the earliest date consistent with your convenience." Boas replied that he desired "to arrange matters" in person, and that he was finishing up and returning soon.[35]

In the midst of the correspondence with Putnam in New York, and with McGee and Powell in Washington, Boas quietly pursued possible employment at Stanford University. He wrote a letter "to President D. S. Jordan, Palo Alto," on June 19, 1895, about his research "among the Indians of the Pacific Coast" with whom he had worked for "a number of summers." Boas admitted that "the conditions under which I am working are not satisfactory. The long distance at which I live from the field of my researches makes the work unnecessarily expensive and often prohibitive to add necessary data." He continued, "Furthermore, the field is too wide for me and I need helpers, which I can only obtain by means of training students for fieldwork." He was inquiring about a position at Stanford because he had received "an offer of Major Powell to enter the B[ureau] of Ethnology." Boas said his "objections which I

Your Orphan Boy

have to that plan are based on" his desire to be located on the west coast, and his need to train student assistants.[36]

Boas's letter landed on Jordan's desk at a troubled time. The U.S. government was suing the Stanford estate in 1894 for fifteen million dollars. While Stanford did, indeed, win the case, this new university was under threat. Keen to have Boas on campus, Jordan asked if "[you] could make Palo Alto your headquarters for work while retaining funds from other sources for the purpose of carrying it on," and, at the same time, "training students and otherwise using your time in research?" Boas had asked Powell if he could be stationed "on the Pacific Coast," while he worked for the Bureau, "so that I might be able to act at the same time as professor at a college." Powell thought that "such an arrangement might be advantageous to all concerned."[37]

Just prior to Boas's return, Putnam had written of his fatigue and of his planned vacation in the White Mountains of New Hampshire. He thought everything would work out in New York. Then, as if in proof of his fatigue, Putnam misspelled the names of the two key players: "I have seen Dr. Jacoby [sic] and President Lowe [sic], and Dr. Jacoby [sic] has also seen President Lowe [sic]." Low wanted to have Boas "connected to Columbia" but didn't know where the money would come from since the budget for the fiscal year had already been determined. Putman said that Low would let him know by the middle of October. Putnam wrote that he thought it likely "that you will be appointed lecturer this year with a professorship another year, but I draw that from the general tone of Mr. Lowe's [sic] conversation, and not from any definite promise he has made me." At this same time, Nicholas Murray Butler, who was a member of the faculty of philosophy, wrote to Columbia College President Seth Low in response to his letter "of the 4th regarding Dr. Boaz [sic]." Butler reviewed Boas's background: "I take pleasure in saying that he is one of the most competent Anthropologists now living. He is by birth and education a German." Butler continued, "His reputation is secure," and he had held "important chairs." Butler conceded, "For [a] year or more I have been strongly urged by some of our own officers and interested outsiders, to suggest to you that Dr. Boaz [sic] be permanently attached to Columbia as Professor of Anthropology." Butler conveyed to Low that he had not done so because "the financial situation" was such as to "make the suggestion inexpedient." Instead, Butler suggested that Boas be secured to deliver "a series of lectures in connection with the Museum of Natural History." Butler intimated that this might lead to a "more permanent connection with Columbia" for Boas.[38]

Finally, on December 6, 1895, Putnam offered Boas a position at the AMNH as "Assistant in the Department of Anthropology of Natural History." Astonishingly, Boas declined the offer. In an incomplete and unsigned draft of his response, Boas wrote, "In reply I beg to say that I cannot accept such a position in the museum because I consider that my place among American Anthropologists entitles me to more than a third class position, and because for that reason I am not inclined to accept directions from anyone except from yourself as Curator of the Museum. The organization of the Museum is such that in the absence of the Curator, the Assistant Curator [Mesoamericanist Marshall Saville] becomes Acting Curator and I cannot accept a position which would in any conceivable way place me under his direction." Boas wrote that he would be "willing to accept the task of taking charge of the Departments of Ethnology and Somatology for the year 1896, . . . as a Special Assistant," to oversee "the material from the North Pacific Coast, from the Eskimo and from the Islands of the North Pacific Ocean so far as possible and to implement the making of groups illustrating primitive life and also to take charge during that period of the somatological collection." He stipulated that the work he undertook "be carried out on a definite plan" agreed upon in advance, and "it must be understood that the work contracted for is done entirely under your personal supervision, not under that of another person who might be charged with the duties of the Curator of the Museum."[39]

In his letter to Putnam on December 9, 1895, Boas referenced conversations of "yesterday and the day before yesterday." Putnam had offered him the "charge of the Ethnographical and Somatological Collection of" the AMNH during 1896 as special assistant. After these conversations, Boas said he was "ready to accept such a contract," with certain stipulations, most particularly that he would be working only "under your personal supervision." The next day Putnam wrote Boas, "President Jesup at my request has appointed you special assistant in charge of the Sections of Ethnology and Somatology in the Department of Anthropology for the year 1896." Putnam closed the letter, "I could have no one better qualified than you to take charge of these important sections of my department and help me to make the department all that our loved science demands it should be." Without a doubt, Putnam had been working just as concertedly to convince Jesup of the wisdom of hiring Boas. Jesup finally "decided to 'take a chance and hire the young man.'" Boas had his break: he was in the employ of the AMNH. At that time in 1895, this was a modest undertaking. As Boas later recalled, "The whole space available for the Department at that period consisted of one hall on the top floor of the Museum, and I believe a gallery in the old building."[40]

Boas's guardian angels, Jacobi and Putnam, had been working persistently for years, and often in confidence, on his behalf. Jacobi had written President Low of Columbia College in 1892 inquiring about a position for Boas and again two years later. In both instances he had received negative responses. Putnam was more visible and more voluble than Jacobi in the role of mentor and supporter of Boas. A combination *macher*—Marie had judged him "'lackadaisical and unreliable'"—and kingmaker, ultimately for Boas he was a kingmaker. While Marie likely missed it, Boas undoubtedly felt it: Putnam cared deeply about Boas. On August 9, 1895, Putnam wrote his daughter Alice, "'You know I have deep affection for Dr. Boas and there is no man for whom I have a greater respect and whose learning I most greatly admire.'" Putnam had been absolutely crucial for Boas's success in obtaining the positions at the AMNH and Columbia College. He wrote Boas in February 1896, "I am very much pleased with the way things have turned out in regard to your appointment. I was so firmly convinced that everything would come out to your satisfaction that I simply urged patience on your part. I am delighted with the results. You see it was worth waiting for." With the hire of Boas, Putnam also felt vindicated for the humiliations he had suffered at the WCE. He wrote his daughter, "'I regard getting Boas as a grand thing, for Boas and myself make a pretty strong team and with [Marshall] Saville, [Harlan] Smith and [George] Pepper to help, you see I have the best equipment of any anthropological museum in the country and I'll show Chicago I can go them one better.'"[41]

In May 1896 President Seth Low wrote Boas, "I am authorized to say that you have been appointed Lecturer in Physical Anthropology in this

University. The appointment extends from July 1st, 1896 to June 30th, 1897, when it expires without further notice, unless definitely renewed." President Low concluded, "The allowance is $1,500 per annum." The next day Low sent Boas official notification that the trustees had appointed him Lecturer in Physical Anthropology. Once Boas signed the letter, Low said he would arrange for Boas to meet with "several officers of the University whose work touches the domain of Anthropology in different parts." He referred to Farrand's lectures on anthropology and to Ripley in the Faculty of Political Science. Low continued,

> You have yourself been appointed under the Faculty of Pure Science. It is evidently necessary that there should be perfect coordination in the treatment of the subject from these different points of view. To that end I have constituted Prof. Cattell, Prof. Giddings, Prof. Woodward, and Prof. Peck a Committee on Anthropology, under whose directions all of the work in Anthropology in Columbia University should be carried on until we are prepared to create such a Department by the appointment of a professor in charge. The gentlemen giving lectures upon this subject in any of its aspects will naturally be connected with the Committee.

Low had also sent Putnam a copy of the letter. Putnam wrote Boas, "I congratulate you on the appointment." This was a success for Putnam and Boas, as well as for Jacobi, behind the scenes as he was. With his never-ending support, Jacobi, and possibly also Boas's Uncle Kobus, had confidentially donated the funding for Boas's first-year salary at Columbia. Putnam informed Jesup that "'a friend of the Museum, of the College & of the Doctor's'" was willing "to donate $1,500 toward Boas's salary, until Columbia could commit itself. . . . Jesup accepted Jacobi's confidential guarantee as a bridge to Columbia's share. Boas had no inkling beyond knowing that Jacobi was lobbying on his behalf. Indeed, he never learned that, without Jacobi's guarantee, he might have missed the offer."[42]

Franz Boas had found his way to Columbia University and the faculty took note. Professor of Psychology James McKeen Cattell wrote, "I congratulate you and the university most sincerely on the appointment," and he invited Boas to dine with him to talk over the courses

Your Orphan Boy

that he would offer the next year. Pioneer of Iranian studies Abraham Valentine Williams Jackson wrote Cattell, "The idea of Dr. Boas' giving a seminar next year on North American Languages is delightful. It will be a valuable acquisition in connection with the introductory course on the Study of Language with which I have been so closely associated during these past three years. I hope that a number of students may be able to take advantage of so good an opportunity." Jackson asked Cattell to convey to Boas how much he would like to meet him "and talk over the subjects for I want the language students to have the opportunity of profiting by this opening." He regretted that he hadn't known about Boas's hire in time to "announce it in connection with our Oriental Division Circular in which the language course is regularly included." In a handwritten note at the top of the letter, Cattell asked Boas if he could write Professor Jackson "regarding work on languages." Boas wrote Jackson and Jackson replied that he was delighted to know "that Columbia next year will have the advantage of your seminar on North American Languages." Jackson concluded, "As soon as the pressure of examinations is over I hope to have the pleasure of calling upon you to say in person as I have in my hand, I am glad of the offer you are making to our linguistic students."[43]

With relief Boas had written Baur, "At last we have found a house at 123 West 82 St. and hope to move in soon. May I count on your help in getting my things shipped from Chicago from the storage warehouse? We shall also need the furniture that we lent you." Months later Boas wrote Baur again: "I do not know whether I wrote you that I am appointed lecturer at Columbia College. That, of course, is only the beginning," he continued, "and I hope that something will come out of it so that I can gradually obtain a sensible position in New York." Boas was poised to marshal his gifts and to draw on his accomplishments. Esteemed by leading anthropologists and ethnologists, Boas had been lauded for his work in physical anthropology, ethnography, fieldwork, and for the courses he would develop. The French physical anthropologist Paul Topinard had written Boas in assessment of his work in anthropometry, "I find that you are the man, the anthropologist I wished for the United States. Your country has plenty of Ethnologists and Prehistoric men, but few real anthropologists. Anthropometry is a hard thing but with great skill of labour gives positive results." At the same time, Frank Hamilton Cushing lauded his ethnographic work as being "more scientific and more significant not only with each new installment, but also, as compared with other current articles than anything I have lately seen in ethnographic lines." For fieldwork, Putnam identified Boas as the person to send to Central America to undertake "the study of the living tribes with the hope of finding some clue to the interpretation of hieroglyphs." Boas was, Putnam asserted, "the right sort of a man, one who has tact to get along with the natives, and one who would thoroughly appreciate the work he is to undertake and the opportunity for ethnological study in an almost unknown region." Putnam continued, "There is no one in the country so well qualified for this work as yourself." J. Walter Fewkes wrote, "I hope your courses . . . will be successful, as I have no doubt they will, and that in at least one of our Universities there will be given that Ethnological and Archaeological training so much needed in America."[44]

The leading nineteenth-century anthropologist E. B. Tylor bestowed the greatest praise on Boas. In 1889 he had written, "You must allow me to say from conversation with you & reading your writings that I have seldom known anyone better qualified for all-round work in Anthropology. If we are to get the native religions & other ideas of the North-West thoroughly investigated, I think you are the anthropologist to carry through this task." In a letter to Boas, Hale quoted Tylor, "Dr. Tylor's last letter has a passage which will gratify you. He writes, 'I was just reading Dr. Boas on the Central Eskimo, published by the Bureau of Ethnology at Washington, a most valuable account and which makes me feel jealous at its being published in the United States and not in Canada or England.'"[45]

Boas's recurrent research on the Northwest Coast—1886, 1888, 1889, 1890, 1891, and 1894—marked him as preeminent in the field of ethnography and also yielded a change in his work. The shift in his approach resulted from the following three factors: his increasing autonomy in determining the territorial and thematic scope of his study; his increasing knowledge of the peoples, languages, and cultures of the area; and his increasing expertise in conducting fieldwork. By 1890 Boas had begun dividing his fieldwork into three categories: linguistic, ethnological, and

Your Orphan Boy

anthropometric. Illustrative of this tripartite division of his research, Boas wrote in a letter to his parents in 1890, "I finished what I wanted in the linguistic and ethnological fields, and measured ninety-eight persons." Boas's study of languages led him to an appreciation of narratives, though like a snake swallowing its tail, the narratives led back to the language: "The Bella Coolas tell me the most beautiful stories in their own language. The stories themselves are not worth much, but on the other hand the language is very worthwhile." Boas's interest in narratives increased as his knowledge of the complexity of languages and of groups (or what he referred to as "tribes") expanded. He wrote Powell in 1892 of his proposed plans to write up his study of Chinook "in such a form, as to give an ethnographical description of the tribe for use of the Annual Reports of the Bureau." Boas continued, "The most important part of this paper would be a careful discussion of the origin of the Chinook mythology, based on a geographical study of the distribution of myths on the Pacific Coast. The material for this comparison has been largely collected by myself on my previous journeys to the North Pacific Coast, but it will also be necessary to compare material collected in upper Oregon, southern Oregon and northern California." Boas's emphasis on the comparative approach to the study of narrative appeared in an 1890 letter to his parents "about an important legend which has its origin on Lake Superior or thereabouts. Here on the coast it is known only in Bella Coola in this place. It throws a peculiar light on the way legends get around."[46]

Still, Boas was so focused on what he selectively saw as his work that he missed rich opportunities, as is apparent in his note to Marie in 1894: "The chief told me that he was descended from many great chiefs and that the Indians wanted to make him chief when his father died but that he did not want to be chief because he wanted to be humble. In all matters he had to ask the advice of the old people who helped him, and this he had to do in my case too." As an "example of his humility," the chief told Boas about how the government had offered all of the Indians, "saddles, bridles, and tools for farming," but that he did not accept them because "he wanted to have only things which he had earned on his own property with his own hands and with the help of the dear God." Boas concluded, "It is interesting to learn how these people think, but this does not help my work."[47]

Boas had established his reputation in the United States, the United Kingdom, and Europe. With copious assistance from Putnam and Jacobi, Boas had obtained positions at the American Museum of Natural History and at Columbia College. He moved forward in both positions and drew on each to strengthen the other. Boas also endeavored to obtain more security than the year-to-year contract, such as he had with Columbia. His struggle for firm footing and job security was not over, though the shape of the struggle had changed.

Your Orphan Boy

10

The Greatest Undertaking of Its Kind

The Jesup North Pacific Expedition

In 1896 Boas had gained his foothold as assistant curator of ethnology and somatology at the American Museum of Natural History and as lecturer in physical anthropology at Columbia College. He worked concertedly to entice AMNH President Morris K. Jesup with his grand plan for exploring the connections between Asia and America. In 1897 this was launched as the Jesup North Pacific Expedition (JNPE). With Jesup's desire to establish joint appointments for curators and professors at the museum and at the university, Boas drew his work together at the AMNH and at Columbia through his courses, some of which he taught at the museum with the use of the collections. E. B. Tylor had written Boas in 1890, "It seems to me very likely that you may trace an Asiatic-American [connection] by transmission of folk-tales. The longer I live the more sure I feel that American culture is largely due to Asiatic influence." In the spring of 1897, from his position at the AMNH, Boas drew up a plan that extended beyond what Tylor had suggested seven years earlier. The Jesup North Pacific Expedition would encompass two continents, span many years, yield magnificent publications, and engage an international team of researchers. Ultimately the expedition would fatigue its donor, Jesup, and its creator, Boas.[1]

The expedition put into play exactly what Boas had envisioned following his earlier work in Baffin Land: a complex, multiyear study that would cover vast but culturally interconnected territory and multiple linguistic groups. A decade earlier, in January 1886, Boas had written to Bastian about his proposal for research in North America, which he had conceptualized as taking place during the summer for four years:

"The objects of my investigation [are] to be the so little known Indian and Eskimo tribes of the British Northwest." Insisting that "these tribes must be studied in relation to one another," Boas made his appeal "to you, father of all ethnographic studies." He concluded, "I would not again make one isolated trip, but can only consider it worthwhile if the whole thing can be done as a related unit." Bastian declined to fund this proposal.[2]

Boas wrote to Tylor two years later in 1888 with a similar plan. In a draft of the letter Boas stated, "I should gladly avail myself of this opportunity to devote my time more fully than I have done so far to ethnology and to carry on my researches on the Canadian tribes in a systematical way." He estimated that "about 3 years would be sufficient to study the ethnology of B.C. in reasonable detail." Revising the draft two days later Boas stressed, "You will undoubtedly be aware that the inquiry, if to be done at all, must be done at the earliest possible date, as what little there is left of native culture is disappearing rapidly." In place of the systematic, multiyear project that Boas had proposed, Tylor and others in the BAAS funded Boas annually for field trips to the Northwest Coast when Boas was available.[3]

Boas's vision for the grand sweep of fieldwork and collections depended on cooperation between the AMNH and Columbia University. As he wrote Jesup, "I believe that through co-operation with the Museum, Columbia University may have the opportunity of educating almost the whole future generation of anthropologists." Boas continued, "I am training my students by the help of the material accumulated in the Museum for field work, and they will necessarily become the investigators for this Institution and for the Bureau of Ethnology." Boas straddled the AMNH and Columbia University, with one foot initially more firmly planted in the museum, whose collections formed the basis for university instruction. As Boas wrote in 1901 to Zelia Nuttall, with respect to his "general plans and the scope of the work which I have laid out for myself,"

> since I took hold of the work in New York, I have tried to develop the same in such a way that it will ultimately result in the establishment of a well-organized school of anthropology, including all the different branches of the subject. I consider this one of the fundamental needs of our science, because without it we can never hope to thoroughly investigate and explore all the numerous prob-

lems of American anthropology. For this reason, I am trying to develop the collections of this Museum in such a way that they will ultimately form the basis of university instruction in all lines of anthropological research. This aim of course must be combined with the general education aims of the Museum, but I find that both are very easily harmonized.

At the museum, Boas focused on honing and sharpening "each department to such a point that within a very short time it will demand the care of a specialist." At that point, he would seize "the opportune moment for introducing instruction in each particular line in Columbia University."[4]

A man of vision and energy, President Jesup was drawn to "big projects and major problems." Not an academic, Jesup frequently said of himself, "'I am a plain, unscientific business man.'" His mind grasped a challenge and his spirit demanded an efficient solution. In his remarks to the AMNH Trustees on December 31, 1896, Jesup spoke of "the theory that America was originally peopled by migratory tribes from the Asiatic continent." Echoing Boas's caution, Jesup remarked that "the opportunities favorable for solving this problem are rapidly disappearing and I would be deeply gratified if some friend or friends of the Museum may feel disposed to contribute means for the prosecution of systematic investigations."[5]

Boas had pitched the ambitious plan to Jesup—to explore the connections between the native peoples of Asia and the north Pacific Coast—and Jesup caught it with immediate enthusiasm. Boas was catapulted into putting flesh on the bones of his plan within a two-month time frame. On January 19, 1897, Boas had written Jesup a letter outlining his research plan: "'One of the most important problems of American anthropology is that of the influence between the cultures of the Old and of the New World.'" Fragmentary evidence pointed to "'certain cultural elements in common to all the tribes of this region,'" tribes that speak "'a great diversity of languages.'" Boas proposed "'a systematic investigation of the whole question.'" He suggested conducting "'an ethnographical study and the making of ethnographical collections of the tribes on the American side'" by doing the same on "'the Asiatic side,'" and by excavating "'the immense shell mounds'" and the "'ancient monuments on the North Pacific coast of both continents.'"[6]

Three weeks later Jesup had called Boas to his office to tell him, as Boas wrote Putnam, "'that he wished to take up the general plan of exploration on the North Pacific Coast," and that he had instructed Boas to consult with Putnam on "'a detailed scheme of work for the carrying out of the plan.'" Enthusiastic about the project, Jesup had decided to fund it himself, since no one else had responded to his call at the meeting of the trustees on December 31, 1896. Jesup envisioned this undertaking as a means for the AMNH to make a mark for itself: "'Mr. Jesup looks at this proposed expedition in the light that it will be the greatest thing ever undertaken by any Museum either here or abroad and that it will give the Institution an unequalled standing in scientific circles.'" A day after Boas had met with Jesup, John H. Winser, secretary and assistant treasurer of the AMNH, had written to Putnam, "'Mr. Jesup has about concluded to take up the cost of the Bering Sea explorations. He would like you to have the matter in mind and be prepared to give your views.'" Putnam wrote Boas, "I have sent to Jesup a letter about our great plan, Asia-America, for him to read at the meeting of the Executive Committee tomorrow."[7]

On March 13, 1897, Boas was quoted in a "press dispatch from Albany to THE NEW YORK TIMES," about "Mr. Jesup's Expedition." The subtitle of the article stated, "Three Parties of Scientists to Start for the North Pacific this Spring Exploring Both Coasts." The article continued, "Dr. Boas will personally conduct the West American coast party, and will be assisted by Harlan I. Smith, an attaché of his department in the museum. His other assistants will be employed in the field." The leaders of the other two parties in Siberia had "not yet been determined." The article made clear Jesup's commitment to the undertaking: "While it is expected that the object of the exploration can be accomplished in about six years, Mr. Jesup has set no limit to the time which must be consumed, and has declared his intention of seeing this matter through no matter what cost or length of time are required." The next day, on March 14, 1897, as if to give Putnam equal exposure, the *New York Times* issued a dispatch from Cambridge, Massachusetts: "Prof. F. S. [*sic*] Putnam, the celebrated Cambridge archaeologist, has formulated the plans for the exploration of Northwestern North America and Eastern Asia."[8]

There were also announcements in scientific publications. "Proposed Explorations on the Coasts of the North Pacific Ocean" appeared in *Sci-*

ence on March 19, 1897, with a discussion of the "systematic manner" of the investigation, the need to fill in the "gaps" in "the ethnology of the Pacific Coast of Siberia," and the "almost incredible" linguistic diversity of the area. The article concluded, "The whole field of research is a vast one, and it is to be expected that the enterprise inaugurated by Mr. Jesup will lead to results which will clear up many of the obscure points regarding the early history of the American race." In his letter to *Globus* in May 1897, Boas began, "Since the message given in the newspaper does not quite correspond to the facts, I take the liberty to inform you" that the Jesup Expedition would "not be a collecting trip, but a thorough study of the northern part of Pacific coasts." Boas concluded, "My plan is to make the relations of the neighboring peoples the leitmotif of the whole investigation."[9]

In May 1897, prior to his departure for the first season of fieldwork for the JNPE, Boas wrote his parents, "'I go west better equipped than ever before.'" Boas traveled with his colleague from Columbia, psychologist Livingston Farrand, a novice to anthropology and so keen to learn about fieldwork that he paid his own travel expenses. Joining them was Harlan Smith, who had worked first with Boas at the WCE in 1893 and in 1895 was hired by Putnam as staff member at the AMNH, where he remained until 1911. They arrived in Vancouver at the beginning of June. "Farrand," Boas wrote Marie, "was very surprised to learn how well known I am in Victoria." Boas wrote his parents, "We three fellows get along fine." They were headed to Spences Bridge, BC: "Today we say goodbye to civilization and from tomorrow on we will live in the back woods. . . . You must think of me in a woolen shirt with corduroy pants and a big hat. And, of course, with pad and pencil in hand."[10]

Two days later Boas, Farrand, and Smith met up with the fourth member of their team, James Teit. Born in the Shetland Islands, Teit had come to Spences Bridge in March 1884, just one month before his nineteenth birthday, to help his uncle, John Murray, with his store. In 1892 he married Lucy Antko, a Thompson Indian woman, who died of pneumonia in 1899 and left him feeling "'greatly cut up about it,'" and, as he wrote to Smith, "'it will take me a long time to get over the loss.'" Engaged in seasonal farming and operating the ferry, Teit was a "skilled outdoorsman" who explored the "remote regions of southern and central British Columbia." He also "hunted and fished with the Indians, learned from them the location of the best hunting grounds and this led to him becoming a guide for the hunting parties which came to British Columbia from all over the world." Teit's son from his second marriage, Sigurd, recounted what a Thompson River Indian had said of his father: he was "so fluent in the language and his accent so good . . . that in a dark room 'you couldn't tell him from an Indian speaking.'"[11]

On first meeting Teit during his 1894 fieldwork, Boas described him as "a treasure! He knows a great deal about the tribes. I engaged him right away." In December 1894 Boas wrote Marie again about Teit: "My informant is a very nice man. He comes from the Shetland Islands. . . . He is very much interested in the Indians and is writing a report for me about this tribe [the Thompson Indians], which will be very good, I hope. He will also make a collection for me." This encounter with Boas in 1894 marked a "turning point" in his life. "Admittedly Teit had the potential," Banks writes, "but it was largely Boas who developed Teit the anthropologist." Boas remained supportive and appreciative of his work. As he wrote in 1902, "Mr. Teit commenced work for the Museum in 1895. He has also worked off and on for the Jesup North Pacific Expedition. . . . He is a very exceptional man, and his Memoir published in the Jesup Expedition Series is being quoted everywhere with the highest appreciation."[12]

Teit had done preparatory work for the team: "Early in the year 1897 he collected notes on the Thompson River Indians for the use of the Jesup Expedition . . . mainly bearing upon the art of the Indians, their language and their physical characteristics." On arrival in Spences Bridge, Boas, Farrand, and Smith found that "Teit has prepared everything for us very well. The Indians were ready for us yesterday afternoon, and we could not work quickly enough to finish with all of them." With a four-person team—soon to be five when they would meet up with George Hunt in Bella Coola the next month—Boas was able to delegate responsibilities. While Boas included Fillip Jacobsen as a member of the 1897 group, Jacobsen did not join in the fieldwork, but rather collected items for the AMNH. To Marie Boas wrote, "I let Farrand and Smith make the casts ready for shipping. This afternoon Jimmy Teit and I went down to the village and collected melodies." He continued, "The phonograph works very well, and we got ten good songs. The rhythms seem to be rather difficult, although the songs themselves are very simple." He recounted, "There were two women whom I could not get to sing at first. However, they did sing after all when all the men had left the house." To test the phonograph, and perhaps also to induce some reluctant women to participate, Boas recorded his own song. Into the horn of the recording mechanism, Boas sang a snippet of the popular song, "Sweet Rosie O'Grady":

Sweet Rosie O'Grady,
My own darling Rose,
She's my steady lady,
As everyone knows.

Thomas Ross Miller notes that this recording was "the first sound ever recorded in the North Pacific."[13]

Teit was crucial to the work of the research team. Because he spoke the language of the Thompson River Indians, he could explain to the people what the anthropologists wanted in terms of taking pictures, making plaster-of-paris casts of their faces, and recording their songs. Familiar with the area, Teit also guided Smith to several archaeological sites on the Thompson River. As the archaeologist for the British Columbia portion of the expedition, Smith was left on his own from June 12 to August 11, after which he rejoined the team in Port Essington. Finding that Spences Bridge was "not the most favorable place for excavations," he explored sites "at the confluence of the Fraser and Thompson Rivers." Smith also photographed Indians, made casts, and collected ethnographic objects.[14]

With four riding horses, five packhorses, and three guides who traveled on foot, Boas, Farrand, and Teit left on horseback and headed north for Chilcotin and Bella Coola. The goal of this "lengthy trip northward" was twofold: "To investigate the physical characteristics of the Indians inhabiting the banks of the Fraser River north of Lytton, and to study the customs and physical characteristics of the Chilcotin, the most southern Athapascan tribe of British Columbia." From "fifteen miles below Lillooet," Boas wrote Marie, "The trip is very good for me. We are outdoors all the time and I have no intellectual work worth mentioning. . . . This morning we rode horseback through a valley about 2,000 feet high. . . . Horseback riding is not as hard on me as I thought. We go very slowly because the heavily laden horses cannot go fast on these steep trails." The next day, drenched by incessant rain, they followed the Indian trails down the one-thousand-foot descent of the canyon walls to the Frazer River, the longest river in British Columbia. Neither Boas nor Farrand were experienced riders. "We both try hard to handle the horses," Boas wrote. "I can already saddle mine but I cannot load them the right way." By choice, Boas rode "behind the pack-horses because it is boring to go together with them in one line. I will be an experienced horseman when I come back." Then he admitted, "Yesterday, however, I was thrown when the horse suddenly shied."[15]

The rain continued. All their supplies were soaked, and their frustrations mounted. The Indians whom they had planned to study were little in evidence; they lived in scattered settlements. By the time he had reached Puntzi Lake, after a month of traveling on horseback, Boas was more heartened. As they "rode through the woods from one little village to another," they encountered Indians who lived along the road. Boas recounted to his parents, "It was really funny how they all accompanied us and how we finally arrived [at Puntzi Lake] with a cavalcade of twenty horses." With satisfaction, he remarked, "My work here has turned out successfully, against all expectations. At first it looked as if I would not get any measurements but then I hired an interpreter and everything went as well as possible." Since he "found the tribes here so interesting," he decided to leave Farrand behind to work with the Chilcotin "for at least one month. . . . I am glad I can give him the opportunity of working completely independently for a while because that makes the trip more advantageous for him." Farrand focused his research in the larger villages of Chilcotin, but he also traveled to "the isolated families, which live on the shores of Tatla Lake and in the mountains."[16]

After seven weeks on the trail, "our guide with his horse, Teit, our Indian Sam with four pack-horses and myself" arrived at the summit over-looking Bella Coola, five thousand feet below. Boas wrote of the approach, "Finally about three miles from the Bella Coola River the valley narrowed into a gorge. We left it and rode along the northern side of the mountain until we arrived at the foot of a pass, which leads into the Bella Coola valley." After a wet and windy night, that "threatened to blow our tents away," they awoke to "the most beautiful mountain country. Deep in the valley was the Bella Coola, and we rode slowly toward it along the side of the mountain. The view was gorgeous. There were steep mountaintops with huge glaciers, and in the valley a sea of clouds through which one could see the river." The party rode down the steep descent: "Here the deep and rapid river had to be crossed. The party built a raft, on which an Indian embarked in order to fetch a canoe that was seen on the other side. In this the men crossed the river, while the horses swam over."[17]

Boas related, "I rode ahead alone because I wanted to be sure of arriving that evening. I had written to George Hunt that I would arrive between the fifteenth and the twentieth, and I wanted to keep my word. I was glad to find him here and to find that he had everything well prepared. That assured the success of my trip." Responsible for leading the pack train back over the mountains to Fraser River, Teit let the horses rest for two days and then departed on July 23 for a four-week ride home to Spences Bridge. Keen to study the Bella Coola, particularly since their "customs and beliefs had never been subjected to systematic inquiry," Boas began his research with Hunt. In addition, he worked on his and Hunt's Kwakiutl materials. He wrote Marie and his parents, "I went over the whole collection Hunt had made; I got the names of all items, and a number of stories." Together they reviewed "all the old Kwakiutl manuscripts . . . a great task because I have to write out two hundred and thirty pages of manuscript after his dictation." Boas was happy with what he had collected: "The material I have now is *very* beautiful." Of the Bella Coola, he wrote, "This tribe has veritable gods who live in Walhalla and to whom are entrusted the lives and the fates of men as well as nature."[18]

On the day of departure from Bella Coola, Boas reflected, "I finished the texts with George Hunt, two hundred and forty-four pages, and a number of songs on seventy-two more pages. That really was hard labor." While Boas left for Port Essington, George Hunt remained behind to collect for another two weeks. Boas added, with satisfaction, "I think I will then have a very good collection." After two days in the fishing village of Namu, Boas was able to take the steamer to Port Essington where Harlan Smith had been waiting for him for six days. He wrote Marie, "Last night at nine o'clock we finally arrived. Smith was on the dock in the pouring rain." Boas and Smith resumed their work together: "Smith started right in to make castings and since yesterday I have joined him. We already have sixteen, partly Haida, partly Tsimshian, and one Tlingit woman." While Smith took photographs of the people, Boas worked with Charles Edenshaw, the "most highly regarded Haida artist of his time." Accolades regarding Edenshaw's work abound. Charles Frederick Newcombe, medical doctor and Indian art collector, described him in 1902 as "the best carver in wood and stone." As Aldona Jonaitis and Robin Wright note, Edenshaw belonged to a Haida family of noble lineage. At the age of fourteen, he had been bedridden, and he passed his time by carving totem poles from argillite. "His skills developed," Jonaitis writes, "and before long he was a master carver of both argillite and wood, as well as a talented gold- and silversmith." He was also a very talented painter. Boas showed Edenshaw the photographs he had made in the Smithsonian, at the AMNH, and that he had obtained from Ottawa. "I am able to identify many objects," Boas wrote, "with his help." Boas also asked Edenshaw to make "several crayon drawings which he ultimately used as illustrations in his Northwest Coast art publications."[19]

On August 20 Boas sent Smith to Bella Bella to make facial casts with Farrand, who was already there, and to take photographs of people and of old houses. Farrand would remain for the rest of the summer in Bella Bella, "studying the social organization and arts of this tribe." Boas, Smith, and Hunt traveled by boat to Rivers Inlet to work with the Kwakiutl. There they stayed together for nine days, during which time they tried—with little success—to find some people with whom to work. They wanted to make facial casts, to photograph, and to collect stories. Boas wrote his parents, "It is so annoying to sit around with nothing to do while being surrounded by the most interesting material." He added, "The people are very difficult to handle. For tomorrow one has promised to tell me a tale. I will be surprised if he does come." Hunt did not "know the dialect well enough" to be of help. With little work to do, Boas sent Smith south to Victoria, where he would resume his archaeological excavations.[20]

Intent on fostering goodwill among the Indians for his work, Boas employed his "oft-used trick" of inviting "all the Indians to a feast." He wrote Marie, "Tonight I finally gave the Indians a speech in my house, saying what a great friend of theirs I was and what good things I have done for them!! I *hope* that tomorrow I shall get some promises, otherwise I don't know what I shall do here all the time." It was successful. People began to work with Boas. "I am really busy now," he wrote Marie. "This morning at 8 I started to translate. From 10 until 3 o'clock I took dictation and afterwards I made a few castings. That is how I like to work! . . . Now the people come of their own accord to have castings made." Boas wrote his parents, "All my attention is focused on the Indians now. This makes my travels so relaxing for me, that I am able to concentrate completely on one subject and forget everything else."[21]

In mid-September Farrand journeyed by steamer to Rivers Inlet. Boas and Hunt joined him on board the Tees, and the three traveled south to Alert Bay. With plans to return home, Hunt disembarked only to receive sad news: "One of his children, an eight-year-old boy, was very ill, and possibly dead by the time the news finally reached him." Boas regretted that the news had not been conveyed earlier, since he "would have sent him home." As they continued their journey south on board the Tees, Boas spent the night talking with Farrand, "whom I had hardly seen since July." Boas wrote Marie, "He did not *do* very much but assembled quite a few things." Farrand assured Boas that his Bella Coola collection had been loaded on board a steamer in Namu, bound for Victoria. "Little by little all my material is piling up in Victoria," he wrote Marie. "I now have twenty boxes there and I have eight here, fourteen in Namu, and eight in Alert Bay. I hope that they will all arrive safely in New York."[22]

In addition to his concern about the safe transport of what would be a total of 125 boxes of field collections, Boas had begun to worry about how his work would be received. To his parents he wrote, "I am very anxious to find out whether Jesup will be satisfied with the results of my trip. I think he ought to be because I am." Along with the angst, he was excited about his return. He had "all sorts of new plans for the Museum," and he hoped "to find the new wing of the Museum almost ready to put in everything." Boas continued, "My gallery is supposed to be finished by May at the latest. . . . This really spurs me on." Boas ended the first season of the JNPE in Victoria on September 16, 1897, when he departed for home with a stop-over in Chicago for a visit with Donaldson and to the cemetery, to his baby Hedwig's grave. Boas was fatigued with "these trips into the wilderness," and with being away from his wife and children for extended periods of time.[23]

Boas was pleased with the results of the season. He and his team "had made over a hundred plaster-of-Paris facial casts and many more body measurements." Boas published the results of his research on art, which he had conducted with Edenshaw, in the first volume, part 1, of the *Jesup North Pacific Expedition*, as "Facial Paintings of the Indians of Northern British Columbia." Working with Hunt, he had revised over three hundred pages of text and had gathered new material, all of which appeared in the first volume, part 2, of the *Jesup North Pacific Expedition*, as "The Mythology of the Bella Coola Indians." When Boas and Farrand returned home, Smith carried on his excavations through November.[24]

At the start of the season, his intention had been to train Farrand and Smith so that they could take over the fieldwork portion of the research in the Pacific Northwest. In fact, this was the result of their work together. In the second season in the summer of 1898, Farrand and Smith traveled to Washington State, while Boas remained at the AMNH to organize the Siberian portion of the JNPE. Smith carried out excavations at the shell mounds of Puget Sound and along the west coast of Washington. Farrand worked with the Quilleute and the Quinault. Roland B. Dixon, after completing his MA at Harvard in 1898, worked with Farrand at Quinault and then moved on to work in BC at the mouth of the Fraser River and later joined Smith for work in Lillooet territory. Teit conducted research with the Lillooet, and Hunt continued collecting artifacts among the Kwakiutl. In the third season, in 1899, Smith "turned his attention to the shell mounds and burial-cairns of Washington" and carried out excavations on Vancouver Island, and Hunt and Teit continued their investigations.[25]

In 1900 Boas returned for the fourth season of work on the Northwest Coast: "the last on the American side of the Jesup Expedition." He joined Teit for six days in Nicola Valley and then headed north by steamer to Alert Bay, where he stayed with the Spencers, George Hunt's sister and brother-in-law. To Marie he wrote, "I have a bed in a pleasant little room upstairs where I am writing just now. The food is also good." Hunt and his whole family were in Alert Bay at work in the cannery. During the day, with the help of an interpreter, Boas revised texts collected in previous years, and worked on "the grammar of the language"; in the evening, he conferred with an artist who was helping him to understand "the art of these tribes." He was only able to work with Hunt during the evenings and on Sundays, when the cannery was closed. "The most laborious part," he wrote, "is the revision of the texts which I am doing with George Hunt. I can't do more than eight pages per hour and I cannot stand this pace too long. I have now revised 187 pages and still have 495 to go."[26]

Repeatedly, Boas expressed the sentiment that "the language is terribly hard and complicated. The Chinook and Tsimshian are easy in comparison." He remarked, "The Kwakiutl is much harder than I thought. It is the first Indian language I have worked with which has irregular verbs, etc., and they are terribly difficult to handle." In another letter to Marie he bemoaned, "I spent the whole afternoon over the tense of a verb, a very complicated business." Even when he came to understand "the structure of the language quite well," he still found it hard. He wrote Marie, "I think it is even harder than Eskimo." Boas began working with women on what he called "kitchen menus, Küchenzettel, kitchen list, and the preparation of food," and on medicines. He was also making a collection of plants. To his mother, he wrote, "The scientific result of this summer is most satisfactory. I will finally be able to publish the [Kwakiutl texts], which I have been collecting for six years. I will start with this right after my return while the language is fresh in my memory. Then I hope I will have enough material to make a detailed description of the manners and customs of the Indians." He concluded, "I also have enough material for the language part," and added, "but the editing of it will take years, of course."[27]

While the investigations included archaeology and physical anthropology, Boas had a predilection for language, texts, and art. He stressed this in his 1897 remarks from the field: "I am rather satisfied with the results of my work here. We now have twenty-five castings, ten Haida and fifteen Tsimshian. I have also measured all these people. However, although I would like to get more measurements, I think that the ethnological work is more important so that I cannot use too much time for measurements." Even with "a very interesting series of face measurements, fifty-six altogether," Boas was thinking in terms of his research on "clues to the meaning of the local [ornamentation]." He anticipated linking this to his work on facial painting. To his parents, Boas summed up the intent of his work: "My purpose here is to collect more material on the art of the Indians." On board the Tees, en route to Rivers Inlet, Boas expanded on his interest in facial painting and symbolism: "You might remember that I planned to collect paintings done on hard-to-decorate materials in order to study the symbolism of the Indians. For this purpose, I chose face paintings and paintings on edges of blankets." Boas was pleased with the results, "because I found just what I had expected; that is, strong stylization and stressing of symbols."[28]

At the initial stages of planning for the JNPE, Jesup had stipulated the importance of finding "'the right man for the work.'" Boas was in accord, though for him this would need to be an accomplished scientist. As he wrote Putnam, "'Our prime endeavor now must be to impress Mr. Jesup with the necessity of having *trained specialists* do the work, and not give it to adventurers or people with superficial knowledge.'" Boas had first anticipated sending two expeditions to Asia in 1898, one to "Asiatic Siberia," and the other to the Amur River Cultures. He was, however, only able to send one party to the Amur River, and that with difficulty, due to the challenges of identifying leaders for the expeditions.[29]

In 1895, when first thinking about organizing fieldwork in Siberia, Boas had conferred with Wilhelm Grube, a sinologist and an expert in the languages of the Amur Region with whom Boas had worked at the Royal Ethnological Museum in Berlin. Grube suggested Bertold Laufer, who had studied at the University of Berlin in 1893–95 with Adolf Bastian, Felix von Luschan, and Eduard Seler, and who had also studied in the Seminar for Oriental Languages in 1894–95. Laufer received his doctorate at the University of Leipzig in 1897, with a doctoral dissertation on a Tibetan text. His focus during his university years was the study of Asian languages and ethnology. When he met with Laufer, Boas learned of his military obligation and advised him to fulfill it as soon as possible, "so that he would be available should a Siberian worker be required."[30]

On May 19, 1897, Boas had extended a formal offer to Laufer to lead the expedition on the east coast of the Sakhalin Island and in the Amur River region. He received Laufer's acceptance while still in the Northwest Coast during the first season of the JNPE. Arriving early in New York to prepare for the expedition, Laufer was ready to depart in March, when "the museum received word that his visa had been refused by the Russian Interior Ministry." Laufer was a German Jew, and thus would not be allowed into Siberia. "Boas had just arranged a large farewell reception for the traveler," Cole writes, "and Laufer might never be able to leave." Working with urgency, "Boas went to Washington to meet with officials at the State Department, where, in Jesup's name, he pulled all possible strings." Ethan A. Hitchcock, the U.S. minister to St. Petersburg, spoke with the Russian minister of the interior. The Russian official was adamant: Dr. Laufer was a German Jew and would not be permitted into Siberia. Hitchcock did not give up. He spoke with "W. Radloff, director of the Museum of Anthropology and Ethnography of the Imperial Academy of Sciences, who called upon the Grand Duke Constantin, President of the Academy, who in turn directed Radloff to contact the Governor General of Siberia, then in St. Petersburg." The intractable problem was solved. Jesup received the following notification from the Imperial German Embassy: "Referring to your favor of Jan. 7, 1898, I beg leave to inform you that the Imperial Embassy in St. Petersburg has been instructed by the Department of State of the German Empire to make application to the Imperial Russian Government in favor of Dr. Laufer, director of the expedition which your Museum has sent to investigate the tribes of the Siberian coast." Cole writes, "Word reached New York that Laufer had by special permission of Tsar Nicholas II, been authorized to visit Sakhalin and the Amur River."[31]

The anxious wait was over. Laufer was on his way to Vladivostok, where he and Gerard Fowke, who had been hired as archaeologist for this portion of the JNPE, arrived on June 19, 1898. Together, Laufer and Fowke traveled north to Khabarovsk on the Amur River and then separated. Fowke, as Boas wrote in his AMNH report, "descended the Amur in a boat, investigating the remains along both banks of the river." Laufer journeyed down the Amur by steamer "and crossed to the Island of Sakhalin." While Fowke conducted excavations with little success along the Amur River and then, in Japan, Laufer spent eight months of rigorous fieldwork—from July 10, 1898, to March 21, 1899—on Sakhalin Island among the Gilyak, Tungus (Evenki), and Ainu peoples. He then crossed back to the mainland, where he worked for an additional five months with the Goldi and Gilyak from March to October 1899.[32]

In October 1898, while visiting a Gilyak village, located twelve miles inland on Sakhalin Island, Laufer was struck down with a flu that progressed to pneumonia. Boas wrote, "When hardly well enough to resume his work, he journeyed southward, at first on horseback and then on reindeer-sledges, visiting the Tungus and Ainu of the central and southern parts of the island." As if severe illness were not enough of a challenge, Laufer received a telegram from "the Russian Governor, informing him of the presence of a band of desperadoes, who had built a fort in that region and had terrorized the whole country." Laufer turned back north and, as he wrote, faced even more harrowing challenges: "'At one time I narrowly escaped drowning when crossing the ice at the foot of a steep promontory. I broke through the ice. . . . Fortunately, my guide happened to upset his sledge at the same moment when I broke through. Thus it was that he saw my situation, and extricated me with his staff.'" Journeying the last sixty-seven miles on horseback, Laufer reached the point of Sakhalin Island, just opposite Nikolayevsk-on-Amur on March 21, 1899, in time to cross the ice to the mainland before it broke up. Traveling by sledge and arriving once again at Khabarovsk, Laufer stayed with the Tungus from March 25 until late May, when the Amur River flowed free of ice. Going downriver, back toward Nikolayevsk-on-Amur, he visited villages where the Goldi (Nanai) and Gilyak lived; and then from Nikolayevsk-on-Amur, he journeyed east to visit Goldi peoples along the Amgun River. On October 19, 1899, Laufer departed Vladivostok for Japan, and, after that, returned to New York.[33]

Fowke's archaeological results were abysmal. He attributed his difficulties to the changing course of the Amur River and the dense vegetation. He wrote Boas with a description of the riverside: "'Out of the timber, the grass was from 4 to 7 feet high and thick as timothy in a meadow; where grass did not grow, weeds flourished. . . . Flies that bite like mosquitoes . . . swarmed in millions: mosquitoes were in clouds.'"[34] Laufer himself thrived on the challenges of fieldwork. Laufer wrote good-naturedly from Khabarovsk, "I have now taken here a lodging built of rough planks and resembling a coffin, and have begun to engage myself in a linguistic and anthropological study of the Gold, of whom I have fortunately met a good many excellent representatives in this place." Prevented from traveling by "the terrible hurricanes of this season and deficiency of roads," Laufer would remain at Khabarovsk until the ice melted and the rivers were navigable. He wrote Boas of his "'very good success'" in recording songs from the Gilyak and Tungus. "The ghosts are in the machine," the people remarked. "I took phonographic records of songs," Laufer conveyed to Boas, "which created the greatest sensation among the Russians as well as among the natives. A young Gilyak woman who sang into the instrument said, 'It took me so long to learn this song, and this thing has learned it at once, without making any mistakes. There is surely a man or a spirit in this box which imitates me!' and at the same time she was crying and laughing with excitement."[35]

Laufer did not, however, have the same success in obtaining anthropometric data for Boas. Laufer recounted, "The people were afraid that they would die at once after submitting to this process. Although I had their confidence, I failed in my efforts in this direction, even after offering them presents which they considered of great value. I succeeded in measuring a single individual, a man of imposing stature, who, after the measurements had been taken, fell prostrate on the floor, the picture of despair, groaning, 'Now I am going to die tomorrow!'" Boas was delighted with Laufer's work and particularly with the extensive collection of art and artifacts that he had sent to the AMNH. Laurel Kendall, in her evaluation of Laufer's work, found his collections heavily weighted toward ritual objects and replete with "rich embroideries and appliqué work of the Nanai and their neighbors." Laufer acknowledged his fascination with the "Tungus . . . wooden idols and amulets made of fish-skin which are quite new to science."[36]

In his 1898 trip to Europe, Boas had identified the leaders of the northeastern Siberian expedition. "In the fall of 1898," Nikolai Vakhtin writes, "Boas went to Berlin, where, for the first time, he had an opportunity to meet Radloff in person and to make the acquaintance of Jochelson, who was still in Switzerland working on his doctoral examinations." Professor Dr. Wilhelm Radloff, who had assisted Laufer in obtaining special permission to travel to the Amur River region, suggested Vladimir Jochelson and Vladimir Bogoras.[37] Jochelson wrote Boas, "In regard to my friend Bogoraz, I beg to repeat that he is by far the best man for the investigation of the Chuckchee and the other tribes of the Bering Peninsula. . . . Mr. Bogoraz speaks Chukchee fluently. He is well prepared to conduct ethnological work, and he is willing to start at once, if so required."[38]

Careful to avoid causing additional problems with the Russian government, Boas had been circumspect in writing about Bogoras's and Jochelson's revolutionary activity and gave only a superficial review of their expertise. They "had for several years," Boas wrote, "carried on important studies in Siberia under the auspices of the Imperial Geographical Society." In fact, Bogoras's and Jochelson's extensive knowledge of Siberia had come from their ten years of political exile. Jochelson had been in solitary confinement from 1885 to 1887, and then in exile in eastern Siberia from 1887 to 1897, during which time he became interested in the Yukagir. Bogoras had been imprisoned for three years and then exiled to eastern Siberia, to the Kolyma region. Jochelson and Bogoras had belonged to "'a radical, populist, and terrorist political party,'" part of the movement based on "'the identification of the intellectuals with the simple folk.'" While Laufer and Fowke had been novices to the region, "Bogoras and Jochelson were veterans of several years of Siberian research when they joined the Jesup Expedition; a good bit of their experience was with the tribes that Boas wanted studied."[39]

Arriving in New York in March 1900, Jochelson and Bogoras spent time working with Boas. As Bogoras had expressed, "Before my parting for Chukchee, I would stay some months in America for the use of learning American methods of anthropologic measurement." Boas had mirrored Bogoras's wishes: "'My intention is to have both Mr. Jochelson and Mr. Bogoras here for a few months in order to make sure that the work on physical anthropology will be done according to the same methods, so that our results may be comparable.'" In addition, Boas provided instructions on "the production of phonograph records and 'a good collection of anthropological photographs and plaster casts' as top collecting priorities." Jochelson particularly enjoyed the gatherings on Friday mornings to work on linguistics: "I think the idea of them is excellent."[40]

Boas was close to having met his match with the two Russian ethnographers. Jochelson and Bogoras had, as Vakhtin writes, "their own ideas as to where and how to do research in Siberia." Once in New York, Jochelson and Bogoras consulted with Boas and were able to arrive at a suitable compromise for the expedition. Cole notes, "Boas found them 'very curious' men, 'so different in personality from western Europeans.'" Less dispassionate than Boas, "Marie did not particularly like either, in part because they kept Franz until late in the evening and everything was put on hold at home 'until the Russians go.'" For his part, Jochelson was grateful for the kind reception: "It is a particular pleasure to me to look back upon your recent hospitality. Please thank Mrs. Boas cordially and I hope to thank you in person."[41]

Jochelson and Bogoras left New York in late March 1900 for San Francisco. They sailed to Nagasaki and then to Vladivostok, where they arrived on May 16. Because Bogoras had facility with spoken and written English, Jesup had appointed him as head of the northeastern Asia expedition. Boas wrote, "Mrs. Jochelson and Mrs. Bogoras, who were to share the hardships of the journey with their husbands, and to undertake part of the work of the expedition, had gone to Vladivostok by way of the Trans-Siberian Railway." While Sofia Bogoras and Dina Jochelson-Brodsky—who had been studying medicine at the University of Berne, Switzerland—worked diligently and suffered enormous privations, the expenses they incurred were "deducted from their husbands' salaries at the expedition end."[42]

The group divided into two parties. One was comprised of Vladimir and Sofia Bogoras; the other, of Vladimir Jochelson and Dina Jochelson-Brodsky, with Norman Buxton, in charge of collecting zoological materials, and Alexander Axelrod, a Russian who had been studying in Zurich, as general assistant and "engineer in training." The four members of the Jochelson party were bound for "the small Russian town of Gizhiga on the coast of the Sea of Okhotsk," to study the Koryak; but they were not able to depart until July 24, 1900, due to political unrest in China.[43] This division into two parties was meant to be fluid. As Jochelson described in a letter to Boas, "Mr. Bogoras came overland on a visit from Anadyr, and spent the month of December with us. During this time, he was engaged in studies of the Koryak language. After his arrival, I sent Mr. Axelrod to Anadyr to take charge of Mr. Bogoras's station until his return. Mr. Bogoras completed his linguistic studies and then proceeded to visit the villages of northern Kamchatka. After his return, Mr. Axelrod stayed with him at Anadyr."[44]

Tsar Nicholas II ostensibly supported Jochelson's and Bogoras's research. In his letter of introduction on November 17, 1899, he wrote, "'All institutions and persons under the jurisdiction of the Ministry of the Interior are herewith commanded to render the bearer of this all possible aid with their lawful powers.'" Erich Kasten and Michael Dürr note, "Orders were sent simultaneously to the local authorities calling for surveillance of their work." Timed to coincide with the beginning of the research, this "secret order" from the Russian minister of the interior dated April 28, 1900, to the "Chiefs of the District Police of the Yakutsk Province," instructed "'a secret surveillance over the acts of Waldimir Bogoras and Wladimir Jochelson, former administrative exiles.'" Further, it stated that due to their past "anti-government activity," it was "unwarranted to render them assistance of any kind in the scientific work assigned to them."[45] Jochelson and his party were, in particular, affected by this order. Boas noted, "On his whole journey overland to the Kolyma, and from there through the district of Yakutsk, certain Russian officials, following a secret order issued by the Minister of the Interior, did all they could to hinder the progress of the expedition and to thwart its success." In an intentionally subdued critique of the Russian minister of the interior and of "certain Russian officials," Boas continued, "This action seems difficult to understand, in view of the hearty support and assistance rendered by the Imperial Academy of Sciences and the open letters issued by the Russian Government requesting the officials of Siberia to render assistance whenever possible." Boas was candid in his letter to AMNH Director Bumpus: "'I have rather slurred over Jochelson's and Bogoras's difficulties. . . . These men will return to Russia and . . . a severe arraignment of the action of the Russian Government may have most serious consequences for them.'" In his letter to Jesup, Boas was more direct: "'You will appreciate how difficult the work of both Mr. Bogoras and Mr. Jochelson was made by these secret orders; and the full success of their investigation deserves, for this reason, the highest praise.'" Boas continued, "'I hope that the publication of the results of their work will make the Russian Government ashamed of the manner in which they have acted.'"[46]

Vladimir and Sofia Bogoras left Vladivostok on June 14, 1900, on the Russian mail steamer, Baikal, bound for Mariinsky Post, at the mouth of the Anadyr River, to study the Chukchi. They arrived five weeks later. En route and offshore the Kurile Islands, Bogoras wrote Boas, "Pray excuse my writing this letter on the leaves torn out of my note book, since . . . I cannot find any more proper letter paper. The steamer is small and shaky and I have to finish that letter before our coming to Petropavlovsk." He continued, "I [am] carrying with me on board 30,000 pounds of goods." An additional thirty tons had gone under separate passage, including copious quantities of leaf tobacco, flour, hardtack bread, brick tea, sugar, and dried fruit. He had taken one camera and left the other for Mr. Axelrod, who would arrive in Anadyr in late fall, as well as "one set of anthropometrical instruments, one graphophone with a hundred blank cylinders and . . . one thermometer." Bogoras would send half of the supplies "up river for . . . Buxton and Axelrod who have to come to the Anadyr River in the beginning of the following winter."[47]

Bogoras had already studied the Chukchi language during his exile in Siberia, but he planned to conduct a comparative study of the language spoken by the people along the coastline. While still in St. Petersburg, prior to beginning on the JNPE, he wrote Boas of his expectation that "the principal part of work certainly must be devoted to making collections, photographs, and anthropo[metrical] measurements." While Bogoras had anticipated arriving to fair weather, lots of reindeer, "and maritime Chukchee and some other natives too," instead he arrived in the midst of a devastating epidemic of measles that resulted in a 30-percent death rate among the Chukchi. With the steamer on the verge of departing, Bogoras hastily conveyed that "I am writing in my hut sitting on the ground and holding the writing desk on my knee and for that . . . I hope you will excuse the irregularity of my scribbling." He continued, "In all that I decided to spend here the first three months of my working time, wandering among the burrowing camps and making every kind of collecting I [can] think of." The next day, Bogoras wrote,

> I end this letter in the . . . small room of the large . . . house that . . . serves for the common living place for the all Cossacks in Anadyr mouth. A half-drunk Chukchee is sitting behind my back and [asked] me [for] a little brandy. I interrupted this letter, since one of my new acquaintances, blind . . . , in some way a shaman, come to sing to phonograph. It was performed however not without trouble, since he got excited and would not leave off, and afterwards I had to spend half an hour to quiet again his feelings.

Bogoras told Boas about having people paint designs. One man, in particular, wanted to paint with European colors and not deer blood. Bogoras gave him a blue pencil and he came the next day with something "all painted blue and smeared over and over with my pencil, as if he was painting war. His mouth too was coated with blue, because he used his saliva to moisten the pencil." Bogoras concluded, "From these few specimens you can form a notion, how is employed my time and attention, while in these days."[48]

At the end of October 1900 Bogoras set off with a Cossack and a native guide, with the eventual destination of northern Kamchatka, where he planned to join up with Jochelson's team; "traveling mostly by dog sled, Bogoras was on the move for the rest of his 12 ½ months in northeastern Asia." Remaining no more than four weeks in any location and traveling through treacherous terrain, Bogoras became so ill with influenza "that his Cossack asked where to deliver his body and official papers in case he died on route."[49]

With their focus on the Koryak, Yukagir, and Yakut, the Jochelson party arrived at the small village of Kushka at the mouth of the Gizhiga River on August 16, 1900. They also encountered a population devastated by the epidemic of measles: "The Reindeer Koryak, who usually wintered there, had moved far into the mountains to escape the epidemic." With no Koryak to be found, the Jochelsons traveled overland to the villages of the Maritime Koryak, on Penzhina Bay. In his letter to Boas, Jochelson described the underground dwellings in which they lived: "'The smoke, which fills the hut, makes the eyes smart. . . . Walls, ladder and household utensils are covered with a greasy soot, so that contact with them leaves shining black spots on hands and clothing. . . . The odor of blubber and of refuse is almost intolerable; and the inmates, intoxicated with fly agaric, add to the discomfort of the situation.'" From the "squalor" of underground dwellings to the "winter tents of the Reindeer Koryak" that were so cold they could not work in them, the Jochelsons faced nearly insurmountable challenges. Their packhorses and saddle horses became mired in mud; they were separated from their Cossack guide and interpreter and lost on the trail for two days "without food, fire or protection against wind and frost"; they were stranded by a snowstorm for three days; their skin boats were driven by "the tempestuous seas" into a bay where they had to stay for five days, "almost without any provisions." Their journey on horseback over the Stanovoi Mountains was "the most difficult one that it was ever my fate to undertake," Jochelson wrote. "Bogs, mountain torrents, rocky passes and thick forests combined to hinder our progress." With rotting provisions and horses exhausted to the point of death, Jochelson made the decision to divide the party. Three Yakut guides took the horses and the remaining provisions overland, and Jochelson, his wife, and the rest of his party took one day to build a raft. What was to have been a two-day descent down the Korkodon River was stretched to nine days by the "'numerous rapids and short bends, by the rocky bands and by jams of driftwood.'"[50]

Jochelson wrote, "'In all my journeys I was accompanied by Mrs. Jochelson, who being a candidate for the degree of medicine at the University of Zürich, took charge of the anthropometrical and medical work of the expedition and of most of the photographic work.'" Jochelson summarized the results of their journey: "'The distance covered by myself and Mrs. Jochelson from Gishiga to Irkutsk amounted to nearly eight thousand miles. The results of our work are complete studies of the ethnography and anthropology of the Koryak and Yukaghir, illustrated by extensive collections.'" He enumerated, "'These collections embrace three thousand ethnographical objects, forty-one plaster casts of faces, measurements of about nine hundred individuals, twelve hundred photographs, one hundred fifty tales and traditions, phonographic cylinders, and skulls and archaeological specimens from abandoned village sites and from graves.'"[51] Jochelson recounted the reaction of people to the phonograph: "'Often a hundred persons would crowd into the house where we put up our phonograph, and gather around it in a ring.'" After Jochelson had given two agaric fungi with hallucinogenic properties to a Reindeer Koryak, "'he began to sing in a loud voice, gesticulating with his hands. I had to support him, lest he fall on the machine; and when the cylinder came to an end, I had to tear him away from the horn, when he remained bending over it for a long time, keeping up his songs.'"[52]

In June 1901 Bogoras made his tortuous way from Indian Point to the mouth of the Anadyr: "Since no steamer could be induced to take me back, I will have to construct a skin-canoe of a moderate size and to try to make the trip myself with my men. It was not very convenient, since I had to dispose of 100 dogs with a considerable loss of value." Purchasing "'the frame of a native boat'" and having "'it covered with walrus hides,'" Bogoras recounted, "'Our journey in this boat lasted thirty-two days, and we arrived at Mariinsky Post on July 28, 1901, ten days before the arrival of the annual postal steamer which took us back to Vladivostok.'" From Vladivostok, Bogoras shipped the extensive collection of ethnographic objects he and his wife had gathered from the Chukchi and the Asiatic Eskimo to New York via the Suez Canal. He and Sofia Bogoras returned to St. Petersburg on the Trans-Siberian Railway: "'There I was unfortunately taken ill, and was unable to return to New York until April 17, 1902.'" Jocheslon's remarks about the departure of the rest of the team convey his sense of abandonment: "'While Mr. Bogoras's party was returning to Vladivostok from Mariinsky Post, and while Mr. Buxton was waiting for the steamer that was to take him back, I had to stay another year in northeastern Siberia, the object of my further investigation being the study of the Yukaghir of the Kolyma.'"[53]

With the glow of success in the initial stages of the JNPE, Jesup had written to Putnam, "'I am ever so much pleased with Dr. Boas' memoirs of the Jesup Expedition. It is a wonderful well written paper & I hope it will do good.'" Two years later Jesup's enthusiasm had deflated. He was not mollified by the numerous compliments he had received regarding the JNPE during the celebration of his seventieth birthday on June 21, 1900. He complained to Boas about the rising cost of the expedition. In a draft of a letter to Jesup, Boas wrote, "I beg to say that I am doing my best to carry on a great scienfitic inquiry with due circumspection. The plan is on a large scale and, in consequence, it takes long to obtain final results." He continued, "I believe you would feel greater confidence in the ultimate results if you would see the numerous remarks on the expedition, which is referred to by scientists of highest standing as the greatest undertaking of its kind. Even now the 'Jesup Expedition' is known the world over. The expressions of good wishes and of gratitude that you received from foreign scientific societies on your recent anniversary are further proof of the esteem in which the expedition is held." Boas assured Jesup, "The 'eclat' is increasing with every new publication. It is thanks to the publications of the Jesup Expedition that the Museum has become [known] in all countries as standing in the front rank of Anthropological Institutions." Closing his letter with an apology, Boas wrote, "I can only regret that my efforts in behalf of the Expedition for which I am sacrificing every other inspiration do not seem to meet with your approval."[54]

The expenses for the expedition had ballooned. While Boas had initially planned on finding one scientist for northeastern Siberia, instead he ended up with two experienced ethnographers, Jochelson and Bogoras, both of whom negotiated higher salaries than Boas had originally budgeted. Jesup had approved all of this. "I had an interview with Mr. Jesup last Monday," Boas wrote Putnam, "in which he authorized me to engage the two Russian gentlemen in connection with the Jesup North Pacific Expedition, and to go on with the American work of the Expedition." The appropriation has been "increased by $20,000."[55]

Boas couldn't resist the suggestion made by the curator of the Department of Mammalogy and Ornithology at the AMNH that a zoologist should accompany the expedition to collect specimens, thus increasing the transportation budget by three thousand dollars. Then Bogoras and Jochelson were to assemble "a small geological collection," for an additional six hundred dollars. And since Jochelson would be returning via the land route, "through the interior of Siberia to Yakutsk and to Irkutsk," he would be in the "territory inhabited by one of the most interesting Central Siberian tribes, the Yakut." While they were technically outside the area of the JNPE, Boas wrote Jesup that the Yakut were important because they had "swayed the fates of northern Asia and eastern Europe for centuries." An additional one thousand dollars would allow Jochelson to collect "highly ornamented garments and implements." Jesup authorized the additional expenditures for this collection.[56]

With original plans to publish "12 quarto volumes," seven volumes had been published by 1908. Boas remarked, "We realize that there is too much information for the planned size of the publication. However, I hope we will reach a satisfying conclusion for the exploration Mr. Jesup so generously organized by publishing its complete results." Jesup had not lived to know of Boas's September 1908 summary address on the JNPE, presented at the Sixteenth International Congress of Americanists in Vienna. He had died nine months earlier on January 22, 1908. For years prior to his death, a point of contention for Jesup—always a gentleman and always polite in expressing his disappointments—had been Boas's failure to write the volume *Summary and Final Results*. Boas's 1908 address, "The Results of the Jesup Expedition," was a step along the path, though the final volume was never realized.[57]

By 1930 the last volume of *The Jesup North Pacific Expedition* was published, with Bruno Oetteking's *Craniology of the North Pacific Coast.* Oetteking had begun work on "the osteological collections of the" JNPE in October 1913 at the AMNH. He wrote in the 1930 JNPE volume, "The skeletal material collected by the various members of the Jesup Expedition was entrusted in the autumn of 1913 by Professor Boas, to the present author for systematic investigation." While his work had been interrupted by the war, he said, "it was the author's good fortune, however, to have handled the material in the condition it was brought in from the field, and in which unprepared state it had been stored in the Museum for future examination."[58]

The 1930 Memoir of the AMNH listed on the front cover the published volumes of the JNPE, and those that had not been published. The latter included Boas's *Summary and Final Results*, Lev Shternberg's *Sociology of the Amur Tribes*, and Dina Brodsky-Jochelson's *Anthropometry of Siberia.* Shternberg's and Brodsky-Jochelson's manuscripts had been submitted to the JNPE series but not published. Krupnik and Fitzhugh note, "Even Boas became daunted by the immensity of the task and by the dragging performance of many of his associates." In 1999 the American Museum of Natural History published Shternberg's *The Social Organization of the Gilyak*, edited by Bruce Grant, not as part of the JNPE publications, but as part of the papers of the AMNH.[59]

There was a stalemate between the businessman, Jesup, expecting specific results for his investment, and the scientist, Boas, tormented by trying to draw a synthesis from what he felt was insufficient information. Boas's life work was always open-ended. He was eternally in search of synthesis. In sum, he avoided closure because he feared he would overlook something significant and would distort the facts. As Douglas Cole wrote, "To AMNH President Morris K. Jesup, the expedition had, by the time of his death in early 1908, become a matter of 'many disappointments,' 'an enterprise that has involved expense and anxiety out of all proportion to the representations that were originally made.'" Boas wrote his mother that he wished he could "'simply dump the whole Jesup Expedition and concern myself no further with it.'"[60]

Initially, Boas had taken pride in the JNPE publications. He wrote Jesup in April 1900, "I had the pleasure of sending to you to-day the first copy, just received of the new publication of the Jesup North Pacific Expedition. We have now in press and ready for press all the material required for completing the first volume, and I hope to be able to hand to you a copy of the complete volume about the middle of May." He had "the material in hand for two papers of the second volume," that would include Farrand material collected in 1897, and Harlan Smith's on "the archaeology of the State of Washington."[61] In January 1900 Teit had sent Boas the manuscript of all that he had "up to the end of last year." Teit wrote, "I have been working most days of this month on the supplementary paper Thomp[son] Indians." He had finished the paper on tattooing and was halfway through the paper on facial and body painting. Laufer planned to write "a number of monographs on the four tribes" he had studied, with the addition of "extensive amount of illustration." To Jesup, Boas wrote,

> It is necessary to decide now what is to be done in regard to future publication, and I beg to suggest that it would be best to continue without delay to bring the matter before the public. If you will authorize me to do so, we can begin at once printing the second volume of the Jesup Expedition, and can have the first number ready before the summer; and we can also begin with the preparation of illustrations for Dr. Laufer's papers. Estimates of the price of publishing each volume were submitted to you in connection with the general estimate of the expedition.[62]

At the end of the year Boas was still pressing Jesup about the importance of charting an expeditious publication schedule: "I beg leave to call your attention *once* more to the importance of pushing the publications of the Jesup North Pacific Expedition as much as possible, and to the desirability of using the winter months for publication." Boas stressed that "if we continue . . . at the present rate, it will take about fifteen years to finish the publication of . . . results of the Jesup Expedition. We have so many scientists now at work on this undertaking that we are perfectly able to push publication much faster." He emphasized the importance of the work that deserves "to be brought before the scientific public as quickly as we can, and I feel that we ought to close the whole undertaking in four or five years." He asked for authorization "to proceed at once with the publication of 1. *The Quinault Indians*, by Livingston Farrand, estimated cost, $300.00; [and] 2. Kwakiutl Texts, by Franz Boas, estimated cost $2500.00." AMNH Director Bumpus responded to Boas's letter, "In reply to your communication of December 22nd, addressed to President Jesup, I would reply as follows," and Bumpus laid out the order for the publication of the Kwakiutl Texts. In language that was bound to grate on Boas, Bumpus wrote that he was "given authority over the question of printing," and that he would need "to see the contract before it is finally signed."[63]

Boas was attempting to cajole manuscripts from Jochelson and Bogoras. Jochelson had come to New York in November 1902 to work at the AMNH on the material he had collected. He returned to Europe in 1904 without having completed his work. Jochelson had concluded that there was no hope for permanent employment at the AMNH because of the disagreements between Boas and Bumpus and Jesup. Bogoras had returned to St. Petersburg in 1904 and found himself in the midst of a revolution. Boas wrote, "'I fully appreciate the excitement of the present time, and the difficulty in concentrating yourself on scientific work; but if events like the present happen only once in a century, an investigation by Mr. Bogoras of the Chukchee happens only once in eternity, and I think you owe it to science to give us the results of your studies.'" Bogoras responded, "'You must believe us, that we here do not forget our good friends in America. . . . But the events of the time are so stirring. The blood is flowing, the best blood of the country, and no result is seen so far.'" On November 27, 1905, Bogoras was arrested in Moscow. Boas wrote Bumpus, "On Nov. 29 a cablegram is received from Mr. Bogoras informing me of his arrest." The cable read, "'Am arrested, reasons unknown.'" From Jochelson, Boas learned that Bogoras had been arrested for taking part in the Farmers' Congress in Moscow.[64]

For Boas, the fight with Bumpus over JNPE publications rendered lasting disappointment that remained as the sour aftertaste of what had been the glorious and monumental Jesup North Pacific Expedition. Boas had failed to gain support for his position at the AMNH from President Jesup. In July 1905 Boas resigned as curator of the anthropology department but agreed to stay on to complete "researches and publications relating to the Jesup Expedition and the Asiatic work of the Museum." Jesup appointed him "in Charge of the Scientific Work of the Jesup North Pacific Expedition, and the East Asiatic Research." Admittedly "not very sanguine" that this new accord would last, Boas wrote Bogoras, "I rather look upon my present position as a means of winding up the scientific work that I have in hand." With the present arrangement "very insecure," Boas implored him with urgency "to get your manuscripts into my hands."[65]

Despite the tumult of the revolutions in Russia and his multiple arrests, Bogoras completed seven monographs, four of which were on the Chukchi. Even in his collections, Bogoras surpassed all others. Stanley Freed, Ruth Freed, and Laila Williamson note, "No modern anthropologist has ever collected such a diversity of data." Boas noted in 1903 that Bogoras and his wife had "collected ethnographic data, linguistic notes and 150 texts, 5,000 ethnographic artifacts, skeletal material, plaster casts of faces, archeological specimens, 95 phonographic records, and somatological measurements of 860 individuals."[66]

William Fitzhugh and Igor Krupnik place the JNPE as "the first, and as yet the most coordinated, single study ever undertaken of the peoples and cultures of the North Pacific region." They continue, "Boas was decades ahead of his time. He instructed the members of the team he assembled to gather masses of ethnological data, including facial casts, body measurements, photographs, folklore texts, wax recordings, archaeological artifacts, and linguistic records. He dispatched his field crews to the Northwest Coast . . . and Siberia with the imprimatur of the AMNH and with funds provided by Morris Jesup together with his own detailed instructions on data collecting. Fieldwork lasted from several summer months (for Boas, Dixon, and Farrand, in North America) up to two full years (for the Jochelsons in Siberia)." Krupnik and Fitzhugh conclude that "the expedition's greatest accomplishment was to gather invaluable collections and publish masses of ethnographic data that documented cultural practices of the North Pacific peoples at a transitional time in their history."[67]

Boas grounded his meticulous planning of the JNPE on the importance of collaboration. He drew on individuals who either showed promise of developing expertise—a promise he saw in Teit, Farrand, Hunt, and Smith—or who were scholars with established expertise, as with Laufer, Jochelson, and Bogoras. As he consistently did, Boas forged relationships with international scholars. For the JNPE, these relationships were with

American, Canadian, German, and Russian scientists. Replicating his earlier desire for multiyear fieldwork in the Northwest Coast, Boas had a grand sweep to his vision for the JNPE.[68]

Fitzhugh and Krupnik note that Boas's "last (and practically his only) general review of the expedition's outcomes, methodology, and theoretical framework was presented in German in [September] 1908 as the opening address at the 16th International Congress of Americanists in Vienna." This address was not published in English until 2001, as "The Results of the Jesup Expedition," in *Gateways: Exploring the Legacy of the Jesup North Pacific Expedition, 1897–1902.* Beginning his remarks with a review of attempts by anthropologists to explain the similarities shared by widely dispersed cultural groups—either through "parallel evolution of humankind in all parts of the globe," or through uniform "psychological laws"—Boas gave his own perspective: "In opposition to these views is a more individualized theory in which culture is a product of a specific history and development that relies not only on the mental and physical accomplishments of a people but also acknowledges that new ideas and modes of living arise through contact with neighboring peoples and external forces. Supporters of this theory tend to attribute cultural similarities between discrete areas to a common history." Boas explained the difficulty in producing a synthesis from such complexity: "One should demand a gradual exploration of a problem that is of such sweeping importance." The success of the JNPE lay in "the wealth of ethnographic information" gathered, not in the search for the origins of the peoples, the routes of diffusion of culture traits, or the culture history. Boas concluded, "As expected, the members of the expedition have collected a wealth of ethnological, linguistic, and anthropological data."[69]

The heart of Boas's approach lay in finding the people's view of their life, from their own cultural perspective: "Aside from the geographic comparison, no research method now seems more promising than surveying how different tribes perceive their own customs and interpret their own traditions. If it is true that a large part of every tribe's culture is acquired, then it is no less true that the acquisition only becomes a genuine part of the culture if it fuses with the native perceptions into a comprehensive whole which has a more or less expressed character. In other words, the foreign element in a culture becomes native by being permeated by the spirit or style of the native culture." Thus, for Boas, the anthropologist needed to see the people's own "point of view." Such an approach, Boas posited, would give "the people's own interpretation of their traditions. It thus seemed supremely important to document the anthropological material through uncensored accounts of natives in their own words and in their own language, to preserve the original meaning."[70]

In a resounding understatement Freed, Freed, and Williamson note, "Jesup and the American Museum may have put too much emphasis on Boas's failure to write the summary volume." Indeed, Krupnik and Fitzhugh state that "the Jesup Expedition [was] one of the most extensively published anthropological projects ever," with "11 Jesup Expedition volumes comprising 31 separate reports on detailed ethnographic descriptions, folklore, and physical anthropology, [and] several dozen external articles and other monographs." In "A Jesup Bibliography," Krupnik examines the complexity of the JNPE publications and divides these into thirteen thematic sections. The total page count alone of the eleven volumes in the JNPE *Series/Memoirs of the* AMNH (1898–1930) is 6,037 pages.[71]

In *The Museum at the End of the World*, Alexia Block and Laurel Kendall write of their 1998 journey to the Russian Far East as a much later tracing of the JNPE. In appraisal of the JNPE in Siberia, they write of the "monumental" work of the ethnologists: "Traveling by horse, dogsled, skin boat, and raft, and camping for long and short periods in Native villages, Bogoras, Jochelson, and Laufer gathered data for a shelf of ethnographic monographs, including some 'classics,' substantial archives of photographs and correspondence, wax cylinders of songs and stories in Native languages, head casts and body measurements, and uniquely comprehensive collections documenting the lifeways of the Native people of the Russian Far East." The Northwest Coast portion of the JNPE was parallel to the Siberian expedition, though less traumatic, absent the Tsarist political intrigue. The results were equally bountiful and spectacular. Laurel Kendall and Krupnik write in the introduction to *Constructing Cultures Then and Now: Celebrating Franz Boas and the Jesup North Pacific Expedition*, "Boas and his colleagues collected about half of the American Museum's 16,755 Northwest Coast artifacts under the auspices of the Jesup Expedition. Although the numbers themselves are noteworthy, it is their diversity, comprehensiveness, and documentation that make the Jesup Expedition acquisitions so valuable. The American Museum's Northwest Coast collection is generally regarded as the world's strongest, holding artifacts from every known group and nation in this culture region. For over 100 years, this collection has been studied by almost every anthropologist, art historian, and historian engaged in research of any magnitude on the Northwest Coast native cultures."[72]

Krupnik remarks, "With the emphasis upon concerted teamwork of field and museum ethnography, linguistics, physical anthropology, and archaeology, the Jesup Expedition was clearly at the root of everything produced in Arctic/North Pacific anthropology for the next 100 years." Krupnik also emphasizes the feat of "an international anthropological project" that was "disseminated skillfully in three languages—English, Russian, and German—to both international and domestic audiences." The century following the Jesup Expedition served up tumultuous events in the United States, Germany, and Russia that washed over the accomplishments of the anthropologists who had joined forces on two continents: revolutions in Russia in 1905 and two in 1917; two world wars; the Cold War; the warming of perestroika in the 1980s; and the breakup of the former Soviet Union in 1991. Finally, there has been recognition of what had been left to us by the Jesup legacy. *Drawing Shadows to Stone* (1997) examines, as the subtitle indicates, *The Photography of the Jesup North Pacific Expedition, 1897–1902*. The bridge of cooperation between Siberia and Alaska was opened with the September 18, 1988, exhibit *Crossroads of Continents: Cultures of Siberia and Alaska* at the Smithsonian Institution's National Museum of Natural History. All of this led up to the two Jesup celebrations to mark the centenary, which yielded important publications examining both historical aspects of the JNPE and "coordinated research activities in the Greater North Pacific Region." Gavril Nikolaevich Kurilov and Vladimir Karlampovich Ivanov translated Jochelson's 1926 *The Yukaghir and the Yukaghirized Tungas* into the Russian and Yukaghir languages. Laurel Kendall writes, "They saw Jochelson's work as a testimony to the richness of Yukaghir culture before Soviet times; an accessible translation would help the Yukaghir recapture pride in their own history and culture after decades of forced assimilation." Recently, in "Jochelson and the Jesup North Pacific Expedition: A New Approach in the Ethnography of the Russian Far East," Erich Kasten and Michael

Dürr have shown continued interest in the JNPE by stressing the value and importance of the original publication by Vladimir Jochelson on the Koryak. Kasten has edited a book on the *"etnotroika"* of *Jochelson, Bogoras and Shternberg: A Scientific Exploration of Northeastern Siberia and the Shaping of Soviet Ethnography.*[73]

The very magnitude of the Jesup North Pacific Expedition could not be appraised close up. The perspective of time was needed to perceive the results. All of this rich tapestry comes to us through the years because Franz Boas had the amplified vision to dream on a large scale, to plan without a foregrounded fear of failure, and the courage to dare. Morris Jesup may have died disappointed in the endeavor bearing his name, but he lives on in the monumental work that he so generously funded. As Boas had written Jesup in 1900, this was, indeed, "the greatest undertaking of its kind."[74]

Taking Hold in New York

From the AMNH to Columbia University

Boas's institutional affiliation shifted from his grounding at the American Museum of Natural History with a lesser affiliation at Columbia University to, finally, a solid affiliation with the university. This changing center of activity emerged more from issues of personality than from his own strategic planning. From his beginnings at the AMNH in 1896 to his ultimate falling out with Morris K. Jesup and Herman Bumpus in 1905 and his final resignation in 1906, Boas's battles were many. He struggled with Jesup over the benefactor's demands that Boas produce the promised volumes on the JNPE, particularly the summarizing volume, and with Bumpus over issues of bureaucratic control at the AMNH. His institutional struggles also extended to Washington DC, to his work with W J McGee over the formation of the American Anthropological Association; and to William H. Holmes, who had been appointed BAE chief in 1903, over financial support of linguistic research.

Boas's battle with leaders at the AMNH and the BAE was set against a shifting national institutional landscape. There was a change in power centers associated with East Coast cities to broader, more national educational and geographical concerns. Boas was explicit about his intent to balance geographical and institutional representation. He wrote Frederick Hodge about the meeting of the Council of the American Anthropological Association to be held in New York City on October 29, 1903, "We shall have statements from California, Cambridge, New Haven, Brooklyn, New York, and I presume from Chicago: so it would seem curious not to have a report of the Government." These geographical groupings would come to be called the Washington anthropologists, the Philadelphia crowd, the Boston group, and the New York gang. They would battle over resources and the right to speak for the increasingly important discipline of anthropology, and they would be joined by voices from the Midwest at the University of Chicago and the West Coast at the University of California, Berkeley.[1]

Attempting to entice Kroeber into taking the position of secretary of the newly formed AAA, Boas appealed precisely to the need to balance representation: "The one or two others who might be thought of did not seem desirable, because we want to avoid the appearance of the concentration of the work of the Society in one city." Ultimately, George A. Dorsey of the Field Museum of Natural History in Chicago was named secretary, thus striking a balance midway between the East Coast and the West Coast. Propelled by personality and institutional conflicts, these changes ultimately forced creative developments. Boas took up his full professorship at Columbia University in July 1899 and shifted his time and energy to the Department of Anthropology in the first years of the twentieth century. During this period he emerged as the central figure for educating American anthropologists. What he had written to Jesup in 1898 had come to pass: he was training "the whole future generation of anthropologists" at Columbia University.[2]

"There are two objects to which my life is devoted," Boas wrote Bumpus in 1902. "The one, the establishment of anthropology on a broad basis in our country; the other, the prosecution of researches among the rapidly vanishing people of our continent." He continued, "Until two or three years ago it seems that the Anthropological Department of this Museum in conjunction with Columbia University would give the opportunity to carry out both of these objects, and for this reason I have centered all interests and activities in the promotion of these two institutions." Boas asserted, "the accomplishment of these ends is a matter of great importance to our country and to science."[3]

In 1898 Boas had made a pivotal career choice in order to realize his goal of developing anthropology in the United States. Baron Ferdinand Leopold von Andrian-Werburg had approached Boas about a professorship at the University of Vienna. On August 8, 1898, Boas replied, "I would like to send a word of explanation about our last conversation." He continued, "If I were thinking of returning to Europe and if I may even get a proposal from Vienna, it would be acceptable." Forthrightly, Boas admitted that he was held in place by his "hope to launch a thorough investigation" of tribes threatened with extinction: "I have invested much energy so I must not depart from it until success is ensured." Once his "organizational task" was completed, Boas thought Europe would offer "the most advantageous conditions" for employing his "scientific work," because the teaching and the educational background of the students were better developed than in America.[4]

For Boas, the enticement of a professorship in Vienna contrasted with his constant struggle at the AMNH. To his parents he wrote, "'I am sick and tired of annual bargaining and will try finally to get a secure position.'" He did just that when he successfully finessed the offer from the University of Vienna into a professorship at Columbia University in the newly created department of psychology and anthropology. Boas did not, however, conduct these delicate negotiations alone. Putnam was at his side for advice; Jesup worked with President Seth Low of Columbia to achieve a stronger, shared position for Boas; and ultimately Jacobi finalized the arrangement by anonymously paying $2,500 toward Boas's salary for the first two years.[5]

Boas wrote Putnam about his conversation with Jesup concerning the Vienna offer, "I spoke to him rather freely on the whole organization of the Museum, and in regard to the work of the different departments, as it appears to me. I was particularly anxious to impress Mr. Jesup with the fact that my present position is unsatisfactory in so far as both positions that I am holding are inferior positions, and that consequently I do not meet my colleagues on a basis of equality, and that, furthermore my position has no assurance of permanence." Boas stressed "that the only remedy lies in improving my position at Columbia College, where I feel I ought to have a professorship. If I could obtain that position, it would also improve my income considerably, and thus make my place in every way more desirable."[6]

Summarizing their conversation of November 28, 1898, Boas wrote Jesup that "I have delayed replying to the question that was put to me, as to whether I would accept the offer of a professorship in Vienna, because I feel that my field of activity here in the Museum and at Columbia College, may become a very satisfactory one." Boas continued, "On the other hand, I cannot feel satisfied with the present arrangements, because both positions that I am holding are inferior in character, and do not give me the opportunity to work to best advantage. The uncertainty of the continuity of my work is its most unsatisfactory feature." He had been told that his work at Columbia University "is only tentative, and by no means certain to be continued." Additionally, since he was not "a member of the faculty," he was hampered in "the development of my department of instruction." In his view, the strength of his position lay precisely in drawing together his work at the AMNH and at Columbia: "I am training my students by the help of the material accumulated in the Museum for field work, and they will necessarily become the investigators for this Institution and for the Bureau of Ethnology. But this work can be carried out, only if Columbia University really develops its Anthropological Department. This development is of great importance to the Museum since we must get our field workers from among the men training or trained in the University." Boas desired two things: to have support for "the carrying out of scientific work that it will take a series of years to complete. . . . for an investigation of those tribes of North America that are doomed to speedy extinction" and "to be appointed to a professorship at the University." He concluded, "If these two points can be favorably settled, I feel that I shall be justified in declining the offer from Vienna."[7]

From December 1898 through February 1899, Boas, Jesup, Putnam, and Low exchanged numerous letters that explored how the museum and the university might work more closely together, and how the professorship could be established. On December 31, 1898, Boas responded to Jesup's request "to indicate in writing what work is practicable in this department of the Museum, in connection with the work of instruction at Columbia University." Boas wrote, "Under the present conditions we are able to give students opportunity to do extended research work in physical anthropology and in ethnology. Our collections of crania, skeletons, and masks [plaster casts], are very extensive, and give good opportunity for a great variety of work. Our ethnological collections are now well arranged, and can be used to advantage for advanced instruction and for research." With respect to "modification in University courses . . . to make the work at the Museum available," Boas continued, "Dr. Farrand, in his courses at the University, has prepared a few men for advanced work, and it is likely that several of these will desire to avail themselves of the opportunities offered in the Museum. One of my students, who is working at the Museum this year, will probably continue to work here, and I expect that another one will desire to take up work in this Institution." While there were only a few students who benefited from "the opportunities offered in the Museum," this was linked directly to the length of time that Farrand and Boas had been training students: "Dr. Farrand's work has extended over four years only, my work over three years only. Students were hardly prepared to do advanced work before this time." Boas assured Jesup that his plan for "the closer affiliation of the work of the University and of the Museum" could be accomplished through a combination of opening the facilities at the AMNH to students and broadening "the preparatory work at Columbia University" and that the plan needn't be put into place all at once.[8]

Boas replied to Low's letter of February 20, 1899, "I am very thankful for the interest you have taken in the advancement of the subject of anthropology, and for the success of your endeavor." He went on, "I only hope that I may be able to gradually develop anthropology in such a way that it may become a strong department of the University, and that it may materially contribute to the advancement of scientific research and of the scientific spirit in this country." Boas assured Low that Jesup also desired "the fullest co-operation between the Museum and the University, so that I presume no obstacle will be put in my way in regard to giving the University a full equivalent in the way of instruction."[9]

Finally, in May 1899, President Low wrote Boas, "It gives me pleasure to inform you that the Trustees at their meeting held to-day, unanimously adopted the following resolution: *Resolved*, That from and after July 1st, 1899, Franz Boas, Ph.D. be and hereby is appointed Professor of Anthropology, for the term of two years, or during the pleasure of the Trustees, at a salary of $2,500 per annum." The letter continued, "The chair of Anthropology has been assigned to the Department of Psychology, making that . . . the Department of Psychology and Anthropology." Low concluded: "Hoping that this appointment, though in its terms limited to two years, may lead in some way to a permanent provision for the chair."[10]

As he had so often done, Jacobi kept watch over Boas's struggles and progress from the sidelines and stepped in at just the right time. Douglas Cole recounts, "He had written to Low with an offer to pay $2,500 toward Boas's professorial salary for two years. His sole condition was 'that Dr. Boas should never know about this correspondence.' . . . Boas had heard, accidently, from his niece, Nandi Meyer, that Putnam had called on Jacobi to discuss his professorship. The thought that Jacobi should still be assuming financial responsibility at this time in his life was painful." Boas spoke with Jacobi, who, "'in his redeeming way, declined all responsibility.'" As Boas wrote his parents, "'I can do nothing about it except to make the most of the opportunity.'"[11]

When Boas first began to teach at Columbia in 1896, Alfred Louis Kroeber was a graduate student. He was teaching a course in eighteenth-century literature in the English department and freshman composition classes in the rhetoric department, and he was writing his MA thesis in English on "The English Heroic Play" (1897). Kroeber found his way to Boas's seminar on American Indian languages. Theodora Kroeber writes, "Kroeber and two other young men enrolled." Boas had the students "come each Tuesday evening to his home on 82nd Street, close to the museum, where, at the dining table lighted by a fringe-shaded lamp, he held his class." Kroeber remarked on his two classmates that "one was an archaeologist from the Museum," and the other "an adventurous non-descript who soon after rolled himself out of anthropology as suddenly as he had rolled in, and who required some quarts of beer in a can from the nearest saloon to overcome the tension of a two hours' session with Chinook or Eskimo." As Kroeber recounted to his wife, Theodora, "'We spent about two months each on Chinook, Eskimo, Klamath, and Salish, analyzing texts and finding the grammar (with help and some straight-out presentation by Boas). I was enormously stimulated. Grammatical structure was interesting as presented; but to discover it was fascinating.'" Later in the course, Boas brought Esther Bein to the Tuesday night class to dictate, as Theodora Kroeber recounted, in "her dialect of Eskimo," for the students to record it phonetically.[12]

Esther, an Inuit woman from Labrador, had come to the United States at the age of sixteen with her parents, Abile and Helena, and fifty-seven Inuit recruited by the promoters, Ralph Taber and Lyle Vincent, for exhibition at the Eskimo Village at the 1893 World's Columbian Exposition. While most of the Labrador Inuit returned home following the closing of the WCE, Abile, Helena, Esther, and her daughter, Nancy Columbia, who had been born in Chicago at the WCE, traveled the country. They were on exhibition in 1894 at the Austin and Stone's Museum in Boston, the Eskimo Village exhibit at Huber's Museum in New York, and at the Midwinter Exposition in San Francisco, and they visited the White House in May 1895.[13] Finally, in 1895, at the end of their travels, the family came to New York City, where Esther met and married German-American Charles Bein, who hauled freight with his horse-drawn lorry. Undoubtedly, Boas, Abile, Helena, and Esther had met in Chicago at the WCE, where Boas had visited the Eskimo Village. In January 1896 Esther Bein sent Boas a letter: "I write you these few lines to let you know that my mother is not feeling very well." Esther was hoping to be able to send her parents back home. In March Esther wrote, "I am pleased to hear that you are going to try your best to help them to get home." In May Esther asked for a loan of "a few dollars that I can save for Doctor" for her mother. She asked if Boas knew when her parents could leave for home.[14]

As Kenn Harper and Russell Potter note, "With the family penniless and Helena recovering from a serious illness, Ralph Taber and Franz Boas . . . provided means for their passage home. Friends provided Abile with a parting gift—a hunting outfit, including a new gun—to allow him to start afresh in Labrador." Boas apparently wrote Taber about Esther Bein's desire to send her family home. Taber responded, "My arrangements have not yet been completed and I cannot say definitely whether I shall visit Labrador this summer or not." He continued, "I would advise you to take the necessary steps for the return of the Eskimo, and when you have secured a sufficient sum for this purpose, I will aid you in arranging for their transportation and in getting them started." He concluded, "You may count upon me to contribute $25 for their return." Boas purchased the tickets for Esther's mother, father, and daughter. Harlan Smith accompanied them to the wharf and saw them safely aboard the Silva, bound for Labrador.[15]

As Harper recounts, when Boas had joined the AMNH in 1896 as assistant curator, "he asked Peary to bring back from his summer's cruise one Inuk for a year's stay." Likely reflecting on the Bella Coola Indians with whom he had worked in Berlin and the Labrador Eskimos from whom he and others had collected materials in Chicago, Boas thought, as Harper related, that "such a thing had previously been done ... without the individual suffering from it." In May 1897, just as he was preparing to depart for the first season of the JNPE Northwest Coast fieldwork, Boas repeated the request that he had made to Robert Peary the previous year: "'I beg to suggest to you that if you are certain of revisiting North Greenland next summer, it would be of the very greatest value if you should be able to bring a middle-aged Eskimo to stay here over winter. This would enable us to obtain leisurely certain information which will be of the greatest scientific importance.'" As Ludger Müller-Wille conveyed to me, Boas undertook continuing work on Inuit language and culture, particularly "Der Eskimo-Dialekt des Cumberland-Sundes" (The Eskimo dialect of the Cumberland Sound, 1894); his publications on folklore and religion (1894, 1900); and his volumes, "a long time in preparation," on "The Eskimo of Baffin Land and Hudson Bay" (1901, 1907). Müller-Wille adds, "This is to say that he had a particular interest to have Inuit come and reside close by to be available for research."[16]

Peary brought not one "middle-aged Eskimo," but "'three men, one woman, a boy, and a girl'"—Qisuk and his young son Minik; Atangana and her husband Nuktaq with their adopted daughter Aviaq; and Uisaakassak.[17] Peary used the Eskimo as a means to raise funds for another voyage to the Arctic and charged an entrance fee for the thousands of people who boarded the Hope to see what was called "the Peary Eskimo." As related in an article in the *New York Times*, "All of the Eskimos will leave the ship to-day and go to the Museum of Natural History, where they will arrange the exhibit of their implements. They will remain here until Lieut. Peary starts for the North again, which will be in July of next year." Since Peary had made the decision on his own to bring the Eskimos to the United States, Jesup was in the uncomfortable position of finding that his museum was to serve as host for the unexpected guests. A memo from Bumpus noted, "'It was felt that it would be unwise to place the Eskimos in an asylum or in a hospital because the artificial, and to them, unnatural confinement of such places would prove unfavorable.'" Jesup authorized the assignment of rooms for the "'temporary occupancy of the Eskimos, who were placed in the custody of Mr. Wallace.'" Initially, the six individuals, sometimes referred to as "the Peary Eskimos," were housed in a basement room at the AMNH. Throngs of New Yorkers came to the museum to see them. As reported in the *New York Times*, every visitor went "through a process of vigorous handshaking." When "disappointed . . . that the Eskimos were not on exhibition," some members of the crowd stretched out prone and peered through the grate into the basement room where the Eskimos were housed. Jesup turned to AMNH Building Supervisor William Wallace to find appropriate housing for the six individuals. Wallace moved them to his sixth-floor apartment in the museum that he shared with them.[18]

Within one month, all the Eskimos had been admitted to Bellevue Hospital from colds that had progressed to pneumonia.[19] Some recovered enough to return to the museum, but others were not so fortunate. Harper relates, "On February 17, 1898, Dr. Boas received a letter from Bellevue Hospital—Qisuk [the father of Minik] was dying and the other Eskimos, who were all in the hospital again, should be removed from the institution and placed in a private house. Then, suddenly, Qisuk died that very day, before the move could be made." Jesup owned a house in Highbridge in the Bronx, with a cottage on the property. The Eskimos were moved to the cottage and, as reported in the *New York Tribune*, "after some searching there was found in the city a woman from Labrador who could talk with the Esquimaus, though with some difficulty, for she was not familiar with many peculiarities of their dialect. This woman was engaged as housekeeper, and she has been in charge of the Esquimaus' cottage ever since." This was Esther Bein. Less than a month after they had moved to Jesup's cottage, Atangana, the mother of the young girl Aviaq, died. As reported in the *New York Tribune*, the following question was posed to Boas: "'When you found they were sick so much, didn't you think of sending them North again?'" He replied, "'Yes, but there was no opportunity to send them. There were ships going north as far as Newfoundland and Labrador, but that would not have been anywhere near their home, and we could not land them in a strange country. When Lieutenant Peary starts on his trip this summer he will take them back with him.'" Boas said, "'We are very sorry about the deaths of the man and woman, but we know that everything was done for them to keep them well.'"[20] Of the six Smith Sound Eskimo that Peary brought to

New York, all died save for Minik, the young boy, and Uisaakassak. On July 2, 1892, Uisaakassak sailed back home on the Windward. He came to be called "the big liar," because no one would believe his stories about New York, where "'people lived up in the air like auks on a bird cliff. The houses are as big as icebergs . . . and they stretch inland as far as you can see . . . with innumerable canyons that serve as roads.'"[21]

Jesup valued his stature in the community and the respect that came to him from his position as president of the AMNH. With the glare of publicity, he felt himself unwillingly drawn into the tragedy of the Smith Sound Eskimos. Almost simultaneously he became aware of Wallace's shady dealings, which involved kickbacks from contractors he had employed for work at the AMNH. Jesup spent $71,000 of his own money to settle claims against the museum, some of which dated to the 1890s. Wallace resigned from the AMNH on January 11, 1901. Seven months later, Jesup was still reeling from the ordeal, as he wrote Osborn and Bumpus on July 24, 1901: "'The only mistake I have made . . . is in trusting and placing confidence in a man that I believed was honest, and trustworthy and loyal.'" He continued, "'I am not strong in body or mind just now: this trouble has un-nerved me.'" Undoubtedly Jesup had been spurred by his negative experience with Wallace to promote Henry Osborn to vice president and to hire Herman Bumpus as director of the AMNH in 1901, both of whom were to keep a careful eye on all administrative details. Precisely at this time, Bumpus, in Jesup's stead, began scrutinizing Boas's expenditures for the JNPE, and Boas felt his collegial relationship with Jesup disintegrating.[22]

The reporter of the *New York Tribune* depicted Boas as being "in charge of the Esquimaus." Boas explained, "'It was believed that much valuable information of an ethnological character could be obtained from them, and that their presence here would be very instructive to scientists interested in the study of the Northern races. This has, in fact, proved true. Many things theretofore unknown have been learned regarding their language, their traditions and their personal characteristics.'" Due to the demands on his time for the organization of the JNPE, Boas did not himself work with the Smith Sound Eskimos but encouraged his student, Kroeber, to do so after they had moved to Jesup's cottage in Highbridge:

My dear Mr. Kroeber,

I went up to see the Eskimos last night, and everything is ready for you to continue your work. . . . They are located on Feather-Bed Lane, which you reach by taking the cars to Washington Bridge, crossing Washington Bridge, and then taking the street to the north. . . . You will come to a parting of the roads, and there you will see to the right, a small brownish frame house. The Eskimos live in this house. . . .

Please let me know what arrangements you have made. I think I shall be able to go out with you once a week or so, and we will make some appointment for a time to discuss the material that you are going to obtain.

Working as housekeeper for the Smith Sound Eskimos, Esther Bein also served as Kroeber's translator for his work on Eskimo folktales. Drawing partially from this collecting, as well as from bibliographical research, Kroeber presented a paper at the American Folklore Society meetings at Columbia University in 1898, published as "Animal Tales of the Eskimo" in the *Journal of American Folklore* (1899). He then published "Tales of the Smith Sound Eskimo" (1899), also in the *Journal of American Folklore*. In the latter article he began, "The following tales were collected during the winter of 1897–98 from the Smith Sound Eskimo then in New York city, in charge of the American Museum of Natural History." In "The Eskimo of Smith Sound" (1900) Kroeber wrote, "The following pages consist in the main of the results of investigations carried on in the winter of 1897–98, under the direction of Dr. F. Boas, among six Eskimo from Smith Sound, brought to New York by Lieut. R. E. Peary." He continued, "The boy Minik, ten years old. . . . called the ghost of a dead person . . . a torngang"; and if one saw such a ghost, one would die immediately. The Smith Sound Eskimo, Kroeber related, said that the *angakoq* (shaman) had no power in the United States because there were no *tornat*, or spirits of the dead, in this land. Kroeber had quoted Minik, the youngest of the Smith Sound Eskimo and the least knowledgeable of the intricacies of his native culture, but the individual who had acquired the greatest facility with English.[23]

In September 1908 the consul-general of Denmark wrote Boas at the suggestion of William Wallace to inquire about Minik, "I have seen Mr. Wallace and the boy, and the last mentioned declared to me that he was very anxious to get home." He continued, "The Danish Government, as you will perhaps be aware, takes a paternal interest in the welfare of the Eskimos, and has instructed me, after the case had been brought to its notice, to make full inquiries and report, but before doing so, I should be very grateful if you would give me whatever particulars you have about this case so as to enable me from outside sources to get an independent opinion respecting the particulars as to the manner in which these people were originally brought here and kept in New York." Boas replied that he would be happy to talk with him, but there is no further correspondence in the Boas Papers.[24]

Minik returned to Greenland in August 1909. Word spread among the inhabitants of North Star Bay that Minik, the son of Qisuk, about whom all had heard stories, had come back. Gustav Olsen, a Dane and the first missionary to the Polar Eskimo, wrote in his diary of the arrival of the Jeanie, "'On that ship was an Eskimo named Minik who was returning home. He was one of the ones that Peary had taken away when he was a child. He has completely forgotten his language. He came ashore here but we have seen very little of him. He has only the clothes on his back.'" While he was able to relearn the language and the ways of his people, Minik never really found his place among them, nor did he find it in the United States. The Arctic explorer Peter Freuchen, who had met Minik, observed, "'In America he had longed for Greenland, and now that he was in Greenland he wanted to be back in America.'" Minik sailed south, one of the few passengers on board the decrepit Cluett. He arrived in New York harbor on September 21, 1916. Two years later, on October 29, 1918, Minik died from bronchial pneumonia as a complication from the Spanish influenza that he had contracted while working as a lumberjack in Pittsburgh, New Hampshire. Afton Hall, Minik's close friend from the sawmill where they worked, had taken Minik to his home after they both contracted influenza. A nurse and doctor looked after Minik, Afton, his mother, and his father, who were all ill. Afton buried Minik in the Indian Stream Cemetery on October 30, 1918.[25]

While Minik and Wallace had repeatedly petitioned the AMNH for the burial of Minik's father, it was not until July 1993 that, as Harper writes, "the bones of four Polar Eskimos were loaded aboard an American military transport aircraft at Maguire Air Force Base in New Jersey and transported to Thule Air Base in northern Greenland. The journey that had taken over a month in 1897 was accomplished in a few short hours." The repatriation of the bodies resulted from the attention attracted by Harper's *Give Me My Father's Body: The Life of Minik, the New York Eskimo*, first published in 1986.[26]

What remains for us of the stories from Qisuk, Atangana, Nuktaq, Aviaq, Uisaakassak, and Minik? Is it the pathos of these six Eskimos taken from their homeland by the explorer Peary? Is it outrage over the abuse of power by scientists and administrators with respect to the disposition of the dead bodies of the four Eskimos? Is it recognition that the press both kept the story alive and sensationalized it for their readership? Or is it, as Edmund Carpenter reflects, knowledge triumphing over misbegotten belief? There are no easy answers to these questions, but there clearly was a trail of travesty, and the sad end to this trail leads to the cemetery in Qaanaaq, Greenland, where a bronze plaque declaims, "They have come home."[27] In a communication to me, Müller-Wille highlighted the difficulty as to "how these events can be assessed and evaluated 120 years later," and he posed another question: "What went on in the heads of Peary, Boas, Kroeber, Wallace, Jesup, and Bumpus—all were *Kinder ihrer Zeit* (children of their time). That is not to say that people did not reflect, certainly Boas did if not as explicitly and extensively as we sometimes hope for. . . . Clearly, he did adhere to the overpowering premise that prevailed in the 19th century that things needed to be done in the name of and to the advancement of science."

In May 1901 Boas had written to Zelia Nuttall about his plans and vision for the development of American anthropology. Among other points in his detailed letter, he emphasized the important place of the BAE for work in linguistics:

I have, furthermore, always retained a certain connection with the Bureau of Ethnology, through which I have been enabled to expand our work over lines which do not properly fall in the scope of work in the Museum. I refer particularly to work in linguistics. One of the most important steps that I have taken in this direction is to suggest to the bureau the publication of a handbook of American languages, which I am to edit. . . . Through this undertaking I hope to be put in a position to push the necessary linguistic and ethnological work very considerably.[28]

In April 1901 Boas had begun a correspondence with McGee about "publishing a handbook of North American languages." Boas wrote, "I think I have trained now a sufficient number of young men to make it possible to take up work of this kind . . . and I should like to suggest to you that the Bureau take up this work with a plan of bringing out a publication of this sort say in about five or six years." With McGee positively disposed to his idea, Boas summarized their recent discussions: "I will undertake to prepare for the Bureau of Ethnology a handbook of North American languages, which is to contain descriptions of all the fundamental languages, taking on in order what ideas are expressed in each language, what material and processes are used, and how these are applied for the expression of certain ideas. Each sketch is to be accompanied by a number of pages of texts, fully explained by means of grammatical notes." Boas proffered his article on "Sketch of Kwakiutl" as a template for the work on the *Handbook of American Indian Languages* (1911). He wrote McGee, "What I have in mind [is] to describe the language in an analytical way, giving the fundamentals of the phonetics, grammatical processes, and grammatical categories." He continued, "It would be my wish to follow the sketch of each language with a text of about a thousand words or so, fully annotated, and with references to the corresponding paragraphs of the grammatical sketch."[29]

Secretary of the Smithsonian Institution Samuel Pierpont Langley appointed Boas as honorary philologist of the BAE, effective July 1, 1901. In May 1901 Boas wrote BAE ethnologist-in-charge McGee, "I have made the final arrangements for linguistic field-work for the coming summer. According to our agreement, I shall pay the men who are to do the work all of their travelling expenses, the total amount to be expended from sources not coming from the Bureau of Ethnology being at least equal to the amount expended by you." With such an expansive undertaking,

Boas stressed the need to draw on the cooperation of many institutions: "For this reason the work during the past year has been organized in co-operation with the American Museum of Natural History, Columbia University, Harvard University, and the University of California."[30]

Ever mindful of the need to work toward the professionalization of anthropology, Boas joined forces with McGee in creating a national and professional journal of anthropology. Together they drafted and signed the co-ownership agreement for the *American Anthropologist*. "I am in hopes," Boas wrote, "that the establishment of the journal may prove beneficial to the development of anthropology on our continent." Initially with 156 subscribers, Boas and McGee struggled to maintain the journal financially. Ultimately, they found themselves divided in opposition as to the disposition of the journal that they had birthed, coddled, and owned.[31]

The Anthropological Society of Washington, founded in 1879, had begun publishing the *American Anthropologist* in 1888. However, as Daniel Lamb writes, "the needs of anthropology in America had outgrown the media of publication," and the Anthropological Society of Washington, with "limited financial resources . . . could not afford to increase the size of its magazine, or make it national in scope." At the 1897 winter meeting of Section H of the AAAS, a committee was appointed to consider the creation of an anthropology journal. By February 1898, with McGee as president of Section H and undoubtedly with the support of Boas, the decision was made to retain the title *American Anthropologist*, with the sole distinction of the addition "New Series." On the last page of the last issue of the old series of the *American Anthropologist*, the editors noted that "it has been the aim of the Anthropological Society of Washington to render the new journal all the aid that lies in its power; and its officers and members, in expressing their appreciation of the support given its own journal during the eleven years of publication, urge that its subscribers extend their patronage to the new and enlarged series."[32]

In January 1899 Boas and McGee signed the document of incorporation for the *American Anthropologist*, New Series. They were "equal partners in the constructive ownership of the said Editorial Board for and during the year 1899," and for three years from the date of signing.[33] Boas was consumed in a flurry of work on the *American Anthropologist*: well over half of his 1899 professional correspondence—222 of 329 letters—

dealt with the journal. Financial problems began at once: "It was soon obvious that subscriptions would not cover the costs the first year, even with the lump sum contributions" from the Anthropological Society of Washington.[34]

As co-owners of the *American Anthropologist*, Boas and McGee were responsible for raising funds to cover the deficit; in the first year, that was approximately $1,000. With characteristic focus and energy, Boas threw himself into fund-raising. In an effort to increase interest in the *American Anthropologist*, Boas attempted to revive the all-but moribund American Ethnological Society. He wrote the twenty people living in New York City who had been affiliated with the society, "It is now several years since the American Ethnological Society has held any meetings, and still longer since the society has done any active work." Boas invited them to attend a meeting in his office at the AMNH on December 14, 1899, "to consider ways and means for a re-organization of this society." Hoping to augment the numbers, Boas was including those who had been attending the Anthropology Club, which had been informally meeting in his home since 1896. On this topic Boas wrote Jesup, "I spoke to you last week on a plan which I have in mind, to develop what anthropological interest there is or can be around in this City in such a way, as to make it useful to the Museum." Boas planned to propose to the members of the Anthropology Club, and to those who met to revive the AES, "that the old society make over all its property which is at present deposited in the Museum, to the Museum," and that the Anthropology Club combine membership with the AES. Boas concluded his letter to Jesup, "Anthropology is developing so rapidly that a society of this kind is bound to come, and I believe, it is a wise move to affiliate it with the Museum now, as long as we can control the movement."[35]

By 1900 the AES had increased from the twenty people Boas had contacted for the original meeting to seventy-one members of the revived society. Sadly, however, this did not yield the financial benefit in paid subscriptions. The summary of Boas's activities in 1900 noted that "his correspondence with the Treasurer who was quite irresponsible, failed to pay bills or collect dues or keep appointments with [Boas]. After [the] meeting of [the] Board was called, he left town and his brother took over. Meanwhile [Boas] paid some of the bills himself." In October 1900 Boas reported a deficit of $550: "We shall therefore have to raise again a very considerable amount."[36]

So it continued with Boas cajoling friends and colleagues to contribute to the *American Anthropologist* and repeatedly reminding them of promises made but not fulfilled. He also enlisted others to take part: Stewart Culin to raise money in Philadelphia, Dorsey to fulfill his promise to raise money in Chicago, and Hodge to see if Jesse Walter Fewkes had written to the philanthropist Augustus Hemenway. Then there were the letters to follow up on the reminders. Noting the need for an additional one hundred subscriptions, Boas prodded Stewart Culin regarding his promise to obtain subscriptions from Philadelphia, "The *American Anthropologist* is in a very bad financial position at the present time, and I do not know whether it will be necessary for us to discontinue the publication." With the additional subscriptions promised by Culin from Philadelphia, "we may hope to carry the unavoidable deficit a few years longer, until the subscription-list is still further increased."[37]

With the *American Anthropologist* scarcely viable financially, McGee proposed to Boas the formation of a national anthropology society, linked to the journal and perhaps eventually able to provide enough members for "the maintenance of the journal." Referring to his conversation with James McKeen Cattell, who served as editor of the AAAS publication *Science*, McGee wrote, "On thinking over the matter discussed . . . in the course of a conversation with Professor Cattell in which he quite independently suggested that the time has come for the establishment of an American Anthropological Society, it has seemed to me that the present may offer an auspicious occasion for moving toward a national organization of anthropologists."[38]

McGee seized the initiative and wrote to all who had attended the meeting that had been held in Chicago in Dorsey's office at the Field Museum of Natural History on December 31, 1901. They had gathered, McGee wrote, to discuss "the subject of American Anthropology and the possible means of securing better coordination of effort among American anthropologists." The participants included "Dr. Franz Boas and Dr. Livingston Farrand, representing a delegation from the American Ethnological Society in New York; Dr. George A. Dorsey, Dr. George G. MacCurdy, Dr. Frank Russell, Professor Frederick Starr, and Dr. Stewart

Culin, representing a delegation on behalf of Section H of the American Association; and Dr. J. Walter Fewkes and myself." In his copy of the letter, Boas had penciled the marginal notation "Roland B. Dixon, representing a delegation from the Anthropological Society of Washington." This discussion "turned on the condition and prospects of *the American Anthropologist*." McGee continued, "Had the duration of the conference permitted, the question would have been raised by either Dr. Boas or myself, whether the time has not come for definite movement in the direction of a national organization of anthropologists." McGee maintained that those at the Chicago meeting were "thoroughly representative of American anthropology in personnel and in object." He continued, "I venture to propose that the participants in this conference constitute themselves a nucleus of an American anthropologic association, and proceed toward the organization of such a body." Moving quickly to formalize his proposal, McGee drafted a constitution, which covered three main points—first, that the society would work with local organizations; second, that the proposed council would be "large enough to include all active professional workers in anthropology in the country"; and, third, that the association would "assume the issue of the *American Anthropologist* in case such course be deemed wise by the new body and agreeable by the present owners and editorial board."[39]

In his response, Boas suggested that "it might be better to wait a year or two" before attempting to organize a national anthropological society. Boas felt very strongly the need to "bring in all the financial aid that we possibly can," but he expressed the fear "that, if the national society is established on the proposed basis, we may endanger the permanent interests of science by yielding to our temporary needs." Wary of duplicating the work of the AAAS, Boas was particularly concerned about diluting the force of the professional anthropologist: "It seems to my mind that what is most urgently needed is a national society of anthropologists in which the amateur element is rigidly excluded."[40]

The battle lines were drawn. McGee did not have formal training in science, let alone in anthropology. A strong supporter of the contributions to science by local societies, McGee embraced an inclusive approach. He envisioned making room for local societies and amateur anthropologists. With his unrelenting push for professionalism in anthropology,

Boas insisted on an exclusive approach, one in which admittance to the society would be based on members having "contributed to the advancement of anthropology either by publication or by high-grade teaching." Boas expressed his view succinctly: "By admitting the general public to a national society, its scienfitic character would be at once endangered; and I consider this the prize end in such a society." George Stocking remarks that Boas "viewed the founding of the Association not in narrow organizational terms but rather as part of a much broader process, to which he devoted the better part of his adult life: the professionalization of American anthropology." Stocking continues, "By virtue of his position [at the BAE] McGee was the organizer of much of the anthropological work in this country. Considering his own origins and his long association with and leadership in the A.S.W., an organization of quite broad character with a large amateur element . . . , McGee was hardly likely to be receptive to arguments for professional exclusiveness. He was in fact fighting for the birth of an organization built along lines with which he was familiar and in which his own leadership would be assured."[41]

There was more at stake for McGee than the founding of a national anthropology society. As Curtis Hinsley delineates, McGee's position at the BAE was in peril with the decline of John Wesley Powell's health before his death on September 23, 1902. McGee's place in government had been directly linked to Powell. When Powell retired from the U.S. Geological Survey and moved to the Bureau in 1893, he brought "McGee as protégé and heir apparent." In 1894 Powell had a second operation on his right arm, where he was wounded during the Civil War. During this period, from 1894 to 1902, McGee operated as "ethnologist-in-charge," a title that he had given to himself, not thinking "ethnologist," was sufficient for his position. Hinsley remarks, "As Powell withdrew, his protégé took control of the Bureau, dictating Powell's correspondence and composing the annual reports. 'I knew it all,' he testified. 'I drafted every plan of operations, and wrote every report, and drafted every important letter, letters from Major Powell as well as from myself.'" As Powell's stenographer noted, after 1895 Powell "did not dictate 'more than the smallest percent' of the letters he signed. During the summers, when Powell was in Maine, 'every particle of control' remained in McGee's hands." Hinsley quotes McGee's letter to Powell's widow:

In his office life I knew the condition better than anyone else, and sought in every way to have his best side kept outward. The fact remains that since the final operation on his arm in Baltimore [in 1894] the Major never wrote a report or any other important official paper; for while sometimes he was undoubtedly able to do so, he was oftener unable, and even in his best hours the strain of the work and the need for gathering half-forgotten details would have been injurious . . . during the later years of the Bureau he seldom saw the reports until they were shown to him in printer's proofs.[42]

McGee found validation through affiliation with scientific societies. When McGee had moved to Washington in 1883, he immediately joined the Anthropological Society. Over the years, he delivered twenty-two papers there and served as officer for fifteen consecutive years. He was the "driving force" in the National Geographic Society, the Geographical Society of America, the Columbian Historical Society, and, of course, the organizing force behind the AAA. As Hinsley writes, "At the founding of the Washington Academy of Sciences in 1898, McGee was the only person belonging to all twelve constituent societies." Despite the society affiliations, "McGee never felt accepted in Washington. His daughter remembered that 'for years my environment had no more use for my father than if he had been a coal-heaver.'"[43]

Having taken an almost immediate dislike to McGee, Secretary of the Smithsonian Langley was determined that McGee would never succeed Powell as the director of the BAE. One month after coming to the BAE, McGee had challenged Langley on a budgetary issue. As Hinsley recounts, "Langley grew to despise and distrust the new ethnologist. While Powell lived, the tense and suspicious relations between the Smithsonian staff and the BAE did not erupt into open conflict, despite accusations of shoddy business methods in the Bureau." In 1902, with Powell's health in decline, Langley wrote Daniel Coit Gilman in the latter's capacity as the founding president of the Carnegie Institution (1902–4) "that after Powell's death he intended to purge the Bureau." Langley wrote similarly to his aide Richard Rathbun, "'The possible death of Major Powell is so near a contingency, and the unfortunate affairs of the Bureau have aroused such opposition in Congress to its continuance . . . that I am more disposed than heretofore, if possible, to say that Mr. McGee must not hope to occupy [the directorship] while I am responsible for his official acts.'"[44]

McGee read the tea leaves correctly: that with Powell's death he would lose much of his power. Likely, McGee saw the organization of the AAA as a way of maintaining his otherwise threatened position in anthropology. In a veiled reference McGee wrote Boas, "As you surmise there *was* a reason why I was most anxious for early action, yet it was one which I hesitated to explain fully in semi-public writing. I am convinced that when you come down you will deem it a weighty one, even if you do not share my feeling that it was paramount."[45] While Boas would be fiercely supportive of McGee with respect to his position at the BAE, he nonetheless resisted McGee's efforts to found the American Anthropological Association. Across the divide of difference, McGee urged Boas to the view "that the contemplated Association should live for tomorrow as well as today, and strengthen the science of man by activity in other directions as well as in the narrow path represented by meetings of working anthropologists with attendant publication."[46]

McGee sent letters to the other anthropologists who were voting on the formation of the American Anthropological Association, with strategic sequencing. In this way, he managed to garner support for his point of view. Stocking opines that McGee had "no subtlety," and that, in McGee's view, his position "was the only correct one." McGee, Stocking surmises, "attempted what in historical retrospect seems like a rather transparent flanking maneuver." By submitting his proposal "first to those conferees definitely favoring the inclusive policy, and to MacCurdy and Starr, whose positions had wavered, McGee had succeeded in getting the signatures of six of the ten conferees before the convinced opponents of inclusiveness had even seen the revised document." Boas called McGee on his manner of soliciting opinions: "I fear that the method of correspondence which has been selected by necessity in order to bring out opinions is not the best, because I should assume with the same certainty with which you express your opinion that all these men are decidedly of my opinion."[47]

With an "almost fanatical perseverance," McGee successfully achieved his goal of gathering the support for the creation of the American Anthropological Association. In his carefully designed move to collect the necessary signatures before presenting the draft constitution to Boas, McGee wrote that "it now begins to look as though the movement will mature, and that we shall have a satisfactory organization within a few months." In an attempt to assuage Boas, he concluded: "I regret exceedingly that all are not in complete harmony as to policy," but never has there been "perfect agreement among the organizers in the preliminary stages." Far from being assuaged, Boas was livid. He fired off a letter to McGee:

> I confess that your mode of procedure surprised me very much, and I wish to express my strongest disapproval of it. You have not treated me with that openness to which I am accustomed from you. After all that had preceded, I had a right to see your draught of incorporation, which was not sent to me, and to be advised of the proposed meeting. The method which you have adopted of nego- tiating with the members of the Committee that met in Chicago has not allowed a fair expression of opinion, and it seems to me that the methods which you have employed are those to which we are accustomed in the warfare of political parties, but not among scientists who have the advancement of common interests at heart.

From Boas's perspective, it was "entirely inadmissible to force the consti- tution representing points of view of a small group of individuals upon the anthropologists of the country."[48]

In his concerted attempt to garner support, McGee had made sure that his views were widely disbursed to the scientific community. In "An American Senate of Science," published in *Science*, McGee argued for the formation of a national organization through a selection of "delegates chosen by the voluntary scientific associations of the country." In 1902 McGee continued his appeal through announcements in the *American Anthropologist*, "Proposed American Anthropologic Association," and "Anthropology at Pittsburgh." Boas, in turn, presented his views to the Anthropological Society of Washington on the formation of a national anthropological society and published a copy of this address in *Science*. Boas wrote McGee, "I wish that a copy of this paper would be sent to all those whom you invited to co-operate in the establishment of an anthro- pological society, together with your propositions."[49]

Stocking opines that McGee "was more nearly right in his estimate of future developments than was Boas." But, he reflects, "in achieving his goal, he seems to have been willing to go quite far—one feels without completely realizing how far—in the direction of political 'sharpness' and even duplicity." On March 24, 1902, the articles of incorporation for the American Anthropological Association were signed by "Stewart Culin of Philadelphia, George A. Dorsey of Chicago, J. Walter Fewkes of Washington, W J McGee of Washington, and Joseph D. McGuire of Washington," and recorded in the "Office of Recorder of Deeds, Washington, D.C." The officers of the new society were elected on June 30, 1902, at the organizational meeting held in conjunction with the AAAS in Pittsburgh. With, as Hodge represented McGee, "almost unlimited ambition, and ever ready, whatever the cost, to resent any seeming interference with it," McGee had cunningly and strategically maneuvered against Boas, who had his own surfeit of stubbornness. McGee won the day. The American Anthropological Association was established, and McGee was elected president for the first three years.[50]

McGee had secured his position nationally with anthropologists almost simultaneously with his loss of power at the BAE. In 1902, in McGee's first year as president of the American Anthropological Association, his mentor and supporter John Wesley Powell died. "On September 15, Mrs. Powell," as Hinsley writes, "summoned McGee to be with the old Major in his final hours; he passed away on September 23." Powell had wanted McGee to succeed him as director of the BAE, and most American anthropologists, along with McGee, had assumed that this would happen. Langley was of a different mind. As Regna Darnell writes, "Langley, however, considered McGee a second-rate scientist and an unreliable administrator." He appointed Holmes as chief of the BAE. With this one administrative appointment, Langley dissolved the position of director, diminished the importance of the BAE, and strengthened his own decision-making powers, as secretary of the Smithsonian, over the BAE. In a letter to Boas, Langley emphasized that the bureau had developed as "a personal creation of Major Powell's, over which he had a personal charge unusual in other Government bureaus." As Powell's health declined, Langley was advised by his superiors "that no one should be again placed exactly in his position or termed 'Director' as he was with the implications the word covers."[51]

With a "clear preference" for McGee as director of the BAE, Boas expressed "support for his linguistic and mythology work, and hoped for its continuance; he was fully prepared to befriend McGee against [Holmes], the man who had taken his place in Chicago; and he deplored the possible domination by the [U.S. National Museum]." Boas mounted an ambitious but fruitless campaign in support of McGee. To President of the Carnegie Institution Daniel Coit Gilman, Boas wrote in October 1902 that the "subordination" of the BAE to the Smithsonian was "a most unfortunate step, which will hinder the advance of anthropology." Boas continued, "We are justly proud of the work of the Bureau of American Ethnology, which has often been held up by foreign anthropologists as a model for their governments." In his November 1902 article in *Science* Boas wrote, "Since 1893 Dr. W J McGee has been acting for Major Powell, and training to become his successor. According to all principles of good government, he should have been advanced to the position of director. The appointment of another man, no matter how good he may be, to the position brings about discontinuity in the work of the bureau, which I consider dangerous, not alone to the best interests of anthropology, but to those of science in general." Anthropologists, Boas noted, "respect Dr. McGee for the ability, straightforwardness and success with which he had conducted the bureau under peculiarly difficult conditions." Boas added, in a cutting critique of Langley, "Personal inclination of the appointing officer has once more outweighed the principles of continuity and stability."[52]

In spring 1903 Holmes uncovered irregularities in the office of accounts and property. Chief Clerk Frank M. Barnett was charged with misappropriation of BAE funds and summarily fired, and by the summer he was on trial for forgery and embezzlement. By July this had led to "a general inquiry by Smithsonian officials into the operations of the Bureau during the Powell-McGee tenure." Throughout the long, hot Washington summer, the committee compiled over one thousand pages of testimony from, among others, Boas in his capacity as honorary philologist, Matilda Coxe Stevenson, Frank Hamilton Cushing, William Dinwiddie, Jesse Walter Fewkes, and, of course, McGee. Hinsley writes, "The investigation ranged widely but returned again and again to McGee's shortcomings as administrator and scientist. Boas returned to New York after his testimony, convinced that the investigation was a witch-hunt. The records tend to confirm his suspicion."[53]

In his testimony, Boas stressed the cooperative nature of the work undertaken by the BAE, the AMNH, and Columbia University. As Curtis Hinsley and Bill Holm write, "The collaborations, he explained, had provided linguistic material for the BAE and ethnographic data for the Museum at a minimum cost." The committee members scrutinizing the BAE understood very little about the Powell-McGee-Boas partnership. Boas attempted to explain his students' fieldwork: "'They get specimens; they get explanations of the specimens; they get connected texts that partly refer to the specimens and partly refer simply to abstract things concerning the people; and they get grammatical information. The line of division is clear; the grammatical material and the texts go to the Bureau, and the specimens with their explanations go to the New York Museum. There is no conflict of any sort.'" The officials of the Smithsonian Institution were intent on remaking the BAE into an institution of practical purpose. They found Boas's "methods unorthodox," and the funding of the endeavors with government money suspect. They were particularly befuddled by Boas's "constant recall of materials." In sum, not only had McGee's position at the BAE been imperiled, but also Boas's partnership. Hinsley and Holm note, "That lack of understanding eventually helped to undermine Boas' joint enterprises with Washington, and indeed contributed to the demise of Bureau anthropology as a stimulating source of activity in the first decade of the new century."[54]

In a last desperate attempt to solicit assistance, Boas wrote to Carl Schurz, a family friend and well-connected in political circles, "Evidently the appointment of the new chief implied disapproval of Mr. McGee and the opinion that he was responsible for defects which in a great measure were the outcome of Secretary Langley's failure to remedy the faulty organization of the Bureau. In June or July of this year almost a year after the new appointment was made the Secretary appointed a Committee of employees of the Smithsonian Institution to investigate the former administration of the Bureau and to make suggestions for an improvement." No help for McGee was forthcoming. Hinsley concludes,

"The committee's verdict was predictable. . . . The blistering indictment found him guilty of unsystematic financial methods, carelessness and possible corruption in purchasing manuscripts, chiefly from Boas and Fletcher; gross negligence of the manuscript collections; and hostility toward Langley."[55]

Langley had written a note to himself in preparation for his testimony before the committee: "'On [Powell's] death a new day begins for the Bureau.'" Aware of Langley's wishes, McGee wrote Boas that Langley and Holmes were "trying to make things so impossible for me as to compel me to get out." McGee referred to Boas's struggle in Chicago when Holmes was appointed director of the anthropology department at the Field Museum of Natural History, a position Boas had regarded as rightfully his. He wrote, "You saw Holmes' cloven foot in Chicago but I see both of them and the forked tail as well." Langley and Holmes succeeded in driving McGee out of the BAE and away from Washington. McGee wrote Boas, "After a session with 'the Committee' yesterday, the least disagreeable by the way of the series, . . . I tendered my resignation from the Bureau . . . and today the resignation is accepted." Boas expressed shock at McGee's resignation and despair over his absence from the Bureau. Hinsley surmises, "The committee placed entire responsibility for the shortcomings of the Bureau on McGee. As Boas pointed out, this was not completely just, since McGee had worked within limits set by Powell. Boas concluded that 'whatever was good went to the credit of Powell and whatever was bad went to the discredit of McGee.'" Leaving Washington "under a heavy cloud," McGee went to St. Louis as chief of the department of anthropology at the Louisiana Purchase Exposition.[56]

Boas had been wary about the geographical concentration of power for anthropology in the United States, a concern shared by other anthropologists. Daniel Brinton had been a strong dissenter in allowing the Anthropological Society of Washington to affiliate with the *American Anthropologist*, New Series. In his words, the proposal, "so grasping in character," would make what should be a national journal into "'the scholastic organ' of the Society." In his careful maneuvering to found the American Anthropological Association, McGee was determined to reach anthropologists beyond what he called, the "Chicago nucleus," as well as to protect the Washington anthropologists. When Boas suggested that the Anthropological Society of Washington simply be converted into a national society, McGee expressed doubts that this proposition would be received favorably. Washington anthropologists, McGee wrote, were concerned about "feelings against Washington sometimes encountered in other parts of the country." For his part, Boas expressed his "strongest disapproval" of McGee's methods of canvassing anthropologists by referencing "the old objection to the application of political methods by the Washington scientists, and the belief in an endeavor of undue centralization of power in Washington."[57]

At the turn of the twentieth century Boas felt poised to establish a professional basis for anthropology in the United States. Deliberative in the implementation of his plans, Boas responded to a letter from Zelia Nuttall, who was serving as intermediator for her friend, Phoebe Apperson Hearst, the first woman on the University of California Board of Regents. Hearst wanted to know, as Nuttall related, whether Boas "would consider the possibility of *your* going to California" and undertaking the founding of a museum and department of anthropology at the University of California. Nuttall added, "This would not exclude Mr. Kroeber, whose assistance would be needed, I should think." Boas responded with a detailed letter about his work in New York and his plans for anthropology. At Columbia he had undertaken "a number of special lines . . . for carrying on field-work, and here I lay particular stress upon a training in linguistics, a general ethnological training, and knowledge of certain field methods of physical anthropology." He continued, "I am confident that in this manner we shall be able inside of a very few years to give a young man a thorough all-round schooling, which cannot be had at the present time anywhere. Neither Berlin with its five anthropological professorships, nor Paris with its anthropological school, nor Holland with its colonial school, could give a proper training to the observers whom we need."[58]

Boas surmised, "By pursuing this method, I have been able to train a small number of young men who are able to do pretty good work." However, in his estimation, there was not a single ethnologist who had the fullness of training necessary to undertake the task of establishing anthropology in California. "I am very anxious," Boas wrote, "that those who do take up the work should not be as unprepared as most of our generation have been." Boas continued, "If you were to ask me at this moment who to put in charge of the whole field of Californian ethnology, I should be unable to name any man in this country whom I should consider capable of doing so. . . . I am very confident that five years hence either Mr. Dixon or Mr. Kroeber will have gained sufficient experience to do so."[59]

Boas had wanted to retain "a certain amount of control" for a period of time. Whether this was for the establishment of the American Anthropological Association or for the development of the department and museum of anthropology at the University of California, Boas felt that he needed to exercise oversight: "I have the conviction that in certain lines at least I know exactly what is needed for furthering our knowledge of American ethnology, and I believe that the method which I am pursuing is more systematic than that followed by many others. It is only for this reason that I have ventured to concentrate in my hands a considerable part of the ethnological work that is being done on our continent."[60]

Zelia Nuttall did not share Boas's caution. With a sly move in her role as intermediator and likely working under the influence of Putnam, Nuttall wrote Hearst that Boas advised the immediate hire of Kroeber: "'In the interest of science alone he advocates the employment, as soon as possible, of Mr. Kroeber. . . . I hope, that if at all possible this chance of securing this promising young man will not be missed and that he may be lost to us by being employed by another institution.'" Indeed, Kroeber was being considered for other positions, one as curator at the Field Museum of Natural History, and another, through Boas's recommendation, for a four-month continuation of research in Berlin on his Arapaho work.[61]

Phoebe Apperson Hearst was keen to establish a museum for the antiquities that she had collected in her 1899 tour of Egypt, and Alfred Louis Kroeber was poised to step out on his own. Playing the role of institutional matchmaker as he had for Boas, Putnam wired Hearst, "'Would your work for Kroeber be permanent character.' He mentioned the Berlin offer, adding that Kroeber preferred California and that an immediate reply was necessary." Hearst sent a telegram to Kroeber: "The position here permanent. Hope this message will reach you in good time." Kroeber snapped up the offer, "I took California [because it offered] greater independence and a larger chance for activity."[62]

In his reservations about the founding of the American Anthropological Association and his concerns about Kroeber taking up the development of anthropology in California, Boas exhibited his inherently cautious nature. Still, Boas accorded respect and autonomy to the younger scholars he had trained. When Putnam requested from Boas a critique of Kroeber's "Languages of the Coast of California South of San Francisco," Boas replied, "I beg leave to say that I consider Mr. Kroeber perfectly competent to judge of the value of the results of his researches. He has fully mastered methods of research, and at the present time is better posted on the languages of California than anyone else. For this reason, I believe that it would be an injustice on my part to edit his paper, and I return it without any remarks." Boas concluded, "It seems to my mind that it is in the best interests of science to let young men who have had a good training develop without interference, because new points of view, which are so essential to a healthy development of science, are much more likely to develop among students who work independently."[63]

With the clashes of personalities and the cacophony of voices, Boas could not clearly fathom the inexorable shift in institutional forces. He himself did not realize what he had already built—a sound footing for the development of professional anthropology in the twentieth century. With loss came gain. Putnam left his part-time position in New York for another in Berkeley and to give a "good part" of his time "to further the development of the department at the University." He looked forward to being "instrumental in the work of another great centre of anthropology and California is the place for it."[64] Simultaneous with Putnam leaving the AMNH, Powell died, and McGee left Washington after he had been passed over for Holmes in the appointment as chief of the BAE. Boas had lost much of the financial support for his research from the BAE, and his relationship with Jesup at the AMNH had shredded. With these shifting institutional forces, Boas was pushed ever more firmly into the halls of Columbia University. From the museum and the bureau to academe, Boas would establish his base to build out the profession of anthropology in the twentieth century.

Conclusion

From his childhood to his teenage years, Franz Boas developed a firm educational foundation in science. With his botanizing box, his hammer to uncover fossils, his glass herbarium, and his rooftop garden at home, Franz studied nature and cultivated his interests. His mother and father paid close attention to their son's education and encouraged him to pursue his hobbies in natural science. They closely monitored his educational achievements, as well as his challenges, which resulted from his recurrent illnesses as a young child. In the botanical garden at the University of Jena, Franz learned, as he wrote at the age of nineteen, "that true science does not consist in describing single plants but in the knowledge of their structure and lives and in the comparison of all classes of plants with one another." He was fascinated from an early age with comparing "isolated things with each other." He also learned his limitations—for instance, when he attended Kuno Fischer's lectures on aesthetics at the Ruprecht-Karls-Universität in Heidelberg. He had difficulty, he admitted, in following "abstract things," in separating "the essential from the inessential." The pathway was in place that would lead Boas from his focus on mathematics to physics, cultural geography, and then to ethnography. Keenly interested in languages, he relished learning Latin, Greek, Hebrew, and French at the Gymnasium. He studied English privately and began studying Russian in Heidelberg; he studied Danish and Inuktitut (the Greenlandic variety) in his study in Minden in preparation for his travels to Baffin Land; and later at Clark University, he began the study of Spanish.[1]

Franz cherished his childhood dream of traveling to Africa to study the people and then as a teenager, to the North or the South Pole. When he entered Berlin's scientific circles, he was advised to tell Adolph Bastian that he wanted to travel—the mark of a serious scientist. Boas's *Erstlingsreise*, his first voyage, to Baffin Land, had all the components for what later he would call his fieldwork. He worked hard to capture the Inuit view of the world. He learned their language, ate their foods, traveled with them by skin boat and dog sled. He shifted from physics to the study of living peoples, but he never abandoned cultural geography. Later, among the Bella Coola in the Northwest Coast, Boas found "veritable gods who live in Walhalla." In the course of his work in Baffin Land and the Northwest Coast, as well as in shaping the Jesup North Pacific Expedition, Boas developed his approach to anthropology, which included the following: anthropometry, later called physical anthropology; linguistics; folklore and mythology; ritual and religion; and material culture. In all this, his stress was on collecting from the people. The texts were, Gladys Reichard wrote in her tribute to her mentor, the "strongest rocks" in Boas's work. They reflected "his belief that what people record of themselves in their own words will in the last analysis reveal their motivations and ideas most accurately."[2]

Boas's emphasis on collaborative and long-term research were central to his approach to the study of anthropology. In Baffin Land he worked with James Mutch at the Scottish whaling station; with Ssigna, the Inuit hunter and guide; and with Wilhelm Weike, his assistant in all things. In the Northwest Coast, he developed collaborations with George Hunt and James Teit that lasted for decades. And the Jesup North Pacific Expedition comprised an international, multiteam group of colleagues that spanned two continents and many years. Boas grew into anthropology from his interest in science. By the 1890s his embrace of it was total: his approach to life had become singularly, intensely focused, on anthropology. At eighteen, he had written his sister Toni, "I just want to work until I have achieved something." Achieve something he did, and, in the process, he took a central place in creating a discipline for himself and for his students: that of anthropology.[3]

Notes

Abbreviations

AAA	American Anthropological Association
AA	*American Anthropologist*
AAAS	American Association for the Advancement of Science
AES	American Ethnological Society
AFS	American Folklore Society
DA/AMNH	American Museum of Natural History, Department of Anthropology
ASW	Anthropological Society of Washington
BRC	Boas-Rukeyser Collection
BAAS	British Association for the Advancement of Science
BAE	Bureau of American Ethnology
CU	Columbia University
FB	Franz Boas
JNPE	Jesup North Pacific Expedition
USNM	U.S. National Museum
UCA	University of California Archives
WCE	World's Columbian Exposition

Introduction

1. Müller-Wille, *Franz Boas Enigma*, 43; FB to Toni, February 27, 1874, EM's translation, BFP. Boas always referenced "Baffinland," as was done in Germany at the time of his writing. I will use "Baffin Land," though now it is referred to as "Baffin Island."
2. FB to family, June 18, 1888, BFP.
3. Cole, "Value of a Person," 33.

4. Kroeber, "Franz Boas," 5; Lowie, "Biographical Memoir," 303. The Franz Boas Documentary Project is funded by the Social Sciences and Humanities Research Council of Canada and draws on the cooperative endeavors of the University of Western Ontario, home institution of Director and Editor Regna Darnell; the University of Nebraska Press; the American Philosophical Society; the University of Victoria; and the Musgamagw Dzawada'enuxw Tribal Council (Darnell, *Franz Boas Papers*, ix).

1. Ardently Desired Boy

1. Hedwig Boas Lehmann, "Tante Hete, Reminiscences of Sister," BRC. For Jewish naming customs, see Lévy and Zumwalt, *Ritual Medical Lore*, 89–93; and Dosick, *Living Judaism*, 289–90.

2. Antonie Boas's birth year is variously recorded as July 1853 (Cole, *Franz Boas*, 16); 1865 (Norman Boas, *Franz Boas*, 291); July 14, 1865 (Norman Boas, "Boas Family Genealogy," 5, BFP); 1853 ("Stammbaum der Familie Boas" [Family tree of the Boas family], March 1, 1930, BFP); and July 12, 1857 (http://www.franz-boas.de/download/geschlechterbuch.pdf, accessed July 23, 2018). I elect to follow the date given on the 1880 census for Minden, Westphalia, that records the following, "Antonie, 12 July 1854," and that Müller-Wille sent me.

3. Curriculum vitae (CV), 1, BFP; see also "Salient Dates of Early Life," BFP. In the CV that Boas composed as a requirement for exit from Gymnasium at the age of nineteen, he wrote that his baby brother Ernst lived for "four months" (CV, 1, BFP). Norman Boas, in his genealogical research on the Boas family notes, "Ernst Boas died at the age of one on July 11, 1861" ("Boas Family Genealogy, 1650–1985," 5, BFP).

4. Cole, *Franz Boas*, 17; FB to father, November 9, 1869, BFP.

5. Brilling, "Vorfahren," 103, 105; Norman Boas, *Franz Boas*, 289, 290; Norman Boas, Genealogy, 2, BFP; Cole, *Franz Boas*, 10.

6. Brilling, "Vorfahren," 106, EM's translation.

7. Brilling, "Vorfahren," 106; Herzig, *Jüdisches Leben*, 12, RLZ's translation; "Stammbaum der Familie Boas," BFP.

8. The first name is spelled variously in genealogies as Karoline and Caroline. The anglicized spelling is Carolyn. Kaufmann, "Stammbaum der Familie Boas," RLZ's translation, BFP; notes by Ernst Boas of conversation with Franz Boas, 1940 or 1941, BFP; "Seal: Kingdom of Westphalia," BFP.

9. Brilling, "Vorfahren," 106, RLZ's translation; Cole, *Franz Boas*, 10, 294n5; see "Geschlecterbuch Heinemann (Chajim)/Boas, http://www.franz-boas.de/download/geschlechterbuch.pdf, accessed March 14, 2014; "Notes by Hedwig Lehmann, Sister of F. Boas, 1944," EM's translation, BFP. Blumenthal

notes that "Jews were forced to buy the output of the Prussian king's beloved porcelain factories—far above market prices, taking a loss on the resale" (*Invisible Wall*, 7).

10. "Notes by Hedwig Lehmann, 1944," EM's translation, BFP.

11. Cole (*Franz Boas*, 11) quotes *Mindische Fama*, Beilage zum 37, Stöck des [Mindener] *Sonntagsblatt*, September 8, 1836.

12. Brilling, "Vorfahren," 107, 108, RLZ's translation.

13. Brilling, "Vorfahren," 108; Norman Boas, "Boas Genealogy," 12, BFP. Menke is an abbreviated form of the Hebrew first name Menachem, which means "the comforter" (Brilling, "Vorfahren," 111n27).

14. "Sophie Boas Collected from Letters to her Brother Salomon Meyer Approximately 1843–1845," EM's translation, BFP; see also Cole, *Franz Boas*, 10, 11–12; and Norman Boas, "Boas Family Genealogy," BFP.

15. Cole, *Franz Boas*, 13; "Sophie Boas Collected from Letters to her Brother Salomon Meyer," EM's translation, BFP. See Dosick, *Living Judaism*, 178–79, for a discussion of the confirmation ceremony that was adopted by Reform Judaism.

16. Herzig, *Abraham Jacobi*, 14, RLZ's translation; Cole, *Franz Boas*, 14.

17. Cole, *Franz Boas*, 19, 14; see also Wellhäußer, "Political Activism," n41. Herzberg's last name was also spelled "Hertzberg."

18. Cole, *Franz Boas*, 14, 15; Wellhäußer, "Political Activism"; Herzig, *Abraham Jacobi*, 23; Herzig, *Jüdisches Leben*, 70.

19. Cole, *Franz Boas*, 15, quoting Sophie Meyer to Abraham Jacobi, March 8–12, 1851.

20. Truax, *Doctors Jacobi*, 155; Herzig, *Abraham Jacobi*, 69, EM's translation; Wellhäußer, "Political Activism."

21. "Sophie Boas Collected from Letters to her Brother Salomon Meyer," BFP; Truax, *Doctors Jacobi*, 146; Sperber, *European Revolutions*, xix–xx; Cole, *Franz Boas*, 16.

22. Truax, *Doctors Jacobi*, 157; Norman Boas, "Boas Family Genealogy," BFP, 13.

23. Cole, *Franz Boas*, 8–9, 16. Herzig, *Jüdisches Leben*, 65, RLZ's translation.

24. Boas, "Franz Boas," 19; Stocking, "From Physics to Ethnology," 149. "An Anthropologist's Credo" was first published in the *Nation* (1938) and later revised and reprinted under the title of "Franz Boas," in *I Believe*, edited by Clifton Fadiman, in 1939. George Stocking reprinted it in *The Shaping of American Anthropology*.

25. Weston, *Friedrich Froebel*, 1, 7, 13; Sophie Boas to Dr. A. Braun, March 13, 1862, BFP.

26. CV, 1–2, BFP; "Notes by Ernst Boas of Conversation with Franz Boas, 1940 or 1941," BFP. Boas rendered the spelling "Wagener" in his CV. The reference

is to Hermann Wagner, a prolific author of nature books, many of them for children. In the Fröbel approach, the young child was not introduced to reading until age five.

27. Lehmann's footnote to "Sophie Boas Collected from Letters to her Brother Salomon Meyer," EM's translation, BFP; Cole, *Franz Boas*, 13, quoting Lehmann's "Reminiscences," and Toni Boas Wohlauer, "Reminiscences of Franz Boas"; FB to parents, December 6, 1877, EM's translation, BFP; FB to parents, June 25, 1877, BFP.

28. Lehmann, "Reminiscences," RLZ's translation, BFP; FB to Toni, October 5, 1876, EM's translation, BFP.

29. Cole, *Franz Boas*, 13; FB to uncle, January 1, 1870, BFP.

30. Boas, "An Anthropologist's Credo," 201; Boas, "Franz Boas," 19; Lehmann, "Reminiscences," RLZ's translation, BFP; Brilling, "Vorfahren," 111n28a.

31. Cole, *Franz Boas*, 13; Volkov, "'Verbürgerlichung' of the Jews," 367, 370, 373; FB to Sophie Boas, September 28, 1879, BFP.

32. Lehmann, "My Memories of my Brother, Franz Boas," EM's translation, BFP; Cole, *Franz Boas*, 10; Norman Boas, "Boas Family Genealogy,"12, 13, BFP; "Notes by Hedwig Lehmann, 1944," BFP. Müller-Wille shared this quotation from the BFP with me, and Linna Weber Müller-Wille translated it.

33. Lehmann, "My Memories of my Brother, Franz Boas," EM's translation, BFP; FB to aunt, April 13, 1870, BFP; FB to Toni, April 6, 1871, RLZ's translation, BFP.

34. Lehmann, "Tante Hete's Reminiscences of Sister. Hedwig Lehmann," BRC; Lehmann, "My Memories of my Brother, Franz Boas," EM's translation, BFP.

35. Liss, "Cosmopolitan Imagination," 163.

36. CV, 2, BFP; Lehmann, "Tante Hete's Reminiscences of Sister. Hedwig Lehmann," BRC; Cole, *Franz Boas*, 18.

37. CV, 2, BFP; Cole, *Franz Boas*, 18, 19.

38. CV, 3, BFP; FB to Toni, December 3, 1870, BFP.

39. Lehmann, "Tante Hete's Reminiscences of Sister. Hedwig Lehmann," BRC; FB to uncle [Jacobi], June 8, [1867], BFP; Cole, *Franz Boas*, 19; Jarausch, *Students, Society, and Politics*, 34–35.

40. FB to Meier Boas, November 8, 1868, February 20, 1869, BFP; FB to uncle, July 14, 1870, BFP; FB to uncle [Jacobi], April 9, 1868, BFP; FB to uncle, September 22, 1869, BFP.

41. CV, 3, 4, BFP; Lehmann, "Tante Hete's Reminiscences of Sister. Hedwig Lehmann," BRC.

42. Lehmann, "Tante Hete's Reminiscences of Sister. Hedwig Lehmann," BRC; FB to Ernst Boas, July 12, 1929, BFP; CV, 4, BFP; Franz to uncle [Salomon Meyer] and aunt, December 27, 1867, BFP.

43. Lehmann, "Tante Hete's Reminiscences of Sister. Hedwig Lehmann," BRC; FB to uncle [Salomon Meyer], January 3, [1868], BFP.

44. CV, 4, BFP; "Memories of my Brother, Franz Boas, by Hedwig Lehmann," EM's translation, BFP.

45. Meier to Sophie Boas, July 31, 1868, RLZ's translation, BFP.

46. CV, 5, BFP.

47. Lehmann, "Tante Hete's Reminiscences of Sister. Hedwig Lehmann," BRC; Cole, *Franz Boas*, 21; CV, 5–6, BFP; FB to Sophie Boas, September 19, 1870, BFP.

48. Cole, *Franz Boas*, 22, quoting FB to Toni, April 6, June 30, 1871, BFP.

49. CV, 6, 7, BFP; FB to aunt, April 13, 1870, BFP; Cole, *Franz Boas*, 22; Lehmann, "Tante Hete's Reminiscences of Sister," BRC.

50. Lehmann, "Tante Hete's Reminiscences of Sister. Hedwig Lehmann," BRC; CV, 6, BFP.

51. CV, 7, BFP; Cole, *Franz Boas*, 23; Meier to Sophie Boas, December 14, 1871, RLZ's translation, BFP.

52. Cole, *Franz Boas*, 23; FB to Sophie Boas, January 5, 1872, EM's translation, BFP; Meier to Sophie Boas, January 8, 1872, RLZ's translation, BFP.

53. Meier to Sophie Boas, January 13, 1872, RLZ's translation, BFP; see also Cole, *Franz Boas*, 23.

54. Meier to Sophie Boas, November 27, 1871, RLZ's translation, BFP; Meier to Sophie Boas, January 1, 1872, RLZ's translation, BFP.

55. CV, 7, BFP; FB to Hete, January 17, 1872, BFP.

56. CV, 9, 13, 15, BFP; Meier Boas to Toni, September 27, 1873, RLZ's translation, BFP. Meier Boas used the phrase "*unentwickelter Knabe*" to describe his son. "*Unentwickelt*" focuses on education, skills, knowledge, while "*unreif*" focuses on character development. Thus, as Müller-Wille clarifies in a personal communication, Boas's father was not making an observation about his son's physical or moral development, but rather his educational preparation.

57. FB to Toni, February 6, 1874, EM's translation, BFP; CV, 15, BFP.

58. The Abitur examination was introduced in response to the "excessive number of students" who wished to pursue university education, an increase that accompanied the "university reforms instituted by the Prussian minister of education Wilhelm von Humboldt (1808–19) (Kampe, "Jews and Anti-Semites," 369). By 1834, the Abitur was the only entrance examination accepted by universities in Prussia.

59. Cole, *Franz Boas*, 26; CV, 16, BFP; FB to Toni, October 1, 1876, RLZ's translation, BFP; FB to Toni, October 5, 1876, RLZ's translation, BFP; FB to Toni, October 12, 1876, EM's translation, BFP. "*Ich hab's gewagt*" is a phrase associated with Ulrich von Hutten (1488–1523), humanist and poet, who used it

in a stanza of his poetry and for whom it became a personal motto. Müller-Wille told me, "This well-known phrase is used when one has set a goal which one has missed, still one was proud to have tried."

60. Cole *Franz Boas*, 26–27, parentheses in original, quoting FB to Toni, February 21, 1877, BFP; FB to Theodor [Meyer], February 27, 1877, RLZ's translation, BFP.

61. Müller-Wille sent me a copy of Zeugnis der Reife, BFP, and translated it for me; Cole, *Franz Boas*, 28.

62. Sophie Boas to Abraham Jacobi, February 15, 1877, BFP.

63. Lehmann, "My Memories of my Brother, Franz Boas," EM's translation, BFP; FB to Toni, September 27, 1873, EM's translation, BFP; CV, 20, BFP.

64. Lehmann, "My Memories of my Brother, Franz Boas," EM's translation, BFP; Sophie Boas to Abraham Jacobi, February 15, 1877, BFP.

65. Sophie Boas to Abraham Jacobi, February 15, 1877, BFP.

66. Sophie Boas to Toni, late February 1877, EM's translation, BFP; FB to Toni, March 18, 1877, EM's translation, BFP.

67. CV, 2, 6, BFP.

68. CV, 7, BFP; FB to Toni, March 18, 1877, RLZ's translation, BFP.

69. FB to Toni, June 20, 1871, EM's translation, BFP; FB to Toni, May 3–4, 1874, EM's translation, BFP; FB to Toni, February 27, 1874, EM's translation, BFP.

2. Student Life into Deepest Depths

1. FB to Sophie Boas, April 24, 1877, EM's translation, BFP; FB to Toni, April 23, 1877, RLZ's translation, BFP; see also FB to Sophie Boas, April 23, 1877, BFP; FB to parents, June 30, 1877, EM's translation, BFP.

2. Püschel, "Franz Boas," 81, RLZ's translation; Sophie Boas to Jacobi, February 15, 1877, BFP; Sophie Boas to Jacobi, March 2 ,1877, BFP; FB to Toni, April 18, 1877, RLZ's translation, BFP; FB to parents, abstracts of letters, April 21, 1877, BFP; Cole, *Franz Boas*, 39.

3. FB to Toni, April 18, 1877, EM's translation BFP; FB to Sophie Boas, April 19, 1877, EM's translation, BFP; FB to parents, April 20, 1877, EM's translation, BFP; FB to Krüer, April 22, 1877, BFP.

4. FB to Sophie Boas, April 19, 1877, BFP; FB to parents, April 20, 1877, RLZ's translation, BFP; FB to parents, abstracts of letters, April 19, 20, 1877, BFP; FB to Sophie Boas, April 19, 1877, RLZ's translation, BFP.

5. FB to parents, April 22, 1877, BFP; FB to Sophie Boas, April 24, 1877, RLZ's translation, BFP; FB to parents, May 3, 1877, BFP; Cole, *Franz Boas*, 39; FB to Sophie Boas, April 21, 1877, BFP; Cole, *Franz Boas*, 40; FB to Sophie Boas, April 28, 1877, BFP; FB to parents, June 13, 1877, EM's translation, BFP; FB to Toni, April 23, 1877, EM's translation, BFP.

6. FB to Krüer, April 22, 1877, BFP.

7. FB to Krüer, April 22, 1877, BFP; FB to parents, abstracts of letters, April 21, 1877, BFP; FB to Sophie Boas, April 21, 1877, EM's translation, BFP; FB to Sophie Boas, April 28, 1877, RLZ's translation, BFP.

8. FB to Sophie Boas, April 21, 1877, RLZ's translation, BFP; FB to Sophie Boas, April 30, 1877, RLZ's translation, BFP; FB to parents, May 3, 1877, RLZ's translation, BFP; FB to parents, April 28, 1877, BFP.

9. FB to parents, May 3, 1877, EM's translation, BFP; FB to parents, abstracts of letters, May 3, 1877, BFP; FB to parents, May 26, 1877, EM's translation, BFP.

10. Cole, *Franz Boas*, 39, 297n5; FB to parents, abstracts of letters, May 3, 1877, BFP; Cuddihy, *Ordeal of Civility*, 4, 227; Glick, "Types Distinct," 553; Cohen, "German Jewry," xxiv, emphasis in original.

11. Trilling, "Afterword," 316. Trilling was writing about New York City in the 1930s and the split between German Jews and Eastern European Jews, "generally called Russian" Jews. CV, 1, BFP.

12. FB to parents, May 3, 1877, BFP; FB to Sophie Boas, April 28, 1877, RLZ's translation, BFP; FB to parents, May 26, 1877, BFP.

13. FB to parents, May 26, 1877, RLZ's translation, BFP; FB to parents, May 26, 1877, RLZ's translation, BFP; FB to parents, May 10, 1877, RLZ's translation, BFP; FB to Sophie Boas, May 28, 1877, EM's translation, BFP; FB to Krüer, June 8, 1877, BFP.

14. FB to Krüer, June 8, 1877, BFP; FB to Krüer, June 22, 1877, BFP; FB to Krüer, June 27, 1877, BFP.

15. Twain, *Tramp Abroad*, vol. 1, 32, 33, 43.

16. FB to Krüer, June 27, 1877, and postscript July 19, 1877, BFP; FB to Krüer, July 25, 1877, BFP; FB to Krüer, July 29, 1877, BFP.

17. Lehmann, "My Memories," RLZ's translation, BFP.

18. FB to Sophie Boas, June 25, 1877, EM's translation, BFP; FB to Krüer, July 29, 1877, BFP.

19. FB to parents, July 21, 1877, EM's translation, BFP; FB to parents, July 23, 1877, RLZ's translation, BFP.

20. Jarausch, *Students, Society, and Politics*, 82; Cole, *Franz Boas*, 43.

21. FB to parents, July 30, 1877, EM's translation, BFP; Meier Boas to FB, July 31, 1877, emphasis in original, EM's translation, BFP.

22. Cole, *Franz Boas*, 43. Cole quotes the *Mindener Zeitung*, August 25, 1877, 2, and August 27, 1877; *Jahresbericht des Evangelischen Gymnasiums und der Realschule zu Minden*, 1878, 10.

23. FB to Sophie Boas, July 8, 1877, RLZ's translation, BFP; FB to parents, July 23, 1877, RLZ's translation, BFP.

24. Müller-Wille sent me this excerpt from the handwritten (German script) of the Leaving Certificate (October 27, 1877, BFP).

25. Cole, *Franz Boas*, 4; FB to parents, December 6, 1877, EM's translation, BFP; FB to parents, November 11, 1877, EM's translation, BFP. See Twain, *Tramp Abroad*, vol. 2, 284–89, for an account of "The College Prison" in Heidelberg.

26. Cole, *Franz Boas*, 44; Lehmann, "My Memories," 3, EM's translation, BFP.

27. Cole, *Franz Boas*, 45; FB to parents, February 15, 1878, EM's translation, BFP.

28. FB to Sophie Boas, March 7, 1878, EM's translation, BFP.

29. Cole, *Franz Boas*, 46; FB to Sophie Boas, February 19, 1878, EM's translation, BFP.

30. FB to parents, February 10, 1879, RLZ's translation, BFP; FB to parents, February 19, 1879, EM's translation, BFP.

31. FB to parents, July 10, 1879, EM's translation, BFP.

32. FB to parents, February 14, 1879, RLZ's translation, BFP; FB to parents, August 27, 1879, RLZ's translation, BFP.

33. FB to Sophie Boas, September 28, 1879, RLZ's translation, BFP; Cole, *Franz Boas*, 54–55; FB to parents, October 27, 1879, BFP.

34. Seelig, *Deutsche Jugend*, 176, RLZ's translation; Cole, *Franz Boas*, 55, 51, quoting FB to parents, emphasis in original; Jungnickel, *Theoretical Mastery of Nature*, 218; FB to parents, November 6, 1880, LMW's translation, BFP.

35. Mills, *Biological Oceanography*, 14; Cole, *Franz Boas*, 52,

36. FB to parents, January 31, 1881, EM's translation, BFP; Cole, *Franz Boas*, 52, 53, quoting FB to parents, June 12, 1880, November 12, 1880, March 11, 1881; FB to parents, November 6, 1880, EM's translation, BFP.

37. Lehmann, "My Memories," 12–13, RLZ's translation, BFP; FB to parents, May 1, 1881, BFP; FB to parents, January 8, 1881, EM's translation, BFP; FB to parents, January 8, 1881, RLZ's translation, BFP. In a personal communication, proverb scholar Wolfgang Mieder commented on this "very popular" German expression, "*mit seinem Latein zu Ende sein*" (to be at one's wits end), as a proverbial phrase.

38. FB to parents, January 18, 1881, RLZ's translation, BFP; FB to Toni, February 2, 1881, RLZ's translation, BFP; FB to parents, March 11, 1881, EM's translation, BFP.

39. FB to parents, May 30, 1881, EM's translation, BFP.

40. Cole, *Franz Boas*, 59, quoting Meier Boas to FB, November 17, 1880, BFP; Glick, "Types Distinct," 550; Telman, "Adolf Stoecker," 94, 102.

41. Cole, *Franz Boas*, 60, quoting FB to father, November 18, 1880, BFP; FB to Papa, November 18, 1880, EM's translation, BFP.

42. FB to parents, January 18, 1881, EM's translation, BFP; see Glick, "Types Distinct," 553; Cole, *Franz Boas*, 59.

43. Kampe, "Jews and Anti-Semites," 357–58; FB to Sophie Boas, April 6, 1881, BFP.

44. FB to parents, April 26, 1881, BFP; FB to Sophie Boas, July 8, 1881, BFP; FB to parents, July 8, 1881, RLZ's translation, BFP; FB to Sophie Boas, July 11, 1881, EM's translation, BFP. As Müller-Wille conveyed to me, Boas's remark that he was no longer a student referenced his position as not being registered for the 1881 summer term since all that remained for him was the examination.

45. FB to parents, July 15, 1881, parentheses in original, BFP; FB to Meier Boas, July 24, 1881, BFP; FB to parents, July 18, 1881, and July 23, 1881, BFP.

46. FB to Meier Boas, July 24, 1881, BFP; FB to parents, August 12, 1881, LMW's translation, BFP; FB to parents, August 9, 1881, LMW's translation from Latin, BFP.

47. FB to parents, May 30, 1881, EM's translation, BFP; FB to parents, January 18, 1881, LMW's translation, BFP; Boas, *Beiträge zur Erkenntniss*, 8, 1, 24–31, 34–42, RLZ's translation.

48. Boas, *Beiträge zur Erkenntniss*, 31, 42, table 1, EM's translation.

49. Cole, *Franz Boas*, 53, quoting FB to parents, May 30, 1881; FB to Sophie Boas, August 9, 1881, BFP; FB to parents, May 14, 1881, EM's translation, BFP; FB to Meier Boas, August 12, 1881, BFP; Meier Boas to FB, August 12, 1881, LMW's translation, BFP.

50. van Gennep, *Les rites de passage*, 13; see Turner, "Betwixt and Between"; Jarausch, *Students, Society, and Politics*, 19; FB to Krüer, June 8, 1877, BFP.

51. McAleer, *Dueling*, 3, 5, 119; Hobsbawm, "Mass-Producing Traditions," 293, 294.

52. McAleer, *Dueling*, 141; FB to Krüer, July 25, 1877, BFP; Cole, *Franz Boas*, 46; FB to parents, February 14, 1879, EM's translation, BFP.

53. McAleer, *Dueling*, 125; Cole, *Franz Boas*, 45; FB to parents, February 19, 1878, EM's translation, BFP. See Liss, "The Cosmopolitan Imagination," 76–80, for letters from Boas to his family about the fervent pleasure of belonging to the fraternal organization; and 68–82, for an informative discussion of the German fraternal organizations and of Boas's membership in the Burschenschaft Alemannen.

54. McAleer, *Dueling*, 138–39.

55. Cole, *Franz Boas*, 57–58, 60; Jarausch, *Students, Society, and Politics*, 98, 100.

56. Tal, *Christians and Jews in Germany*, 32, 63; Mosse, *German Jews*, 6–7; Glick, "Types Distinct," 549.

57. Jarausch, *Students, Society, and Politics*, 10, 82, 97, 100; Mosse, *German Jews*, 2; Liss, "Cosmopolitan Imagination, 69n11; Kampe, "Jews and Anti-Semites," 358–59.

58. Jarausch, *Students, Society, and Politics*, 100, parentheses in original; Fischer to FB, December 21, 1884, RLZ's translation, BP; see also Cole, *Franz Boas*, 60.

59. Jarausch, *Students, Society, and Politics*, 19; Mosse, *German Jews*, 3.

60. Fishberg, "The Boas Anniversary," 647. Boas's letter of thanks to "Mr. President, Friends, and Colleagues" is included in Fishberg, 646–47.

61. FB to Toni, March 13, 1877, RLZ's translation, BFP.

3. In Heaven, In Love, and Separation

1. Norman Boas, *Franz Boas*, 24; Lehmann, "Reminiscences." RLZ's translation, BFP.

2. FB to Marie, May 29, 1883, BFP; Marie to FB, July 7, 1883, BFP; Marie to FB, July 7, 1883, BFP; Cole, *Franz Boas*, 69–70, parentheses and question mark in original.

3. FB to Sophie Boas, October 1, 1881, BFP; Cole, *Franz Boas*, 64; FB to parents, June 23, 1878, RLZ's translation, BFP; FB to Sophie Boas, July 11, 1881, BFP.

4. FB to Jacobi, January 3, 1882, BP; Sophie Boas to Salomon Meyer, December 26, 1881, RLZ's translation, BFP.

5. FB to Jacobi, January 2, 1882, parentheses in original, BP.

6. Jacobi to FB, March 9, 1882, BP; Gilman to FB, April 8, 1882, emphasis in original, BP.

7. Fischer to FB, April 3, 1882, RLZ's translation, BP.

8. FB to Jacobi, April 10, 1882, BP.

9. FB to Jacobi, April 10, 1882, BP.

10. FB to Toni, May 14, 1882, emphasis in the original, BFP; Sophie Boas and FB to Jacobi, July 22, 1882, BP.

11. Lehmann, "Reminiscences," RLZ's translation, BFP. Meier Boas to FB, July 18, 1882, BFP.

12. FB to parents, August 26, 1882; August 28, 1882, BFP; FB to parents, September 3, 1882; September 10, 1882, BFP.

13. FB to parents, November 11, 1882, BFP. The article to which Boas referred was published as "*Über die ehemalige Verbreitung der Eskimos*" in 1883.

14. FB to Sophie Boas, November 11, 1882, BFP; FB to parents, October 20, 1882, BFP. In Germany, holding the thumbs is for good luck, equivalent to crossing the fingers in Anglo-American tradition.

15. Boas, "Rudolf Virchow's Anthropological Work," 441, 442; Lowie, *History of Ethnological Theory*, 30; Tylor, "Professor Adolf Bastian," 141.

16. FB to parents, November 17, 1882, BFP; FB to parents, October 24, 1882, BFP; FB to Sophie Boas, October 22, 1882, BFP.

17. FB to parents, October 24, 1882, BFP.

18. FB to parents, November 9, 1882, BFP.

19. FB to parents, November 17, 1882, BFP.

20. FB to Jacobi, November 26, 1882, BP.

21. FB to Jacobi, November 26, 1882, BP.

22. FB to Jacobi, November 26, 1882, BP.

23. FB to parents, November 17, 1882, BFP; FB to parents, January 13, 1883, BFP; FB to parents, January 21, 1883, BFP.

24. FB to parents, January 13, 1883, BFP; FB, copy of incomplete typescript, BP, Ernst Boas's translation of pages 3, 4, 6, 7, with other pages missing. While Ernst penciled in "when written?," it is clear from the internal dates that it followed Boas's acceptance of the position as assistant editor at *Science* in January 1887.

25. FB to parents, January 23, 1883, parentheses in original, BFP.

26. FB to parents, January 23, 1883, BFP. See Müller-Wille, *Franz Boas Enigma*, 56–68, for discussion of the *Berliner Tageblatt* and Boas's series of articles published in this newspaper.

27. FB to parents, January 24, 1883, BFP; Cole and Müller-Wille, "Franz Boas' Expedition," 42; Müller-Wille, *Franz Boas among the Inuit*, 37; Müller-Wille, *Franz Boas Enigma*, 58, 56.

28. The International Polar Year was a multinational effort directed toward standardizing and synchronizing data for one annual cycle (Müller-Wille and Weber Müller-Wille, "Inuit Geographical Knowledge," 218). See also Müllller-Wille, *Franz Boas Enigma*, 23–24, 53.

29. FB to parents, February 2, 1883, BFP.

30. FB to parents, February 2, 1883, BFP; FB to parents, February 8, 1883, BFP.

31. Lehmann, "Reminiscences," RLZ's translation, BFP; Müller-Wille and Gieseking, *Inuit and Whalers*, 216, 218.

32. FB to parents, January 24, 1883, BFP; FB to parents, February 8, 1883, BFP; Müller-Wille and Gieseking, *Inuit and Whalers*, 13; Müller-Wille, *Franz Boas among the Inuit*, 44, quoting from Wilhelm Weike diary, June 18, 1883.

33. FB to parents, February 25, 1883, BFP; FB to parents, March 6, 1883, BFP.

34. FB to "Angel," May 14, 1882, parentheses in original, BFP; FB to Hedwig, September 6, 1882, BFP; Marie to FB, June 3, 1883, BFP.

35. Emilie Krackowizer to Sophie Boas and Toni, February 8, 1883, BFP.

36. FB to parents, February 8, 1883, BFP; FB to parents, February 20, 1883, emphasis in original, BFP; Willy Meyer to FB, April 16, 1883, RLZ's translation, BFP.

37. Müller-Wille, *Franz Boas Enigma*, 61–62. See Müller-Wille, *Franz Boas among the Inuit*, 160–61, for the trial articles that Boas wrote for the *Berliner Tageblatt* on "Third German Assembly of Geographers." See also Cole and Müller-Wille, "Franz Boas' Expedition," 41, for discussion of the German Northern Polar Expeditions (1868 and 1869–70) and the First International Polar Year (1882–83).

38. FB to parents, April 3, 1883, BFP; FB to Marie, June 1, 1883, BFP; FB to Marie, May 28, 1883, BFP; Marie to Toni, April 2, 1883, BFP.

39. Marie to Toni, April 2, 1883, emphasis in original, BFP.

40. FB to Jacobi, May 2, 1883, BP.

41. FB to Marie, April 27, 1883, BFP.

42. Marie to FB, May 3, 1883, BFP; FB to Marie, May 9, 1883, BFP.

43. Marie to Toni, May 27, 1883, emphasis in original, BFP.

44. FB to Marie, June 8, 1883, BFP; FB to Marie, May 28, 1883, second letter, BFP; FB to Marie, May 28, 1883, first letter; BFP.

45. FB to Marie, June 4, 1883, BFP; Marie to FB, July 7, 1883, BFP; Marie to FB, June 6, 1883, BFP; FB to MK, June 17, 1883, BFP.

46. FB to Marie, May 28, 1883, first letter, BFP; FB to Marie, May 28, 1883, second letter, BFP.

47. FB to Marie, May 29, 1883, BFP; Marie to FB, May 31, 1883, BFP.

48. Marie to FB, May 31, 1883, BFP.

49. Emilie Krackowizer to FB, May 31, 1883, BFP.

50. FB to Marie, June 8, 1883, BFP; FB to Marie, June 2, 1883, BFP; Marie to FB, June 4, 1883, BFP; FB to Marie, June 1, 1883, BFP; FB to Marie, June 4, 1883, BFP; FB to Marie, June 7, 1883, BFP. As Müller-Wille conveyed to me, Boas had chosen the colors of the German Imperial flag, which was comprised of stripes from top to bottom of black, white, and red.

51. FB to Marie, June 9, 1883, BFP; FB to Marie, June 11, 1883, BFP; FB to Jacobi, May 9, 1883, BP; FB to Marie, June 18, 1883, BFP.

52. FB to family, June 19, 1883, BFP; FB to Marie, June 19, 1883, BFP.

53. FB to family, June 21, 1883, BFP; Lehmann, "Reminiscences, RLZ's translation, BFP."

54. Emilie Krackowizer to Sophie Boas, June 12, 1883, BFP; Marie to Sophie Boas, June 13, 1883, BFP; FB to family, June 19, 1883, BFP.

55. Marie to FB, June 9, 1883, BFP; Marie to Boas family, October 13, 1883, BFP.

56. FB to Marie, June 11, 1883, BFP; Marie to FB, July 9, 1883, BFP; FB to Marie, June 4, 1883, BFP.

57. FB to Jacobi, April 10, 1882, BP; Stocking, "From Physics to Ethnology," 141, 142, parentheses in original, quoting letter from Fischer to FB, April 3, 1882; Fischer to FB, February 24, 1878, BP.

58. Müller-Wille, *Franz Boas Enigma*, 27, 23, 31, 33, quoting Boas, *Baffin-Land*, 65; FB to Jacobi, November 26, 1882, BP; FB to parents, January 13, 1883, BFP.

59. FB to Jacobi, May 9, 1883, BP; FB to parents, June 24, 1883, BFP.

60. FB to Jacobi, May 9, 1883, BP; Müller-Wille, *Franz Boas among the Inuit*, 1998, 42, diary entry, June 9, 1883, emphasis in original.

4. Creating a Future for Us

1. Müller-Wille, *Franz Boas among the Inuit*, 50, FB/MK, June 30, 1883, emphasis in original.

2. FB to parents and sisters, June 22, 1883, on back of envelope, BFP; FB to parents, June 23, 1883, BFP; FB to parents, June 24, 1883, BFP; Müller-Wille, *Franz Boas among the Inuit*, 50, 51.

3. Knötsch, "Franz Boas' Research Trip," 9; Müller-Wille, *Franz Boas and the Inuit*, 21, 46–47; Cole, "Value of a Person," 16; Letter Diary, FB to Marie, June 23, 1883, 38, BFP. Müller-Wille conveyed to me his concept of "multi-layered and often parallel letters and journals." After Boas's departure on June 20, 1883, Boas sent and received mail infrequently and in the following way, as Müller-Wille writes: "Before the winter of 1883–4, this occurred on 22 June 1883 off Heligoland via the pilot boat and on 27 June in Pentland Firth off the island of Stroma via fishing boat; he sent letters from Kekerten Whaling Station on 16 September direct to Hamburg with the *Germania* and off Middleaktuk Island in the southern part of Cumberland Sound on 3 October with the *Catherine* via Dundee (Scotland) to Minden i.W. and to New York" (*Franz Boas among the Inuit*, 21). In turn, Marie Krackowizer, the Boas family, and their employees would send letters to Boas and Weike via Peterhead, Scotland, by early August 1883, for the Catherine, Crawford Noble's supply ship, to take to Kekerten, where she arrived on September 7 and returned to Peterhead on October 3, before the Cumberland Sound was frozen over for the winter (Müller-Wille, *Franz Boas among the Inuit*, 21–22, 110–11, 269; Müller-Wille and Gieseking, *Inuit and Whalers*, 41; and Müller-Wille, personal communication). Because of William Barr's translation from German to English in Müller-Wille's *Franz Boas among the Inuit of Baffin Island 1883–1884*, I cite this material, though I also use the translations of the letters done by Helene Boas Yampolsky in BFP. I cite the latter by date and page number of the Yampolsky translation. Müller-Wille has published the original German versions in the following works: his 1992 article, "Franz Boas: Auszüge aus seinem Baffin-Tagebuch"; and his 1994 book, *Franz Boas: Bei den Inuit in Baffinland*.

4. Letter Diary, FB to Marie, July 19, 1883, 51, BFP; Letter Diary, FB to Marie, July 4, 1883, 21, BFP; Letter Diary, FB to Marie, July 19, 1883, 51, BFP; Müller-Wille, *Franz Boas among the Inuit*, 61, FB/MK, 5 Aug. 1883.

5. FB to parents and sisters, June 21, 1883, BFP; Letter Diary, FB to Marie, August 5, 1883, 51, 52, BFP; Müller-Wille and Gieseking, *Inuit and Whalers*, 30n15; Letter Diary, FB to Marie, July 4, 1883, 3, 4, BFP; Letter Diary, FB to Marie, July 21, 1883, 40, BFP; Letter Diary, FB to Marie, July 5, 1883, 22, BFP.

6. Müller-Wille, *Franz Boas among the Inuit*, 52; Müller-Wille and Gieseking, *Inuit and Whalers*, 31–32, 9 July 1883; Letter Diary, FB to Marie, July 9, 1883, 27, BFP. For an account of his attempts to surprise "Herr Dr Boas" with his birthday

presents, see Weike's letter to Mathilde Nolting and Linna, maids in the Boas home in Minden (Müller-Wille and Gieseking, *Inuit and Whalers*, 43–44).

7. Letter Diary, FB to Marie, July 10, 1883, 29, BFP; Letter Diary, FB to Marie, July 11, 1883, 30, BFP.

8. Müller-Wille, *Franz Boas among the Inuit*, 59; Letter Diary, FB to Marie, August 10, 1883, 54, BFP; Letter Diary, FB to Marie, August 13, 1883, 56, BFP.

9. Letter Diary, FB to Marie, August 14, 1883, 56, 57, BFP; Letter Diary, FB to Marie, August 28, 1883, 63, BFP. The official spelling was Kekerten. Boas frequently spelled it "Kikkerton"; other authors use various spellings.

10. Letter Diary, FB to Marie, September 2, 1883, 63, BFP; Norman Boas and Doris Boas, *Arctic Expedition*, 17, quoting Boas, September 14, 1883. Boas, "Im Eise des Nordens."

11. Letter Diary, FB to Marie, September 2, 1883, 64, BFP; Müller-Wille, *Franz Boas among the Inuit*, 72; Eskimo Story, 12, BFP; Letter Diary, FB to Marie, September 2, 1883, 64, BFP. Of the "Eskimo Story," Franziska Boas said that she and her siblings were always intrigued because the story ended in mid-sentence. See Knötsch, "Franz Boas' Research Trip," 11–12, 13–14, for a perceptive analysis of what she calls Boas's "First Contacts and Ventures (August–September 1883)."

12. FB to Marie, April 27, 1883, BFP; see also Müller-Wille, *Franz Boas among the Inuit*, 38–40, 92; and Cole and Müller-Wille, "Franz Boas' Expedition," 44; Müller-Wille and Gieseking, *Inuit and Whalers*, 225.

13. Cole, "Value of a Person," 19; Norman Boas and Doris Boas, *Arctic Expedition*, 17–18; Knötsch, "Franz Boas' Research Trip," 15.

14. Letter Diary, FB to Marie, September 9, 1883, BFP; see also Cole and Müller-Wille, "Franz Boas' Expedition," 45; Letter Diary, FB to Marie, September 3, 1883, 65; FB to Marie, September 19, 1883, BFP.

15. Müller-Wille, *Franz Boas among the Inuit*, 72, 83, 86, 87, 89.

16. Cole, "The Value of a Person," 14; Harper, "Collecting at a Distance," 89–90; Harper, "Collaboration of James Mutch and Franz Boas," 55; Boas, "Journey in Cumberland Sound," 247.

17. FB to parents, October 31, 1883, BFP; Müller-Wille and Gieseking, *Inuit and Whalers*, 73; Müller-Wille, *Franz Boas among the Inuit*, 22, 96, 99, 91, FB/ parents, sisters, 12 Sept. 1883; Letter Diary, FB to Marie, September 19, 1883, BFP; FB to parents, September 19, 1883, BFP. See also Cole and Müller-Wille, "Franz Boas' Expedition," 48. For Boas's research during his time in the Cumberland Sound, see Cole and Müller-Wille, "Franz Boas' Expedition," 44–45, wherein the authors reproduce Boas's plans as of May 1883. Boas spelled the name "Ssigna" and he was called "Jimmy" by the Scottish whal-

ers. In advance of his trip, Boas had inquired about the appropriate payment for Inuit assistants. Paul Hegemann, captain of the second German North Pole Expedition (1869–70) had informed him "that an Eskimo receives 32 lbs of ship's biscuit, 1 gallon of molasses, 2 lbs coffee and 12 oz. of tobacco as payment for 4 weeks" (Müller-Wille, *Franz Boas among the Inuit*, 37).

18. FB to parents, October 31, 1883, BFP; Letter Diary, FB to Marie, September 3, 1883, 65, BFP; Müller-Wille, *Franz Boas among the Inuit*, 79, 81–82.

19. "Journey in Cumberland Sound," 244; see also Müller-Wille, *Franz Boas Enigma*, 109, 110; Müller-Wille and Weber Müller-Wille, "Inuit Geographical Knowledge," 220, quoting Boas, "Baffin-Land."

20. Boas, "Eskimos of Baffin Land," 1, Ernst Boas translation, typescript, BFP; Boas, "Journey in Cumberland Sound," 253, 270.

21. Boas, "Journey in Cumberland Sound," 244.

22. Letter Diary, FB to Marie, September 24, 1883, BFP; Müller-Wille, *Franz Boas among the Inuit*, 14; Letter Diary, FB to Marie, October 19, 1883, BFP; Letter Diary, FB to Marie, September 22, 1883, BFP; Müller-Wille, *Franz Boas among the Inuit*, 99, FB/MK, 23 Sept. 1883.

23. Müller-Wille, *Franz Boas among the Inuit*, 134, FB/MK, 5 Nov. 1883; 135, 6 Nov. 1883; 133; see also Cole and Müller-Wille, "Franz Boas' Expedition," 51–52.

24. Müller-Wille and Weber Müller-Wille, "Inuit Geographical Knowledge," 221, parentheses in original; Müller-Wille, *Franz Boas among the Inuit*, 127, 130, 133. See also Cole and Müller-Wille, "Franz Boas' Expedition," 53; Letter Diary, FB to Marie, September 24, 1883; Boas, "Under the Arctic Circle," 13, BFP. Ernst Boas had translated his father's article from the German as published in the Sunday supplement, *New Yorker Staatszeitung*, January 13, February 1, February 22, March 2, 1885.

25. Müller-Wille and Weber Müller-Wille, "Inuit Geographical Knowledge," 220, 221; Cole and Müller-Wille, "Franz Boas' Expedition," 62, citing Boas, "Eskimo-Dialekt," 97.

26. Cole and Müller-Wille, "Franz Boas' Expedition," 57; Letter Diary, FB to parents, November 18, 1883, BFP; Müller-Wille, *Franz Boas among the Inuit*, 133, 139, 140, FB/MK, 18 Nov. 1883; Letter Diary, FB to Marie, January 23, 1884, BFP.

27. Müller-Wille, *Franz Boas among the Inuit*, 128, 130, FB to parents and sisters, October 26, 1883; Boas, *Central Eskimo* (1964), 204.

28. Cole, *Franz Boas*, 301n29, identifies the disease that afflicted the dog population of Baffin Land as resembling "distemper or 'fox encephalitic' of domestic fox farms." Müller-Wille, *Franz Boas among the Inuit*, 211, FB to parents, April 20, 1884; Boas, "Journey in Cumberland Sound," 257; Boas, Eskimo Story, 56, BFP.

29. Müller-Wille, *Franz Boas among the Inuit*, 117, FB to Marie, October 1883; Boas, "Eskimo Story," 35, BFP.

30. Müller-Wille, *Franz Boas among the Inuit*, 131, FB to parents and sisters, October 31 1883; 146, brackets in Müller-Wille; Letter Diary, FB to Marie, December 9, 1883, 27, emphasis in original, BFP.

31. Boas, "Journey in Cumberland Sound," 253; Müller-Wille, *Franz Boas among the Inuit*, 163, FB/MK, December 30, 1883.

32. Müller-Wille, *Franz Boas among the Inuit*, 136; Müller-Wille and Gieseking, *Inuit and Whalers*, 102.

33. Boas, "Eskimo Story," 50, 51, 52, BFP; Boas, *Central Eskimo* (1964), 196–97.

34. Fragment on Sedna, BFP. Boas, *Central Eskimo* (1964), 176, (1888), 584.

35. Letter Diary, FB to Marie, November 5, 1883, BFP; Letter Diary, FB to Marie, September 19, 1883, BFP; Müller-Wille, *Franz Boas among the Inuit*, 171, FB/MK, January 22, 1884; 140, FB to parents, November 18, 1883.

36. Müller-Wille, *Franz Boas among the Inuit*, 117, FB/MK, October 11, 1883.

37. Boas 1884, "Journey in Cumberland Sound," 258; Cole, "Value of a Person," 29, December 16, 1883; 30, December 19, 1883.

38. Müller-Wille, *Franz Boas among the Inuit*, 156; Boas, "Journey in Cumberland Sound," 259, 260; Müller-Wille and Gieseking, *Inuit and Whalers*, 125. There is a discrepancy in dates recorded in Boas's account, "A Journey in Cumberland Sound," and those entered in Boas's diary and in Weike's diary. In the 1884 article, Boas identified the early morning departure for this ill-fated trek as December 21 ("Journey in Cumberland Sound," 259), while the diary entries for both Boas and Weike note the date of departure as December 20, and the arrival in the Inuit camp of Anarnitung as December 21. Likely the correct date was recorded in the diaries of Boas and Weike.

39. Müller-Wille and Gieseking, *Inuit and Whalers*, 116, 116n63, 126–27, 127n24, 248; Boas, "Journey in Cumberland Sound," 260. Müller-Wille conveyed to me his reflection on the import of the first aid administered to Weike by Ocheito and his wife.

40. Müller-Wille, *Franz Boas among the Inuit*, 160; Müller-Wille and Gieseking, *Inuit and Whalers*, 139.

41. Müller-Wille, *Franz Boas among the Inuit*, 159, quotations and emphasis in original; Cole, "Value of a Person," 33, emphasis in original; Letter Diary, FB to Marie, December 23, 1883, emphasis in original, BFP. *Bildung* and *Herzensbildung* have been translated elsewhere with different English words. Müller-Wille suggests to me that *Bildung* be translated as "(educational, cultural, spiritual) formation," and that *Herzensbildung* be translated as "nobleness of the heart."

42. Müller-Wille, *Franz Boas among the Inuit*, 212, FB/parents, 30 Apr. 1884; Boas, "Under the Arctic Circle," 14–15, BFP.

43. Müller-Wille, *Franz Boas among the Inuit*, 181, FB to Marie, February 14, 1884; 182, FB/MK, 15 Feb. 1884.

44. Letter Diary, FB to Marie, October 2, 1883, BFP; Boas, "Journey in Cumberland Sound," 261; see also Cole and Müller-Wille, "Franz Boas' Expedition," 57–58.

45. Müller-Wille, *Franz Boas among the Inuit*, 185, 201, 203; Knötsch, "Franz Boas' Research Trip," 34.

46. Letter Diary, FB to Marie, October 2, 1883, BFP; Pöhl, Assessing Franz Boas' Ethics," 37–38; Müller-Wille, *Franz Boas among the Inuit*, 116.

47. Müller-Wille, *Franz Boas among the Inuit*, 203, 215, quoting Weike's diary entry, May 6, 1884; 218, May 14, 1884, emphasis in original; Letter Diary, FB to Marie, May 8, 1884, BFP; Boas to Arnold Jacobi, January 22, 1913, BP. James Mutch arranged to have the two boxes retrieved that Boas had left on the trail, and had them shipped to the German Polar Commission, whose property they were (Müller-Wille, *Franz Boas among the Inuit*, 219).

48. Müller-Wille, *Franz Boas among the Inuit*, 227 (FB to Marie, June 6, 1884), Boas's emphasis; 229 (FB to Marie, June 1, 1884); 230 (FB to Marie, June 11, 1884); Letter Diary, FB to Marie, June 5, 1884, 169; May 16, 1884, 175; June 6, 1884, 171. BFP; FB to parents, September 20, 1884, BFP.

49. Müller-Wille, *Franz Boas among the Inuit*, 255 (FB to Marie, August 20, 1884), parentheses in original; FB to parents, September 20, 1884, BFP.

50. FB to parents, September 20, 1884, BFP; Müller-Wille, *Franz Boas among the Inuit*, 230 (FB to Marie, June 11, 1884), 258 (August 26, 1884), 258 (August 29, 1884), 267.

51. Müller-Wille, *Franz Boas among the Inuit*, 260, 265; Marie to FB, September 10, 1884, BFP; FB to parents, September 8, 1884, BFP.

52. FB to Marie, September 11, 1884, BFP; FB to Marie, September 16, 1884, BFP; FB to parents, September 11, 1884, BFP; FB to Marie, September 16, 1884, BFP.

53. FB to parents, October 11, 1884, BFP.

54. Aunt Phips to Sophie Boas, September 22, 1884, emphasis in original, BFP; FB to parents, October 11, 1884, BFP.

55. FB to parents, October 11, 1884, BFP. See Norman Boas, *Alma Farm*, for an account of the summer vacation home for the Meyer, Krackowizer, Jacobi, and Boas families.

56. Marie to Franz's people, September 25, 1884, parentheses in original, BFP; FB to parents, September 25, 1884, BFP; FB to parents, October 11, 1884, BFP.

57. Müller-Wille, *Franz Boas among the Inuit*, 53–54 (FB/MK, July 11, 1883), emphasis in original; Letter Diary, FB to Marie, July 11, 1883, 31, BFP; Letter Diary, FB to Marie, October 2, 1883, BFP.

58. FB to parents, April 30, 1884, BFP; Krupnik, "One Field Season," 73, 80, 81.

59. Cole and Müller-Wille, "Franz Boas' Expedition," 45, 51, 54. Cole and Müller-Wille note that Boas had a model for his approach to the Baffin Island project. Charles Francis Hall was, as Boas had said, "the first one to prove how much one could achieve in arctic areas by adopting completely the Eskimo mode of life" (Boas, "Baffin-Land," 35).

60. Müller-Wille, *Franz Boas among the Inuit*, xi, 14; Müller-Wille and Weber Müller-Wille, "Inuit Geographical Knowledge," 223; Müller-Wille and Gieseking, *Inuit and Whalers*, 266.

61. Müller-Wille and Weber Müller-Wille, "Inuit Geographical Knowledge," 220; Müller-Wille, *Franz Boas among the Inuit*, 14.

62. In the early 1970s Müller-Wille and Weber Müller-Wille had begun collecting place names among the Inuit of Naujaat or Aivilik (Repulse Bay): "At that time the Inuit remarked that their names for places did not appear on official maps" (Müller-Wille and Weber Müller-Wille, "Inuit Geographical Knowledge," 225).

63. Müller-Wille and Weber Müller-Wille, "Inuit Geographical Knowledge," 227. As Müller-Wille conveyed to me, Etuangat Aksayook (1901–1996) "was highly esteemed for his extensive and deep knowledge of the land, the people and their own history." Intrigued by the maps with the accompanying place names, Etuangat began to talk about his life: "He was born in 1901, grew up in Kingait Fiord, lived at Kekerten whaling station, and finally at Pangnirtung. His father, born around 1850 . . . in Padli on the coast of Davis Strait . . . moved to Cumberland Sound. [His father] was around 30 years old when Boas and Weike were on Baffin Island, thus he and his family must have known them." Müller-Wille continued to recount to me how Etuangat reflected "that he had heard about Boas and Weike but could not give any more details."

64. Müller-Wille and Weber Müller-Wille, "Inuit Geographical Knowledge," 217, 226.

65. Müller-Wille, *Franz Boas Enigma*, 40; Lowie, *Biographical Memoir of Franz Boas*, 313–14.

66. Müller-Wille, *Franz Boas Enigma*, 40, emphasis in original. Ludger Müller-Wille conveyed to me this added perspective on Boas's year-long research. See William Barr, "Expeditions of the First International Polar Year," 2–5.

67. Müller-Wille and Gieseking, *Inuit and Whalers*, 17.

68. Cole and Müller-Wille, "Franz Boas' Expedition," 48, 50.

69. Müller-Wille and Weber Müller-Wille, "Inuit Geographical Knowledge," 221.

70. Boas, "Second Report"; Harper, "Collaboration of James Mutch and Franz Boas," 54, 58, 59; see also Harper, "Collecting at a Distance," 89–91.

71. Boas, "Under the Arctic Circle," 1, 8, BFP; Müller-Wille and Weber Müller-Wille, "Inuit Geographical Knowledge," 225.

72. Knötsch, "Franz Boas' Research Trip," 22; Herskovits, "Some Further Notes," 116; Müller-Wille, *Franz Boas Enigma*, 32.

5. Divided Desires

1. FB to parents, November 18, 1884, BFP; FB to parents, October 7, 1884; FB to parents and sisters, October 11, 1884, BFP; FB to Marie, November 25, 1884, BFP.

2. FB to parents, October 7, 1884, emphasis in original, BFP; FB to Marie, October 2, 1884, BFP.

3. FB to parents, October 7, 1884, BFP; FB to parents, November 13, 1884, BFP; FB to parents and sisters, October 3, 1884, emphasis in original, BFP; FB to parents, October 12, 1884; see Müller-Wille, *Franz Boas Enigma*, 84.

4. FB to Marie, October 13, 1884, BFP; FB to parents, November 27, 1884, BFP.

5. Hough, "Otis Tufton Mason," 662; FB to Marie, October 15, 1884, BFP; FB to Marie, October 25, 1884, BFP; FB to parents, November 25, 1884, BFP; FB to Marie, November 26, 1884.

6. FB to Marie, November 28, 1884, BFP; FB to Marie, November 25, 1884, BFP; FB to Marie, November 26, 1884, BFP. Established by an act of Congress in 1879, the Bureau of Ethnology changed to the Bureau of American Ethnology in 1897. I elect, however, to refer to it as the BAE.

7. FB to parents, November 30, 1884, BFP. FB to parents, November 7, 1884, BFP.

8. FB to Marie, November 26, 1884, emphasis in original, BFP; see also Müller-Wille, *Franz Boas Enigma*, 83–84; Rood to Jacobi, January 30, 1885, BP; FB to parents, November 21, 1884, BFP. Carl Schurz, a fellow '48er with Jacobi, was at the time of Boas's writing editor of the *New York Evening Post* (1881–84).

9. FB to Marie, April 2, 1885, emphasis in original, BFP; Müller-Wille, *Franz Boas Enigma*, 91; FB to Marie, May 4, 1885, BFP; FB to parents, May 4, 1885, BFP.

10. FB to Marie, November 29, 1884, BFP; FB to Marie, October 16, 1884, BFP; FB to parents, October 22, 1884, BFP.

11. FB to parents, October 22, 1884, BFP; FB to parents, December 2, 1884, BFP; FB to parents, December 22, 1884, BFP.

12. Fischer to Toni, October 26, 1884, BFP; Fischer to Toni, September 7, 1884, EM's translation, BFP; Fischer to Toni Boas, December 30, 1884, EM's translation, BFP.

13. Fischer to FB, December 21, 1884, EM's translation, BP.

14. Fischer to FB, December 21, 1884, EM's translation, BP.

15. FB to Jacobi, January 7, 1885, BFP; Jacobi to Sophie Boas, December 23, 1884, EM's translation, BFP.

16. Sophie Boas to Jacobi, February 4, 1885, BFP.

17. FB to Jacobi, January 13, 1885, BFP.

18. Jacobi to FB, January 17, 1885, EM's translation, emphasis in original, BP.

19. Jacobi to FB, January 17, 1885; EM's translation, BP.

20. FB to parents, December 22, 1884, BFP; FB to parents, November 13, 1884, BFP; FB to Marie, November 28, 1884, BFP; FB to Marie, December 4, 1884, BFP.

21. FB to Marie, January 14, 1885, BFP.

22. FB to Marie, January 14, 1885, emphasis in original, BFP.

23. FB to parents, January 18, 1885, BFP.

24. FB to Marie, January 18, 1885, BFP.

25. FB to Jacobi, January 18, 1885, BP.

26. FB to Jacobi, January 18, 1885, BP.

27. FB to Marie, January 18, 1885, BFP; FB to parents, January 20, 1885, BFP.

28. FB to Marie, February 11, 1885, BFP; FB to parents, February 12, 1885, BFP; FB to Marie, February 18, 1885, BFP; Boas, "Melville's Plan," 248.

29. FB to Marie, February 15, 1885, BFP; FB to Marie, February 19, 1885, BFP; FB to Marie, February 20, 1885, BFP; FB to Jacobi, February 12, 1885, BFP; FB to Marie, February 18, 1885, BFP; FB to Marie, February 24, 1885, BFP; FB to Marie, January 19, 1885, BFP.

30. FB to parents, February 5, 1885, BFP; FB to parents, November 13, 1884, BFP.

31. FB to Marie, March 26, 1885, BFP; FB to Marie, March 27, 1885, BFP; Cole, *Franz Boas*, 86.

32. Fischer to FB, March 26, 1885, BP; FB to Marie, April 2, 1885, BFP; Cole, *Franz Boas*, 86; FB to Marie, April 10, 1885, BFP; FB to parents, April 13, 1885, BFP. Boas's paper from the *Deutscher Geographentag* appeared as "*Die Eskimo des Baffinlandes*" (1885). See Müller-Willer, *Franz Boas Enigma*, 165, 90–91; and Cole, *Franz Boas*, 302n9. Müller-Wille pointed me to the letter from Boas to his parents in which he identified Hermann Wagner as the preeminent methodologist in geography (FB to parents, April 13, 1885, BFP).

33. Sophie Boas to Jacobi, April 20, 1885, BFP.

34. FB to Jacobi, April 20, 1885, BFP.

35. Müller-Wille, *Franz Boas Enigma*, 91, 165; FB to Marie, April 21, 1885, BFP; FB to Marie, May 4, 1885, BFP.

36. FB to Jacobi, April 20, 1885, BFP; FB to Marie, May 11, 1885, BFP. Concerning the editorship at the Viennese Geographisches Institut, which was under the direction of Eduard Hölzel, see also notes by translator appended to the latter letter.

37. Müller-Wille, *Franz Boas Enigma*, 32, 93–94, 97, 165; FB to Marie, June 12, 1885, BFP; FB to Marie, December 12, 1885, BFP; FB to Marie, April 21, 1885, BFP.

38. FB to Marie, June 5, 1885, emphasis in original, BFP; FB to Marie, September 22, 1885, BFP.

39. Clark, *Academic Charisma*, 80; FB to Marie, September 22, 1885, BFP; Fischer to FB, June 19, 1885, EM's translation, BP.

40. FB to Marie, July 3, 1885, BFP; FB to Marie, May 17, 1886, BFP; Müller-Wille, *Franz Boas Enigma*, 39.

41. Fischer to FB, June 19, 1885, EM's translation, BP; Cole, *Franz Boas*, 89; Fischer to FB, September 21, 1885, BP.

42. FB to Marie, July 24, 1885, BFP. Müller-Wille offered a more accurate translation for the passage of this letter, originally translated in the version on file in APS as, "modern (*naturwissenschaftlichen*) environmental tendency." See Müller-Wille, *Franz Boas Enigma*, 101, for the original handwritten script of Boas, and the English translation by Müller-Wille and Weber Müller-Wille of "The visit to Kiepert's or The Amiable Professor" (100).

43. FB to Marie, August 10, 1885, BFP; Kirchhoff to FB, February 15, 1886, emphasis in original, RLZ's translation, BP; Fischer to FB, February 27, 1886, RLZ's translation, BP.

44. FB to Marie, November 20, 1885, BFP; see also Müller-Wille, *Franz Boas Enigma*, 98; FB to Marie, January 14, 1886, BFP.

45. Cole, *Franz Boas*, 90, 91; Kiepert to FB, January 22, 1886, RLZ's translation, BP; see also FB to Marie, January 25, 1886, BFP; FB to Marie, March 9, 1886, BFP.

46. Boas, *Kwakiutl of Vancouver*, 307; FB to Marie, October 9, 1885, parentheses in original, BFP; FB to Marie, November 23, 1885, BFP; FB to Marie, January 19, 1886, BFP; FB to Marie, February 28, 1886, BFP; FB to Marie, March 12, 1886, BFP.

47. Müller-Wille, *Franz Boas Enigma*, 57; Haberland, "Nine Bella Coolas," 337; Lutz, "Introduction," xiii–xiv.

48. Haberland, "Nine Bella Coolas," 337–38, 340, 362–63; see also Bland, "Bernard Fillip Jacobsen"; Cole, "Franz Boas and the Bella Coola," 115, 117; FB to Marie, January 14, 1886, BFP. Carl Stumpf published *"Lieder der Bellakula Indianer"* (Songs of the Bella Coola Indians) in 1886 based on his work with the Bella Coola in Berlin in 1885.

49. Cole, "Franz Boas and the Bella Coola," 123n1, n4; 199, quoting Boas; FB to Marie, February 5, 1886, BFP. As Cole notes, this article was not listed in Andrews, "Bibliography of Franz Boas," nor was it in the clippings book of *Berliner Tageblatt* articles on file among the Boas Papers at the American Philosophical Society. Cole provides an English translation of Boas's "Captain Jacobsen's Bella Coola Indians" (119–22).

50. Cole, "Franz Boas and the Bella Coola," 119, 120, 122, quoting Boas; FB to Marie, February 28, 1886, emphasis in original, BFP; FB to Marie, January 14, 1886, BFP.

51. FB to Marie, May 17, 1886, BFP; FB to Marie, May 28, 1886, BFP; FB to Marie, June 6, 1886, BFP; FB to Papa, June 7, 1886, BFP.

52. FB to Marie, February 28, 1886, BFP.

53. FB to Marie, December 20, 1885, BFP; FB to Marie, April 16, 1886, BFP; FB to Marie, March 14, 1886, BFP; FB to Marie, May 9, 1886, BFP.

54. FB to parents, March 28, 1886, BFP; FB to Marie, April 23, 1886, BFP.

55. FB to Marie, May 9, 1886, BFP.

56. Müller-Wille, *Franz Boas Enigma*, 31, 39, emphasis in original. For a listing of Boas's publications during this period, see Müller-Wille, *Franz Boas Enigma*, 162–67; and Andrews, "Bibliography of Franz Boas," 68–69.

57. FB to Marie, October 15, 1884, BFP; FB to Marie, October 2, 1885, BFP; FB to Marie, December 12, 1885, BFP.

58. FB to Marie, December 25, 1885, BFP; FB to Marie, April 6, 1886, BFP.

59. FB to father and Anne, June 17, 1886, BFP; FB to parents, July 15, 1886, BFP.

60. FB to Marie, June 15, 1886, BFP; FB to Marie, July 8, 1886, BFP; FB to parents, July 15, 1886, BFP.

6. West to the Indians

1. FB to Marie, September 13, 1886, BFP; FB to parents, September 7, 1886, BFP; FB to parents, September 2, 1886, BFP.

2. FB to Marie, August 15, 1886, BFP; FB to Marie, August 18, 1886, BFP; FB to Marie, August 20, 1886; FB to parents, August 24, 1886, BFP.

3. FB to Marie, September 17, 1886, BFP; Rohner, *Ethnography of Franz Boas*, 20, quoting FB to parents, September 18, 1886; Jacknis, "Franz Boas and Photography," 5.

4. FB to Marie, September 23, 1886, BFP; Boas, "Boas' Introduction," 6, parentheses in original; Rohner, *Ethnography of Franz Boas*, 21, quoting FB to parents, September 19, 1886; Rohner, *Ethnography of Franz Boas*, 29, quoting FB to parents, September 30, 1886.

5. Rohner, *Ethnography of Franz Boas*, 31–32, quoting FB to parents, October 5, 1886.

6. Rohner, *Ethnography of Franz Boas*, 33–34, quoting FB to parents, October 7, 1886.

7. Rohner, *Ethnography of Franz Boas*, 42–43, quoting FB to parents, October 19, 1886. In "Kwakiutl of Vancouver Island," Boas described the mode of "Travel and Transportation," with a focus on the types of canoes, paddles, and sails used (444–46).

8. Rohner, *Ethnography of Franz Boas*, 43, 44, 45, 46, quoting FB to parents October 19, 1886.

9. FB to Marie, November 1, 1886, BFP; Rohner, *Ethnography of Franz Boas*, 50, quoting FB to parents, October 31, 1886; 49, quoting FB to parents, October 28, 1886; Jacknis, "Franz Boas and Photography," 5; Rohner, *Ethnography of Franz Boas*, 52, quoting FB to parents, November 4, 1886. Jacknis notes that O. C. Hastings had purchased the photography studio from Stephen Allen Spencer, who had left Victoria for Alert Bay in the late 1880s and had married Annie Hunt, the sister of George Hunt, who was to become Boas's longtime collaborator in work on the Kwakiutl.

10. Rohner, *Ethnography of Franz Boas*, 53–54, quoting FB to parents, November 6, 1886; 57, quoting FB to parents, November 9, 1886; 60, quoting FB to parents, November 15, 1886.

11. Rohner, *Ethnography of Franz Boas*, 58, 59, quoting FB to parents, November 12, 1886; FB to Marie, December 2, 1886, BFP; Rohner, *Ethnography of Franz Boas*, 60, quoting FB to parents, November 15, 1886; 66–67, quoting FB to parents, November 27, 1886.

12. FB Field Notebooks, Diary, September 19, 1886, BP; FB to Marie, September 21, 1886, BFP; Rohner, *Ethnography of Franz Boas*, 74, quoting FB to parents, December 12, 1886; 75, quoting FB to parents, December 16, 1886; FB to Marie, December 16, 1886, BFP.

13. FB to Marie, December 16, 1886, parentheses in original, BFP; Rohner, *Ethnography of Franz Boas*, 61, quoting FB to parents, November 17, 1886. Boas was referring to the lecture he would be required to give as Privatdozent at Friedrich-Wilhelms-Universität in Berlin. As Müller-Wille told me, "To maintain the docentship one had to give at least one lecture course per term, usually for free, all depending upon agreement with the faculty."

14. FB to Marie, December 17, 1886, BFP; FB to Marie, December 17, 1886, emphasis in original, BFP.

15. FB to parents, January 4, 1887, BFP. While Boas doesn't identify the article, it was "*Zur Ethnologie Britisch-Kolumbiens*," a five-page article with one map (1887).

16. FB to Marie, January 8, 1887, BFP; FB to Marie, August 18, 1886, BFP.

17. FB to parents, January 10, 1887, BFP; FB to Marie, January 12, 1887, BFP; Hodges to FB, January 26, 1887, January 27, 1887, BP; Hodges and Boas contract, February 1, 1887, BP.

18. FB to parents, January 28, 1887, BFP; Gatschet to FB, January 30, 1887, BP; Bell to FB, February 7, 1887, BP; Dawson to FB, February 5, 1887, BP.

19. FB to parents, January 28, 1887, BFP.

20. FB to parents, January 25, 1887, BFP; Norman Boas, *Franz Boas*, 81, quoting Emilie Krackowizer to Sophie Boas, February 6, 1887, BFP.

21. Cole, *Franz Boas*, 106.

22. Cole, *Franz Boas*, 105; FB to family, telegram, March 10, 1887, BFP; invitation to reception, 1887, BFP. The town of Sing Sing changed its name to Ossinging in 1901 to differentiate it from the infamous prison. Marie's father, Ernst Krackowizer (1821–75), died in the town of Sing Sing as a result of typhoid and was buried in the town's cemetery.

23. FB to Helene, July 15, 1919, BFP.

24. Letterhead of *Science,* November 1887, BP; Fischer to FB, March 13, 1887, RLZ's translation, BP; Wagner to FB, July 15, 1887, RLZ's translation, BP; Cole, *Franz Boas,*108; Kiepert to FB, June 6, 1887, BP.

25. Cole, *Franz Boas*, 107; Boas, "American Ethnological Society," 7; Bieder, "From Ethnologists to Anthropologists," 13; Cotheal to FB, November 17, 1887, BP; Smith, "Centenary of the American Ethnological Society," 183. See also Lesser, "American Ethnological Society"; and Stocking, *Shaping of American Anthropology*, 304, for Boas's letter to Jacobi, September 2, 1909, where Boas referred to reviving the American Ethnological Society in 1900.

26. Newell to FB, December 17, 1887, BP; Bell, "William Wells Newell," 10; Newell to FB, January 11, 1888, BP; FB to parents, January 3, 1888, BFP.

27. Hale to FB [December 30, 1887], BP; Gruber, "Horatio Hale," 20, 23.

28. Hale to FB [December 30, 1887], BP; see also Gruber, "Horatio Hale," 24–25.

29. FB to Hale, February 1, 1888, BP; FB to Hale, February 25, 1888, BP; FB to parents, March 6, 1888, BFP.

30. FB to Charles Scribner's, n.d., BP. Boas wrote this draft by hand on the back of another letter that was dated February 9, 1888. While he did not designate the addressee, it is apparent from his other drafts and letters that he was writing to Charles Scribner's Sons (FB [to Charles Scribner's Sons], n.d., BP); FB [to Charles Scribner's Sons, c. February 1, 1888], BP.

31. Charles Scribner's Sons to FB, February 9, 1888, BP; FB to Charles Scribner's Sons, February 6, 1888, BP.

32. FB to parents, February 6, 1888, BFP; Bell to FB, April 3, 1888, BP.

33. FB to parents, March 23, 1888, BFP; FB to parents, March 30, 1888, BFP. The foregoing citations were taken from the summary of "1888 FB and MB to parents," compiled by Helene Boas Yampolsky, hereafter referred to as HBY summary.

34. Henshaw to FB, March 5, 1888, BP; Dawson to FB, March 19, 1888, BP.

35. FB to parents, May 26, 1888, HBY summary, BFP; FB to parents, HBY summary, May 25, 1888, BFP; FB to Powell, February 25, 1888, BP; Hale to FB, April 30, 1888, BP; Hale to FB, May 21, 1888, emphasis and quotation marks in original, BP.

36. Hale to FB, [December 30, 1887], BP; FB to parents, June 18, 1888, BP; FB to Hale, February 25, 1888, BP; Hale to FB, March 1, 1888, BP; Hale to FB, May 21, 1888, BP; Gruber, "Horatio Hale," 28–29.

37. FB to parents, July 23, 1889, BFP; FB to parents, July 28, 1889, BFP; Hale to FB, July 13, 1889, BP; Gruber, "Horatio Hale," 31.

38. Hale to Boas, May 21, 1890, BP; Gruber, "Horatio Hale," 31; Fenton, "Hale," 1; Hale to Dawson, November 26, 1888, emphasis in original, BP.

39. Rohner, *Ethnography of Franz Boas*, 107, 109, quoting FB to Marie, July 23, 1889.

40. Rohner, *Ethnography of Franz Boas*, 95, quoting FB diary, June 29, 1888; FB to Marie, June 4, 1888, quotation in original, BFP; Rohner, *Ethnography of Franz Boas*, 91, quoting FB diary, June 13, 1888 and FB diary, June 14, 1888. Norman Boas dates Franz Boas's first acquaintance with George Hunt to 1886 (*Franz Boas*, 95). However, the record of Boas's fieldwork indicates the date of their initial work together as 1888. Rohner writes, "George Hunt, Boas' major Kwakiutl informant, was born in February 1854, to a Scot father and Tlingit mother. He was raised among the Kwakiutl at Fort Rupert and learned Kwak-wala . . . as his first language. Boas met Hunt in Victoria in June 1888, but the latter did not become Boas' major informant until after the World Columbian Exposition at Chicago in 1893" (*Ethnography of Franz Boas*, 244n2). As Judith Berman ("Hunt, George") and Ira Jacknis ("George Hunt," 177) note, George Hunt's father Robert Hunt was born in Dorsetshire England.

41. Rohner, *Ethnography of Franz Boas*, 93, 95, 102, quoting FB diary, June 21, 1888, June 29, 1888, July 18, 1888; FB to Marie, July 17, 1888, BFP.

42. Rohner, *Ethnography of Franz Boas*, 88, 90, 93, quoting FB diary, June 8, 1888, June 12, 1888, June 24, 1888; see also Jacknis, "Franz Boas and Photography," 5–6; FB to parents, June 10, 1888, BFP.

43. Rohner, *Ethnography of Franz Boas*, 88, 90, quoting FB diary, June 6, 1888, June 7, 1888, June 11, 1888.

44. Rohner, *Ethnography of Franz Boas*, 89, 95, quoting FB diary, June 9, 1888, June 29, 1888, parentheses in original; see also Jacknis, "Franz Boas and Photography," 6.

45. Rohner, *Ethnography of Franz Boas*, 88, 98, FB diary, June 7, 1888, July 9, 1888; HBY summary of Marie to FB's parents, July 19, 1888, BFP; Cole, *Franz Boas*, 120; FB to Powell, August 8, 1888, BP.

46. Sutton to FB, November 15, 1888, parentheses in original, BP.

47. Sutton to FB, January 23, 1889, BP; Donaldson to FB, September 21, 1894, BP; Donaldson to FB, October 1, 1894, BP; Dorsey to FB, July 1, 1896, quotation marks and emphasis in original, BP.

48. Cole, *Franz Boas*, 112; Hodges to FB, August 1, 1888, BP.

49. FB to Toni, November 30, 1888, HBY summary, BFP; FB to parents, December 7, 1888, HBY summary, BFP.

50. FB to Powell, August 8, 1888, BP; FB to parents, August 27, 1888, HBY summary, BFP; Ross, *G. Stanley Hall*, 179; Koelsch, *Clark University*, 17.

51. FB to Tylor, August 15, 1888, draft, BP; FB to Tylor, August 17, 1888, second draft, BP; Tylor to FB, September 11, 1888, BP.

52. Hale to FB, October 3, 1888, BP; Hale to FB, October 18, 1888, parentheses in original, BP.

53. FB to Hodges, January 30, 1889, BP; Hodges to FB, January 30, 1889; FB to parents, January 15, 1889, BFP; Cole, *Franz Boas*, 113.

54. Sophie Boas to FB, February 11, 1889, BFP; Sophie Boas to FB, March 26, 1889, BFP; Cole, *Franz Boas*, 115.

55. Sophie Boas to FB and Marie, June 24, 1889, BFP.

56. FB to parents, June 10, 1888, BFP.

57. FB to Marie, July 28, 1889, BFP; FB to Marie, August 29, 1889, BFP; FB to Marie, August 12, 1889, BFP; FB to Marie, August 7, 1890, BFP; FB to Marie, August 29, 1889, BFP; FB to Marie, September 3, 1889, emphasis in original, BFP; FB to Toni, June 19, 1888, BFP.

58. FB to Hale, September 18, 1888, BP.

59. FB to parents, January 15, 1889, BFP.

60. FB to parents, January 15, 1889, BFP; Schmeltz to FB, January 23,1888, January 29, 1888, BP; see also Cole, *Franz Boas*, 108; Boas, "Game of Cat's Cradle," 229–30; "Game of Cat's Cradle" (1889), 52.

61. FB to parents, January 15, 1889, BFP; FB to parents, October 19, 1888, BFP.

62. FB to parents, June 10, 1888, BFP; Rohner, *Ethnography of Franz Boas*, 21, quoting FB to parents, September 19, 1886; Jacknis, "Franz Boas and Photography," 5.

63. FB to Powell, November 1888, draft, BP; Rohner, *Ethnography of Franz Boas*, 74, quoting FB to parents, December 12, 1886; FB to Powell, October 19, 1891, BP.

64. Rohner, *Ethnography of Franz Boas*, 29, quoting FB to parents, September 30, 1886, and 45, 46.

65. FB to Marie, August 25, 1889, BFP; Rohner, *Ethnography of Franz Boas*, 113, quoting FB to Marie, September 8, 1889.

66. FB to parents, October 11, 1889, emphasis in original, BFP.

67. FB to parents, October 18, 1889, BFP.

68. FB to parents, October 11, 1889, BFP.

7. All Our Hopes Came to Disgrace

1. FB to parents, October 11, 1889, BFP.

2. Ross, *G. Stanley Hall*, 193, 194, 195, 198, 202; Hall, "Contemporary University Problems," 15; Hall, *Life and Confessions*, 264, 288–89; Donaldson Papers, "Memories of My Boys," 1930, 94, APS. Georg Baur's last name was frequently rendered as "Bauer."

3. Webster, "Remarks," 60; Ross, *G. Stanley Hall*, 203.

4. Ross, *G. Stanley Hall*, 189, 203; Hall, *Life and Confessions*, 338.

5. Hall, *Life and Confessions*, 271–72. See Koelsch, *Clark University*, 24–25, for discussion of the introduction of the *Privatdocent* (current German spelling is *Privatdozent*), as derived from German universities, and the similarities of Johns Hopkins and Clark with the emphasis on "the primacy of research." See also Clark, *Academic Charisma*, 46.

6. Hall to FB, August 8, 1889, BP; FB to Hall, August 21, 1889, BP; Hall to FB, August 30, 1889, BP.

7. Hall to FB, August 8, 1889, BP; FB to Hall, August 21, 1889, BP; Hall to FB, August 30, 1889, BP.

8. FB to Hall, October 11, 1889, parentheses in original, BP; FB to Hall, October 22, 1889, BP.

9. Clark University, *Register* (1891), 65, 67, 68.

10. Clark University, *Register* (1891), 55, 53.

11. Clark University, *Register* (1891), 55; Boas, "Alexander Francis Chamberlain," 326; Chamberlain to FB, June 9, 1890, BP; Chamberlain to FB, June 18, 1890, BP.

12. Hall to FB, August 8, 1889, BP; FB to Hall, June 4, 1891, BP.

13. Marie to parents-in-law, April 17, 1890, RLZ's translation, BFP; Powell to FB, March 10, 1890, BP; Rohner, *Ethnography of Franz Boas*, 117, FB diary to parents, June 14, 1891; Dawson to FB, June 18, 1890, BP; FB to Hale, August 3, 1890, BP; Hale to FB, August 15, 1890, BP.

14. Hall to FB, April 6, 1891, BP; Wilson to FB, May 23, 1890, BP; Wilson to FB, February 18, 1891, BP.

15. Hall to FB, September 1, 1890, BP. Hall patterned his report on faculty research activity on President Gilman's practice at Johns Hopkins. In his autobiography, Hall recounted how Gilman established "the custom of printing in the Register the academic record of each professor and graduate student, and also calling attention in his annual reports . . . to the special achievements in research in each department" (Hall, *Life and Confessions*, 252n5).

16. Ross, *G. Stanley Hall*, 207; see Hall, *Life and Confessions*, 293; Washburn to Gilman, January 22, 1887, Daniel Coit Gilman Papers, Series 1, John Hopkins University.

17. Albert B. Southwick, "The Times, the Globe, and the T & G," *Telegram*, August 8, 2013, http://www.telegram.com/article/20130808/column21

/308089994/1020, accessed February 8, 2014. Frank H. Lancaster and Ernest F. Birmingham, "Worcester's Welcome to Advertisers and Advertiser Agencies, The Fourth Estate," May 27, 1922, in *Fourth Estate: A Weekly Newspaper for Publishers, Advertisers, Advertising Agents and Allied Interests*, 799. Fourth Estate Publishing Company. https://play.google.com/books/reader?id=66saaqaamaaj&printsec=frontcover&output=reader&authuser=0&hl=en&pg=gbs.ra5-pa35, accessed February 8, 2014.

18. "Dogs Vivisected, Scientific Torture at Clark University," *Worcester Telegram*, March 9, 1890; Koelsch, *Clark University*, 33.

19. Hall, *Life and Confessions*, 292.

20. "If He Be a Cur, Cut Him Up, The Psychology and Ethics of Cruelty at Clark University," *Worcester Sunday Telegram*, March 16, 1890.

21. "Dogs Vivisected," *Worcester Telegram*, March 9, 1890. See Liss, "Cosmopolitan Imagination," 294–95, for a discussion of the articles in the *Worcester Telegram* and *Worcester Sunday Telegram*. See also Ross, *G. Stanley Hall*, 210.

22. "Dr. Franz Boas of Clark University," *Worcester Telegram*, March 5, 1891.

23. Cole, *Franz Boas*, 142–43. While Cole cites the *Worcester Daily Telegraph* (March 5, 1891), this newspaper was in circulation only from 1847 to 1848. The only newspaper published in Worcester during the period of time cited by Cole was the *Worcester Telegram*; thus his attribution to the *Worcester Daily Telegraph* must necessarily be incorrect.

24. Cole, *Franz Boas*, 143, quoting FB to parents, April 19, 1891, BFP; Liss, "Cosmopolitan Imagination," 295n23, quoting Marie to Sophie Boas, March 20, 1891, BFP.

25. Ross, *G. Stanley Hall*, 211–12; Hall, *Life and Confessions*, 299.

26. Ross, *G. Stanley Hall*, 221; Donaldson Papers, "Memories of My Boys," 1930, 95, APS.

27. Thurs., January 21, 1892, BP; Copy, Clark University, January 21, 1892, BP. The signatories of the letter were the following: Albert A. Michelson, Prof. of Physics; C. O. Whitman, Prof. of Zoology; Henry H. Donaldson, Assist. Prof. of Neurology; Warren P. Lombard, Assist. Prof. of Physiology; John Ulric Nef, Assist. Prof. of Organic Chemistry; Franklin P. Mall, Adjunct Prof. of Anatomy; Oskar Bolza, Associate Prof. of Mathematics; G. Baur, Docent in Comp. Osteology & Paleontology; Franz Boas, Docent in Anthropology.

28. Notes from February 2, 1892, BP; Goulding, secretary of the corporation, to President Hall, February 1, 1892, BP; Ross, *G. Stanley Hall*, 227. See also Koelsch, *Clark University*. For the list of proposals presented by "the concerned faculty" to the faculty as a whole, see "Propositions Presented in the Faculty Meeting," January 1892, BP.

29. Ross, *G. Stanley Hall*, 226; Cole, *Franz Boas*, 145; Donaldson Papers, "Memories of My Boys," 1930, 96, APS.

30. Hall, *Life and Confessions*, 296–97, parentheses in original. See also Koelsch, *Clark University*, 24.

31. Goodspeed, *History of the University of Chicago* 195, 212.

32. Cole, *Great American University*, 30–31; Geiger, *To Advance Knowledge*, 11; Ross, *G. Stanley Hall*, 227.

33. Browman and Williams, *Anthropology at Harvard*, 175; Goodspeed, *History of the University of Chicago*, 201–2, 204, 208, 486–88. Browman and Williams do not cite a specific source for their assertion that Boas did not have the requisite national reputation sought by Harper. They reference Ross, *G. Stanley Hall*, 220, but Ross makes no mention of Harper's assessment of Boas's national reputation.

34. Cole, *Franz Boas*, 141; FB to parents, March 6, 1891, BFP; Marie to parents-in-law, January 2, 1890, February 4, 1890, February 11, 1890, March 4, 1890, RLZ's translation, BFP.

35. Sanford to FB, March 4, 1909, BP; Boas, "Psychological Problems in Anthropology"; Hall, *Life and Confessions*, 332–33; see also Ross, *G. Stanley Hall*, 386–93.

36. Rosenzweig, *Freud, Jung, and Hall*, 44, 252; Jung, *Memories, Dreams, Reflections*, 366, quoting Jung to Emma Jung, September 6, 1909; Freud, *An Autobiographical Study*, 93–94, 95.

37. Hall, *Life and Confessions*, 333; see Freud, *Lectures*, vi–viii; Hall to FB, June 30, 1909, BP.

38. FB to Hall, September 10, 1920, BP; Hall to FB, January 27, 1921, BP.

39. Cole, *Franz Boas*,146, 150–51, quoting FB to father, October 30, 1892, BFP; Sophie Boas to FB and Marie, September 17, 1892, BFP.

8. World's Columbian Exposition

1. Putnam, "Prefatory," x; Putnam to Crawford, March 7, 1894, BP; Dexter, "Putnam's Problems," 317; FB to Putnam, February 18, 1894, BP.

2. Dexter, "Putnam's Problems," 315; Jacknis, "Northwest Coast Indian Culture," 91.

3. Fagin, "Closed Collections," 249, 250, 253; see Hinsley, *Smithsonian and the American Indian*, 27–28, fig. 9; Mason, "Ethnological Exhibit," 211; see also Holmes, "World's Fair Congress," 432.

4. Fagin, "Closed Collections."

5. Hinsley, "Anthropology as Education," 13.

6. De Wit, "Building an Illusion," 46, 49, 85; Nye, "Electrifying Expositions," 146–47.

7. Gilbert, "Fixing the Image," 101. *Rand, McNally's Handbook* provided a detailed description of the Midway Plaisance and glossed it as "the homes

of peoples of many climes" (*Rand, McNally's*, xvi); Aberdeen, "The Midway Plaisance," 206–20.

8. De Wit, "Building an Illusion," 63–64, quoting Frederick Law Olmsted; Benedict, *Anthropology of World's Fairs*, 30; Appelbaum, *Chicago World's Fair*, iv–v; Johnson, *History of the World's Columbian Exposition*, 340; Aberdeen, "The Midway Plaisance," 212–14.

9. Cole, *Franz Boas*, 154, quoting FB to parents, May 28, 1893; Johnson, *History of the World's Columbian Exposition*, 315, 316; Dexter, "Putnam's Problems," 316, quoting Putnam in the *Chicago Daily Tribune*, May 31, 1890; 323, quoting Putnam to Alice.

10. Hinsley, "Anthropology as Education," 27; "Prof. Putnam's Hard Luck, His Difficulties with the Anthropological Exhibit," *New York Times*, May 22, 1893, http://timesmachine.nytimes.com/timesmachine/1893/05/22/106825338 .html?pageNumber=9, accessed January 7, 2015.

11. "Prof. Putnam's Hard Luck."

12. Dexter, "Putnam's Problems," 318; Hinsley, "Anthropology as Education," 2.

13. Johnson, *History of the World's Columbian Exposition*, 316; Putnam, "Ethnology, Anthropology, Archaeology," 415.

14. Johnson, *History of the World's Columbian Exposition*, 316, 318, 333, 334; Scott, "Village Performance," 53. See Scott for an account of the Eskimo Village, also referred to "as the Husky Village or the Innuit Colony," and for accounts of eighteen other "villages" at the World's Columbian Exposition. See also Hinsley, "Anthropology as Education," 40–46; and Harper, "Inuit at the World's Fair."

15. Cole, *Franz Boas*, 152, quoting FB to parents, April 3, 1891, BFP; Johnson, *History of the World's Columbian Exposition*, 317, 329, 331.

16. Johnson, *History of the World's Columbian Exposition*, 344, quoting Boas; Jacknis, "Northwest Coast Indian Culture," 111–12.

17. Jacknis, "Northwest Coast Indian Culture," 94, quoting Frederic W. Putnam to George R. Davis, Monthly Report for October 1891, 13, WCE Correspondence, FWPP; 103; Cole, *Captured Heritage*, 124, 126, 127.

18. Johnson, *History of the World's Columbian Exposition*, 355, quoting Boas; Cole, *Captured Heritage*, 123, quoting Deans; Jacknis, "Northwest Coast Indian Culture," 97–98.

19. Cole, *Captured Heritage*, 127; Jacknis, "Northwest Coast Indian Culture," 103–4; Cole, *Franz Boas*, 153, 311n3, quoting from Putnam's monthly report on WCE.

20. Dexter, "Putnam's Problems," 316, quoting Putnam to Fletcher, July 25, 1891; 317; Cole, *Franz Boas*, 158, quoting FB to parents, December 31, 1893.

21. Boas, "Kwakiutl of Vancouver Island," 308; Berman, "George Hunt," 438.

22. Smith to FB [April 1894], BP.

23. Smith, "Notes on Eskimo Traditions," 210n1, citing Rink, *Tales and Traditions of the Eskimo*, 56; 210n2; Boas, *Central Eskimo*, 583.

24. FB to Newell, n.d., BP; Boas, "Notes on the Eskimo," 205.

25. Fillmore, "Harmonic Structure," 299–300, 304; McNutt, "John Comfort Fillmore," 66; Fillmore, "What Do Indians Mean to Do," 139; Fillmore to FB, December 24, 1893, BP. See Jacknis "Franz Boas and the Music," 107, for Boas's work with Fillmore in recording Kwakiutl songs at the World's Columbian Exposition.

26. Fillmore, "A Woman's Song," 285, 286.

27. Fillmore to FB, December 29, 1893, BP; FB to Fillmore, January 29, 1894, BP; Fillmore to FB, January 30, 1894, RLZ's bracketed translation, BP; FB to Fillmore, April 16, 1894, BP.

28. Boas, "Songs of the Kwakiutl," 1; Boas, "Social Organization and the Secret Societies," 315; Rohner, *Ethnography of Franz Boas*, 179, quoting FB to Marie, November 15, 1894; Miller, "Songs from the House of the Dead," 247–48.

29. Harris, "Memory and the White City," 3; see also Hinsley and Wilcox, *Coming of Age*, xv; and De Wit, "Building an Illusion," 43, quoting *Chicago Evening Post*, February 10, 1891.

30. Hinsley, "Anthropology as Education," 15; Flinn, *Official Guide*, 27; Dexter, "Putnam's Problems," 317.

31. Dexter, "Putnam's Problems," 317, quoting Higinbotham to Salisbury, February 18, 1896; 324; Hinsley, "Anthropology as Education," 23.

32. Putnam to Samuel A. Crawford, March 7, 1894, BP.

33. Putnam to Crawford, March 7, 1894, BP; Jacknis, "Northwest Coast Indian Culture," 92; Putnam, "Prefatory," x; Putnam to FB, April 30, 1894, BP; Putnam, April 16, 1894, extract from meeting, DA/AMNH.

34. FB to Putnam, February 18, 1894, BP; Cole, *Franz Boas*, 161, quoting Rainey.

35. FB to Putnam, February 18, 1894, BP; Hinsley and Holm, "Cannibal in the National Museum," 311, quoting Chamberlin to Holmes, January 27, 1894.

36. FB to Putnam, February 18, 1894, BP; Cole, *Franz Boas*, 162, quoting FB to parents, February 21, 1894.

37. Cole, *Franz Boas*, 157; FB to Putnam, February 18, 1894, BP.

38. Skiff to FB, February 19, 1894, BP; FB to Skiff, February 19, 1894, BP; Holmes to FB, February 21,1894, BP; McGee to FB, March 21, 1894, BP.

39. Cole, *Franz Boas*, 163, 313n36, quoting Holmes to Skiff, March 31, 1894, FCM; 163, quoting FB to parents, May 11, 1894.

40. FB to Putnam, February 18, 1894, BP; De Wit, "Building an Illusion," 43; Dexter, "Putnam's Problems," 319.

41. Cole, *Franz Boas*, 162.

42. Mark, *Four Anthropologists*, 131, 155, 156, 169n84, citing Holmes, Random Records, VII, 32.

43. Putnam to FB, May 7, 1894, BP; Putnam to FB, May 14, 1894, BP; Cole, *Franz Boas*, 163, 164.

44. Putnam to FB, May 14, 1894, BP; Newell to FB, May 14, 1894, BP; Brinton to FB, May 20, 1894, BP; Baur to FB, June 29, 1894, BRC; Hale to FB, June 22, 1894, BP.

45. FB to McGee, December 5, 1893, BP; Pepper to FB, December 2, 1893, BP; Cornelius Stevenson to FB, December 4, 1893, BP; Cole, *Franz Boas*, 158; Allen to FB, December 13, 1893, BP.

46. See Donaldson to FB, September 7, 1893; July 5, 1895, BP; Donaldson to FB, August 18, 1894, BP; Stocking, *Shaping of American Anthropology*, 219. While referring to the period of time in Chicago following the World's Columbian Exposition, Stocking includes the phrase in quotes—that Boas did not "'take direction' well"—but he does not give a citation and thus it is not clear if these were Stocking's own words or if he was quoting someone who knew of Harper's assessment of Boas.

47. Cole, *Franz Boas*, 158–59; 165, quoting FB to parents, May 22, 1894; Rohner, *Ethnography of Franz Boas*, 164, quoting FB to Marie, October 24, 1894.

48. Cole, *Franz Boas*, 159, 160.

49. Donaldson to FB, May 20, 1894, BP; Cole, *Franz Boas*, 165, quoting Marie to FB, May 16, 1894.

50. Mark, *Four Anthropologists*, 2, 10.

51. Dexter, "Putnam's Problems," 315.

52. Dexter, "Putnam's Problems," 321.

53. Jacknis, "Franz Boas and Exhibits," 76, 82; Hinsley and Holm, "Cannibal in the National Museum," 306–7; Jacknis, "Northwest Coast Indian Culture," 101.

54. Sophie Boas to FB, January 1, 1894, BFP; Sophie Boas to FB, March 30, 1894, BFP; Sophie Boas to FB, November 19, 1894, BFP.

9. Your Orphan Boy

1. FB to Baur, June 15, 1894, BRC; Cole, *Franz Boas*, 167, quoting Marie and FB to parents, [May 1894].

2. Cole, *Franz Boas*, 166, 167, 313n1, quoting FB to parents [May 1894]; Hinsley and Holm, "Cannibal in the National Museum," 311.

3. Donaldson to FB, May 26, 1894, BP; FB to Baur, June 15, 1894, BRC; "Morris K. Jesup," *New York Times*, May 28, 1899, http://query.nytimes.com/mem

/archive-free/pdf?res=9e06e1dc1430e132a2575bc2a9639c94689ed7cf, accessed November 9, 2017; [Jesup] to FB, June 16 [1894], BP; Donaldson to FB, June 14, 1894; Donaldson to FB, June 18, 1894, BP; FB to Bowditch, December 9, 1893, BP.

4. Putnam to FB, August 21, 1893, BP; Stocking, *Shaping of American Anthropology*, 220; Putnam to FB, May 18, 1894, BP; Cole, *Franz Boas*, 168.

5. Boas, "Human Faculty," 4, 5.

6. Stocking, *Shaping of American Anthropology*, 220; Boas, "Human Faculty," 28; see Zumwalt and Willis, *Franz Boas and W. E. B. Du Bois*.

7. Putnam to FB, April 30, 1894, BP; Putnam to FB, May 14, 1894.

8. Putnam to FB, June 25, 1894, BP; Putnam to FB, July 16, 1894, BP.

9. Putnam to Jesup, November 8, 1894, DA/AMNH.

10. Sophie Boas to FB and Marie, December 25, 1893, BFP; FB to Putnam, January 4, 1893, BP; Mark, *Four Anthropologists*, 14, 36.

11. Cole, *Franz Boas*, 169, quoting FB to parents, June 20, 1894; Hale to FB, June 5, 1894, BP; Putnam to FB, July 16, 1894, BP; Harrel to FB, March 25, 1895, BP.

12. Putnam to FB, August 25, 1894, BP; Putnam to FB, August 3, 1894, BP; FB to Putnam, July 25, 1894, BP; Mason to FB, June 5, 1895, BP; Smith to FB, August 2, 1894, BP; see also FB to Powell, July 28, 1895, BP; FB to Goode, June 3, 1895, BP; FB to McGee, July 29, 1895, BP.

13. FB to Putnam, August 28, 1894, BP; Glass, "Frozen Poses," 92.

14. FB to parents, September 21, 1894, BFP; FB to Marie, September 30, 1894, BFP; Rohner *Ethnography of Franz Boas*, 142, quoting FB to Marie, September 23, 1894.

15. Wilson to FB, May 23, 1890, BP; Hale to FB, October 7, 1891, BP; Powell to FB, March 10, 1890, BP; Henshaw to FB, April 9, 1891; Henshaw to FB, July 9, 1890, BP.

16. Wilson to FB, March 21, 1891, BP; Hale to FB, December 19, 1890, BP; Hale to FB, January 12, 1891, BP; FB to Hale, April 16, 1894, BP.

17. Rohner, *Ethnography of Franz Boas*, 133, quoting FB to Marie, September 12, 1894; 134, quoting FB to Marie, September 13, 1894; 144, quoting FB to Marie, September 29, 1894; 152, quoting FB to Marie, October 6, 1894; 152, quoting FB to Marie, October 6, 1894, brackets in Rohner.

18. Boas, "Indians of British Columbia," 232, 233; FB to Marie, November 15, 1894, BFP; Rohner, *Ethnography of Franz Boas*, 177–78, quoting FB to Marie, November 17, 1894.

19. FB to Marie, November 17, 1894, BFP; FB to Marie, November 15, 1894; Rohner, *Ethnography of Franz Boas*, 187, quoting FB to Marie, November 28, 1894.

20. FB to parents, December 11, 1894, BFP; FB to Baur, December 20, 1894, BRC; Rohner, *Ethnography of Franz Boas*, 139, quoting FB to Marie, September 21, 1894.

21. Cole, *Franz Boas*, 172, quoting FB to parents, January 13, 1895; Maclarn, President's Secretary, to FB, January 14, 1895, BP. See Boas, "Anthropometric Observations on the Mission Indians of Southern California."

22. Cole, *Franz Boas*, 172, quoting FB to Marie, December 23, 1894; 173, quoting FB to Marie, December 30, 1894, January 8, 1895; FB to parents, January 24, 1895.

23. Putnam to Jesup, December 8, 1894, DA/AMNH.

24. Donaldson to FB, February 4, 1895, BP; Cole, *Franz Boas*, 199, 173; FB to Marie, September 29, 1894, BFP.

25. McGee to FB, June 11, 1894, BP; Cole, *Franz Boas*, 174, quoting FB to Putnam, May 21, 1894; Goode to FB, February 5, 1895, emphasis in original, BP.

26. FB to Putnam, July 25, 1894, BP; Putnam to FB, February 18, 1895, BP.

27. FB to Putnam, August 28, 1894, BP; Glass, "Frozen Poses," 94, 104; Hinsley and Holm, "Cannibal in the National Museum," 306; Jacknis, *Storage Box of Tradition*, 100, quoting Boas, *Ethnological Collections*, 1900.

28. FB to Goode, March 27, 1895, BP; Cole, *Franz Boas*, 179; FB to Hamburg-American Packet Co., February 21, 1895, BP.

29. Mason to FB, June 5, 1895, BP; FB to McGee, July 29, 1895, BP.

30. FB to Powell, June 19, 1895, BP; McGee to FB, June 14, 1895, BP; Cole, *Franz Boas*, 182; Putnam to FB, June 8, 1895, Telegraphie des Deutschen Reiches, BP; FB to Powell, June 19, 1895, BP; Powell to FB, July 3, 1895, BP.

31. Putnam to FB, June 19, 1895, BP; Cole, *Franz Boas*, 182, quoting Marie to FB, July 26, 1895.

32. Putnam to FB, June 19, 1895, BP.

33. FB to Putnam, July 16, 1895, BP; FB to Powell, July 28, 1895, BP; Boas, *Kathlamet Texts*, 5.

34. Putnam to FB, August 9, 1895, BP.

35. FB to Putnam, September 6, 1895, BP; McGee to FB, August 19, 1895, BP; FB to McGee, August 23, 1895, BP.

36. FB to Jordan, June 19, 1895, BP.

37. Jordan to FB, July 6, 1895, BP; FB to Jordan, October 29, 1895, BP. The United States sued to establish a claim against Stanford's estate for money loaned by the United States to the Central Pacific Railroad Company to aid in construction of the railway. Leland Stanford had been president of the Central Pacific and of its successor, the Southern Pacific Railway Company. In his history of Stanford, Elliott writes, "At the graduation festivities held at the Stanford's Nob Hill estate in San Francisco in May 1895, Mrs. Stanford told those gathered that if the government suit was successful, the university would have to close" (*Stanford University*, 121).

38. Putnam to FB, October 4, 1895, BP; Butler to Low, October 5, 1895, Central Files, Box 318, Folder 1, Columbia University Rare Books and Manuscripts.

39. FB to Putnam, December 9, 1895, draft letter, BP.

40. FB to Putnam, December 9, 1895, BP; Putnam to FB, December 10, 1895, BP; Kennedy, "Philanthropy and Science," 138, quoting Jesup to Putnam, January 23, 1895, AMNH; FB, Anthropological Notes, BP.

41. Low to Jacobi, September 7, 1892, BP; Secretary to the president to Jacobi, February 28, 1894, BP; Cole, *Franz Boas*, 179; Putnam to FB, February 4, 1896, BP; Dexter, "Role of F. W. Putnam in Developing Anthropology," 305, 306, quoting Putnam to Alice Putnam, December 25, 1895.

42. Low to FB, May 5, 1896, BP; Low to FB, May 7, 1896; Putnam to FB, May 9, 1896, BP; Cole, *Franz Boas*, 183.

43. Cattell to FB, May 9, [1896], BP; Jackson to Cattell, May 22, 1896, BP; Jackson to FB, May 30, 1896, BP.

44. Summary of letters of FB to Dr. Baur, FB to Baur, January 3, 1896, BRC; FB to Baur, July 14, 1896, BRC; Topinard to FB, December 21, 1894, BP; Cushing to FB, December 5, 1894, BP; Putnam to FB, March 11, 1895, BP; Fewkes to FB, October 11, 1896, BP.

45. Tylor to FB, December 9, 1889, BP; Hale to FB, October 10, 1890, BP.

46. Rohner, *Ethnography of Franz Boas*, 117, quoting FB to parents, July 7, 1890; 50, quoting FB to parents, October 28, 1886; 122, quoting FB to parents, July 16, 1890; FB to Powell, October 19, 1891, BP.

47. Rohner, *Ethnography of Franz Boas*, 135–36, quoting FB to Marie, September 16, 1894.

10. The Greatest Undertaking

1. Kennedy, "Philanthropy and Science," 111–12; Tylor to FB, October 9, 1890, BP.

2. FB to Bastian, January 5, 1886, BP. Boas had requested a total not to "exceed 9,000 Mark per year." One of the Boas children, who had translated this letter but who was not named, added a note, "This request was denied by Bastian."

3. FB to Tylor, August 15, 1888, BP; FB to Tylor, August 17, 1888, BP.

4. FB to Jesup, December 2, 1898, DA/AMNH; FB to Nuttall, May 15, 1901, BP.

5. Freed, "Capitalist Philanthropy," 9; see also Cole, *Franz Boas*, 31; Brown, *Morris Ketchum Jesup*, 152; Jesup, "Twenty-eighth Annual Report," 24–25.

6. Cole, "'Greatest Thing Undertaken,'" 48, 65, appendix A, quoting Boas to Jesup, January 19, 1897.

7. Cole, "'The Greatest Thing Undertaken,'" 66, appendix B, quoting Boas to Putnam, February 11, 1897; Brown, *Morris Ketchum Jesup*, 169; Vakhtin,

"Franz Boas and the Shaping of the Jesup Expedition," 74, quoting Winser to Putnam, February 12, 1897; Putnam to FB, March 5, 1897, DA/AMNH.

8. "Mr. Jesup's Expedition," *New York Times*, March 13, 1897. "Mr. Jesup's Expedition, To Trace the Origin of the American Indian and the Eskimo," *New York Times*, March 14, 1897.

9. *Science*, "Proposed Explorations," 455–57; Boas, "Jesup-Boas-Expedition," 342, RLZ's translation.

10. Cole, "'The Greatest Thing Undertaken,'" 33, quoting FB to parents, April 9, 1897; FB to Marie, June 3, 1897, BFP; FB to parents, June 3, 1897, BFP.

11. Jonaitis, *Land of the Totem Poles*, 190, quoting Teit to Smith, March 12, 1899; Wickwire, "'They Wanted Me . . . to Help Them,'" 300; Banks, "Comparative Biographies," 48, 96.

12. Rohner, *Ethnography of Franz Boas*, 139, quoting FB to Marie, September 21, 1894; 196, quoting FB to Marie, December 15, 1894; Banks, "Comparative Biographies," 46; FB to Bumpus, April 29, 1902, DA/AMNH.

13. Boas, "Jesup North Pacific Expedition," 78; Rohner, *Ethnography of Franz Boas*, 202–3, quoting FB to Marie, June 5, 1897; quoting FB to Marie, June 6, 1897; FB to Marie, June 6, 1897, BP; Miller, "Songs from the House of the Dead," 140; Zumwalt, "The Personalized Voice in the History of Folklore Scholarship," 21; 54–139-F, IU Archives of Traditional Music.

14. Thom, "Harlan I. Smith's Jesup Fieldwork," 141, 142; Boas, "Jesup North Pacific Expedition," 78.

15. FB to parents, June 15, 1897, BP; Boas, "Jesup North Pacific Expedition," 81; FB to Marie, June 14, 1897, BP.

16. Boas, "Jesup North Pacific Expedition," 81, 82; Rohner, *Ethnography of Franz Boas*, 206, quoting FB to Marie, June 18, 1897; FB to parents, July 12, 1897, BP.

17. FB to Marie and parents, July 21, 1897, BP; Boas, "Jesup North Pacific Expedition," 85.

18. Rohner, *Ethnography of Franz Boas*, 214, quoting FB to Marie and parents, July 21, 1897; 216, quoting FB to Marie and parents, July 30, 1897; Boas, "Jesup North Pacific Expedition," 81; FB to Marie, August 2, 1897, emphasis in original, BP.

19. FB to Marie, August 5, 1896, BP; FB to Marie, August 2, 1897, BP; Rohner, *Ethnography of Franz Boas*, 223, quoting FB to Marie, August 11, 1897; Jonaitis, *Land of the Totem Poles*, 202; Wright, "Edenshaw, Charles"; FB to Marie, August 13, 1897, BP.

20. Thom, "Harlan I. Smith's Jesup Fieldwork," 143; Boas, "Jesup North Pacific Expedition," 85; Rohner, *Ethnography of Franz Boas*, 235, quoting FB to parents, August 30, 1897; 234, quoting FB to Marie, August 31, 1897; 232, FB to Marie, August 28, 1897.

21. FB to parents, August 30, 1897, BP; FB to Marie, August 30, 1897, emphasis in original, BP; FB to Marie, September 1, 1897, BP.

22. FB to Marie, September 5, 1897, emphasis in original, BP.

23. Rohner, *Ethnography of Franz Boas*, 243, quoting FB to Marie, September 13, 1897, emphasis in original; 207, FB to Marie, September 5, 1897, BP; FB to Marie, September 7, 1897, BP; FB to parents, September 2, 1897, BP; FB to Marie, July 6, 1897, BP.

24. Cole, *Franz Boas*, 34.

25. Boas, "Jesup North Pacific Expedition," 89–90; Cole, *Franz Boas*, 34.

26. Cole, *Franz Boas*, 36; FB to Marie, July 5, 1900, BP; FB to Marie, July 23, 1900, BP.

27. FB to Marie, July 10, 1900, BP; FB to Marie, July 14, 1900, BP; FB to Marie, August 7, 1900, BP; Rohner, *Ethnography of Franz Boas*, 251, quoting FB to Marie, July 19, 1900; 262, quoting FB to Sophie Boas, August 16, 1900; FB to Marie, July 23, 1900, BP.

28. FB to Marie, August 15, 1897, BP; Rohner, *Ethnography of Franz Boas*, 231, quoting FB to Marie, August 26, 1897.

29. Vakhtin, "Franz Boas and the Shaping of the Jesup Expedition," 74, quoting Winser to Putnam, February 12, 1897; Cole, "'The Greatest Thing Undertaken by Any Museum,'" 66, appendix B, emphasis in original, quoting Boas to Putnam, February 11, 1897.

30. Hummel, "Berthold Laufer," 101; Cole, "'The Greatest Thing Undertaken by Any Museum,'" 36.

31. FB to Marie, September 5, 1897, BP; Cole, "'The Greatest Thing Undertaken by Any Museum,'" 36; Freed, "Capitalist Philanthropy," 13; Holleben to Jesup, April 28 [1898], BP.

32. Boas, "Jesup North Pacific Expedition," 94.

33. Boas, "Jesup North Pacific Expedition," 94; 97–98, quoting Laufer to FB, March 4, 1899; Andrews to FB, June 13, 1903, DA/AMNH.

34. Freed, Capitalist Philanthropy," 15, quoting Fowke to FB, September 15, 1898.

35. Laufer to FB, April 19, 1899, DA/AMNH; Miller, "Songs from the House of the Dead," 39; Boas, "Jesup North Pacific Expedition," 97, quoting Laufer to FB, March 4, 1899. The April 18, 1899, letter from Laufer to Boas was part of a synopsis made by Boas's secretary, Miss Harriet A. Andrews, to assist Boas in writing his report on the JNPE for the *American Museum Journal* (Andrews to FB, June 13, 1903, DA/AMNH).

36. Boas, "Jesup North Pacific Expedition," 94, 96, 97; Cole, "'The Greatest Thing Undertaken by Any Museum,'" 37; Kendall, "Young Laufer on the Amur," 104.

37. Vakhtin, "Franz Boas and the Shaping of the Jesup Expedition," 80, quoting Boas to Jesup, October 4, 1898, AMNH-L. I follow the guidance of Fitzhugh

and Krupnik for the orthography of Russian names: "The names of the Russian members of the expedition, including Waldemar Bogoras, Waldemar Jochelson, his wife, Dina Jochelson (Jochelson-Brodsky), and Leo [Lev] Shternberg, have been spelled in many different ways in various languages." Fitzhugh and Krupnik follow "the long-established spelling used in their English publications and in major reference bibliographies: Bogoras, Jochelson, Jochelson-Brodsky, and Shternberg," but they note the differences in spelling in some German and Russian sources (Fitzhugh and Krupnik, "Introduction," 11). In like manner, I will use English convention in the spelling of these names, unless I am quoting from a Russian or German source, where the names are rendered as follows: Waldemar, Bogoraz, Jochelson-Brodskaya, and Sternberg.

38. Jochelson to FB, November 3, 1898, BP.

39. Boas, "Jesup North Pacific Expedition," 98; Vakhtin, "Franz Boas and the Shaping of the Jesup Expedition," 78; Freed, "Capitalist Philanthropy," 15, citing Krader, 17.

40. Bogoras to FB, August 18, 1899, BP; Vakhtin, "Franz Boas and the Shaping of the Jesup Expedition," 83, quoting FB to Radloff, April 18, 1899, DA/AMNH; Miller, "Songs from the House of the Dead," 57n19, quoting Boas to Jochelson, March 26, 1900, AMNH; Jochelson to FB, March 15, 1900, BP.

41. Vakhtin, "Franz Boas and the Shaping of the Jesup Expedition," 83, 85. Cole, "'Greatest Thing Undertaken by Any Museum,'" 38, quoting FB to Sophie Boas, March 6, 1900; quoting Marie to Sophie Boas, March 23, 1900; Jochelson to FB, March 15, 1900, BP.

42. Boas, "Jesup North Pacific Expedition," 101; FB Summary of 1900, BP; Vakhtin, "Franz Boas and the Shaping of the Jesup Expedition," 85.

43. FB to Abbe, March 14, 1900, BP. This was the time of the Boxer Revolution and, as Boas noted, all forms of transport were commandeered for the military (Boas, "Jesup North Pacific Expedition," 101–2).

44. Boas, "Jesup North Pacific Expedition," 103, quoting Jochelson.

45. Freed, "Capitalist Philanthropy," 17, quoting Tsar Nicholas II, November 17, 1899, AMNH; Kasten, *The Koryak*, 86; Freed, "Capitalist Philanthropy," 17, citing the English translation of a Russian article published in *Osvobozhdenie, Emancipation*. The article, "Double-Faced Janus," included the letters from Tsar Nicholas II and the circular to the chiefs of the district police. While the author was listed as "Docent," Vakhtin notes that Jochelson wrote the account when he returned to St. Petersburg in January 1903 ("Franz Boas and the Shaping of the Jesup Expedition," 86). Karsten and Dürr note that it was

published by Jochelson anonymously in Stuttgart in 1903. See Kasten, *Jochelson, Bogoras, and Shternberg.*

46. Boas, "Jesup North Pacific Expedition," 109; Freed, "Capitalist Philanthropy," 17, quoting FB to Bumpus, June 29, 1903; quoting FB to Jesup, March 1, 1903.

47. Bogoras to FB, June 19, 1900, BP. This letter had been transcribed, since it was on AMNH stationery.

48. Bogoras to FB, March 22, 1899, BP; Bogoras to FB, June 19, 1900, BP; Bogoras to FB, July 25, 1900, BP; Bogoras to FB, July 26, 1900, BP.

49. Freed, "Capitalist Philanthropy," 17, 19; see also Freed, "Jesup Expedition and its Analogues," 92.

50. Boas, "Jesup North Pacific Expedition," 102, 103, 104, quoting Jochelson; 107, quoting Jochelson; Freed, "Capitalist Philanthropy," 20.

51. Boas, "Jesup North Pacific Expedition," 103, 108–9, quoting Jochelson.

52. Kasten, *The Koryak*, 19.

53. Bogoras to FB, June 18, 1901, BP; Boas, "Jesup North Pacific Expedition," 114–15, quoting Bogoras; 104, quoting Jochelson.

54. Putnam to FB, June 21, 1898, BP; Summary of 1900, BP; FB to Jesup, draft, October 25, 1900, BP.

55. See Vakhtin, "Franz Boas and the Shaping of the Jesup Expedition," 80–81; FB to Putnam, December 1, 1898, DA/AMNH.

56. FB to Jesup, March 9, 1900, BP; FB to Jesup, March 26, 1900, BP.

57. Boas, "Results of the Jesup Expedition," 24.

58. FB to Wissler, October 27, 1913, BP; Oetteking, *Craniology of the North Pacific Coast*, 1.

59. Oetteking, *Craniology of the North Pacific Coast*; Krupnik, "Introduction," 3.

60. Cole, "'Greatest Thing Undertaken by Any Museum,'" 29, quoting Jesup to Osborn, April 30, 1906, AMNH, File 293b; 29, quoting FB to Sophie Boas, March 18, 1909, BFP.

61. FB to Jesup, April 16, 1900, DA/AMNH. See Krupnik, "Jesup Bibliography," 297–316 for the publications of the JNPE and information for the Farrand and Smith contributions.

62. Teit to FB, January 14, 1900, BP; FB to Jesup, April 16, 1900, DA/AMNH.

63. FB to Jesup, December 22, 1900, emphasis in original, DA/AMNH; Bumpus to FB, January 5, 1901, DA/AMNH.

64. Kasten, *The Koryak*, 14; Freed, "Capitalist Philanthropy," 19, quoting, Boas to Bogoras, April 22, 1905, DA/AMNH; quoting Bogoras to FB, May 13, 1905, DA/AMNH; quoting Bogoras to FB, January 10, 1906, BFP; Notes on Museum Work, May 25–December 1905, BP.

65. FB to Jesup, May 23, 1905, BP; FB to Holmes, May 24, 1905, BP; Jesup to FB, May 24, 1905, BP; FB to von den Steinen, May 25, 1905, BP; FB to Bogoras, May 25, 1905, BP.

66. Krupnik, "Jesup Bibliography," 299; Boas, "Jesup North Pacific Expedition," 115; Freed, "Capitalist Philanthropy," 20.

67. Krupnik, "Introduction," 1, 3, parentheses in original.

68. See Krupnik, "Jesup Genealogy," 199.

69. Krupnik, "Introduction," 9; Boas, "Results of the Jesup Expedition," 18, 19, 24.

70. Boas, "Results of the Jesup Expedition," 19.

71. Freed, "Capitalist Philanthropy," 22; Krupnik, "Introduction," 3; Krupnik, "Jesup Bibliography," 298–99.

72. Block, *Museum at the End of the World*, x; Kendall and Krupnik, "Introduction," 4.

73. Krupnik, "Jesup Genealogy," 200, 201; Fitzhugh, "Heritage Anthropology," 295; Krupnik and Fitzhugh, "Introduction," 3; see also Kendall and Krupnik, "Introduction"; Kendall, "Afterword," 103–4; see Kasten, "Jochelson and the Jesup North Pacific Expedition," 7, and *The Koryak*. These works are part of the Kulturstiftung Sibirien. See http://www.kulturstiftung-sibirien.de /bibliothek_E.html, accessed January 6, 2019

74. Draft of FB to Jesup, October 25, 1900, BP.

11. Taking Hold in New York

1. See Darnell, "Development of American Anthropology," 141; Hinsley and Wilcox, *Coming of Age in Chicago*, xxxiv; FB to Hodge, October 16, 1903, BP. See FB to Putnam, January 27, 1906, for reference to the Washington group: "I think the prospects for the next Christmas meeting are also very bad, because the Washington anthropologists are so hard to induce to attend any meetings." Dixon wrote Boas about "the Washington crowd," not one of whom would likely attend the celebration to honor F. W. Putnam on his seventieth birthday (Dixon to FB, March 5, 1909, BP).

2. FB to Kroeber, November 2, 1903, BP; FB to Jesup, December 2, 1898, BP.

3. FB to Bumpus, February 21, 1902, DA/AMNH.

4. FB to von Andrian-Werberg, August 8, 1898, EM's translation, BP.

5. Cole, *Franz Boas*, 213, quoting FB to parents, November 22, 1898, BFP; Low to FB, May 1, 1899, BP.

6. FB to Putnam, December 1, 1898, DA/AMNH.

7. FB to Jesup, December 2, 1898, DA/AMNH. Boas variously referenced Columbia College and Columbia University. The college oversaw undergraduate instruction, and the university, graduate instruction.

8. FB to Jesup, December 31, 1898, DA/AMNH.

9. FB to Seth Low, February 25, 1899, BP.

10. Low to FB, May 1, 1899, BP.

11. Cole, *Franz Boas*, 213, quoting FB to parents, February 17, 1899.

12. Theodora Kroeber, *Alfred Kroeber*, 45, 46, 47, parentheses in original; Steward, "Alfred Louis Kroeber," 1042–43; Steward, "Alfred Kroeber," 196–97; Kroeber, "Franz Boas: The Man," 15.

13. Harper, "Early Arctic Films."

14. Bein to FB, January 27, 1896, BP; Bein to FB, March 3, 1896, BP; Bein to FB, May 24, 1896, BP.

15. Taber to FB, [illegible] June 1896, DA/AMNH. Kenn Harper pointed out this letter from Taber to Boas. Smith to FB, July 13, 1896, BP.

16. Harper, *Minik*, 8; Harper, *Give Me My Father's Body*, 25, quoting FB to Peary, May 24, 1897, DA/AMNH.

17. Harper, *Give Me My Father's Body*, 26.

18. "The Big Meteorite Landed," *New York Times*, October 3, 1897, http://timesmachine.nytimes.com/timesmachine/1897/10/03/105954363.html?pageNumber=24, accessed April 5, 2016; Harper, *Give Me My Father's Body*, 22, 24, 27, quoting Bumpus memo, April 1909, AMNH; Thomas, *Skull Wars*, 79; "Too Warm for Eskimos," *New York Times*, October 11, 1897, https://timesmachine.nytimes.com/timesmachine/1897/10/11/issue.html, accessed August 26, 2018.

19. Autopsies also revealed that the Smith Sound Eskimo had contracted tuberculosis.

20. Harper, *Give Me My Father's Body*, 33; "Going Home to Greenland," illustrated supplement, *New York Tribune*, March 27, 1898, http://chroniclingamerica.loc.gov/lccn/sn83030214/1898–03–27/ed-1/seq-33/, accessed May 17, 2016.

21. Harper, *Give Me My Father's Body*, 41, 173–74, quoting Knud Rasmussen.

22. Harper, *Give Me My Father's Body*, 55, 64, 65.

23. "Going Home to Greenland," *New York Tribune*, March 27, 1898; Zumwalt, *American Folklore Scholarship*, 75, quoting FB to Kroeber, December 10, 1897, UC Archives; Kroeber, "Tales of the Smith Sound Eskimo," 166; Kroeber, "The Eskimo of Smith Sound," 304, 305, 306.

24. Consul-General of Denmark to FB, September 24, 1908, BP; FB to J. Cun, Consul-General of Denmark, October 1, 1908, BP.

25. Harper, *Give Me My Father's Body*, 155, quoting Olsen, 189, quoting Freuchen, *Arctic Adventure*, 1935; 206, 215, 217–19.

26. Harper, *Give Me My Father's Body*, 227.

27. Carpenter, "Dead Truth, Live Myth," 29. Kenn Harper conveyed to me the following information about the inscription on the plaque: "The text of the plaque is in Greenlandic. It reads, 'Nunamingnut uteqihut,' which translates simply as 'They have come home.' This is followed by the names of the four Eskimos with details of their birth and death dates, and the statement, '1897 New York-Imut, 1993 Qaanaamut.'" Of the reception of his work in Greenland, and particularly in Qaanaaq, Harper responds to a query from me: "My book was published in Danish in the 1980s, so bilingual Greenlanders had access to it. . . . It was also republished in another Danish edition, and in 2001 in Greenlandic. I lived in Qaanaaq for two years and was a regular visitor to the community for many years thereafter. The elders of the community were tremendously interested in the story and often thanked me for solving what to them had been the mystery of Minik."

28. FB to Nuttall, May 16, 1901, BP. Boas had met Zelia Nuttall in 1886 when he attended the AAAS meeting in Buffalo just after he had returned to the United States from Germany. Boas and Nuttall also had first met Putnam at this meeting.

29. FB to McGee, April 4, 1901, BP; McGee to FB, April 5, 1901, BP; FB to McGee, April 4, 1901, BP.

30. Langley to FB, May 23, 1901, BP; FB to McGee, May 14, 1901, BP; FB to McGee, June 18, 1902, BP.

31. Memorandum of Understanding between Boas and McGee, January 5, 1899, BP; FB to Low, April 14, 1899, BP; FB to Hodge, January 20, 1899, BP.

32. Lamb, "Story of the Anthropological Society of Washington," 576; American Anthropologist, "American Anthropologist, New Series," 390. See Stocking, "Franz Boas and the Founding of the American Anthropological Association," 1–2.

33. "Memorandum of Agreement between Franz Boas, PhD of the City of New York and Professor W J McGee of the City of Washington, parties of the first part, and G. P. Putnam's Sons . . . Parties of the second part. Signed by Franz Boas, W J McGee and G. P. Putnam," January 5, 1899, BP.

34. Summary of 1899, BP. The summary was compiled by one of his children, who was unnamed and who organized his 1899 professional correspondence.

35. Circular sent out to those interested in reviving the AES, December 12, 1899; BP; FB to Jesup, December 12, 1899, BP. Since McGee lived in Washington, he was not involved in Boas's New York fund raising efforts.

36. Summary of 1900, BP; FB to Hodge, October 11, 1900, BP.

37. FB to Culin, December 17, 1900, BP; FB to Dorsey, December 17, 1900, BP; FB to Hodge, December 21, 1900, BP; FB to Dorsey, January 21, 1902, BP; FB to Culin, November 19, 1901, BP.

38. McGee to FB, February 19, 1902, BP; McGee to FB, January 4, 1902, BP.

39. McGee, per E. R. Smedes, secretary, to FB, January 21, 1902, BP.

40. FB to McGee, January 25, 1902, BP.

41. Hinsley, *Smithsonian and the American Indian*, 234; FB to McGee, January 25, 1902, BP; Stocking, "Franz Boas and the Founding of the American Anthropological Association," 1, 8.

42. Hinsley, *Smithsonian and the American Indian*, 236, 238, 246, quoting McGee.

43. Hinsley, *Smithsonian and the American Indian*, 234. Hinsley is quoting from a personal interview with Klotho McGee Lattin, December 31, 1973.

44. Hinsley, *Smithsonian and the American Indian*, 238, 248, 249. Hinsley is quoting from a draft, Langley to Rathbun, confidential note, February 15, 1902, BAE Records of 1903 Investigation of the Bureau of American Ethnology.

45. McGee to FB, March 28, 1902, emphasis in original, BP. For further reference to external pressures necessitating a speedy decision, see McGee to FB, March 26, 1902, BP, where he wrote that "a certain circumstance transpired," making "early action requisite" for the formation of the society.

46. McGee to FB, February 12, 1902, BP.

47. Stocking, "Franz Boas and the Founding of the American Anthropological Association," 4; FB to McGee, February 28, 1902, BP.

48. Hodge, "W J McGee," 686; McGee to FB, March 10, 1902, BP; FB to McGee, March 25, 1902, BP.

49. McGee, "An American Senate of Science," 278; McGee, "Proposed American Anthropologic Association"; McGee, "Anthropology at Pittsburgh"; Boas, "Foundation of a National Anthropological Society"; FB to McGee, March 27, 1902, BP; FB to McGee, May 15, 1902, BP.

50. Stocking, "Franz Boas and the Founding of the American Anthropological Association," 8; *American Anthropologist*, "American Anthropological Association," 181–82, 184–86; Hodge, "W J McGee," 686; Darnell, "Anthropology and the Development of Folklore Scholarship," 38.

51. Hinsley, *Smithsonian and the American Indian*, 249; Fletcher to FB, October 14, 1902, BP; Darnell, *And Along came Boas*, 126; Langley to FB, October 13, 1902, BP.

52. Hinsley, *Smithsonian and the American Indian*, 215; FB to Gilman, October 29, 1902, BP; Boas, "The Bureau of American Ethnology," 830.

53. Langley, *Annual Report of the Board of Regents of the Smithsonian Institution*, 46; Hinsley, *Smithsonian and the American Indian*, 253; O'Sullivan, "Series VIII: Records Relating to the 1903 Investigation of the BAE," 119.

54. Hinsley and Holm, "Cannibal in the National Museum," 313, 314, quoting BAE-IN: Boas testimony, 922.

55. FB to Schurz, end of November 1903, handwritten draft, BP; Hinsley, *Smithsonian and the American Indian*, 255.

56. Hinsley, *Smithsonian and the American Indian*, 252, quoting the BAE Records of the 1903 Investigation of the Bureau of American Ethnology, "Strictly private memorandum of what I am saying to Mr. Cannon," 255, 261n106, parentheses in original; McGee to FB, June 16, 1903, BP; McGee to FB, August 1, 1903, BP; FB to McGee, August 3, 1903, BP.

57. Brinton to FB, June 4, 1898, BP; McGee to FB, February 19, 1902, BP; McGee to FB, February 27, 1902, BP; FB to McGee, March 25, 1902, BP.

58. Thoresen, "Paying the Piper and Calling the Tune"; Nuttall to FB, May 14, 1901, emphasis in original, BP; FB to Nuttall, May 15, 1901, BP.

59. FB to Nuttall, May 15, 1901, BP.

60. FB to Nuttall, May 15, 1901, BP.

61. Thoresen, "Paying the Piper and Calling the Tune," 264, quoting Nuttall to Hearst, May 19, 1901.

62. Thoresen, "Paying the Piper and Calling the Tune," 264; Zumwalt, *American Folklore Scholarship*, 76, quoting Hearst to Kroeber, July 29, 1901, Kroeber Papers; Kroeber, February 23, 1905, Kroeber Papers.

63. FB to Putnam, May 17, 1902, UC Archives.

64. Putnam to Hearst, May 2, 1902, Bancroft Library. Letter appears on the Bancroft Library website, "Foundations of Anthropology at the University of California," http://bancroft.berkeley.edu/Exhibits/anthro/4establish3.html #item1, accessed June 12, 2016.

Conclusion

1. CV, 2, 6, BFP; FB to parents, May 3, 1877, RLZ's translation, BFP.

2. FB to Marie, August 2, 1897, BP; Reichard, "Franz Boas and Folklore," 55.

3. FB to Toni, EM's translation, October 12, 1876, BFP.

Bibliography

Archives

American Museum of Natural History (AMNH)
> Department of Anthropology (DA/AMNH)

American Philosophical Society (APS)
> Elsie Clews Parsons Papers
> Franz Boas Papers (BP)
> Franz Boas Family Papers (BFP)
> Boas-Rukeyser Collection (BRC)

Bancroft Library, University of California, Berkeley
> Alfred Louis Kroeber Papers
> Robert Lowie Papers

Columbia University Archives (CUA)

Columbia University Oral History Research Office

Columbia University Rare Books and Manuscripts

Johns Hopkins University, Special Collections
> Daniel Coit Gilman Papers

University of California, Berkeley Archives (UC Archives)

Vassar College
> Ruth Benedict Papers

Published Sources

Aberdeen, Ishbel. "The Midway Plaisance." In *Rand, McNally's & Co.'s Handbook of the World's Columbian Exposition*, 212–20. Chicago: Rand, McNally, 1893. https://play.google.com/books/reader?id=TFU6AAAAMAAJ&printsec=frontcover&output=reader&authuser=0&hl=en&pg=GBS.PA3, accessed August 13, 2014.

American Anthropologist. "American Anthropologist, New Series." *American Anthropologist* 11, no. 12 (1898): 389–90.

———. "The American Anthropological Association." *American Anthropologist* 5 (1903): 178–90.

Appelbaum, Stanley. *The Chicago World's Fair of 1893: A Photographic Record.* New York: Dover, 1980.

Baick, John S. "Reorienting Culture: New York Elites and the Turn Toward East Asia." PhD diss., New York University, 1998.

Baker, Lee D. *From Savage to Negro: Anthropology and the Construction of Race, 1896–1954.* Berkeley: University of California Press, 1998.

Banks, Judith Judd. "Comparative Biographies of Two British Columbian Anthropologists: Charles Hill-Tout and James A. Teit." Master's thesis, University of British Columbia, 1970.

Barnett, Ferdinand Lee. "The Reason Why." In *The Reason Why the Colored American Is Not in the World's Columbian Exposition,* edited by Robert W. Rydell. Urbana and Chicago: University of Illinois Press, [1893] 1999. http://digital.library.upenn.edu/women/wells/exposition/exposition.html, accessed August 18, 2014.

Barr, William. "The Expeditions of the First International Polar Year." *The Arctic Institute of North America,* Technical Paper 29 (1985). Calgary: University of Calgary.

Bell, Michael J. "William Wells Newell and the Foundation of American Folklore Scholarship." *Journal of the Folklore Institute* 10 (1973): 7–21.

Benedict, Burton. "Rituals of Representation: Ethnic Stereotypes and Colonized Peoples at World's Fairs." In *Fair Representations: World's Fairs and the Modern World,* edited by Robert W. Rydell and Nancy Gwinn, 28–61. Amsterdam: VU University Press, 1994.

Benedict, Burton, and Marjorie M. Dobkin. *The Anthropology of World's Fairs: San Francisco's Panama Pacific International Exposition of 1915.* Berkeley: Robert H. Lowie Museum of Anthropology, Scolar, 1983.

Berman, Judith. "George Hunt and the Kwak'wala Texts." *Anthropological Linguistics* 36 (1994): 482–514.

———. "Hunt, George (Xawe, 'Maxwalagalis, K'ixitasu, Nolq'oḷala)." In *Dictionary of Canadian Biography,* vol. 16. University of Toronto/Université Lavla, 2003, www.biographi.ca/en/bio/hunt_george_16E.html, accessed December 31, 2018.

Bieder, Robert E., and Thomas G. Tax. "From Ethnologists to Anthropologists: A Brief History of the American Ethnological Society." In *American Anthropology: The Early Years,* edited by John V. Murra, 11–22. 1974 Proceedings of the American Ethnological Society. St. Paul MN: West, 1976.

Bland, Richard L. "Bernard Fillip Jacobsen and Three Nuxalk Legends." *Journal of Northwest Coast Anthropology* 46, no. 2 (2012): 143–66. http://northwestanthropology.com/article_files/46(2)%20website.pdf, accessed May 26, 2015.

Block, Alexia, and Laurel Kendall. *The Museum at the End of the World: Encounters in the Russian Far East*. Philadelphia: University of Pennsylvania Press, 2004.

Blumenthal, W. Michael. *The Invisible Wall: Germans and Jews, A Personal Exploration*. Washington DC: Counterpoint, 1998.

Boas, Franz. "Alexander Francis Chamberlain." *Journal of American Folklore* 27 (1914): 326–27.

———. "The American Ethnological Society." *Science* 97 (1943): 7–8.

———. "An Anthropologist's Credo." *Nation* 147 (August 1938): 201–4.

———. "The Anthropology of the North American Indian." In *Memoirs of the International Congress of Anthropology*, edited by C. Staniland Wake, 37–49. Chicago: Schulte, 1894.

———. "Anthropometrical Observations on the Mission Indians of Southern California." *Proceedings of the American Association for the Advancement of Science* 44 (1895): 261–69.

———. "Baffin-Land: Geographische Ergebnisse einer in den Jahren 1883 und 1884 ausgeführten Forschungreise. Mit zwei Karten und neun Skizzen im Text" (Baffin Land: Geographical results of a research trip conducted in 1883 and 1884. With two maps and nine sketches in the text). *Petermanns Mitteilungen* supplement 80 (1885): 1–100.

———. *Beiträge zur Erkenntniss der Farbe des Wassers* (Contributions to the knowledge of the color of water). PhD diss., Christian-Albrecht-Universität in Kiel, 1881.

———. "Ein Beweis des Talbot'schen Satzes und Bemerkungen zu einigen aus demselben gezogenen Folgerungen" (A proof of Talbot Principles and remarks on some conclusions drawn from it). *Poggendorffs Annalen der Physik und Chemie* 16 (1882): 359–62.

———. "Boas' Introduction." In *The Ethnography of Franz Boas: Letters and Diaries of Franz Boas Written on the Northwest Coast from 1886 to 1931*, editor Ronald P. Rohner, 3–13. Translated by Hedy Parker. Originally published as "Über Seine Reisen in Britisch-Columbien" (About his travels in British-Columbia). *Verhandlungen der Gesellschaft für Erdkunde zu Berlin* 16 (1889): 257–68. Chicago: University of Chicago Press, 1969.

———. "The Bureau of American Ethnology." *Science* 16 (1902): 828–31.

———. *The Central Eskimo*. 1888. Sixth Annual Report of the Bureau of Ethnology. Washington DC: Bureau of American Ethnology. Facsimile of the first edition, with an introduction by Henry B. Collins. Lincoln: University of Nebraska Press, 1964.

———. "Der Eskimo-Dialekt des Cumberland-Sundes" (The Eskimo dialect of the Cumberland Sound). *Mittheilungen der Anthropologischen Gesellschaft in Wien* 24, no. 14 (1894): 97–114.

———. "The Eskimo of Baffin Land and Hudson Bay: from notes collected by George Comer, James S. Mutch, and E. J. [Edmund James] Peck." *Bulletin of the American Museum of Natural History* 15, article 1 (1901): 1–370. New York: American Museum of Natural History. http://digitallibrary.amnh.org/discover?scope=%2F&query= Boas%2C+Franz+the+Eskimo+of+Baffin+Land&submit=Go.

———. *Eskimo Story (Written for my Children): My Arctic Expedition 1883–1884,* edited by Norman Boas. Mystic CN: Seaport Autograph, 2007.

———. "Eskimo Tales and Songs." *Journal of American Folklore* 10 (1894): 109–15.

———. "Facial Paintings of the Indians of Northern British Columbia." *The Jesup North Pacific Expedition,* Vol. 1, 13–24. *Memoirs of the American Museum of Natural History.* New York: G. P. Putnam's, 1898–1900.

———. "The Foundation of a National Anthropological Society." *Science* 15 (1902): 804–9.

———. "Franz Boas." In *I Believe: The Personal Philosophies of Certain Eminent Men and Women of Our Time,* edited by Clifton Fadiman, 17–29. New York: Simon & Schuster, 1939.

———. "The Game of Cat's Cradle." *Internationales Archiv für Ethnographie* 1 (1888): 229–30.

———. "The Game of Cat's Cradle." *Internationales Archiv für Ethnographie* 2 (1889): 52.

———, ed. *Handbook of American Indian Languages.* Part 1. Smithsonian Institution, Bureau of American Ethnology, Bulletin 40. Washington DC: Government Printing Office, 1911.

———. "Human Faculty as Determined by Race." *Proceedings of the American Association for the Advancement of Science* 43 (1894): 3–29.

———. "Im Eise des Nordens. Kikkerton, 14 September 1883" (In the ice of the North. Kikkerton, 14 September 1883). *Berliner Tageblatt,* First Supplement, Sunday, November 4, 1883, Vol. 12, No. 517, 4–5.

———. "Die Eskimo des Baffinlandes" (The Eskimos of Baffin Land). *Verhandlungen des fünften Deutschen Geographentages zu Hamburg am 9, 10 und 11.* 101–12. April 1885.

———. "The Indians of British Columbia." *Journal of the American Geographical Society of New York* 28 (1896): 229–43.

————. "Die Jesup-Boas-Expedition nach Nordwest-Amerika" (The Jesup-Boas-expedition to northwest America). *Globus* 71, no. 21 (1897): 342.

————. "The Jesup North Pacific Expedition." *American Museum Journal* 3, no. 5 (1903): 73–119.

————. "The Jesup North Pacific Expedition, Introduction." *The Jesup North Pacific Expedition, Memoirs of the American Museum of Natural History, Anthropology* Vol. 1, 3–6. New York: G. P. Putnam, 1898.

————. "A Journey in Cumberland Sound and on the West Shore of Davis Strait in 1883 and 1884." *Journal of the American Geographical Society of New York* 16 (1884): 242–72.

————. *Kathlamet Texts.* Bulletin 26, Smithsonian Institution Bureau of American Ethnology. Washington DC: Government Printing Office, 1901.

————. "The Kwakiutl of Vancouver Island." *The Jesup North Pacific Expedition*, Vol. 5, Part 2, 301–522. Leiden: E. J. Brill, 1909.

————. "The Language of the Bilhoola of British Columbia." *Science* 7, no. 161 (1886): 218.

————. "Melville's Plan of Reaching the North Pole" (letter to the editor). *Science* 5, no. 112 (1885): 247–48.

————. "The Mythology of the Bella Coola Indians." *The Jesup North Pacific Expedition: Memoirs of the American Museum of Natural History, Anthropology* Vol. 1, 25–127. New York: G. P. Putnam's, 1898.

————. "Notes on the Eskimo of Port Clarence, Alaska." *Journal of American Folklore* 7 (1894): 205–8.

————. "Operations of the Expedition in 1897." *The Jesup North Pacific Expedition: Memoirs of the American Museum of Natural History, Anthropology* Vol. 1, 7–11. New York: G. P. Putnam's, 1898.

————. "Psychological Problems in Anthropology." Lecture delivered at the Twentieth Anniversary of Clark University, September 1909. *American Journal of Psychology* 21, no. 3 (1910): 371–84.

————. "Religious Beliefs of the Central Eskimo." *Popular Science Monthly* 57 (October 1900): 624–31.

————. "The Results of the Jesup Expedition, Opening Address at the 16th International Congress of the Americanists, Vienna 1908." In *Gateways: Exploring the Legacy of the Jesup North Pacific Expedition, 1897–1902*, edited by Igor Krupnik and William W. Fitzhugh, 17–24. Translated by Saskia Wrausmann. Washington DC: Smithsonian, 2001.

————. "Rudolf Virchow's Anthropological Work." *Science* 16 (1902): 441–45.

———. "Die Sagen der Baffin-Land-Eskimos" (The tales of the Baffin Land Eskimos). *Verhandlungen der Berliner Gesellschaft für Anthropologie, Ethnologie und Urgeschichte* 17 (1885): 161–66.

———. "Second Report on the Eskimo of Baffin Land and Hudson Bay, from Notes Collected by Captain George Comer, Captain James S. Mutch, and Rev. E. J. Peck." *Bulletin of the American Museum of Natural History* 15, no. 2 (1907): 371–570. New York: American Museum of Natural History.

———. "Sketch of the Kwakiutl Language." *American Anthropologist* 2 (1900): 708–21.

———. "The Social Organization and the Secret Societies of the Kwakiutl Indians, based on Personal Observations and on Notes made by Mr. George Hunt." *Report of the U.S. National Museum for 1895*, 311–738. Washington DC: U.S. Government Printing Office, 1897.

———. "Songs of the Kwakiutl Indians." *Internationales Archiv für Ethnographie* 9 (1896): 1–9.

———. "The Study of Geography." *Science* 9 (1887): 137–41.

———. "Über die ehemalige Verbreitung der Eskimos im arktisch-amerikanischen Archipel" (About the former spread of the Eskimos in the Arctic-American archipelago). *Zeitschrift der Gesellschaft für Erdkunde zu Berlin* 18, no. 2 (1883): 118–36.

———. "Über eine neue Form des Gesetzes der Unterschiedsschwelle" (A new form of the law of the difference threshold). *Pflüger's Archiv* 26 (1881): 493–500.

———. "Reisen in Britisch-Columbien" (Travels in British Columbia). *Verhandlungen der Gesellschaft für Erdkunde zu Berlin* 16 (1889): 257–68. http://archive.org/stream/verhandlungende17berlgoog /verhandlungende17berlgoog_djvu.txt, accessed February 7, 2018.

———. "Zur Ethnologie Britisch-Kolumbiens" (On the ethnology of British Columbia). *Petermanns Mitteilungen* 33, no. 5 (1887): 129–33. Gotha: Justus Perthes.

———, and George Hunt. *Kwakiutl Texts: Jesup North Pacific Expedition*. Vol. 3. Memoirs of the American Museum of Natural History. Leiden: E. J. Brill, 1905.

———, and Henrik Rink. "Eskimo Tales and Songs." *Journal of American Folklore* 2 (1889): 123–32.

Boas, Norman Francis. *Franz Boas, 1858–1942: An Illustrated Biography*. Mystic CT: Seaport Autographs, 2004.

———, and Barbara Linton Meyer. *Alma Farm: An Adirondack Meeting Place*. Mystic CT: Boas & Meyer, 1999.

———, and Doris W. Boas, ed. *Arctic Expedition 1883–1884: Translated German Newspaper Accounts of My Life with the Eskimos*. Translated by Rita Terris and Thomas Huber. Mystic CT: Norman Boas, 2009.

Bolz, Peter, and Hans-Ulrich Sanner. *Native American Art: The Collections of the Ethnological Museum Berlin.* Seattle: University of Washington Press, 1999.

Brilling, Bernhard. "Die Familiennamen der Juden in Westfalen" (The surnames of the Jews in Westphalia). *Rheinisch-Westfälische Zeitschrift für Volkskunde* 5, nos. 3–4 (1958): 133–62.

———. "Die Familiennamen der Juden in Westfalen" (The surnames of the Jews in Westphalia). *Rheinisch-Westfälische Zeitschrift für Volkskunde* 6, nos. 1–2 (1959): 91–99.

———. "Die Vorfahren des Professors Franz Boas" (The ancestors of Professor Franz Boas). *Mitteilungen des Mindener Geschichts und Museumsvereins* 38 (1966): 103–12.

Browman, David L., and Stephen Williams. *Anthropology at Harvard: A Biographical History, 1790–1940.* Cambridge MA: Peabody Museum Press, 2013.

Brown, William A. *Morris Ketchum Jesup: A Character Sketch.* New York: Charles Scribner's Sons, 1910.

Carpenter, Edmund. "Dead Truth, Live Myth." *Native American Studies* 11, no. 2 (1997): 27–29.

Chamberlain, Alexander. *The Language of the Mississaga Indians of the Skūgog: A Contribution to the Linguistics of the Algonkian Tribes of Canada.* Philadelphia: MacCalla, 1892.

Clark, William. *Academic Charisma and the Origins of the Research University.* Chicago: University of Chicago Press, 2006.

Clark University. *Clark University, Worcester, Mass. Register and Second Official Announcement.* Worcester: Clark University, 1890.

———. *Clark University, Worcester, Mass. Register and Third Official Announcement.* Worcester: Clark University. 1891.

Cohen, Gerson D. "German Jewry as Mirror of Modernity: Introduction to the Twentieth Volume." *Leo Baeck Institute Year Book* 20 (1975): ix–xxxi.

Cole, Douglas. *Captured Heritage, The Scramble for Northwest Coast Artifacts.* Norman: University of Oklahoma Press, 1985.

———. "Franz Boas and the Bella Coola in Berlin." *Northwest Anthropological Research Notes* 16, no. 2 (1982): 115–24.

———. *Franz Boas: The Early Years, 1858–1906.* Seattle: University of Washington Press, 1999.

———. "Franz Boas, Morris Jesup, and the North Pacific Expedition." In *Gateways: Exploring the Legacy of the Jesup North Pacific Expedition, 1897–1902,* edited by Igor Krupnik and William W. Fitzhugh, 29–70. Washington DC: Smithsonian, 2001.

———. "The Value of a Person Lies in his *Herzensbildung*, Franz Boas' Baffin Island Letter-Diary, 1883–1884." In *Observers Observed*, edited by George W. Stocking Jr., 13–52. Madison: University of Wisconsin Press, 1983.

———, and Ludger Müller-Wille. "Franz Boas' Expedition to Baffin Island, 1883–1884." *Études/Inuit/Studies* 8, no. 1 (1984): 37–63.

Cole, Jonathan. *The Great American University*. New York: Public Affairs, 2009.

Cuddihy, John Murray. *The Ordeal of Civility: Freud, Marx, Lévi-Strauss, and the Jewish Struggle with Modernity*. Boston: Beacon, 1987.

Darnell, Regna. *And Along Came Boas: Continuity and Revolution in Americanist Anthropology*. Amsterdam: John Benjamins, 2000.

———. "Anthropology and the Development of Folklore Scholarship: 1890–1920." *Journal of the Folklore Institute* 10, nos. 1–2 (1973): 23–39.

———. "The Development of American Anthropology, 1879–1920: From the Bureau of American Ethnology to Franz Boas." PhD diss., University of Pennsylvania, 1970.

———, ed. *The Franz Boas Papers, Volume 1: Franz Boas as Public Intellectual—Theory, Ethnography, Activism*, edited by Regina Darnell, Michelle Hamilton, Robert L. A. Hancock, and Joshua Smith. Lincoln: University of Nebraska Press, 2015.

De Wit, Wim. "Building an Illusion: The Design of the World's Columbian Exposition." In *Grand Illusions: Chicago's World's Fair of 1893*, edited by Neil Harris, Wim de Wit, James Gilbert, and Robert W. Rydell, 41–98. Chicago: Chicago Historical Society, 1994.

Dexter, Ralph W. "Putnam's Problems Popularizing Anthropology." *American Scientist* 54, no. 3 (1966): 315–32.

———. "The Role of F. W. Putnam in Developing Anthropology at the American Museum of Natural History." *Curator* 19 (1976): 303–10.

———. "The Role of F. W. Putnam in Founding the Field Museum." *Curator* 13 (1970): 21–26.

Dosick, Wayne. *Living Judaism*. San Francisco: HarperCollins, 1998.

Ewald, Grothe. "Model or Myth? The Constitution of Westphalia of 1807 and Early German Constitutionalism." *German Studies Review* 28, no. 1 (2005): 1–19.

Fadiman, Clifton, ed. *I Believe: The Personal Philosophies of Certain Eminent Men and Women of Our Time*. New York: Simon & Schuster, 1939.

Fagin, Nancy L. "Closed Collections and Open Appeals: The Two Anthropology Exhibits at the Chicago World's Columbian Exposition of 1893." *Curator* 27 (1984): 255–63.

Fenton, William N. "Hale, Horatio Emmons." In *Dictionary of Canadian Biography*. Vol. 12. Toronto: University of Toronto/Université Laval, 1990. http://biographi.ca/en/bio/hale_horatio_emmons_12e.html, accessed August 25, 2013.

Fillmore, John Comfort. "The Harmonic Structure of Indian Music." *American Anthropologist* 1 (1899): 297–318.

———. "What Do Indians Mean to Do When They Sing, and How Far Do They Succeed?" *Journal of American Folklore* 8 (1895): 138–42.

———. "A Woman's Song of the Kwakiutl Indians." *Journal of American Folklore* 6 (1893): 285–90.

Fishberg, Maurice, J. Walter Fewkes, N. H. Winchell, Berthold Laufer, and David I. Bushnell Jr. "The Boas Anniversary." *American Anthropologist* 9, no. 3 (1907): 646–62.

Fitzhugh, William W. "Foreword." In *Gateways: Exploring the Legacy of the Jesup North Pacific Expedition, 1897–1902*, edited by Igor Krupnik and William W. Fitzhugh, xiii–xiv. Washington DC: Smithsonian, 2001.

———. "Heritage Anthropology in the 'Jesup-2' Era, Exploring North Pacific Cultures through Cooperative Research." In *Constructing Cultures Then and Now: Celebrating Franz Boas and the Jesup North Pacific Expedition*, edited by Laurel Kendall and Igor Krupnik, 286–305. Washington DC: Arctic Studies Center, National Museum of Natural History, Smithsonian, 2003.

———, and Aron Crowell. *Crossroads of Continents: Cultures of Siberia and Alaska*. Washington DC: Smithsonian, 1988.

———, and Igor Krupnik. "Introduction." In *Gateways: Exploring the Legacy of the Jesup North Pacific Expedition, 1897–1902*, edited by Igor Krupnik and William W. Fitzhugh, 1–16. Washington DC: Smithsonian, 2001.

Flinn, John J., comp. *Official Guide to the World's Columbian Exposition*. Chicago: World's Columbian Exposition, 1893.

Freed, Stanley A. *Anthropology Unmasked: Museums, Science, and Politics in New York City*. Vol. I: The Putnam-Boas Era, and Vol. II: The Wissler Years. Wilmington OH: Orange Frazer, 2012.

———, Ruth S. Freed, and Laila Williamson. "Capitalist Philanthropy and Russian Revolutionaries: The Jesup North Pacific Expedition (1897–1902)." *American Anthropologist* 90 (1988): 7–24.

———. "The Jesup Expedition and its Analogues: A Comparison." In *Constructing Cultures Then and Now: Celebrating Franz Boas and the Jesup North Pacific Expedition*, edited by Laurel Kendall and Igor Krupnik, 89–101. Washington DC: Arctic Studies Center, National Museum of Natural History, Smithsonian, 2003.

Freud, Sigmund. *An Autobiographical Study: The International Psycho-Analytical Library*. Edited by Ernest Jones. No. 26. London: Hogarth, 1946.

———, C. G. Jung, William Stern, H. S. Jennings, Franz Boas, Adolf Meyer, and E. B. Titchener. *Lectures Delivered Before the Department of Psychology, as Part of the Celebration of the Twentieth Anniversary of the Opening of Clark Univer-*

sity, September 1909. Part I. Reprinted from *American Journal of Psychology* 21, nos. 2–3 (1910).

Geiger, Robert L. *To Advance Knowledge: The Growth of American Research Universities, 1900–1940*. New Brunswick NJ: Transaction, 2004.

Gilbert, James. "Fixing the Image: Photography at the World's Columbian Exposition." In *Grand Illusions: Chicago's World's Fair of 1893*, edited by Neil Harris, Wim de Wit, James Gilbert, and Robert W. Rydell, 99–140. Chicago: Chicago Historical Society, 1994.

Glass, Aaron. "Frozen Poses: Hamat'sa Dioramas, Recursive Representation, and the Making of a Kwakwaka'wakw Icon." In *Photography, Anthropology and History: Expanding the Frame*, edited by Christopher Morton and Elizabeth Edwards, 89–116. Farnham, England: Ashgate, 2009.

Glick, Leonard B. "Types Distinct from Our Own: Franz Boas on Jewish Identity and Assimilation." *American Anthropologist* 84 (1982): 545–65.

Goodspeed, Thomas Wakefield. *A History of the University of Chicago: The First Quarter Century*. Chicago: University of Chicago Press, 1916.

Graff, Rebecca S. "Dream City, Plaster City: Worlds' Fairs and the Gilding of American Material Culture." *International Journal of Historical Archaeology* 16, no. 4 (2012): 696–716. DOI 10.1007/s10761–012–0198–6, accessed August 14, 2018.

Green, Fitzhugh. *Peary, The Man Who Refused to Fail*. New York: G. P. Putnam's Sons, 1926.

Gruber, Jacob W. "Horatio Hale and the Development of American Anthropology." *Proceedings of the American Philosophical Society* 111 (1967): 5–37.

Haberland, Wolfgang. "Nine Bella Coolas in Germany." In *Indians and Europe: An Interdisciplinary Collection of Essays*, edited by Christian F. Feest, 337–74. Lincoln: University of Nebraska Press, 1999.

Hall, G. Stanley. "Contemporary University Problems." *Twenty-Fifth Anniversary of Clark University, Worcester, Mass. 1889–1914*, 14–30. Worcester: Clark University Press, 1914.

——— . *Life and Confessions of a Psychologist*. New York: D. Appleton, 1927.

Harper, Kenn. "The Collaboration of James Mutch and Franz Boas, 1883–1922." *Études/Inuit/Studies* 32, no. 2 (2008): 53–71.

——— . "Collecting at a Distance: The Boas-Mutch-Comer Collaboration." In *Early Inuit Studies: Themes and Transitions, 1850s-1980s*, edited by Igor Krupnik, 89–110. Washington DC: Smithsonian, 2016.

——— . *Give Me My Father's Body: The Life of Minik the New York Eskimo*. South Royalton, VT: Steerforth, 2000 [1986].

——— . "Inuit at the World's Fair." In *In Those Days: Collected Writings on Arctic History. Inuit Lives*, Book 1, 97–108. Iqaluit: Inhabit Media, 2013.

————. *Minik, the New York Eskimo.* Hanover NH: Steerforth, 2017.

————. "Nancy Columbia: Inuit Star of Stage, Screen and Camera." *Above & Beyond* 26, no 3 (2014): 23–29. http://arcticjournal.ca/nancy-columbia-inuit -star-of-stage-screen-and-camera/, accessed March 20, 2016.

————, and Russell Potter. "Early Arctic Films of Nancy Columbia and Esther Eneutseak." *NIMROD: The Journal of the Ernest Shackleton Autumn School* 4 (October 2010): 48–105.

Harris, Neil. "Memory and the White City." In *Grand Illusions: Chicago's World's Fair of 1893,* edited by Neil Harris, Wim de Wit, James Gilbert, and Robert W. Rydell, 1–40. Chicago: Chicago Historical Society, 1994.

————, Wim de Wit, James Gilbert, and Robert W. Rydell, editors. *Grand Illusions: Chicago's World's Fair of 1893.* Chicago: Chicago Historical Society, 1994.

Hellman, Geoffrey T. "The American Museum, II." *New Yorker* 44 (December 7, 1968): 65–136.

Herskovits, Melville J. "Some Further Notes on Franz Boas' Arctic Expedition." *American Anthropologist* 59 (1957): 112–16.

Herzig, Arno. *Abraham Jacobi. Die Entwicklung zum sozialistischen und revolutionären Demokraten* (Abraham Jacobi. The development of the socialist and revolutionary democrats). Minden, Germany: Mindener Geschichtsverein, 1980.

————. *Jüdisches Leben in Minden und Petershagen* (Jewish life in Minden and Petershagen). Mindener Beiträge 31. Minden, Germany: Mindener Geschichtsverein, 2012.

Hinsley, Curtis M., Jr. "Anthropology as Education and Entertainment: Frederic Ward Putnam at the World's Fair." In *Coming of Age in Chicago: The 1893 World's Fair and the Coalescence of American Anthropology,* edited by Curtis M. Hinsley and David R. Wilcox, 1–77. Lincoln: University of Nebraska Press, 2016.

————. *The Smithsonian and the American Indian: Making a Moral Anthropology in Victorian America.* Washington DC: Smithsonian, 1981.

————, and Bill Holm. "A Cannibal in the National Museum: The Early Career of Franz Boas in America." *American Anthropologist* 78 (1976): 306–16.

————, and David R. Wilcox, editors. *Coming of Age in Chicago: The 1893 World's Fair and the Coalescence of American Anthropology.* Lincoln: University of Nebraska Press, 2016.

Hobsbawm, Eric. "Mass-Producing Traditions: Europe, 1870–1914." In *The Invention of Tradition,* edited by Eric Hobsbawm and Terence Ranger, 263–307. Cambridge: Cambridge University Press, 1988.

Hodge, Frederick W. "W J McGee." *American Anthropologist* 14 (1912): 683–87.

Holmes, William H. "The World's Fair Congress of Anthropology." *American Anthropologist* 6, no. 4 (1893): 423–34.

Hough, Walter. "Otis Tufton Mason." *American Anthropologist* 10 (1908): 661–67.

Hummel, Arthur W. "Berthold Laufer: 1874–1934." *American Anthropologist* 38 (1936): 101–11.

Jacknis, Ira. "Franz Boas and Exhibits: On the Limitations of the Museum Method of Anthropology." In *Objects and Others, Essays on Museums and Material Culture*, editor George W. Stocking Jr., 75–111. History of Anthropology, Vol. 3. Madison: University of Wisconsin Press, 1985.

———. "Franz Boas and the Music of the Northwest Coast Indians." In *Constructing Cultures Then and Now: Celebrating Franz Boas and the Jesup North Pacific Expedition*, edited by Laurel Kendall and Igor Krupnik, 105–22. Washington DC: Arctic Studies Center, National Museum of Natural History, Smithsonian, 2003.

———. "Franz Boas and Photography." *Studies in Visual Communication* 10, no. 1 (1984): 2–60.

———. "George Hunt, Collector of Indian Specimens." In *Chiefly Feasts: The Enduring Kwakiutl Potlatch*, edited by Aldona Jonaitis, 177–224. New York: American Museum of Natural History, 1991.

———. "Northwest Coast Indian Culture and the World's Columbian Exposition." In *Columbian Consequences*, edited by David Hurst Thomas, 91–118. Vol. 3. Washington DC: Smithsonian, 1991.

———. *The Storage Box of Tradition*. Washington DC: Smithsonian, 2002.

Jarausch, Konrad H. *Students, Society, and Politics in Imperial Germany: The Rise of Academic Illiberalism*. Princeton: Princeton University Press, 1982.

Jesup, Morris K. "Twenty-eighth Annual Report." *The American Museum of History Annual Report of the President for the Year 1896*, 7–31. New York: William C. Martin, 1897.

Jochelson, Vladimir. *The Yukaghir and the Yukaghirized Tungas*. Anthropological Papers of the American Museum of Natural History. Vol. 9. New York: American Museum of Natural History, 1926.

Johnson, Rossiter, ed. *A History of the World's Columbian Exposition Held in Chicago in 1893*. Vol. 2: Departments. New York: D. Appleton, 1897. https://play.google.com/books/reader?id=qyecaqaamaaj&printsec=frontcover&output=reader&authuser=0&hl=en&pg=gbs.pa315, accessed August 16, 2014.

Jonaitis, Aldona. *From the Land of the Totem Poles: The Northwest Coast Indian Art Collection at the American Museum of Natural History*. Seattle: University of Washington Press, 1988.

Jung, Carl Gustav. *Memories, Dreams, Reflections*. New York: Pantheon, 1963.

Jungnickel, Christa. *Theoretical Mastery of Nature: Theoretical Physics from Ohm to Einstein*. Vol. 1. Chicago: University of Chicago Press, 1990.

Kampe, Norbert. "Jews and Anti-Semites at Universities in Imperial Germany (I), Jewish Students: Social History and Social Conflict." In *Leo Baeck Institute Yearbook* 30, no. 1 (1985): 357–94.

Kan, Sergei. *Lev Shternberg: Anthropologist, Russian Socialist, Jewish Activist*. Lincoln: University of Nebraska Press, 2009.

———. "The 'Russian Bastian' and Boas: Or Why Shternberg's 'The Social Organization of the Gilyak' Never Appeared Among the Jesup Expedition Publications." In *Gateways: Exploring the Legacy of the Jesup North Pacific Expedition, 1897–1902*, edited by Igor Krupnik and William W. Fitzhugh, 217–51. Washington DC: Smithsonian, 2001.

Kasten, Erich, and Michael Dürr, eds. "Jochelson and the Jesup North Pacific Expedition: A New Approach in the Ethnography of the Russian Far East." In *The Koryak by Waldemar Jochelson*, 9–34. By Waldemar Jochelson. Verlag der Kulturstiftung Sibirien, SEC. Nordersted: Books on Demand GMBH, 2016.

———. *The Koryak*. Part I: Religion and Myths, and Part II: Material Culture and Social Organization. By Waldemar Jochelson. Verlag der Kulturstiftung Sibirien, SEC Publications. Nordersted: Books on Demand GMBH, 2016.

Kendall, Laurel. "Afterword: The Present and Future of the Jesup Expedition Photographs." In *Drawing Shadows to Stone: The Photography of the Jesup North Pacific Expedition, 1897–1902*, edited by Laurel Kendall, Barbara Mathé, and Thomas Ross Miller, 102–4. New York: American Museum of Natural History.

———. "Young Laufer on the Amur." In *Crossroads of Continents: Cultures of Siberia and Alaska*, edited by William S. Fitzhugh and Aron Crowell, 104. Washington DC: Smithsonian, 1988.

———, Barbara Mathé, and Thomas Ross Miller, editors. *Drawing Shadows to Stone: The Photography of the Jesup North Pacific Expedition, 1897–1902*. New York: American Museum of Natural History, 1997.

———, and Igor Krupnik. "Introduction, A Centenary and a Celebration." In *Constructing Cultures Then and Now: Celebrating Franz Boas and the Jesup North Pacific Expedition*, editors Laurel Kendall and Igor Krupnik, 1–11. Contributions to Circumpolar Anthropology 4, 1–11. Washington DC: National Museum of Natural History, Smithsonian, 2003.

Kennedy, John Michael. "Philanthropy and Science in New York City: The American Museum of Natural History, 1868–1968." PhD diss., Yale University, 1969.

Koelsch, William A. *Clark University, 1887–1987: A Narrative History*. Worcester: Clark University Press, 1987.

Kohlstedt, Sally Gregory, Michael M. Sokal, and Bruce V. Lewenstein. *The Establishment of Science in America: 150 Years of the American Association for the Advancement of Science*. New Brunswick NJ: Rutgers University Press, 1999.

Konner, Melvin. *Unsettled: An Anthropology of the Jews.* New York: Viking Compass, 2003.

Knötsch, Carol Cathleen. "Franz Boas' Research Trip to Baffin Island, 1883–1884." *Polar Geography and Geology* 17, no. 1 (1993): 5–54.

Kroeber, Alfred Louis. "Animal Tales of the Eskimo." *Journal of American Folklore* 12 (1899): 17–23.

———. "The English Heroic Play." Master's thesis, Columbia University, 1897.

———. "The Eskimo of Smith Sound." *Bulletin of the American Museum of Natural History* 12 (1900): 265–327. http://digitallibrary.amnh.org/handle/2246/551, accessed April 17, 2016.

———. "Franz Boas: The Man." In *Franz Boas, 1858–1942*, edited by Ralph Linton. *American Anthropologist* 45, No. 3 (1943): 5–26.

———. "Tales of the Smith Sound Eskimo." *Journal of American Folklore* 12 (1899): 166–82.

Kroeber, Theodora. *Alfred Kroeber: A Personal Configuration.* Berkeley: University of California Press, 1970.

Krupnik, Igor. "A Jesup Bibliography: Tracking the Published and Archival Legacy of the Jesup Expedition." In *Gateways: Exploring the Legacy of the Jesup North Pacific Expedition, 1897–1902*, edited by Igor Krupnik and William W. Fitzhugh, 297–316. Washington DC: Smithsonian, 2001.

———. "Jesup Genealogy: Intellectual Partnership and Russian-American Cooperation in Arctic/North Pacific Anthropology. Part I. From the Jesup Expedition to the Cold War, 1897–1948." No Boundaries: Papers in Honor of James W. Vanstone, *Arctic Anthropology* 35, no. 2 (1998): 199–226.

———. "In Memory of Douglas Cole, 1938–1997." In *Gateways: Exploring the Legacy of the Jesup North Pacific Expedition, 1897–1902*, edited by Igor Krupnik and William W. Fitzhugh, 25. Washington DC: Smithsonian, 2001.

———. "One Field Season and a 50-Year Career: Franz Boas and Early Eskimology." In *Early Inuit Studies: Themes and Transitions, 1850s–1980s*, edited by Igor Krupnik, 73–83. Washington DC: Smithsonian, 2016.

Lamb, Daniel S. "The Story of the Anthropological Society of Washington." *American Anthropologist* 8 (1906): 564–79.

Langley, Samuel P. *Annual Report of the Board of Regents of the Smithsonian Institution Showing the Operations, Expenditures, and Condition of the Institution for the Year Ending June 30, 1903.* Washington DC: Government Printing Office, 1904.

Lerman, Katherine A. "Bismarckian Germany and the Structure of the German Empire." In *German History since 1800*, edited by Mary Fulbrook, 147–67. London: Arnold, 1997.

Lesser, Alexander. "The American Ethnological Society: The Columbia Phase, 1906–1946." In *American Anthropology: The Early Years*, edited by John V. Murra, 126–35. 1974 Proceedings of the American Ethnological Society. St. Paul MN: West, 1976.

Lévy, Isaac Jack, and Rosemary Lévy Zumwalt. *Ritual Medical Lore of Sephardic Women: Sweetening the Spirits and Healing the Sick*. Urbana: University of Illinois Press, 2002.

Liss, Julia E. "The Cosmopolitan Imagination: Franz Boas and the Development of American Anthropology." PhD diss., University of California, Berkeley, 1990.

———. "German Culture and German Science in the *Bildung* of Franz Boas." In *Volksgeist as Method and Ethic: Essays on Boasian Ethnography and the German Anthropological Tradition*, edited by George W. Stocking Jr., 155–84. Wisconsin: University of Wisconsin Press, 1996.

Lowie, Robert H. *The History of Ethnological Theory*. New York: Holt, Rinehart & Winston, 1937.

———. *Biographical Memoir of Franz Boas, 1858–1942*. 300–322. Washington DC: National Academy of Sciences, 1947.

Lutz, Hartmut, Renate Jütting, and Ruth Bradley-St-Cyr. "Introduction." In *The Diary of Abraham Ulrikab*, edited and translated by Hartmut Lutz, xvii–xxvi. King Edward, OTT: University of Ottawa Press, 2005.

Mark, Joan. *Four Anthropologists: An American Science in its Early Years*. New York: Science History, 1980.

Mason, Otis T. "Ethnological Exhibit of the Smithsonian Institution at the World's Columbian Exposition." In *Memoirs of the International Congress of Anthropology*, edited by C. Staniland Wake, 208–16. Chicago: Schulte, 1894. https://play.google.com/books/reader?id=e47vugEnCnac&printsec=frontcover&output=reader&hl=en&pg=gbs.pr3, accessed January 9, 2015.

McAleer, Kevin. *Dueling: The Cult of Honor in Fin-de-Siècle Germany*. Princeton NJ: Princeton University Press, 1994.

McCaughey, Robert A. *Stand Columbia: A History of Columbia University in the City of New York, 1754–2004*. New York: Columbia University Press, 2003.

McGee, W J. "An American Senate of Science." *Science* 14, no. 347 (1901): 277–80.

———. "Anthropology at Pittsburgh." *American Anthropologist* n.s. 4, no. 3 (1902): 464–81.

———. "Proposed American Anthropologic Association." *American Anthropologist* 4 (1902): 352–53.

McNutt, James C. "John Comfort Fillmore: A Student of Indian Music Reconsidered." *American Music* 2, no. 1 (1984): 61–70.

Miller, Thomas Ross. "Songs from the House of the Dead: Sound, Shamans, and Collecting in the North Pacific (1900–2000)." PhD diss., Columbia University, 2004.

Mills, Eric L. *Biological Oceanography: An Early History, 1870–1960*. Toronto: University of Toronto Press, 2012.

Mosse, George L. *German Jews Beyond Judaism*. Bloomington: Indiana University Press, 1985.

Müller-Wille, Ludger. "Franz Boas: Auszüge aus seinem Baffin-Tagebuch, 1883–1884 (19. September bis 15. Oktober 1883)" (Franz Boas: Excerpts from his Baffin Diary, 1883–1884 [19 September to 15 October 1883]). In *Franz Boas: Ethnologe, Anthropologe, Sprachwissenschaftler. Ein Wegbereiter der modernen Wissenschaft vom Menschen*, edited by Michael Dürr, Erich Kasten, and Egon Renner. Ausstellungskataloge, Neue Folge 4:39–56. Wiesbaden: Reichert, 1992.

———. "Franz Boas's English Publications on the Inuit and the Arctic (1884–1926): A Bibliographical Survey." In *Early Inuit Studies: Themes and Transitions, 1850s–1980s*, edited by Igor Krupnik, 83–89. Washington DC: Smithsonian, 2016.

———. *The Franz Boas Enigma: Inuit, Arctic, and Sciences*. Montréal: Baraka, 2014.

———, ed. *Franz Boas among the Inuit of Baffin Island 1883–1884: Journals & Letters*. Translated by William Barr. Toronto: University of Toronto Press, 1998.

———. *Franz Boas. Bei den Inuit in Baffinland 1883–1884. Tagebücher und Briefe* (Franz Boas among the Inuit of Baffin Island 1883–1884). Ethnologische Beiträge zur Circumpolarforschung 1. Edited by Erich Kasten. Berlin: Reinhold Schletzer Verlag, 1994.

———, and Bernd Gieseking. *Inuit and Whalers on Baffin Island through German Eyes: Wilhelm Weike's Arctic Journal and Letters (1883–1884)*. Translated by William Barr. Montréal: Baraka, 2011.

———, and Linna Weber Müller-Wille. "Inuit Geographical Knowledge One Hundred Years Apart." In *Inuit Studies in an Era of Globalization*, edited by Pamela Stern and Lisa Stevenson, 217–29. Lincoln: University of Nebraska Press, 2006.

Nye, David E. "Electrifying Expositions: 1880–1939." In *Fair Representations: World's Fairs and the Modern World*, edited by Robert W. Rydell and Nancy Gwinn, 140–56. Amsterdam: VU University Press, 1994.

Oetteking, Bruno. *Craniology of the North Pacific Coast*. Vol. II, Part 1.: The Jesup North Pacific Expedition. Memoirs of the AMNH, 15. 1930.

O'Sullivan, Catherine. "Series VIII: Records Relating to the 1903 Investigation of the BAE." *Register to the Records of the Bureau of American Ethnology*, 118–19, Smithsonian, National Anthropology Archives, 2007. http://anthropology.si.edu/naa/fa/Bureau_american_ethnology.pdf, accessed June 7, 2016.

Parmenter, Ross. "Glimpses of a Friendship, Zelia Nuttall and Franz Boas, Based on their Correspondence in the Library of the American Philosophical Society in Philadelphia." In *Pioneers in American Anthropology*, edited by June Helm, 83–147. Seattle: University of Washington Press, 1966.

Pöhl, Friedrich. "Assessing Franz Boas' Ethics in his Arctic and Later Anthropological Fieldwork." *Étude/Inuit/Studies* 32, no. 2 (2008): 35–52.

"Proposed Explorations on the Coasts of the North Pacific Ocean." *Science* 5, no. 116 (1897): 455–57.

Pruette, Lorine. *G. Stanley Hall: A Biography of a Mind.* New York: D. Appleton, 1926.

Putnam, Frederic Ward. "Ethnology, Anthropology, Archaeology." In *The World's Columbian Exposition: Chicago 1893*, edited by Trumbull White and William Igleheart, 415–35. Boston: John K. Hastings, 1893.

——. "Prefatory." In *Boas Anniversary Volume: Anthropological Papers Written in Honor of Franz Boas*, edited by Berthold Laufer, ix–xi. New York: G. E. Stechert, 1906.

Püschel, Erich. "Franz Boas (1858–1942). Amerikas großer Ethnologe, als deutscher Student und Assistant. Zum 125. Geburtstag" (America's great anthropologist, as a German student and assistant to the 125th Birthday). *Curare* 6, no. 2 (1983): 8–84.

Rand, McNally's & Co.'s. Handbook of the World's Columbian Exposition. Chicago: Rand, McNally, 1893. https://play.google.com/books/reader?id=tfu6aaaamaaj&printsec=frontcover&output=reader&authuser=0&hl=en&pg=gbs.pa3, accessed February 8, 2018.

Ray, Dorothy Jean. *The Eskimos of Bering Strait, 1650–1898.* Seattle: University of Washington Press, 1975.

Reichard, Gladys A. "Franz Boas and Folklore." *Franz Boas, 1858–1942*, edited by Ralph Linton. *American Anthropologist* 45, No. 3 (1943): 52–57.

Rink, Hinrich. *Tales and Traditions of the Eskimo with a Sketch of their Habit, Religion, Language, and Other Peculiarities.* Translated from Danish by the author. Edinburgh: William Blackwood & Sons, 1875. https://play.google.com/books/reader?id=kdncaaaaiaaj&printsec=frontcover&output=reader&authuser=0&hl=en&pg=gbs.pr3, accessed August 25, 2014.

Rohner, Ronald P., comp. and ed. *The Ethnography of Franz Boas: Letters and Diaries of Franz Boas Written on the Northwest Coast from 1886 to 1931.* Chicago: University of Chicago Press, 1969.

Rosenzweig, Saul. *Freud, Jung, and Hall the King-Maker: The Historic Expedition to America (1909), with G. Stanley Hall as Host and William James as Guest.* Seattle: Hogrefe & Huber, 1992.

Ross, Dorothy. *G. Stanley Hall: The Psychologist as Prophet*. Chicago: University of Chicago Press, 1972.

Rydell, Robert W. *All the World's a Fair*. Chicago: University of Chicago Press, 1987.

———. "A Cultural Frankenstein? The Chicago World's Columbian Exposition of 1893." In *Grand Illusions: Chicago's World's Fair of 1893*, edited by Neil Harris, Wim de Wit, James Gilbert, and Robert W. Rydell, 141–72. Chicago: Chicago Historical Society, 1994.

———, and Nancy Gwinn, eds. *Fair Representations: World's Fairs and the Modern World*. Amsterdam: VU University Press, 1994.

Scott, Gertrude M. "Village Performance: Villages at the Chicago World's Columbian Exposition, 1893." PhD diss., New York University, 1991.

Seelig, Geert. *Eine deutsche Jugend. Erinnerungen an Kiel und den Schwanenweg* (A German youth. Memories of Kiel and Schwanenweg). Hamburg: Alster Verlag, 1922.

Shternberg, Lev. *The Social Organization of the Gilyak*. Edited by Bruce Grant. Papers of the American Museum of Natural History, no. 82, 1999.

Smith, Harlan I. "Notes on Eskimo Traditions." *Journal of American Folklore* 7 (1894): 209–16.

Smith, Marian W. "Centenary of the American Ethnological Society." *American Anthropologist* 45 (1943): 181–84.

Sperber, Jonathan. *The European Revolutions, 1848–1851*. Cambridge: Cambridge University Press, 2005.

Steward, Julian H. "Alfred Louis Kroeber, 1876–1960." *American Anthropologist* 63 (1961): 1038–60.

———. "Alfred Kroeber, 1876–1960." In *A Biographical Memoir*. Washington DC: National Academy of Sciences, 1962. http://www.nasonline.org/publications/biographical-memoirs/memoir-pdfs/kroeber-alfred.pdf, accessed March 17, 2016.

Stocking, George W., Jr. "Franz Boas and the Founding of the American Anthropological Association." *American Anthropologist* 62 (1960): 1–17.

———. "From Physics to Ethnology." In *Race, Culture, and Evolution, Essays in the History of Anthropology*, edited by George W. Stocking Jr., 133–60. Chicago: University of Chicago Press, 1968.

———, ed. *The Shaping of American Anthropology, 1883–1911: A Franz Boas Reader*. New York: Basic Books, 1974.

Tal, Uriel. *Christians and Jews in Germany: Religion, Politics, and Ideology in the Second Reich, 1870–1914*. Ithaca NY: Cornell University Press, 1975.

Telman, D. A. Jeremy. "Adolf Stoecker, Anti-Semite with a Christian Mission." *Jewish History* 9, no. 2 (1995): 93–112.

Thom, Brian. "Harlan I. Smith's Jesup Fieldwork on the Northwest Coast." In *Gateways: Exploring the Legacy of the Jesup North Pacific Expedition, 1897–1902*, edited by Igor Krupnik and William W. Fitzhugh, 139–80. Washington DC: Smithsonian, 2001.

Thomas, David Hurst. *Skull Wars*. New York: Basic Books, 2000.

Thoresen, Timothy H. "Paying the Piper and Calling the Tune: The Beginnings of Academic Anthropology in California." *Journal of the History of the Behavioral Sciences* 11 (1975): 257–75.

Tozzer, Alfred M. *Biographical Memoir of Frederic Ward Putnam, 1839–1915*. National Academy of Sciences, Biographical Memoirs 16 (1933): 129–53. http://www.nasonline.org/publications/biographical-memoirs/memoir-pdfs/putnam-frederic.pdf, accessed August 18, 2014.

Trilling, Lionel. "Afterword." In *The Unpossessed* by Tess Slesinger, 309–33. New York: Avon, 1966.

Truax, Rhoda. *The Doctors Jacobi*. Boston: Little, Brown, 1952.

Turner, Victor. "Betwixt and Between: The Liminal Period in *Rites de Passage*." In *The Forest of Symbols: Aspects of Ndembu Ritual*, edited by Victor Turner, 93–111. Ithaca NY: Cornell University Press, 1967.

Twain, Mark. *A Tramp Abroad*. Vol. 1. New York: Harper & Brothers, [1880] 1907.

———. *A Tramp Abroad*. Vol. 2. New York and London: Harper & Brothers, [1880] 1921.

Tylor, Edward B. "Professor Adolf Bastian." *Man* 5 (1905): 138–43.

Vakhtin, Nikolai. "The Bogoras Project and Yupik Eskimo Linguistics in Russia." In *Early Inuit Studies: Themes and Transitions, 1850s–1980s*, edited by Igor Kupnik, 193–218. Washington DC: Smithsonian, 2016.

———. "Franz Boas and the Shaping of the Jesup Expedition Siberian Research, 1895–1900." In *Gateways: Exploring the Legacy of the Jesup North Pacific Expedition, 1897–1902*, edited by Igor Krupnik and William W. Fitzhugh, 71–89. Washington DC: Smithsonian, 2001.

van Gennep, Arnold. *Les rites de passage*. Paris: Émile Nourry, 1909.

VanStone, James W. *The Bruce Collection of Eskimo Material Culture from Port Clarence, Alaska*. Fieldiana, Anthropology, Vol. 67. Chicago: Field Museum of Natural History, 1976. https://archive.org/stream/brucecollection067vans#page/n7/mode/2up, accessed August 25, 2014.

Volkov, Shulamit. "The 'Verbürgerlichung' of the Jews as a Paradigm." In *Bourgeois Society in Nineteenth-Century Europe*, edited by Jürgen Kocka and Allan Mitchell, 367–91. Oxford: Berg, 1993.

Wake, C. Staniland, ed. *Memoirs of the International Congress of Anthropology*. Chicago: Schulte, 1894.

Warner, Joan. "The Struggle to Be Jewish and German." *Business Weekly*, 1998. http://www.businessweek.com/stories/1998–06–14/the-struggle-to-be -jewish-and-german, accessed February 4, 2018.

Webster, Arthur G. "Remarks." In *Twenty-Fifth Anniversary of Clark University, Worcester, Mass. 1889–1914*, 60–62. Worcester: Clark University Press, 1914.

Wellhäußer, Nadja. "Political Activism and Gender: German Women and the (Im)possibility of Political Activism during the German Revolution (1848– 49)." In Ryukoku University Institutional Repository, *Ryukoku Journal of Humanities and Social Sciences*, September 30, 2005, http://hdl.handle.net /10519/3608, accessed May 17, 2014.

Weston, Peter. *Friedrich Froebel: His Life, Times, and Significance*. London: University of Roehampton, 1998.

Wickwire, Wendy. "'They Wanted Me . . . to Help Them': James A. Teit and the Challenge of Ethnography in the Boasian Era." In *With Good Intentions: Euro-Canadian and Aboriginal Relations in Colonial Canada*, edited by Celia Haig-Brown and David A. Nick, 297–320. Vancouver: UBC, 2006.

Wintemberg, W. J. "Harlan Ingersoll Smith." *American Antiquity* 6 (1940): 63–64.

Wright, Robin K. "Edenshaw, Charles." In *Dictionary of Canadian Biography* 14. University of Toronto/Université Laval, 2003. http://www.biographi.ca/en /bio/edenshaw_charles_14e.html, accessed November 30, 2015.

Zumwalt, Rosemary Lévy. *American Folklore Scholarship: A Dialogue of Dissent*. Bloomington: Indiana University Press, 1988.

———. "The Personalized Voice in the History of Folklore Scholarship." *Folklore Historian* 31 (2014): 9–30.

———, and William Shedrick Willis. *Franz Boas and W. E. B. Du Bois at Atlanta University, 1906*. Philadelphia: American Philosophical Society, 2008.

Index

Boas, Franz (*continued*)

Eskimo of Baffin Land and Hudson Bay, 129; "The Social Organization and the Secret Societies of the Kwakiutl Indians," 225; "Songs of the Kwakiutl Indians," 225; "The Study of Geography," 169; "Über die ehemalige Verbreitung der Eskimos," 68, 340n13; "Über eine neue Form des Gesetzes der Unterschiedsschwelle," 50; "Under the Arctic Circle," 130; unpublished letters of, xx

Boas, Franziska, 344n11

Boas, Hedwig "Hete" (daughter), xix, 173, 236

Boas, Hedwig "Hete" (sister): birth of, 1; on Boas family background, 10; on family home, 13, 14; on FB's collections, 17–18, 19; on FB's departure for Arctic, 90; on FB's student years, 43, 48; on FB's travel for health problems, 18; on FB's working away from the fraternity, 48; on Harz Mountain holiday, 62; on Karoline Frank's family, 3; and link with Marie, 78–79; and marriage to Rudolf Lehmann, 39; on Meyer family, 4–5; on Minden Gymnasium, 16

Boas, Helene (daughter), xx, 172, 185–86, 187, 236

Boas, Helene (sister), 1

Boas, Karoline Frank (grandmother), 3, 4

Boas, Marie (née Krackowizer): about, 79; boat named for, 86; comments on FB's work by, 81; concerns about FB's work by, 198, 203; and declaration of love for FB, 83–84, 86–87, 88–89; expedi-

tionary flag made by, 129; and first child, 176, 177; and frustration with Frederic Ward Putnam, 245, 255–56, 261; and learning about FB, 79; mother's observation of change in, 90–91; on reuniting with FB, 123–24; and romance with FB, 62–63, 80–89, 90, 91, 92

Boas, Meier (father): and age at death of father, 4; on dangers of dueling, 50; as doting father, 19, 22–23; and FB's choices, 27, 28, 158; and financial support for FB, 55, 68, 72, 76, 77–78, 153; as head of Minden Jewish community, 12; home and occupation of, 8, 13–14, 63; illness of, 90, 254; and Jewish dogma, 10; on moving FB to Finsterbusch residence, 22–23; and Zenker Institute, 21–22

Boas, Meyer (great-uncle), 2, 3–4

Boas, Sophie Meyer (mother): on birth of FB, 1; and concerns for FB, 67; education and upbringing of, 5; and FB's education, 26, 29; on FB's studying and army service, 64; and fear of losing FB to America, 139; and Fröbel kindergarten, xvii, 9–10; and frustration with Frederic Ward Putnam, 245; impact of mother's death on, 7; and Jewish traditions, 10; marriage of, 9; political interests and activity of, 7–9; and pride in FB's gifts and accomplishments, 27, 239; and reunions with FB, 147, 185–86

Boas-Hunt collaboration in collecting and transcribing texts, 221, 239, 275, 278–79, 294, 330

Bogoras, Sofia, 285, 290, 295

Crane, Thomas Frederick, 174

Crawford, Samuel A., 228

Cristy, Austin P., 200

Crossroads of Continents (exhibit), 298

Cuddihy, John, 34

Culin, Stewart, 316–17, 322

cultural geography, 131, 329, 330

Cumberland Sound: charts and topographical features of, 104–5, 112–13, 114, 131; FB's first view of, 99

Cushing, Franklin Hamilton, 264

Danish government interest in Eskimos, 311

Darnell, Regna, xx, 322

Davis, George R., 226–27

Dawson, George Mercer, 171, 175, 177, 237

Deans, James, 218, 219, 224

desecration of burial sites, legal action against, 183

Deutscher Gesellig-Wissenschaftlicher Verein von New York (German Social and Scientific Association of New York): FB as secretary of, 185; FB's lecture to, 124, 134

Dexter, Ralph, 212, 220, 226–27, 238

Dietrich, Johann, 21

discrimination against Jews. *See* anti-Semitism

dissertation, FB's: as best dissertation, 53; equipment and methods for, 48–49, 54–55; publication of, 54; topic of, 47, 49

Dixon, Roland B., 278, 317, 327, 370n1

Donaldson, Henry H.: at baby's funeral, 236; on Clark University's faculty, 192, 193; and efforts for FB's employment, 235; as family friend with FB

and Marie, 208; on FB's need to rest, 241; on human races, 242; and offer of lodging, 237; on resignation from Clark, 204, 358n27; at University of Chicago, 207

Dorsey, George A., 183, 239, 301, 316, 322

Drawing Shadows to Stone, 298

DuBois, W. E. B., 242

dueling, student (*Mensur*): description of, 36–38; and dueling associations, 57; and FB's experience, 38–39; FB's scars from, 57; FB tells his parents about, 40–41; goal in, 56–57; parents' concerns about, 50, 52; in student culture, 56

Durkheim, Émile, 57–58

Dürr, Michael, 285–86, 298

Eastern European Jews, 34–35

Edenshaw, Charles, 276, 278

Edler, Rabbi, 5, 12

Erdmann, Benno, 47, 50, 53, 76

"The Eskimo of Baffin Land and Hudson Bay," 307

Eskimos, FB's study of: and access to artifacts, 71; in Berlin after military service, 68–69, 72–73; as case study in methodology, 67; encouraged by Theobald Fischer, 66; and Eskimo folktales, 148; fieldwork preparation for, 72–73, 93; and similarity of eastern and western Eskimos, 223. *See also* Baffin Land fieldwork; Inuit people

"Eskimo Story" (1883), 108, 110, 344n11

Esmarch, Johannes Friedrich August von, 45–46

ethics in ethnography, 155

ethnographic work: augmentation of
cultural geography by, 131; cooperation and demands of science
in, 117–18; FB lauded for, 264; FB's
approach to, 189, 296, 348n59; FB's
immersion as Eskimo in, 116–17;
FB's preference for, 115–16; with
Northwest Coast Indians, 163–68;
and shift in FB's approach, 264–65;
and worldview, 115, 130, 296–97,
330. *See also* Baffin Land fieldwork; Jesup North Pacific Expedition (JNPE); Northwest Coast
fieldwork
Ethnological Museum in Berlin, 153–56
Etuangat, Aksayuk, 126
European universities, strengths of, 302
exotic peoples shows, 153–54, 155
expeditions compared to research
journeys, 127
explorer's naming rights, 104
Exposition Universelle in Paris, 213–14

facial paintings, 278, 279–80
Fagin, Nancy, 212
Farrand, Livingston: facial casts and
photographs of Indians by, 276,
277; and knowledge of anthropology, 256–57; management of
JNPE fieldwork by, 278; at meeting
about national organization, 316;
The Quinault Indians, 293–94; and
responsibilities on JNPE, 276; and
student use of AMNH collections,
303–4; study of Chilcotin by, 273,
274; and travel to JNPE fieldwork, 271
feast invitations to foster goodwill, 165,
249–50, 276–77
Festschrift, presentation to FB, 61

Fewkes, J. Walter, 264, 317, 322
Field, Marshall, 226
Field Columbian Museum. *See*
Columbian Museum of Chi-
cago (Field Museum of Natural
History)
Field Museum of Natural History.
See Columbian Museum of Chi-
cago (Field Museum of Natural
History)
Fillmore, John Comfort, 221, 223–25, 239
Finsterbusch, Ludwig, 22
Fischer, Kuno, 35
Fischer, Theobald: on Carl Ritter and
FB's scientific work, 92–93; on
employment conditions in Ger-
many, 137, 138; to FB on position
at *Science*, 173; on FB's conversion
to Christianity, 60; FB's course-
work with, 42; on FB's interest in
the United States, 137; in FB's oral
examination, 53; and habilitation
process, 76, 150, 151; on Heinrich
Kiepert, 151–52; on Jews and anti-
Semitism, 138; support and advice
from, 47, 65–66; and welcoming FB
home, 146
Fitzhugh, William, 295–96, 297
Foerster, Wilhelm Julius, 71, 152
Fort Rupert: FB's return to, 249–50;
George Hunt raised in, 355n40;
procurement of skeletal remains
from, 182
Fort Rupert tribes and cultures:
exhibit at WCE, 218–19, 220; and
village on Lake Michigan, 239
Fowke, Gerard, 281, 282
Frank, Joseph Meyer (great-
grandfather), 3

Hunt, George: about, 355n40; and collaboration with FB, 272, 330, 353n9; collection of artifacts by, 278; on FB's return to Fort Rupert, 249; and first meeting with FB, 180; and grave illness of child, 277; major contribution of, 221; management of Fort Rupert exhibit by, 218; review and expansion of folklore collection by, 275, 278–79; songs composed by, 225; and village on Lake Michigan, 239

Hutten, Ulrich von, 28, 335–36n59

illnesses and death in Native populations: in Baffin Land, 106–9, 117–18; among Chukchi, 287; FB associated with, 117, 118; of Labrador Eskimos, 155; among Northwest Coast Indians, 277; of visiting Eskimos, 308–9, 311–12, 372n27

indigenous names, 103–4, 106, 125, 348n62

International Congress of Americanists, FB's address to, 291, 296

Internationales Archiv für Ethnographie, 188

International Polar Year, 76, 80, 127, 341n28

Inuit people: and association of FB with illness, 117–18; and communal nature of, 114; and description of women, 100; FB's continuing work on, 307; and FB's learning of Inuktitut, 100, 106, 109, 120; FB's reflection on learning about, 116; illness, death, and mortuary customs of, 106–9; importance of indigenous names to, 126–27; live traveling

exhibit of, 305–6; maps drawn by, 105, 125, 348n63; Sedna festival of, 110–11; and spontaneous settlements for travelers, 112; and value of Eskimos' stay in New York, 309–10

Itlkakuani, 161, 163, 164

Ivanov, Vladimir Karlampovich, 298

Jacknis, Ira, 189, 218, 219–20

Jackson, Abraham Valentine Williams, 263

Jacobi, Abraham (uncle): assistance to newlyweds from, 172; biographical information about, 5–6, 8; career advice from, 133, 139–40; critique of FB's travel plans by, 71–72; and FB's confiding about Marie, 82; and FB's employment in United States *vs.* Germany, 142–44; FB's sharing of plans with, 64–65; on FB's use of English, 242; on FB's WCE work, 239; funding for FB's salary from, 262, 302, 304–5; funding of FB's fieldwork by, 83, 162; on holiday in Harz Mountains, 62, 63; and influence on Meier Boas, 28; and orders for FB to rest, xix, 240; revolutionary activities of, 7–8; securing position for FB, 65, 135, 136, 256, 261

Jacobsen, Bernard Fillip, 153, 154, 272

Jacobsen, Johan Adrian, 153–54, 167–68

Jarausch, Konrad, 60

Jesup, Morris K.: appointment of FB by, 260–61; approval of JNPE costs from, 291; and concern over FB's health, 241; death of, 291; and efforts to secure positions for FB, 255, 257, 302, 303; and enthusiasm for ethnological exhibits, 244;

Jesup, Morris K. (*continued*)
FB's relationship with, 309; on
finding right scientists, 280; funding of JNPE from, xix, 267, 269–70;
and housing for visiting Eskimos,
307–8; on JNPE's impact on AMNH,
270; and JNPE summary volume,
291, 292, 297, 300; legacy of, 299;
and views of JNPE, 290; on visiting
Eskimos tragedy, 309
Jesup North Pacific Expedition
(JNPE): assessments of, 295, 297–
98; and collaboration of experts,
295–96; continuing importance
of, 297–99, 330; costs associated
with, 290–91, 294, 309; FB's vision
of, 299; funding of, xix, 267, 269–
70; goals and scope of, 267–68,
269, 271, 290; Laufer and Fowke's
work in, 280–83; Northwest Coast
portion of, 272–79; publications
resulting from, 292–94, 297; "The
Results of the Jesup Expedition,"
291, 296; scientists' responses to,
290; Siberian portion of, 278, 280,
284–90; summary volume for, 291,
292, 297, 300, 372n34; team makeup
and responsibilities on, 271–73; and
travel to northern field site, 273–75;
wealth of data resulting from, 296;
work of first season of, 272–78
Jewish culture: dietary laws in, 10; and
FB's encounter with *Yiddishkeit*,
34–35; holidays and customs in,
12–13; and secular Judaism, 35
Jewish emancipation, 59, 60
Jewish identity: and assimilation
into German society, 12, 59; and

employment opportunities in Germany, 137–38
JNPE. *See* Jesup North Pacific Expedition (JNPE)
Jochelson, Bogoras and Shternberg (Kasten), 299
Jochelson, Vladimir: about, 283–
84; and costs of JNPE, 291; and
extended stay in Siberia, 290; and
fieldwork challenges, 288–89; and
plans for JNPE work, 284–85; police
surveillance of, 286; results of field-
work by, 289, 294, 297; *The Yukaghir
and the Yukaghirized Tungas*, 298
"Jochelson and the Jesup North Pacific
Expedition" (Kasten and Dürr),
298–99
Jochelson-Brodsky, Dina, 285, 289;
Anthropometry of Siberia, 292
Johns Hopkins University, 357n5,
357n15
Johnson, Rossiter, 218–19
Jonaitis, Aldona, 276
Jordan, D. S., 259
Journal of American Folklore, 174, 175,
223, 310
Jung, C. G., 208–9
Justus Perthes (publisher), 126, 149,
152, 158, 159
J. W. Skiles and Co., 217

Kampe, Norbert, 52, 60
Karsten, Gustav, 47, 49, 53
Kasten, Erich, 285–86, 298
Kaufmann, Richard, 2–3
Keenainak, Josephie, 127
Kekerten (whaling station): departure
from, 118; description of, 100; FB's

welcome in, 102, 111; as fieldwork base, 108, 109; spelling of, 344n9

Kekulé, August, 42

Kendall, Laurel, 283, 297–98

Kiel, Germany, 58–59

Kiel Commission, 47

Kiepert, Heinrich: and exchange with *Science,* 173; on FB's habilitation, 153, 156; FB's view of, 151–52, 153; and view of FB, 152

Kirchhoff, Alfred, 150, 151

Klus forests, 15, 29

Knötsch, Carol, 96, 117, 131

Königliches Museum für Völkerkunde (Royal Museum of Ethnology), 70

Kootenay people, 177, 180, 184

Kortum, Hermann, 42

Koryak people, 285, 288, 289, 299

Krackowizer, Emilie: about Marie and marriage to FB, 79; on FB and Marie's marriage plans, 171; FB letter of intentions to, 86; in Harz Mountains, 62; and letters of concern, 87–88, 90

Krackowizer, Ernst, 354n22

Krackowizer, Marie. *See* Boas, Marie (née Krackowizer)

Kroeber, Alfred Louis: FB's assessment of, 326, 328; on FB's youth, xx; and native languages, 305; role in AAA suggested to, 301; at University of California, 327–28; and work with visiting Eskimos, 309–10

Kroeber, Theodora, 305

Krüer, Reinhard: death of, 41; and letters with FB, 38–39

Krupnik, Igor, 125, 295–96, 297–98; "A Jesup Bibliography," 297

Kurilov, Gavril Nikolaevich, 298

Kwakiutl people: Boas-Hunt collaboration regarding, 221, 239, 275, 278–79, 294, 330; facial casts and photographs of, 276–77; FB's lasting contribution regarding, 238–39; FB's lifelong study of, 93; and Kwakiutl hamatsa (Hamat'sa), 238–39, 253; and language study, 177; modes of travel of, 352n7; and Northwest Coast languages and cultures, 218; recording and transcriptions of songs of, 223–25; at WCE, 220. *See also* Hunt, George

Ladenburg, Albert, 52, 53

Lamb, Daniel, 314

Langley, Samuel Pierpont: appointment of FB by, 313; FB's criticism of, 324; and intent to purge BAE, 319–20, 322–23, 325

languages, FB's study of, 329; and importance of knowing native languages, 130; and Pidgin English, 106; skill and interest in, 16–17, 33, 329; and study of Danish, 68; and study of English, 134, 171, 242; and study of Eskimo language, 68, 73; and study of Inuktitut, 100, 106, 109, 120. *See also* linguistic research

Laufer, Bertold: on Amur River portion of JNPE, 280; fieldwork by and challenges of, 281–83; visa difficulties of, 280–81; wealth of data collected by, 297

Lausalx, Arnold von, 47

lectures given by FB: at Clark University anniversary celebration, 208; at Columbia College, xix, 135, 136, 145, 173, 266; Ethnography of North-

lectures given by FB (*continued*)
western America, 168; FB's skill in,
135–36; in Germany, 77, 79–80, 124,
134–36, 148; for habilitation, 156; as
path to a position, 135, 145, 148; at
Peabody Museum, 199; at Stanford
University, 251
Lehmann, Betty, 39
Lehmann, Hedwig. *See* Boas, Hedwig
"Hete" (sister)
Lehmann, Rudolph (brother-in-law),
39, 161, 245
Lekwiltok people, 167
letter-diary, 95, 96–97, 104–5, 119
Levysohn, Arthur, 75
Leydig, Franz von, 42
Lillooet people, 278
Lindeman, Moritz von, 73, 76
linguistic research: and approach to
studying languages, 190; on Bella
Coola language, 163; in British
Columbia, 167–68, 176–77, 180,
188, 248; and difficulty with Indian
languages, 279; in FB's approach
to anthropology, 330; FB's chal-
lenges to, 105–6; and FB seminar
on American Indian languages,
305; FB's predilection for, 279; and
handbook of North American
languages, 312–13; and teaching at
Columbia College, 263; value of
collaboration to, 324. *See also* Inuit
people; languages, FB's study of
Lipschitz, Rudolph, 42
Liss, Julia, 15, 60
Lizzie P. Simmons (whaling ship),
101–2
Lombard, Warren P., 207, 358n27
Low, Seth, 255, 259, 261–62, 302, 303, 304

Lowie, Robert, xx; *Biographical Memoir of Franz Boas, 1858–1942*, 127

MacCurdy, George G., 316
Mahlstede, August F. B., 75
Mall, Franklin P., 193, 204, 205, 207,
358n27
manhood, rituals of, 56–58
Mark, Joan, 237, 245
Masius, Hermann, 11
Mason, Otis T.: and eagerness to help
FB, 133–34; on ethnological exhibits at WCE, 212–13; and exhibit at
Cotton States Exposition, 246, 252,
254; FB's discussion of BAE collection with, 145; and life model
exhibits at National Museum, 246,
253; and sympathy for FB over Chicago, 252
material culture: in FB's approach to
anthropology, 330; of Haida Indians, 219; as linked to narratives,
190; techniques of research in, 189
mathematics and physics: and differential calculus, 35; and dissertation topic, 47; FB's aptitude for and
interest in, 26–27; FB's move away
from, 66; university study in, 33
McAleer, Kevin, 56, 57
McGee, W J: and affiliation with scientific societies, 319; and attempts
to calm FB, 231; at BAE, 318–20, 325;
and conflict with FB over national
organization, 300, 317–18, 320–
21, 326; as co-owner of *American
Anthropologist*, 314; on FB's offer
at BAE, 254; and incorporation
of AAA, 322; and investigation of
BAE, 323–25; and pressure on FB

to accept USNM offer, 258; and proposal to form national organization, 316–20; on publication of handbook of North American languages, 313; and sympathy for FB over Chicago, 252

McGuire, Joseph D., 322

Melville, George, 144–45

Meyer, Abraham (uncle), 6, 13

Meyer, Adele (cousin), 13, 14

Meyer, Berthe (aunt), 5

Meyer, Fanny (aunt), 6, 7–8

Meyer, Henriette "Jette" (née Menke, grandmother), 4, 5, 7

Meyer, Jacob "Uncle Kobus" (uncle), 6, 13, 172, 262

Meyer, Jonas (grandfather), 4–5, 9

Meyer, Julius (cousin), 13

Meyer, Jürgen Bona, 42

Meyer, Phips (aunt): death of, 172; letters to Sophie from, 67, 122–23

Meyer, Salomon "Uncle Mons": and concerns about FB's travel, 71, 72; and visits to FB, 36; wedding gift from, 172

Meyer, Theodor (cousin), 13

Meyer, Willy (cousin): congratulations from, 80; as lover of natural history, 14, 15–16; and membership in fraternal organization, 43

Michelson, Albert A., 193, 204, 206, 207, 208, 358n27

Midway Plaisance, 214, 217, 223, 359n7

Miller, Thomas Ross, 225, 272–73

Minden, Westphalia: about, 13; homecoming in, 145–46; Jewish population in, 8–9

Minden Gymnasium, 6, 16–17, 22, 27

Minden revolutionary circle, 5, 6

Minden Töchterschule, 22

Minik, 307, 309, 310–12, 372n27

Möbius, Karl Augustus, 47

modern geography, 151, 159–60, 351n42

Mosse, Rudolf, 74

Müller-Wille, Ludger: on anti-Semitic student association, 51; on Baffin Land research, 125–26; on *The Central Eskimo*, 159; on exchanges during Arctic voyage, 343n3; on FB as pioneer, 128; on FB's change to Kekerten, 100; on FB's work on Inuit, 307; on FB's intellectual interests, 26; on FB's linguistic challenges, 105–6; on FB's performance on dissertation, 53; on FB's use of maps, 127; on format of curriculum vitae, 27; on habilitation process, 150; on *Ich hab's gewagt*, 335–36n59; on importance of FB's work to Inuit, 348n63; on importance of Arctic study, 76; on influence of approach to geography, 127–28; "Inuit Geographical Knowledge One Hundred Years Apart," by Linna Weber Müller-Wille and, 105–6; on model for FB's approach to, 348n59; on newspaper's rights to FB's results, 76; on presentation to Inuit of Pangnirtung, 126; on renown of FB's teachers, 27; on requirements of Privatdozent, 353n13; on value of letter-diary, 96; on visiting Eskimos tragedy, 312; on Weike's contributions, 128–29

The Museum at the End of the World (Block and Kendal), 297

music, FB's interest in, 32, 33, 38, 85, 208

Mutch, James Shepherd: abandoned boxes retrieved by, 347n47; and collaboration with FB, 129, 130, 330; experience, expertise, and assistance of, 102; and identification of Inuit with geographic knowledge, 105; loan of skin clothing, 114; and role at whaling station, 100

mythology and folklore: discovering traits of people through, 164, 190; of the Eskimo, 221–22, 310; in FB's approach to anthropology, 330; Kwakiutl collection of, 166, 221, 239, 275; "The Mythology of the Bella Coola Indians," 278; of Northwest Coast Indians, 265, 330; and "Olŭngwa," 222; and relationship with languages, 265; texts of, 330. *See also* Boas-Hunt collaboration in collecting and transcribing texts

Nachojaschi, 103
National Geographic Society, 319
Navaho songs, 223
Nef, John Ulric, 193, 204, 207, 358n27
Neumayer, Georg von: at Assembly of Geographers, 80; and FB's departure to Arctic, 90; travel and research support from, 76–77
Newcombe, Charles Frederick, 239, 276
Newell, William Wells, 174, 175, 234
New York Evening Post publication of opposing views of expedition, 144–45
New York Times: on plans for JNPE, 270; on Putnam and anthropology exhibit, 216, 217; on visiting Eskimos, 307, 308; on WCE's Anthropological Building, 215

New York Tribune on visiting Eskimos, 308, 309
Noble, Crawford, 100, 102
North Sea observation stations, 47
Northwest Coast fieldwork: BAAS funding for, 174–75, 177–83, 184–86, 198, 237, 245, 247, 248; BAE funding for, 198; on Bella Coola Indians, 330; and FB's approach, 189–90, 264–65; FB's attitude toward, 247, 250; FB's reputation from, 187–88; and FB's research blind spots, 265; and FB's return to territory, 248–49, 250, 251; and FB's separation anxiety, 186–87; and first trip, 162, 163–69, 168; summary of work from, xviii

Northwest Coast Indians: exhibit at Ethnological Museum on, 153; exhibit at WCE on, 212. *See also* Bella Coola Indians
Nuttall, Zelia, 326, 327, 372n28
Nye, David: on World's Columbian Exposition, 214

Ocheitu, 103, 114–15, 346n39
Oetteking, Bruno: *Craniology of the North Pacific Coast*, 292
Olmsted, Law, 214
Olsen, Gustav, 311
The Ordeal of Civility, 34
Osborn, Henry, 309

Peabody Museum at Cambridge, 199, 243
Peary, Robert, 306, 307, 308, 312
"Peary Eskimos" tragedy of, 307–12, 372n27
Pentlatch people, 167
Permeier, Herr, 16

recordings and transcriptions of songs: authenticity and accuracy of, 225; among Gilyak and Tungus, 282–83; as inherited property, 225–26; in JNPE, 272–73; method used for, 223–24; and reactions to phonograph, 283, 289

Reichard, Gladys, 330

Reiß, Johann Wilhelm, 69, 70, 71, 148, 152

repatriation of Greenlandic Eskimos, 312

research universities' recruitment practices, 206

Rheinische Friedrich-Wilhelms Universität: coursework at, 42; FB's move to, 41; fraternity at, 43; and student jail sentence, 42–43; and visit to Bonn synagogue, 45–46

Rink, Hinrich Johannes, 73, 148

Ripley, William Z., 256–57

Ritter, Carl, 92

Roach, John, 100, 101, 102–3

Robinson Crusoe, 16

Rockefeller, John D., 205, 206

Rohner, Ronald P., 355n40

Rood, Ogden N., 135

Ross, Dorothy, 192, 194, 205, 206

Royal Museum of Ethnology, 71

Royal Society of Canada, 161

Ruprecht-Karls-Universität: classes at, 31, 32–33, 35; and complaints over studies, 42; FB's view of Jews at, 35–36; lectures on aesthetics at, 329; need for friendships at, 33–34; residence at, 32; and student jail sentence, 40; student life at, 36–41

Russell, Frank, 316

Russian Minister of the Interior, 286

Sakhalin Island peoples, 281

Salish people, 177, 184, 198, 219–20, 248, 305

Sanford, E. C., 208

Schleinitz, Georg von, 75

Schmeltz, Johannes Dietrich Eduard, 188

Schreiber, Emanuel, 45

Schurz, Carl, 162, 171

Science: announcement about JNPE in, 270–71; FB at, xviii, 93, 169–70, 173, 176, 183–84; and FB's resulting network of scientists, 188; FB's writings in, 144–45, 155–56, 321, 323

scientific collaboration, value to science, organizations, and students, 324. *See also* Boas, Franz, career of; Boas-Hunt collaboration in collecting and transcribing texts; Jesup North Pacific Expedition (JNPE); linguistic research; Mutch, James Shepherd; Teit, James

scientific community of East Coast, 237

Scott, Gertrude, 217

Scottish seal hunters, 78

Sedna, legend of, 110–11, 222

Selwyn, Alfred, 161

Shanguja, 103

Shternberg, Lev: *The Social Organization of the Gilyak*, 292; *Sociology of the Amur Tribes*, 292

Sing Sing NY (Ossining), 172, 354n22

skeletons and skulls: collection and sale of, 167, 181–83; investigation of JNPE collection of, 292; and marking provenance, 183. *See also* physical anthropology

Skiff, Frederick J. V., 228, 231–32, 234

Small, A. W., 207

Smith, Harlan: and assistance to Esther Bein's family, 306; facial casts of Indians by, 275–76; as collaborator on JNPE, 270, 271, 273, 276; FB's encouragement of, 221; fieldwork for JNPE, 278; and publication of work, 293

Smith, Marian, 174

Smithsonian Institution: FB hopes for a position at, 145; on FB's methods, 324; FB travel to, 133; WCE exhibits as model for, 238–39. *See also* Bureau of American Ethnology (BAE); Langley, Samuel Pierpont

sociology, as necessary for geographers, 64

Southwick, Albert B., 200

space and spatial organization, visualization of, 127

Ssigna (Inuit guide), 102–3, 114, 330, 344–45n17

Stanford University: FB lecture to, 251; FB's pursuit of position at, 258–59; suit against, 259, 364n37

Starr, Frederick, 207, 316

Stocking, George: on FB's ability to take direction, 362n46; on FB's approach to race, 242; on Fischer and Ritter, 92–93; on import of FB's role in AAAS, 242; on national organization, 318, 320, 322

Stoecker, Adolf, 50

student dueling: anti-Semitic provocation for, 50, 52; FB's writing home about, 44–45; touted as vivisection, 202

student life: as brotherhood, 57–58; and parental authority, 56; and transition from, 58

Stumpf, Carl, 154

Sutton, William and James, 181, 182–83

symbols, use of, 280

Taber, Ralph, 305, 306

Tacoma, Washington, 163

Teit, James: about, 271; FB's collaboration with, 330; and fieldwork with Lillooet, 278; and manuscript of work, 293; preparatory work for JNPE by, 272; as translator and guide, 273, 275

Thompson River Indians, 272, 273

Tlingit people, 166, 180, 220, 276

Topinard, Paul, 263–64

toponyms, collection of, 126. *See also* indigenous names

travel and research: FB's dreams of, xvii, 329–30; funding for, 73–75; to Germany with young family, 185–86; as mark of serious scientist, 93, 330. *See also* Arctic voyage; Baffin Land fieldwork; Jesup North Pacific Expedition (JNPE); Northwest Coast fieldwork

travel to Arctic and back: arrival in Kekerten, 99–100; from Baffin Land to New York, 120–21; from Europe to Kekerten, 95–97; FB's seasickness during, 96, 98; from Greenland to Baffin Island, 96, 97–99; and life aboard *Germania*, 96–97

Trilling, Lionel, 35, 337n11

true science, FB's view of, 21, 329

Tsar Nicholas II, 281, 285–86

Tsimshian people, 184, 219, 276, 279

Tungus people, 281, 282–83

Tylor, E. B.: at BAAS, 175; and funding for Northwest Expedition, 268; praise for FB's work by, 179, 264; program of research proposed to, 184–85; and use of folktales, 267

Uncle Mons. *See* Meyer, Salomon "Uncle Mons"

University of Berlin, habilitation lecture to, 156

University of California: FB's networking with, 251; FB's possible work at, 326–27; Kroeber at, 327–28; Putnam at, 328; support of linguistic research by, 314

University of Chicago: faculty recruitment for, 205, 206–7; FB's views on, 229–30; as new center of power and influence, 237

University of Halle, 150

University of Jena botanical garden, 21, 329

U.S. Army Signal Office, 145

U.S. National Museum (USNM): catalogue of artifacts and life model exhibits at, 252–53; Holmes's role in, 233; Northwest Coast catalogue for, 246; Northwest Coast exhibit at, 246, 298; offer of position at, 255–56; plan for model exhibits at, 253; and report on Northwest Coast artifacts, 254; WCE exhibits as model for, 238

Utütiak (Yankee), 103, 112

Vakhtin, Nikolai, 283, 284

van Gennep, Arnold, 55

Verbürgerlichung (integration into German society), 12

Vereine Deutscher Studenten (Union of German Students), 51, 59

Vincent, Lyle, 305

Virchow, Rudolph: about, 69–70; FB's introduction to, 73; introduction of Bella Coola Indians by, 154; and response to FB lecture, 148

vivisection at Clark University, claims of, 200–202

Volkov, Shulamit, 12

Volksgeist (national spirit), 59

Wagner, Hermann, 10, 29, 147, 151, 173, 333–34n26, 350n32

Walcott, Charles D., 229–30

Wallace, William, 307–8, 309, 312

Washington anthropologists, 300, 370n1

water, FB's work on properties of: in Cumberland Sound, 109–10; as dissertation topic, 47–50, 54–55; and seawater experiments, 93, 96

WCE. *See* World's Columbian Exposition (WCE)

Weber Müller-Wille, Linna, 126

Webster, Arthur G., 193

Weike, Wilhelm: as assistant and companion, 77–78, 102, 330; and description of storm, 110; diary of Arctic journey by, 128, 346n38; and English lessons, 97; FB responsibility for, 90; frostbite suffered by, 113, 114–15, 346n39; and preparation for travel, 78

West, Gerald, 203

Weyer, Georg Daniel Eduard, 47, 53

In the Critical Studies in the History of Anthropology series

To order or obtain more information on these or other University of Nebraska Press titles, visit nebraskapress.unl.edu.